W9-BXW-617

1000 YEARS *of* FAMOUS PEOPLE

KINGFISHER
a Houghton Mifflin Company imprint
215 Park Avenue South
New York, New York 10003
www.houghtonmifflinbooks.com

First published in 2002
2 4 6 8 10 9 7 5 3 1

1TR/0602/CAC/GRS(GRS)/128JMA

LIBRARY OF CONGRESS CATALOGING-IN-PUBLICATION DATA
has been applied for.

PROJECT TEAM
Project Director and Art Editor Julian Holland
Editorial team Rachel Hutchings, Sarah Laver
Designer Nigel White
Research Janet Laver
Picture Research Anne-Marie Ehrlich

FOR KINGFISHER
Editorial Director Miranda Smith
Creative Director Miranda Kennedy
DTP Coordinator Sarah Pfitzner
DTP Operator Primrose Burton
Editor Sheila Clewley
Coordinating Editors Sarah Snavely, Denise Heal
Picture Research Rachael Swann
Artwork Research Wendy Allison, Steve Robinson
Production Managers Jo Blackmore, Debbie Otter

CONTRIBUTORS
Clive Gifford, Julian Holland, Ann Kramer, Jan Laver,
Peter Mellett, Bethan Ryder, Philip Wilkinson

ISBN 0-7534-5540-4

Printed in Hong Kong

1000 YEARS *of* FAMOUS PEOPLE

KINGfISHER
NEW YORK

CONTENTS

CHAPTER SEVEN
ARTISTS AND ARCHITECTS 153

CHAPTER EIGHT
MUSICIANS AND DANCERS 177

CHAPTER NINE
SPORTS STARS 201

CHAPTER TEN
MOVERS AND SHAKERS 225

Introduction

"Everyone will be famous for 15 minutes."

Artist Andy Warhol (1926–1987)

Andy Warhol may well have been right. Most people's fame or notoriety is short-lived. Many of today's musicians, movie stars, or politicians will not be famous next year, let alone a century from now. Some names, however, will live on in history—the people who have achieved something extra special or noteworthy, the people whohave made a real difference. This book brings you the lives and achievements of over 1,500 people whose fame will endure.

The towering genius Leonardo da Vinci, Napoléon the military master of Europe, Nellie Melba and her wonderful voice, Albert Einstein and his theories of relativity, Laszlo Biro and the invention of the ballpoint pen, Ernest Shackleton and his journey across the frozen Antarctic wastelands, Marilyn Monroe and her unique relationship with the camera, Neil Armstrong, the first human to set foot on the Moon—this book includes the everyday, the extraordinary, the exceptional.

Not everyone in this book has enriched human life. Some people are notorious for their evil deeds. Despots, murderers, and war criminals are also famous—or infamous. From Torquemada's excesses in the Spanish Inquisition to the murderous sprees of Billy the Kid and Hitler's notorious "final solution," history is littered with such people, and their deeds sometimes change history irrevocably. Thankfully forces for good usually outweigh those for evil.

Delve into *1000 Years of Famous People* and you will understand the private lives, driving passions, and towering achievements that have shaped our world today.

◀ American movie star Marilyn Monroe (1926–1962)—one of the most famous icons of the 1900s—pictured here at the height of her acting career.

CAPTIONS TO ILLUSTRATIONS

Page 1: Nelson Mandela; Page 3: Napoléon Bonaparte

KEY TO ILLUSTRATIONS ON PAGE 5:

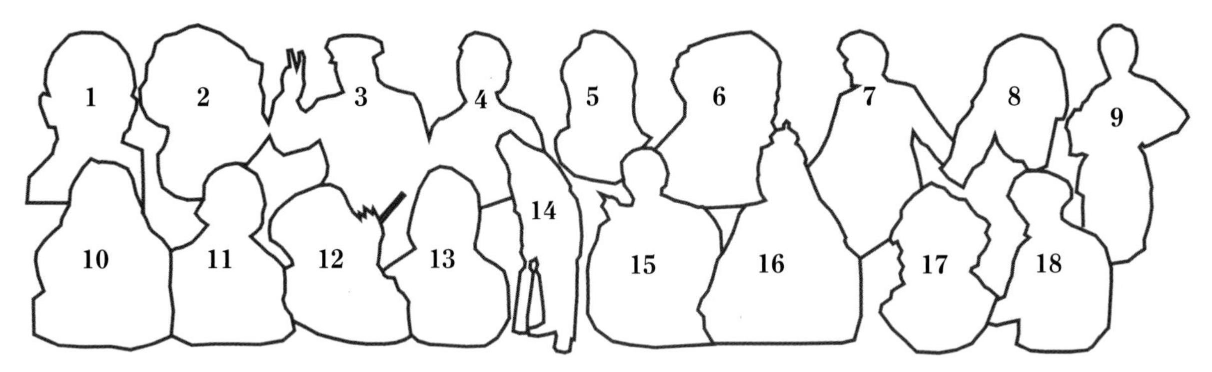

1 Adolf Hitler; **2** Albert Einstein; **3** Winston Churchill; **4** David Livingstone; **5** Alexander Graham Bell; **6** Rudolph Valentino; **7** Leon Trotsky; **8** Greta Garbo; **9** Benito Mussolini; **10** Orville Wright; **11** Isambard Kingdom Brunel; **12** Marlene Dietricht; **13** Grigori Rasputin; **14** W. G. Grace; **15** Oscar Wilde; **16** Queen Victoria; **17** Charles Dickens; **18** Michael Faraday

CAPTIONS TO CHAPTER TITLE PAGES:

p. 9 WORLD LEADERS
French ruler Napoléon Bonaparte (1769–1821) leads his army to victory against the Austrians at the Battle of Marengo (1800).

p. 33 EXPLORERS
Thanks to the work of the Australian photographer, Frank Hurley (1885–1962), Ernest Shackleton's (1874–1922) ill-fated expedition to the Antarctic (1914–1916) was recorded for future generations. Here, Shackleton's ship *Endurance* lies trapped in the ice of the Weddell Sea, only 77 mi. (128km) from its destination.

p. 57 SCIENTISTS
Scottish scientist Alexander Fleming (1881–1955) works in his laboratory. In 1928 he discovered penicillin.

p. 81 ENGINEERS AND INVENTORS
Scottish electrical engineer John Logie Baird (1888–1946) is pictured with one of his early television sets.

p. 105 WRITERS AND REFORMERS
American civil rights leader Martin Luther King, Jr. (1929–1968) acknowledges the assembled crowd in front of the Lincoln Memorial, Washington, D.C., after giving his famous "I have a dream" speech in August 1963.

p. 129 STARS OF STAGE AND SCREEN
American movie star Humphrey Bogart (1899–1957) and Swedish actress Ingrid Bergman (1915–1982) starred in the movie *Casablanca* (1942).

p. 153 ARTISTS AND ARCHITECTS
Dutch artist Vincent Van Gogh (1853–1890) painted many self-portraits.

p. 177 MUSICIANS AND DANCERS
Singapore-born violinist Vanessa-Mae (b. 1978) plays her violin at Bridgewater Hall in Manchester, England, in 2001.

p. 201 SPORTS STARS
American athlete Ed Moses (b. 1955) competes in the 400-m hurdles in 1979.

p. 225 MOVERS AND SHAKERS
The Live Aid charity concert at Wembley Stadium in London, England, on July 13, 1985, was organized by the Irish rock musician Bob Geldof (b. 1954).

CHAPTER ONE

WORLD LEADERS

World leaders before 1000

Human prehistory dates back at least five million years to when the first humanlike mammals—Australopithecines—appeared in central Africa. Prehistoric people probably had leaders, but we know nothing about them. From around 10,000 B.C. humans started farming methods and began settling in fertile areas. They built towns and cities and began trading. From this emerged powerful leaders and rulers and the world's first great civilizations.

▲ The Egyptian pharaoh and his queen received all kinds of gifts from people of other lands—ivory elephant tusks, animal skins, spices, gold, and jewels. Riches like these were placed inside the pharaoh's tomb so that he could use them when he reached the next world.

EGYPT, SUMER, AND BABYLON

One of the first great civilizations developed on the banks of the Nile River in Egypt. Its godlike rulers were called pharaohs. The first pharaoh was **Narmer**, who in around 3100 B.C. united the two kingdoms of Upper and Lower Egypt. The pharaoh **Cheops** (c. 2589–2566 B.C.) built the Great Pyramid. The most powerful pharaohs came from the period known as the New Kingdom (1570–1085 B.C.). They included **Queen Hatshepsut** (c. 1540–c. 1481 B.C.), the only female pharaoh, **Akhenaten** (1300s B.C.), who with his queen **Nefertiti** introduced the worship of one sun god named Aten, and **Ramses II** (1290–1224 B.C.), a military leader who defended Egypt against the Hittites and built the temple of Abu Simbel.

In around 5000 B.C. Sumerians arrived in Mesopotamia, the fertile strip of land between the Tigris and Euphrates rivers. They built the world's first cities. One was Uruk, where in c. 2700 B.C. **King Gilgamesh** reigned.

By 2300 B.C. **Sargon**, king of Akkad, had united the cities and created the Sumerian empire, which stretched from Syria to the Persian Gulf. Around 1900 B.C. the Amorites king, **Hammurabi** (ruled 1792–1750 B.C.), conquered southern Mesopotamia. He produced the world's first system of coded laws and made Babylon a great power and a center of learning and culture.

▶ The Babylonian king Nebuchadnezzar (reigned 605–562 B.C.) built hanging gardens for his wife Amytis.

Other civilizations developed in the Indus Valley (modern-day Pakistan) and in China, where by around 1500 B.C. the kings of the Shang dynasty (ruling family) ruled the Yellow River Valley. In around 1380 B.C. the Hittite military leader and king **Suppiluliumas** created a powerful military empire that lasted until around 1200 B.C.

Between 1200 and 500 B.C. the Chavin and Olmecs created the first American civilizations. Etruscans, Greeks, and Romans developed sophisticated societies in Europe, and Phoenician rulers founded Carthage in Tunisia.

◀ Saul (1000s B.C.), king of the Israelites, conquered the Philistines. Here David cuts off Saul's hem as he sleeps.

In China, Zhou rulers defeated the Shang dynasty, and in the Middle East, **Solomon** (c. 962–922 B.C.), king of Israel, built the Temple of Jerusalem.

ASSYRIANS AND PERSIANS

From the 900s B.C. warlike rulers created the Assyrian empire. An early ruler was **Tiglath-pileser III** (ruled 745–727 B.C.), a warrior king whose armies conquered Syria, Armenia, and Babylonia to make Assyria a world superpower. His successors included **Sargon II** (ruled 721–705 B.C.), who conquered Israel, **Sennacherib** (ruled 705–681 B.C.), who sacked Babylon and built his capital at Nineveh, and **Ashurbanipal** (ruled 668–627 B.C.), the last of the great Assyrian kings.

Under **Nabopolassar** (ruled 626–605 B.C.), Babylon reemerged as a major power. His son, **Nebuchadezzar II** (ruled 605–562 B.C.), rebuilt Babylon and conquered Judah. In around 548 B.C. **Cyrus II** (c. 600–529 B.C.) became king of Persia. He conquered a vast area from Turkey to the borders of India, capturing Babylon in 539 B.C. and founding the Persian Empire. One of his successors, **Darius I** (548–486 B.C.), conquered parts of Egypt and the Indus Valley area and founded Persepolis.

INDIA AND CHINA

In 332 B.C. a nobleman, **Candragupta Maurya**, united much of India and created the country's first empire. His grandson, **Asoka** (ruled 269–232 B.C.), captured the kingdom of Kalinga but was disgusted by the suffering of war. He became a Buddhist and made Buddhism the state religion.

In 246 B.C. a Chinese leader, **Zheng** (259–210 B.C.), became ruler of Qin. From 230 to 222 B.C. he united warring states, and in 221 B.C. he became the first Qin (or Ch'in) emperor of China. He began building the Great Wall to keep out invading tribes from the north. Han emperors replaced the Qin dynasty and governed China until around A.D. 220.

GREECE AND ROME

By the 400s B.C. Greece was an advanced civilization. Athens, the world's first democracy, was the greatest of the city-states. Its leading politician was **Pericles** (c. 490–429 B.C.), who defeated the Persian ruler **Xerxes** (c. 520–465 B.C.) at the Battle of Salamis. In 338 B.C. **Philip II**, king of Macedonia (382–336 B.C.), conquered the Greek city-states. His son, **Alexander the Great** (356–323 B.C.), an excellent general, forged a huge empire, conquering Phoenicia, Judah, Egypt, and Persia.

▼ Using elephants trained for war, the Carthaginian military leader Hannibal (p. 12) crossed the Alps with an army to fight the Romans.

◀ Julius Caesar was an excellent Roman general. He conquered Gaul, making it part of the Roman Empire.

▶ Legend has it that the great Roman emperor Constantine adopted the Christian symbol by painting it on his soldiers' shields before a crucial battle outside of Rome in A.D. 312.

During the 200s B.C. Rome became the most important city in Europe. The Romans conquered Italy and soon clashed with Carthage over trade rights in the Mediterranean. The Punic Wars that followed lasted 60 years. During this period the Carthaginian emperor, **Hannibal** (247–182 B.C.), led his army across the Alps to invade Italy. Following a series of victories by Hannibal, the excellent Roman general, **Scipio** (236–183 B.C.), set off to Africa to attack Carthage. This forced Hannibal to return home, and Scipio finally defeated the Carthaginians, giving the Romans control of Spain and North Africa. In 49 B.C. **Julius Caesar** (c. 100–44 B.C.), a ruthless and ambitious general and politician, became head of the Roman republic. His armies conquered Gaul and invaded Britain. After Caesar's death in 44 B.C. Romans preferred dictatorship to chaos. **Octavian** (63 B.C.–A.D. 14), his successor, gradually took control. He was renamed Augustus ("imposing one"), and he reorganized the government and empire and "imposed" peace. Emperors who followed him included **Claudius** (10 B.C.–A.D. 54), who invaded Britain and added it to the empire, **Trajan** (A.D. 53–117), during whose reign the Empire reached its greatest extent, and **Hadrian** (A.D. 76–138), who built a massive wall across northern Britain to keep out invaders. By A.D. 180, under the rule of the mad emperor **Commodus** (A.D. 161–192), the Empire was under severe strain. The barbarians, Goths, Franks, Alemanni, and Vandals were pressing in, and from A.D. 260 to 272 the Romans had to abandon parts of their empire. In A.D. 286 Emperor **Diocletian** (A.D. 245–313) divided the empire in two, the Greek-speaking east and the Latin-speaking west. He appointed **Maximilian** to rule the western half between A.D. 286 and 305. In A.D. 278 **Constantine** (c. A.D. 274–337) became emperor of the east, made Christianity Rome's official religion, and in A.D. 330 moved the capital to Byzantium, naming it Constantinople.

◀ Boudicca was queen of the Iceni, a British tribe. She led a rebellion against the Roman occupation, killing up to 70,000 of them. The Romans retaliated, and thousands of Iceni were killed. To escape Roman retribution, Boudicca is believed to have poisoned herself in A.D. 61.

BARBARIANS AND THE FALL OF ROME

In the A.D. 400s various people, whom the Romans called barbarians, migrated into

▲ Liu Hsiu (A.D. 6–75) was the first emperor of the Later, or Eastern, Han Dynasty in China.

▼ In A.D. 260 King Shapur I of Persia defeated the Roman emperor Valerian (193–260). He then had him killed, stuffed, and put on display.

▶ Attila was a great warlord and leader of the Huns. In 453 he married a German woman and died suddenly in bed, possibly from poisoning.

Europe and invaded the Roman Empire. **Alaric** (c. 370–410) was king of the Visigoths, a Germanic people. In 410 he besieged and sacked Rome. Another great warlord was **Attila** (c. 406–453), who became king of the Huns in 433. He invaded Europe from Asia and set up a new Hun homeland in Hungary. Under Attila, the Huns devastated the Balkans and Greece, forcing the Romans to pay gold to save Constantinople. After Attila invaded Gaul and northern Italy the western Roman Empire finally collapsed.

EUROPE AND CHARLEMAGNE

After the fall of Rome various kingdoms emerged in Western Europe that would become new nations. One was the kingdom of the Franks in Gaul (France). Their ruler, **Charles Martel** (c. 688–741), defeated invading Muslim armies in Poitier in 732. Charles founded the Carolingian dynasty, and in 771 his grandson, **Charlemagne** (747–814), became king of the Franks. Between 772 and 800 he created a huge empire, defeating the Saxons, the Lombards of Italy, and invading Spain. A devout Christian, he converted his conquered lands, and on Christmas Day in 800 he was crowned Emperor of the West and the first Holy Roman Emperor. Soon after Charlemagne's death his empire collapsed and became two countries—Germany and France.

◀ Charlemagne was king of the Franks. He supported the Roman church, favoring its influence in his kingdom. In return the pope, Leo III (c. 750–816), crowned Charlemagne as the first Holy Roman Emperor in 800. The grand coronation in St. Peter's Church in Rome was a political move to balance the power of the Byzantine Empire to the east.

ANGLO-SAXON BRITAIN

The Romans left Britain in around 410. In 446 the British high king **Vortigern** (ruled c. 425–450) invited German Saxons to help him fight the Picts. The Saxons gained a foothold but were held back by **Arthur**, the legendary king of the Britons. However, after a major battle in 552 the Saxons took control of most of southern and central England. Eventually seven kingdoms were formed, and they frequently fought each other for domination. In 829 **Egbert of Wessex** became the first king of a united England. By the middle of the 800s the Vikings had started settling in England. At that time **Alfred the Great** (849–899) ruled the ancient kingdom of Wessex in southern England. By 886 he had defeated the Vikings, captured London, and divided England into two. He created a legal system that remained unchanged until Norman invaders, led by **William I** (p. 14), conquered the country in 1066.

THE ISLAMIC EMPIRE

During the 500 years of rule by the Abbasid dynasty the Islamic Empire was unified, and its culture flourished. The most famous Abbasid rulers were **Harun al-Rashid** (766–809)—the fifth caliph—and his son **al-Mamun** (786–833). They encouraged learning and the arts and made Baghdad into a world center for astronomy, mathematics, geography, medicine, law, and philosophy.

KINGS AND QUEENS

William the Conqueror

1027–1087

William was the son of Robert, Duke of Normandy, inheriting the dukedom in 1035. He was the nearest adult male heir to the king of England, Edward the Confessor (c. 1003–1066), and in 1051 Edward named William as his successor. But in 1066, as Edward was dying, he changed his mind and named Harold, his brother-in-law, instead. William invaded England to assert his claim. He defeated the Anglo-Saxon army, killing Harold at the Battle of Hastings. On Christmas Day in 1066 William was crowned king of England.

Norman conqueror and king of England (1066–1087); compiler of the Domesday Book

▲ Harold was killed by an arrow through the eye at the Battle of Hastings.

Montezuma II

1466–1520

The Aztec civilization, covering most of what is now Mexico and Central America, was ruled by Montezuma II from 1502 to 1520. In 1519 the Spanish explorer Hernán Cortés (p. 37) arrived in Mexico. Montezuma believed that he was the god king Quetzalcoatl returning from exile. But Cortés took Montezuma hostage, and by June 1520 the Aztecs, doubting that the Spanish were gods, revolted, and Montezuma was killed.

Emperor of the Aztecs 1502–1520

Süleyman the Magnificent

c. 1494–1566

Under Süleyman's rule, the Ottoman Empire spread to its greatest extent and presented a real threat to the West. He conquered lands from the Balkans to Persia, and his navy dominated the Mediterranean, the Persian Gulf, and the Red Sea. In 1529 Süleyman advanced to the heart of the Austro-Hungarian Empire. His last defeat was at the Battle of Valetta, Malta, a year before his death.

Succeeded Selim I, his father 1520; captured Belgrade 1521 and Rhodes 1522; beseiged Vienna unsuccessfully 1529

HENRY V 1387–1422
Crowned king of England in 1413, Henry V dedicated his short reign to reclaiming French lands lost after the death of Edward III (1312–1377). During the Hundred Years' War he won a famous victory against the French in Agincourt in 1415. By the time he died the whole northern half of France was under English rule.

ISABELLA I 1451–1504 AND FERDINAND OF ARAGON 1452–1516
Queen of Castile, Isabella married her cousin Ferdinand of Aragon in 1469. Their united kingdoms established the basis of modern Spain. They drove Moorish invaders out of southern Spain, establishing Spain as a Catholic country. Isabella ensured Spain's share of wealth and trade in the Americas.

Catherine de' Medici

1519–1589

The daughter of Lorenzo de' Medici, the Duke of Urbino, Catherine married Henry II of France (1519–1559) in 1533. Her three sons became kings of France one after the other—Francis II, Charles IX, and Henry III. As regent she ruled France. She was behind the massacre of St. Bartholomew's Day (1572), when Charles IX ordered the killing of the Huguenot (Protestant) leader—Gaspard II de Coligny—and his followers. About 25,000 Huguenots died. Pope Gregory (d. 1187) VIII congratulated Catherine and had a medal made in her honor.

Wife of Henry II of France 1533–1559; regent for her sons Francis II (1559–1560) and Charles IX (1560–1563)

► In 1588 Elizabeth I addressed the sailors at docks near London, England, as the fleet sailed to defeat the Spanish Armada.

Ivan the Terrible

1530–1584

Ivan was crowned Ivan IV of Russia in 1547. Ruthless and clever, he reduced the power of the aristocracy, government, and merchants. On his orders thousands of Russians were executed, and he even murdered his own son in a fit of rage. However, he laid the foundations for modern Russia. Under him the country expanded to include the territories of Kazan, Astrakhan, and Siberia. Moscow was made the capital, and trade relations were established with England.

Assumed power 1547 as first czar; reduced power of nobility in Russia

Elizabeth I

1533–1603

The daughter of Henry VIII and Anne Boleyn, Elizabeth introduced the Act of Religious Settlement in 1559, making Protestantism the lawful religion of England. Much of her reign was spent fighting the Catholic forces of Spain. She imprisoned and later executed the Catholic Mary Queen of Scots for plotting against her. In 1588 Elizabeth's forces defeated the Spanish Armada. She encouraged exploration and financed the voyages of Walter Raleigh (p. 48) and Francis Drake (p. 47).

First Protestant queen of England 1588–1603; presided over flowering of the English Renaissance

Shah Jahan

1592–1666

During Shah Jahan's reign as the fifth Mogul Emperor of India, the empire was at its richest. His reign ended when his son, Aurengzeb (1618–1707), seized the throne, killing two of his three brothers and imprisoning his father. Shah Jahan is probably best known for the Taj Mahal, the white marble mausoleum built after the death of his favorite wife, Mumtaz Mahal.

Emperor of India 1627–1658; great patron of architecture and engineering

HENRY VIII 1491–1547
Founder of the Tudor dynasty, Henry became king of England in 1509. He inherited a huge fortune from his father but spent most of it on foreign wars, making England a great naval power. He is probably best known for having six wives. When the pope refused to grant him a divorce, Henry split from the Roman Catholic Church.

CHARLES V 1500–1558
King of Spain (as Charles I) and Holy Roman Emperor from 1519 to 1556, he inherited the crowns of the Netherlands, Spain, and Austria–Hungary. This empire was challenged by France, the Ottoman Empire, and the Protestant movement. Overwhelmed, Charles gave up his thrones in 1555 to his son Philip II of Spain (1527–1598).

AKBAR THE GREAT 1542–1605
Considered the greatest of the Mughal emperors of northern India, Akbar ruled from 1556 until his death. He was the grandson of Babar, who had founded the Mughal Dynasty in 1526. Akbar's wisdom, administrative abilities, firm rule, religious tolerance, and patronage of the arts led him to be called the "Guardian of Mankind."

Louis XIV

1638–1715

Louis was crowned king of France at the age of four. He went on to reign for 72 years, the longest reign of any king or queen in Europe.

He ruled as an absolute monarch, taking political power for himself after the death of his chief minister, Jules Mazarin, in 1661, declaring *"L'Etat c'est moi"* ("I am the state"). The king had great ambition for France and fought four wars against various alliances of other European countries in order to expand French ownership. In the end the wars were unsuccessful, but he had been able to fight them because of the economic management of Jean Colbert (1619–1683), his finance minister. After Colbert's death the country sank into debt. However, Louis continued to live in expensive splendor in the magnificent palace he had built in Versailles. His court was so dazzling that he became known as the "Sun King." His extreme extravagance and his insistence that all his nobles lived in the royal court fueled the unrest that finally led to the French Revolution in 1789. Louis failed to win on the battlefield, but he encouraged the arts, bringing enormous prestige to France. Writers, artists, and architects all flourished. Many were brought to the king's attention by two of his mistresses, Madame de Montespan (1641–1707) and later Madame de Maintenon (1635–1719). The king secretly married the latter after his queen, Maria Theresa of Spain, died in 1683. A Catholic convert, De Maintenon encouraged the king to drive Protestants out of France.

Longest reigning European monarch 1643–1715; started War of Dutch Devolution 1667–1668; built Palace of Versailles 1676–1708; revoked the Edict of Nantes 1685; signed Treaty of Utrecht 1713

◀ The Palace of Versailles was built between 1676 and 1708 at great expense to the French taxpayers.

CHARLES I 1600–1649
Charles became king of Great Britain and Ireland in 1625. He believed in the Divine Right of Kings—that kings were ordained by God and did not have to answer to the people. His dictatorship was the main cause of the English Civil War (1642–1651). Charles lost the war, was convicted of treason, and was beheaded in 1649.

KARL X OF SWEDEN 1622–1660
A decisive and ruthless military leader, Karl Gustav led Sweden's army during the Thirty Years' War (1616–1648). He became Crown Prince in 1650 and succeeded to the Swedish throne in 1654. His army inflicted crushing defeats on Poland and Denmark. During Karl's reign Sweden's territories expanded to their greatest extent.

William of Orange

1650–1702

William was the son of William II (1626–1650) of Orange, the Protestant Dutch royal house, and Mary (1631–1660), daughter of Charles I of England (p. 16). At the age of 22 William was given the task of resisting the French invasion of the Netherlands. In 1677 he married Mary (1662–1694), daughter of James II of England (1633–1701), a Catholic. In 1688 British statesmen asked him to "rescue" Britain. In what was known as the Glorious Revolution he invaded Britain, James fled to France, and in 1689 William was crowned William III, ruling jointly with Mary. He died after falling off his horse.

As William III, king of Great Britain and Ireland 1689–1702

Frederick the Great

1712–1786

Crowned king of Prussia in 1740, Frederick II (later known as the "Great"), was a strong, efficient ruler, superb military tactician, and renowned patron of the arts. He won Silesia from the Austrians and fought so successfully against the combined forces of Austria, Russia, and France in the Seven Years' War (1756–1763) that his country and its possessions remained intact. Frederick encouraged industry and agriculture, reformed the educational system, and supported religious tolerance. He wrote poetry, played the flute, and composed music. He also corresponded with Voltaire (p. 108), the great French writer and thinker who described him as the "Philosopher King."

King of Prussia and reformer of Prussian educational system, industry, and agriculture 1740–1786

Catherine the Great

1729–1796

A Prussian princess, Catherine married Peter, the Grand Duke of Russia (1728–1762), in 1745. Peter became czar in 1762 but was deposed in a coup and assassinated. Catherine became Empress of Russia, and she ruled with energy and efficiency. During her reign Russia expanded to include the Crimea, parts of Sweden, and most of Poland. She brought European ideas to Russia, built schools and hospitals, promoted education for women, and encouraged religious tolerance. However, Catherine did nothing to help the poor people of Russia. She kept the system of serfdom and harshly defeated peasant revolts.

Empress of Prussia and expanded Russian territory 1762–1796

▲ During her reign Catherine the Great promoted European culture in Russia.

K'ANG-HSI 1661–1722
Under the name K'ang-hsi, Hsuen-yeh was the second Ching emperor of China. Tolerant, frugal, and educated he encouraged learning, literature, arts, and sciences. He invited western missionaries to enter China, legalizing their work in 1692. When he died, there were 300,000 Roman Catholics in China and over 300 churches.

PETER THE GREAT 1672–1725
Czar of Russia from 1682, Peter I expanded his country's borders through successful wars and introduced modern ideas from the West. He traveled to Europe and worked in Dutch and English shipyards to learn the latest technologies. He reorganized the army and navy, encouraged education, and put the Church under state control.

LOUIS XVI 1754–1793 AND MARIE ANTOINETTE 1755–1793
King and queen of France when the monarchy fell during the French Revolution (1789–1799), Louis was influenced by Marie Antoinette, daughter of the Austrian emperor, Francis II (1708–1765). During the Revolution they were both imprisoned, tried, and eventually executed in 1793.

QUEEN VICTORIA

Queen Victoria

1819–1901

During Victoria's reign the British Empire expanded worldwide, making Great Britain the richest country in the world. In 1840 Victoria married her cousin, Prince Albert of Saxe-Coburg-Gotha (1819–1861). He promoted industry and technology and planned the Great Exhibition of 1851. When he died, Victoria went into mourning for years, only coming back into public view to celebrate her Golden Jubilee in 1887.

Queen of Great Britain and ruler of British Empire 1837–1901; introduced modern constitutional monarchy 1840; Empress of India 1876–1901

Cetewayo

c. 1826–1884

Cetewayo's rule of Zululand was dominated by war with the British. In 1879 he led his troops to victory in Islandhwana and Rorke's Drift but was defeated in Ulundi. Zululand was then divided into 13 chieftaincies and Cetewayo exiled. In 1883 some of his powers were restored by the British.

King of Zululand 1873–1883; defeated British in Zulu Wars 1879

Czar Nicholas II

1868–1918

Succeeding to the Russian throne in 1894, Nicholas' reign was a tragic story of repression, incompetence, and mismanagement. He was very influenced by his wife, Alexandra, who in turn was influenced by the religious mystic, Grigory Rasputin (p. 240). After a disastrous war with Japan (1904–1905) and civil unrest the first revolution under his reign took place in 1905. To meet the rebels' demands the Duma, an elected assembly, was set up. It had only met four times when in 1917 the second—and more successful—revolution swept Nicholas from power. He and his entire family were shot by the Red Guards in 1918.

Czar of Russia 1894–1917

Haile Selassie I

1891–1975

Haile Selassie brought western ideas and economic reform to Ethiopia, declaring slavery a crime. In 1916 he became regent and heir to the throne. When the Italians invaded Ethiopia in 1935, he was forced to live in exile in Great Britain. After the British captured Ethiopia from Italy in 1941, Haile Selassie took back his throne. In 1974 he was deposed in a military coup and died one year later. He was also known as Ras Tafari, the "Lion of Judah." Followers of the Rastafarian faith, based on the ideas of Jamaican philosopher Marcus Garvey (p. 127), worship Haile Selassie. They believe he was the Messiah.

Emperor of Ethiopia 1930–1974; introduced democratic government 1955

Emperor Hirohito

1901–1989

The eldest son of Emperor Taisho (1879–1926), Hirohito became the 124th emperor of Japan in 1926, ruling under the name Showa. He did not oppose Japan's aggressive military activities against China or its major role in World War II, but it is believed that he did not approve either. In 1946, during the United States' postwar occupation in his country, he agreed to place all political power in the hands of an elected government. He was the first Japanese emperor to became a symbol of the state rather than a divine ruler.

First Japanese prince to visit the West 1921; Emperor of Japan 1926–1989

POLITICIANS

Oliver Cromwell

1599–1658

A parliamentarian who opposed the despotic power of Charles I (p. 16), Cromwell led his side to victory in the English Civil War (1642–1651). He reorganized his troops into the highly efficient New Model Army, and he never lost a battle. After Charles' execution in 1649 Cromwell declared Britain a Commonwealth (republic), and in 1653 he became the Lord Protector. Although he was considered harsh, his rule increased British prestige abroad.

Organized New Model Army 1642; Lord Protector of Britain 1653–1658

George Washington

1732–1799

In 1774 Washington was a member of the U.S. Continental Congress formed to oppose unfair British policies. During the Revolutionary War (1775–1783) against the British he commanded the forces that won the Battle of Yorktown (1781). Elected president in 1789, he signed the Bill of Rights in 1791, and he was reelected for a second term in 1793.

Helped draw up U.S. Constitution 1787; president of the United States 1789–1797

Abraham Lincoln

1809–1865

Lincoln's career, from humble beginnings to the highest office in the United States is seen as an example of the power of democracy.

In 1847 Lincoln was elected to the U.S. House of Representatives. He gave up politics at the end of his term but returned in 1854. In 1856 he joined the antislavery Republican party, and in 1860 he was elected president. After his election the southern slave states broke away from the Union to form a confederacy. At first he fought the American Civil War (1861–1865) to keep the states united. Later, slavery was the issue, and in 1863 he declared slaves in the south free. He was assassinated by John Wilkes Booth (p. 239) in 1865.

First Republican president 1860–1865; freed American slaves 1863; victor in American Civil War 1861–1865

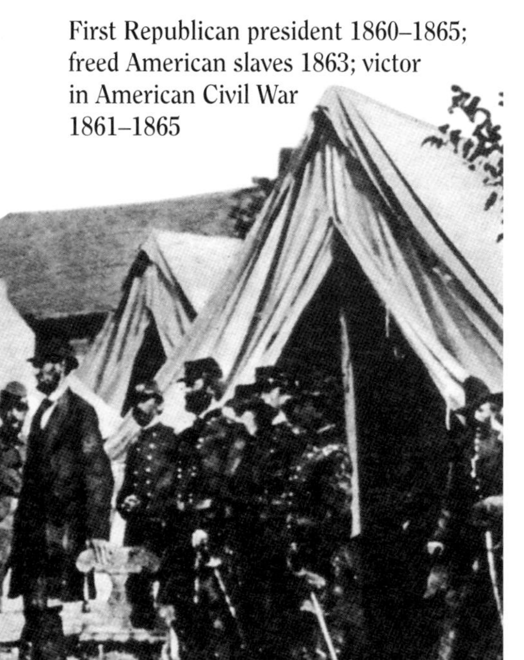

► Lincoln inspects troops during the Civil War.

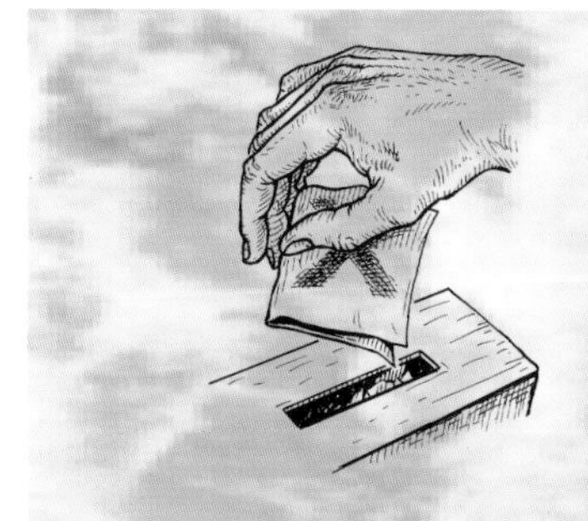

CARDINAL RICHELIEU 1585–1642
Armand-Jean du Plessis, Duc de Richelieu was chief minister to French King Louis XIII from 1624 until his death. Richelieu's aim was to make the monarchy absolute and increase French power in Europe by challenging the Habsburg Empire of Austria. He suppressed rebellions at home and took France into the Thirty Years' War against the Habsburgs. He also founded the French Academy in 1635.

THOMAS JEFFERSON 1743–1826
Thomas Jefferson, a colleague and friend of George Washington (above left), was a member of the first Continental Congress in 1774. He prepared the draft of the Declaration of Independence in 1776, and between 1785 and 1801 he served as U.S. ambassador to Paris, secretary of state, and vice president. He was the third U.S. president from 1801 to 1809.

OTTO VON BISMARCK 1815–1898
This Prussian prince and statesman united the states of Germany, Bismarck was elected prime minister in 1862. He created a German empire, achieving this with a mixture of military force, diplomacy, and political know-how. He successfully fought three wars against Denmark, Austria, and France. After the last victory Bismarck, then known as the "Iron Chancellor," set up the Triple Alliance with Austria and Italy and signed a peace treaty with Russia.

SUN YAT-SEN 1866–1925
A Chinese revolutionary leader, he founded the Nationalist Party in 1894. After years in exile he returned to China in 1911 to join in the revolution that overthrew the corrupt Manchu regime. Sun Yat-sen became the provisional president of the Republic of China in 1912. In 1921, after resigning, he set up an independent republic in Canton, southern China.

Mahatma Gandhi

1869–1948

Gandhi was the leader of the National Congress Party of India. He campaigned for home rule (*swaraj*) and independence from Great Britain.

Born in India, Gandhi studied law in England and worked in South Africa between 1893 and 1914. He returned to India and led two nonviolent campaigns against British rule that led to his imprisonment for conspiracy. After being released from jail in 1931 Gandhi joined talks in London, England, which led to Indian independence. This was eventually achieved in 1947. Gandhi was assassinated in 1948.

Led two campaigns against British rule in India 1919–1920; imprisoned by British 1922–1924 and 1930–1931; founded the Indian State 1947

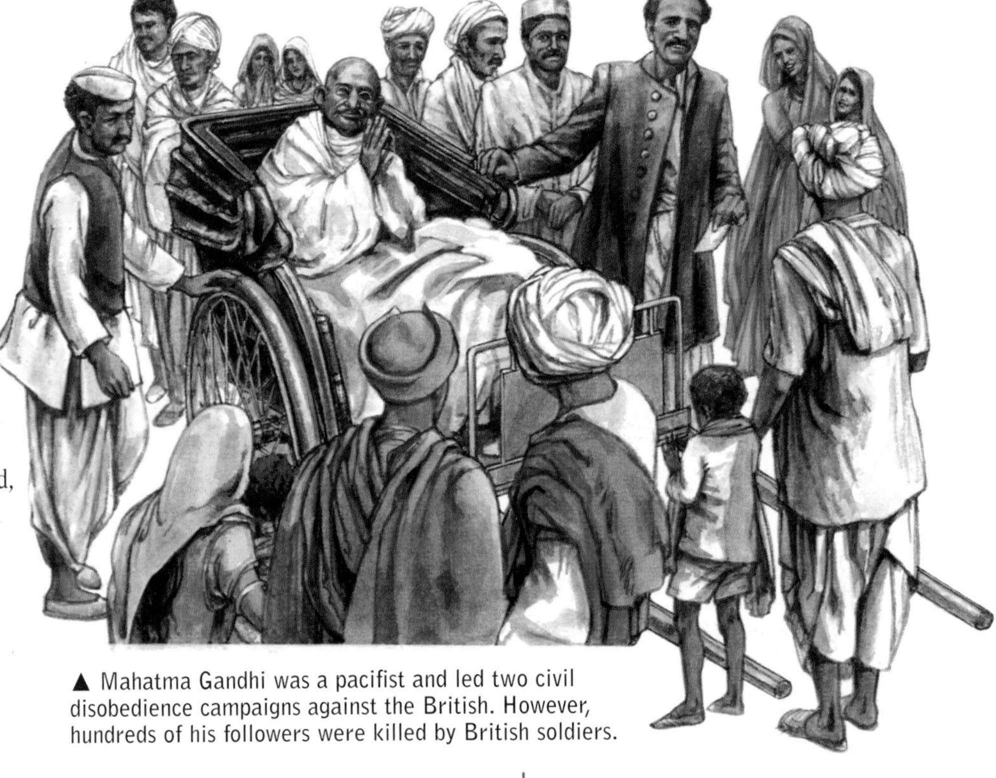

▲ Mahatma Gandhi was a pacifist and led two civil disobedience campaigns against the British. However, hundreds of his followers were killed by British soldiers.

Vladimir Lenin

1870–1924

Vladimir Ilych Ulyanov worked as a lawyer in St. Petersburg, Russia, until 1895, when he was imprisoned for spreading revolutionary ideas. He was then exiled to Siberia until 1900, where he studied the work of Karl Marx (p. 111). In 1903 Lenin's ideas split the Russian Social Democratic Party into two groups: the Bolsheviks, who followed Marxist ideals, and the Mensheviks, who were more moderate. Lenin was a Bolshevik. He was in Switzerland when revolution broke out in 1917 and returned to Russia to lead the Bolsheviks. The revolution succeeded, and Lenin became head of the first Soviet government.

Russian revolutionary 1900–1917; first Communist leader of the newly formed U.S.S.R. 1917–1924

Winston Churchill

1874–1965

Churchill was in and out of British politics from 1900. He belonged to both the Liberal and Conservative parties, and he held many important posts. He was prime minister of a coalition government (1940–1945) during World War II. His speeches made at this time helped the British people withstand defeat and German bombing.

First Lord of the Admiralty 1911–1915; Great Britain's leader during World War II; Conservative prime minister 1951–1955

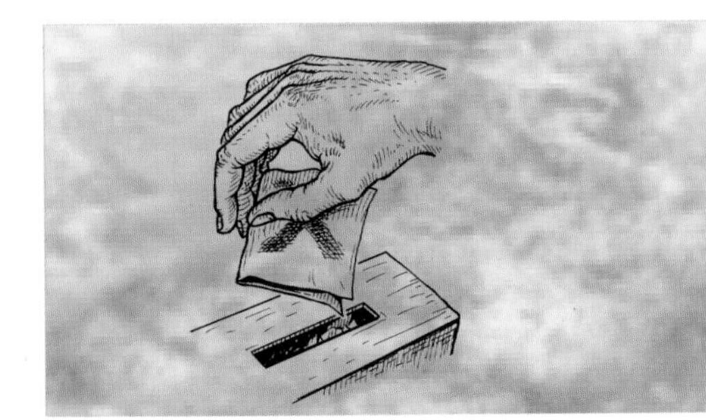

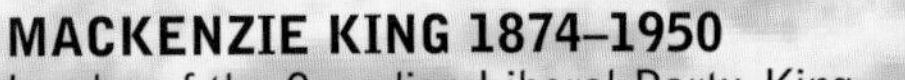

MACKENZIE KING 1874–1950
Leader of the Canadian Liberal Party, King was prime minister of Canada three times between 1921 and 1948. His diplomatic skills kept the English- and French-speaking states of Canada united. As a result of his work, the Statute of Westminster, allowing the Canadian Parliament to pass its own laws, was passed in 1931.

KONRAD ADENAUER 1876–1967
First chancellor of West Germany in 1949, Adenauer was the leader of the Christian Democratic Union. Hitler imprisoned him in 1933 because he opposed the Nazi regime. He also stood against communism. After World War II Adenauer oversaw the rebuilding of his country, and he worked to establish friendly relations with France.

Joseph Stalin

1879–1953

Stalin trained to be a Russian priest, but he was forced out of theological college because of his revolutionary activities. He became a Bolshevik and a member of the October 1917 Revolutionary Committee. After Lenin's death Stalin and Trotsky (p. 30) fought over the leadership. Stalin won, and in 1928 he set up Five-Year Plans to improve industry and agriculture. However, millions died from starvation. Stalin ordered purges to silence opposition—those who disagreed with him were sent to prison or executed. When Germany invaded in 1941, the U.S.S.R. joined the Allies, and Stalin achieved world leader status.

General Secretary of the Communist Party of the U.S.S.R. 1922–1953; Communist dictator of U.S.S.R. 1924–1953

▲ In 1945 Winston Churchill, Franklin D. Roosevelt, and Joseph Stalin met in Yalta to discuss the division of Europe after the end of World War II.

F. D. Roosevelt

1882–1945

Democrat Franklin Delano Roosevelt led the U.S. through the terrible years of the Depression and World War II. When he entered office in 1933, one fourth of the population was unemployed, banks were failing, and people were starving. He provided help for the unemployed, farmers, businesses, and banks. When World War II broke out in Europe in 1939, Roosevelt set up the lease-lend scheme to supply equipment to the Allies. In December 1941, after Japan attacked the American Pacific Fleet in Pearl Harbor, he led his country into the war.

32nd president of the U.S. 1933–1945; architect of the New Deal 1933–1936

Mao Tse-tung

1893–1976

Mao followed the theories of Karl Marx (p. 111) and adapted communism to suit China. In 1931 he set up a Communist Republic in Jiangxi Province. When it was attacked by Nationalist forces in 1934, he led his army on the 6,030 mi. (9,700km) Long March to Shaanxi. Mao became head of the C.C.P., forming an alliance with the Nationalists until 1945. Then after a fierce civil war won by the Communists, Mao established the People's Republic of China in 1949.

One of founders of Chinese Communist Party (C.C.P.) 1921; chairman of C.C.P. 1935–1976; founder and chairman of People's Republic of China 1949–1959

▲ Mao launched the Cultural Revolution in 1966 against liberal forces within China.

KEMAL ATATÜRK 1881–1938
Founder and first president of the Republic of Turkey in 1923, Atatürk brought social and political reform to his country. He wanted to transform the country into a modern European secular republic. His reforms included votes for women, the abolition of polygamy (more than one wife at a time), and improved education for all.

ÉAMON DE VALERA 1882–1975
Born in New York, Irish Republican politician De Valera fought for independence from Great Britain and a united Ireland. In 1926 he helped set up a new political party, Fianna Fail, to achieve these aims. De Valera was prime minister three times between 1932 and 1959 and president of Ireland from 1959 to 1973.

CHIANG KAI-SHEK 1887–1975
Chiang Kai-shek, a leader of the Chinese Nationalist Movement, was part of the revolution that overthrew the Manchu dynasty in 1911. He was president of China twice between 1928 and 1945. In 1948 the Communists drove him out of China to Formosa (Taiwan) where, supported by the U.S., he set up a right-wing government.

Adolf Hitler

1889–1945

Born in Austria, Adolf Hitler rose from humble beginnings to become *Der Führer* ("the Leader") of the German Nazi party.

Based on nationalism and anti-Semitism, the Nazi party grew to become the largest party in the German Parliament, and in 1933 Hitler became chancellor of Germany. He turned the country into a one-party dictatorship, suspending the constitution and murdering opponents. Eager to expand German frontiers, he formed an alliance with fascist Italy in 1936, and in 1938 he invaded Austria and Czechoslovakia. World War II began when he invaded Poland in 1939, and Great Britain and France declared war on Germany. Hitler took personal control of the war and went on to invade Belgium, the Netherlands, France, Denmark, Norway, Romania, Yugoslavia, Greece, and North Africa. Ignoring a pact with the U.S.S.R., he invaded that country in 1941. Hitler ordered the imprisonment and murder of 12 million people—including Jews, homosexuals, and gypsies—who were killed in concentration camps. In 1945, when it was clear that Germany had lost the war, Hitler committed suicide in Berlin.

Chancellor of Germany 1933–1945; architect of the infamous Final Solution and dictator who led Germany into World War II 1939–1945

▲ Hitler married his mistress, Eva Braun, in 1945 only days before they committed suicide.

Jomo Kenyatta

c. 1889–1978

Jomo Kenyatta (born Kamau Ngengi) belonged to the Kikuyu people of Kenya. He was orphaned as a young child and soon became involved in anticolonial politics. In 1922 he joined the Kikuyu Central Association (KCA) and became its president. After lengthy visits to Great Britain and the U.S.S.R. he returned to become president of the Kenya African Union (KAU) in 1947. Kenyatta worked to gain Kenya's freedom from Great Britain, but in 1952 he was jailed for seven years' hard labor, accused of being involved with the Mau Mau terrorists. After another year in exile in north Kenya Kenyatta returned to become a member of parliament in 1961 and then prime minister and first president of the newly independent Kenya. Under his rule Kenya enjoyed a period of peace and economic growth.

Prime minister of Kenya 1963; first president of independent Kenya 1964–1978

Nikita Kruschev

1894–1971

Kruschev rose through the ranks of the Communist party of the U.S.S.R. to become leader in 1953 after Stalin's death. He officially denounced Stalin in 1956 and became premier of his country in 1958. Under Kruschev the U.S.S.R. made the first flights into space (p. 55). During the Cuban Missile Crisis (1962), Kruschev was forced to withdraw Soviet missiles from Communist Cuba. This and his failure to expand the economy led to his forced retirement in 1964.

Chairman of Communist party U.S.S.R. 1953–1964; denounced Stalinism 1956; premier of U.S.S.R. 1958–1964

Salvador Allende

1908–1973

Salvador Allende trained as a doctor, and in 1933 he helped set up the Chilean Socialist party. He held various political posts, and he unsuccessfully ran for president three times. In 1970 he was finally elected leader of the coalition of left wing and socialist parties known as the Unidad Popular (Popular Front). Allende planned to introduce socialism, and he nationalized copper mines owned by U.S. companies. Under Richard Nixon (right) the U.S. did not want a Communist state on their doorstep. In 1973 they backed a coup led by General Pinochet. Allende was shot dead in the presidential palace.

Founded Chilean Socialist party 1933; minister of health 1939–1941; senator 1945–1970; president of Chile 1970–1973

Richard Nixon

1913–1994

The 37th U.S. president, Richard Nixon was elected as a Republican senator in 1946 and was vice president to Dwight Eisenhower (p. 31). He served two terms as president (1969–1974). Nixon opened diplomatic relations with China and the U.S.S.R., and after years of controversy he brought the U.S. war in Vietnam to an end in 1973. He resigned after losing public credibility over the Watergate scandal of 1972.

U.S. vice president 1953–1961; U.S. president 1969–1974; first U.S. president to resign 1974

John F. Kennedy

1917–1963

After serving as a torpedo boat commander in World War II Kennedy served as Democratic senator for Massachusetts in 1952 and won the U.S. presidency in 1960. His New Frontier policy outlined a program of civil rights' reforms, including the desegregation of education, which meant that children from all racial backgrounds could go to school together. In 1961 he backed the unsuccessful Bay of Pigs invasion of Cuba by Cuban exiles opposed to Fidel Castro (p. 32). In 1962 he kept his nerve in a confrontation with the U.S.S.R. and persuaded them to remove missiles from Cuba. In 1963 Kennedy was assassinated, allegedly by Lee Harvey Oswald (p. 246).

Massachusetts senator 1952–1960; youngest and first Catholic president of the U.S. 1960–1963; assassinated 1963

JAWAHARLAL NEHRU 1889–1964
Nehru was the first prime minister of India, from its independence in 1947 until his death in 1964. He was known as "Pandit Nehru." Pandit was his family's caste name and means "teacher." He was president of the Indian National Congress in 1929, supported Gandhi's civil disobedience policy, established democracy in his country, and kept India neutral.

GOLDA MEIR 1898–1978
Born Goldie Mabovitch in Kiev, Russia, she moved to Palestine in 1917 and became active in politics. When Israel was established as an independent state in 1948, she served as ambassador to the U.S.S.R. (1948–1949), secretary of labor (1949–1956), and foreign secretary (1956–1966). Golda Meir was the founder of the Israeli Labor Party (1967) and the first female prime minister of Israel (1969–1974).

DENG XIAOPING 1904–1997
Leader of the Chinese Communist party from 1978 until 1987, Deng's political career was shaped by periods of agreement with—and opposition to—Mao Tse-tung (p. 21). He joined Mao's Long March (1934–1935) but was dismissed during the Cultural Revolution of 1966, accused of having capitalist ideas. After Mao's death in 1976, Deng returned to office. He made many economic reforms but remained politically inflexible.

RONALD REAGAN b. 1911
The 40th president of the U.S., Reagan served two terms from 1981 to 1989. A Hollywood actor between 1937 and 1964, Reagan joined the Republican party in 1962 and was the governor of California (1966–1974). He cut welfare and taxes and increased spending on defense and the military. He survived an assassination attempt in 1981. In 1983 he introduced the strategic defense initiative known as "Star Wars."

Gamal Nasser

1918–1970

Gamal Nasser led the military coup that deposed King Farouk of Egypt in 1952, establishing the country as a republic. He became prime minister in 1954 and was elected president in 1956. In that same year he nationalized the Suez Canal, provoking an international incident. In 1958 Nasser became president of the United Arab Republic, a union of Egypt and Syria that fell apart when Syria withdrew in 1961. Nasser resigned after losing the Six-Day War to Israel in 1967, but he was persuaded to stay in office. He died in 1970, just after signing a cease-fire with Israel.

First president of Egypt 1956–1970; nationalized Suez Canal 1956

Anwar el-Sadat

1918–1981

Sadat served as vice president of Egypt twice. After Nasser's death he took over as president. In 1977 he went to Jerusalem to try and establish peace with Israel. The following year U.S. President Jimmy Carter (b. 1924) invited Sadat and Israeli leader Menachem Begin (1913–1992) to settle their differences. The two leaders were jointly awarded the Nobel Peace Prize. In 1981 Sadat was assassinated by Muslim extremists.

Vice president of Egypt 1964–1970; president 1970–1981

Nelson Mandela

b. 1918

Nelson Mandela has spent his entire adult life fighting racism and the abuse of human rights in South Africa.

Mandela studied law in Johannesburg, and in 1942 he joined the African National Congress (ANC). He traveled around the country organizing resistance to the government's policy of apartheid. For his part in the campaign he was arrested and given a suspended sentence. Throughout the 1950s he worked against white repression and was banned, arrested, and imprisoned many times. After the Sharpeville Massacre in 1960 the ANC was banned, and Mandela organized a three-day national strike. He left the country illegally to set up *Umkhonto we Sizwe* ("Spear of the Nation"). Upon his return in 1964 he was sentenced to life imprisonment for sabotage and treason. Following years of international pressure, President F. W. de Klerk ordered his release in 1990. The ANC was legalized, and in 1991 Mandela was elected its president. In 1993 Mandela and De Klerk agreed on the formation of a government of national unity, and for the first time free elections were held. They were jointly awarded the Nobel Peace Prize, and Mandela became president in 1994, retiring in 1999.

Imprisoned 1964–1990; South Africa's first black president 1994–1999

SIRIMAVO BANDARANAIKE b. 1916
After her husband's assassination in 1959, Mrs. Bandaranaike became leader of the Sri Lankan Freedom Party. In 1960 she was elected the first female prime minister in the world, and she continued her husband's socialist policies. She was expelled from parliament in 1980 for abuse of power.

INDIRA GANDHI 1917–1984
The first female prime minister of India (1966–1977 and 1980–1984), Gandhi was the daughter of Jawaharlal Nehru. In 1975 she was convicted of rigging the elections and was defeated in 1977. Helped by her son Sanjay, she returned to office in 1980, but she was assassinated in 1984 by her own bodyguards.

JULIUS NYERERE c. 1922–1999
First president of Tanzania from 1964 to 1985, Nyerere spent his political life campaigning for African independence. In 1961 he led Tanganyika to independence from Great Britain and became prime minister in 1962. Between 1962 and 1963 he united Tanganyika and the island of Zanzibar to form the republic of Tanzania.

Eva Perón

1919–1952

María Eva Duarte (Evita) de Perón was the second wife of Argentinian president Juan Perón (1895–1974). An actress from a humble background, she was very ambitious and politically shrewd, playing an important part in her husband's political success. Worshiped and adored by the public, she took over the health and labor departments, won the vote for women, and established many charities.

Influential first lady of Argentina 1945–1952

Kenneth Kaunda

b. 1924

Kenneth Kaunda fought for the independence of Northern Rhodesia (today's Zambia). After two years in prison for political activities he became leader of the United National Independence Party (UNIP). The party won the election in 1961, and he served as Minister of Local Government in the first black African government. As president he made UNIP the only political party. Economic decline and unrest forced him to introduce a multiparty system. In 1991 UNIP were defeated, and he lost power.

Secretary general of African National Congress 1953; founded Zambia African National Congress 1958; first president of the Republic of Zambia 1964–1991

Yasir Arafat

b. 1929

Yasir Arafat has always campaigned for an independent Palestinian state. In 1956 he cofounded al-Fatah, the Palestine National Liberation Movement, which became part of the Palestine Liberation Organization (PLO). By the 1980s arguing groups split the PLO, and Arafat almost lost control. In 1990 the PLO recognized the state of Israel, and in 1993 Arafat reached an agreement with Israeli leader, Itzhak Rabin (1922–1995). They and Shimon Peres (b. 1923) were awarded the Nobel Peace Prize. Since then increased fighting between the Israeli government and Palestinian freedom fighters has led to a loss of power for Arafat.

Leader of the Palestinian Liberation Organization since 1969

Mikhail Gorbachev

b. 1931

President of the U.S.S.R. from 1985 to 1991, Gorbachev introduced reforms that ended the Cold War between the U.S.S.R. and the West and led to the breakup of the Soviet Union into independent republics. *Perestroika* ("restructuring") took apart the Stalinist central planning system and mostly affected economic and industrial matters. *Glasnost* ("openness") gave more personal freedom to Russian people. Censorship was abolished, religious tolerance encouraged, dissidents released from prison, freedom of the press allowed information to flow more freely, and relations with the West were encouraged. Gorbachev was praised abroad for his policies and awarded the Nobel Peace Prize in 1990, but he became unpopular at home and resigned in 1991.

President of U.S.S.R. 1985–1991; architect of *perestroika* and *glasnost*

MARGARET THATCHER b. 1925
The first female prime minister of Great Britain, Margaret Thatcher led the Conservative party from 1975 and was elected prime minister three times (1979–1990). She privatized state assets, broke the power of the trade unions, and reduced the power of local governments. She was forced to resign in 1990.

CORY AQUINO b. 1933
President of the Philippines from 1986 to 1992, Corazon (Cory) Aquino was an opponent of the right-wing Marcos regime. Supported by a nonviolent people power movement, she stood against Marcos in the 1986 election. After accusing her opponent of rigging the vote she won the presidency.

DALAI LAMA b. 1935
The Tibetans believe that their leader is reincarnated every generation. As a child the current Dalai Lama was chosen as their leader by Tibetan monks in 1940. In 1959 he fled after the Chinese invaded Tibet, and he has remained in exile in India ever since. He received the Nobel Peace Prize in 1989.

MILITARY LEADERS

El Cid

c. 1043–1099

Born near Burgos in Spain, El Cid is one of his country's national heroes. His real name was Rodrigo Díaz de Vivar, and he earned the name El Cid (from the Arabic *Sayyid* meaning "lord") for his courage and fighting skills. Born an aristocrat, he was in command of the royal army of King Sancho II of Castile by the age of 22. Later, El Cid fought for Sancho's brother Alfonso, leading daring raids against the Muslims, who controlled part of Spain. In 1081 Alfonso exiled El Cid, who had led an unauthorized raid against the Moors, and he switched sides, fighting instead for the Muslims. In 1084 he defeated a much larger Christian army and was richly rewarded by the Muslims. He rejoined Alfonso, and in 1094 he besieged and captured Valencia from the Muslims and ruled it until his death.

Led Spanish Royal Army against Muslims 1065–1081; defected to Muslim army and defeated Christians 1084; ruled Valencia 1094–1099

▲ El Cid was a great leader who attracted an army of courageous and loyal soldiers.

Saladin

1138–1193

An incredible Muslim warrior, Saladin (in Arabic, *Salah ad-Din*) was born of Kurdish ancestry in modern-day Iraq. In 1169 he became chief minister of Egypt, at that time ruled by the Fatimid dynasty. Saladin overthrew Fatimid rule and become sultan.

Saladin expanded Muslim lands by conquering Syria and parts of North Africa. He led a combined force of Syrian and Egyptian Muslims in a *jihad* ("holy war"). Saladin beat the Christians at the Battle of Hattin (1187), captured Acre and Jerusalem, and drove the Crusaders out. In 1189 the Third Crusade left Europe but could not defeat Saladin. Finally, Richard I (below) agreed to a peace treaty, guaranteeing Muslim control of most of the region. A wise leader and cultured man, Saladin united the Muslim Middle East, ending the Crusaders' hopes in the Holy Land.

Sultan of Egypt 1171–1175; sultan of Egypt and Syria 1175–1193; defeated Christians at Hattin 1187; peace treaty with Richard I of England 1192

At the Battle of Hattin in 1187, Saladin tricked the Crusaders onto a hill on a hot day. While they roasted in their metal armor, he surrounded and defeated them.

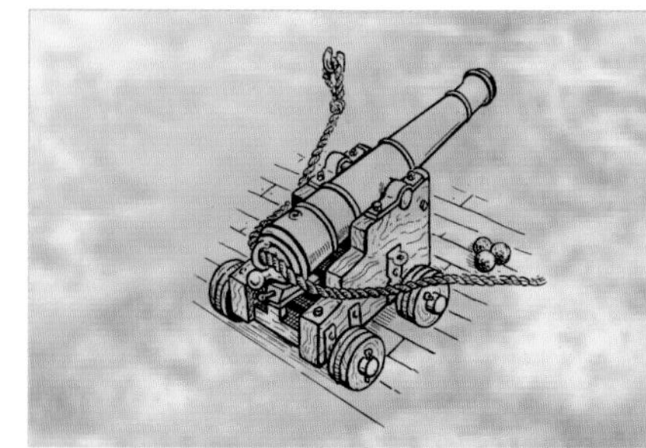

MINIMATO YORITOMO 1147–1199
Yoritomo was a Japanese warlord and the head of the Minimato clan. During a conflict between the different Japanese clans he took over eastern Japan. In 1185 he defeated the Tairo clan at the Battle of Dan No Ura and set up a military government. In 1192 he was given the title shogun ("great general").

RICHARD I 1157–1199
Richard I (known as "the Lionheart") was king of England from 1189 to 1199. In 1190 he went on the Third Crusade against the Muslims and signed a three-year treaty with Saladin. He was captured by Henry VI, Holy Roman Emperor, in 1192, who demanded a huge ransom for his release in 1194. Richard died fighting in France.

Genghis Khan

c. 1162–1227

Originally named Temujin, Genghis Khan was the son of a Mongol chief. When he was about 12, his father died, and he became a skilled warrior and attracted a huge following. He joined forces with the people of eastern Mongolia and helped defend the Chinese borders against the Tatars. His fame grew, and in around 1196 his followers proclaimed him *khan* ("lord" or "ruler")—he chose the name Gengis (or Jenghis). He soon became master of eastern Mongolia. An excellent general, he had also conquered western Mongolia and was proclaimed Great Khan of all the Mongolian tribes by 1206. Under his leadership his armies went on to conquer northern China, Afghanistan, central Asia, and much of Persia (modern-day Iran). His empire was one of the largest in history.

Genghis Khan's armies swept all before them.

Creator and ruler of the Mongol empire 1196–1227

Simón Bolívar

1783–1830

Born in Caracas, Venezuela, Simón Bolívar was a revolutionary leader who liberated much of South America from Spanish colonial rule. In 1810 Bolívar joined the Venezuelan revolution against Spain. He formed an army, but in 1812 his forces were defeated. In 1815 he was forced to flee to the islands of Jamaica and Haiti. In 1817 he returned to Venezuela as commander of the rebel forces. Using guerilla tactics, he and his fighters took the lower Orinoco basin. In 1819 he and his men crossed the Andes mountains into Colombia and defeated the Spanish in Boyaca. He won further victories against the Spanish, capturing Caracas in 1821. By 1824 he had driven the Spanish out of Ecuador, Chile, Peru, and Colombia.

Led South American army to victory against Spanish 1817–1824; president of new republic of Colombia 1819–1830

Tamerlane

1336–1404

Also called Timur, Tamerlane was a Mongolian warrior and ruler. He was born near Samarkand in central Asia and was a descendant of Genghis Khan (above). He became ruler of the Mongol Empire. His army of Turks and Mongols subdued Persia, Georgia, and the Tatar Empire and conquered India, Damascus, and Syria before defeating the Turks in Ankara. Tamerlane died when his forces tried to invade China.

Ruler of Mongol Empire 1370–1405; defeated Ottoman Turks in Ankara 1402

Joan of Arc

c. 1412–1431

Joan believed that God had chosen her to restore the rightful king to the French throne. In 1429 she gained the support of the young king, later Charles VII, and riding at the head of his army defeated the English who were besieging Orléans. Captured by the English, she was tortured, tried, found guilty of heresy and witchcraft, and burned at the stake. In 1456 a court declared her innocent, and in 1920 she was declared a saint.

Defeated English at Orléans 1429; burned at the stake by the English 1431

In 1431 Joan of Arc was burned at the stake in Rouen.

HORATIO NELSON 1758–1805
British admiral Horatio Nelson became a hero for his naval successes in the Napoleonic Wars against France. He defeated the French fleet at the Battle of the Nile in 1798, and in 1805 he was victorious over the French and Spanish fleets at the Battle of Trafalgar. Wounded, he died on his flagship, *Victory*.

SAM HOUSTON 1793–1863
In 1836, a year after Texas declared itself independent from Mexico, a Mexican army besieged the Alamo, killing all 200 Texan defenders. Two months later Houston, leader of the Texan forces, defeated the Mexicans at the Battle of San Jacinto. He became president of an independent Texas, and Houston is named after him.

GEORGE CUSTER 1839–1876
In 1866 American soldier George Custer commanded the U.S. 7th Cavalry against the Native Americans in the Midwest. During his "last stand" at the Battle of Little Big Horn in 1876 he and his troops were wiped out by a combined force of Cheyenne and Sioux led by chiefs Sitting Bull (1834–1890) and Crazy Horse (d. 1877).

Napoléon Bonaparte

1769–1821

One of the world's great military geniuses, Napoléon Bonaparte was born on the French island of Corsica, attended military school in France, and went on to become an excellent general. In the early 1800s he nearly succeeded in conquering all of Europe.

▲ French painter Jacques David (1748–1825) painted the young French general, Napoléon Bonaparte, leading his army through the St. Bernard Pass in the Alps to Italy.

By 1792 revolutionary France was at war with Great Britain, Austria, Russia, and Prussia. In 1795 a weak French government called the Directory was formed. As a young general, Napoléon led a number of successful campaigns, capturing northern Italy in 1797. The Directory relied on him, and he grew popular and powerful. He was asked to invade Great Britain, but he thought that disrupting British trade routes to India was more important. His subsequent invasion of Egypt in 1798 failed when British admiral Horatio Nelson (p. 27) destroyed the French fleet at the Battle of the Nile.

Napoléon returned to France in 1799, dismissed the Directory, and took control. He made himself first consul, and for the next 15 years he ruled France. In 1804 he crowned himself emperor, introducing many reforms, new laws, and better education as well as reorganizing the government. Napoléon had a very large army that by 1815 totaled 2,750,000 soldiers. He used this massive force to try to conquer Europe. His armies defeated Austria and Russia at Austerlitz in 1805, Prussia at Jena in 1806, and Russia faced defeat at Friedland in 1807. Great Britain was saved from invasion by Nelson's defeat of the French fleet at the Battle of Trafalgar (1805). In 1808 French forces invaded Spain, but by 1813 they had been beaten by the British. By 1812 Napoléon had overstretched his armies, and his ill-fated invasion of Russia left over 500,000 French dead. In 1813 he was defeated in Leipzig by a combined European force. France was invaded, and he was sent into exile on the island of Elba in 1814. He escaped and was finally defeated by the British general, Arthur Wellesley, the duke of Wellington (1769–1852) and the Prussian general Gebbard von Blücher (1742–1819) at Waterloo in Belgium. Napoléon died in exile on the island of St. Helena.

First consul of France 1799–1804; emperor of France 1804–1814; Battle of Austerlitz 1805; Battle of Trafalgar 1805; Battle of Waterloo 1815

► One of Napoléon's military successes, the Battle of Austerlitz, was fought against the Austrians and Russians in 1805. Napoléon was a clever and tactical leader, and he inspired his troops with speeches. He modernized warfare, using cannons and large armies.

Guiseppe Garibaldi

1807–1882

In the mid-1800s Italy consisted of different kingdoms, some controlled by Austria and France. From 1848 French-born Garibaldi, who had fought guerrilla wars in South America, led an Italian liberation movement. He fought for the Sardinian king against the Austrians and helped Rome fight the French. His small army of volunteers conquered Sicily and Naples in 1860. In 1861 most of Italy united under Victor Emmanuel II (1820–1878).

Led Italian liberation army 1848–1860; seized Sicily and southern Italy 1860

▲ In 1860 Garibaldi gathered a volunteer army of 1,000 men called Red Shirts.

General Ulysses Grant

1822–1885

When the Civil War began in 1861, Ulysses S. Grant became a brigadier general. In 1862 he captured Fort Henry and Fort Donelson in Tennessee. In the following year he defeated Confederate forces in Vicksburg and Chattanooga. Grant became commander-in-chief and accepted the Confederate surrender from General Robert E. Lee (1807–1870). He was elected president in 1869, but his presidency was marred by corruption and mismanagement.

Commander of Union forces during the Civil War 1864–1865; 18th U.S. president 1869–1877

Geronimo

1829–1909

Geronimo was a Chiricahua Apache leader from Arizona. Mexican raiders killed his mother, wife, and children in 1858. The U.S. government moved the Apaches to a reservation in 1876, and Geronimo fled. He was captured and marched 410 mi. (660km) in chains to the San Carlos Reservation in Arizona. After escaping he carried out repeated raids to free his people. In 1883 U.S. troops forced him to surrender, but in 1885 he led 134 warriors on a final breakout. Captured in 1886, he was deported to Oklahoma.

Chief of Chiricahua Apaches who fought to protect tribal lands from U.S. government and settlers 1875–1886

PAUL HINDENBURG
1847–1934

Born in Germany, Hindenburg was a general during World War I (1914–1918). He was put in charge of German forces in the east, and from 1916 he commanded the entire German army. He achieved a decisive victory against Russia at the Battle of Tannenberg (1914) and stopped the Allied advance in the west along a line known as the Hindenburg Line. In 1918 he launched a counteroffensive against the Allied forces. It failed, and Germany was defeated. Hindenburg was second president of the German Republic from 1925 to 1934.

JAN SMUTS 1870–1950

Jan Christiaan Smuts was a South African soldier and statesman. He was born in Malmesbury, Cape Colony. Of Dutch descent, he commanded Boer (Dutch settlers) forces in the Boer War (1899–1902) between the Boers and the British. Later he worked for cooperation between the British and the Boers and was influential in the Union of South Africa (1910). He was prime minister of South Africa twice, in 1919–1924 and 1939–1948.

MIGUEL PRIMO DE RIVERA
1870–1930

Miguel Primo de Rivera was a Spanish general. He served in the Spanish–American War in 1898 and in Morocco between 1909 and 1913. In 1923 he led a successful military coup against the Spanish government. He seized power and ruled Spain as a dictator until 1930 when he resigned. In 1933 his son, José Antonio (1903–1936), founded the Falange, the Spanish Fascist party but was later executed by Spanish republicans.

Leon Trotsky

1879–1940

Russian revolutionary Leon Trotsky was a follower of Karl Marx (p. 111), and in 1900 he was exiled to Siberia. He fled to London, England, where he met Vladimir Lenin (p. 20). Trotsky took part in the 1905 Russian Revolution and was again exiled. Returning to Russia in 1917, he took a leading role in the Bolshevik revolution that brought Lenin to power. In the civil war that followed, Trotsky was Commissar for War and led the Red Army to victory. Following Lenin's death in 1924, Joseph Stalin (p. 21) and Trotsky struggled for power. Stalin seized control and deported Trotsky, who was later murdered in Mexico City.

One of the leaders of the Russian Revolution 1917; founded Red Army 1918

▲ Trotsky commanded the Red Army, building it up from 7,000 to 5 million men.

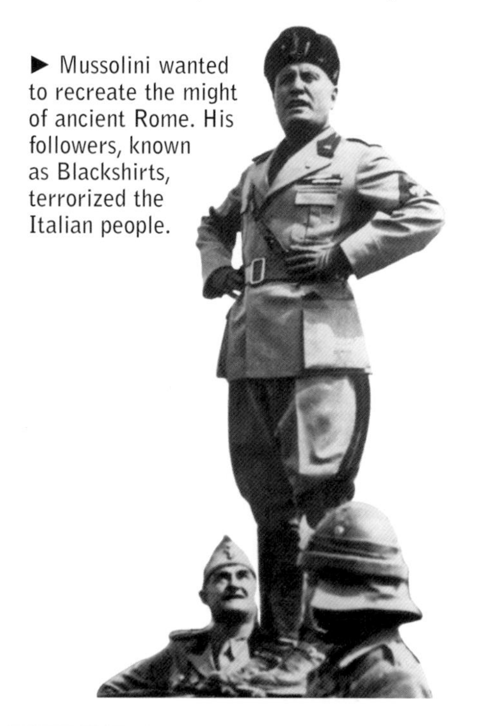

► Mussolini wanted to recreate the might of ancient Rome. His followers, known as Blackshirts, terrorized the Italian people.

Benito Mussolini

1883–1945

In 1922 followers of the Italian Fascist party marched on Rome, and their leader, Benito Mussolini, became prime minister. Mussolini, who called himself *Il Duce* ("the leader"), soon established Fascist rule with himself as dictator. His armies conquered Ethiopia (1935) and Albania (1939). He made an alliance with Germany, and in 1940 he declared war on France and Great Britain. His military campaigns were disastrous, and most Italians turned against him. The Germans protected him, but in 1945 Mussolini was captured and shot by Italian resistance fighters.

Founded Italian Fascist party 1919; Fascist dictator of Italy 1925–1945

Bernard Montgomery

1887–1976

Bernard Montgomery was an English soldier who rose through the ranks to command the British 8th Army during World War II. Under his leadership his army decisively defeated German forces, led by Erwin Rommel (below), at the Battle of El Alamein in North Africa. Further victories eventually drove the Germans out of Africa. In 1944 Montgomery was appointed commander for the ground forces during the Allied invasion of Normandy. His tactics allowed U.S. forces to drive the Germans out of France and Belgium. Following the defeat of Germany, he commanded British forces in Berlin.

Battle of El Alamein 1942; commander of Allied ground forces on D day 1944

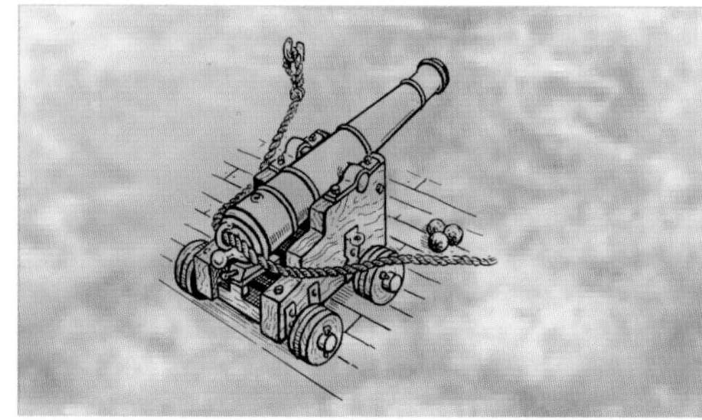

ERWIN ROMMEL 1891–1944
Rommel was one of the most incredible generals of World War II. He commanded the German Afrika Korps in North Africa but was finally defeated by British forces, led by Field Marshall Montgomery (above), at El Alamein in 1942. In 1944 Rommel supported an attempt to assassinate Adolf Hitler. It failed, and he committed suicide.

MENACHEM BEGIN 1913–1992
Born in Poland, Begin was a supporter of a Jewish homeland in Palestine. From 1942 he led the Irgun, an Israeli resistance group. He became Israeli prime minister in 1977 and shared the Nobel Peace Prize with President Sadat of Egypt in 1978. In 1982 he authorized an invasion of Lebanon to destroy Palestinian bases.

General Dwight D. Eisenhower chats to troops during the Allied invasion of Europe in 1944.

Dwight D. Eisenhower

1890–1969

Eisenhower, nicknamed "Ike," graduated from West Point Military Academy in 1915. An excellent organizer, he became famous during World War II (1939–1945). In 1944 he became supreme commander of the Allied D-day cross-channel invasion of mainland Europe. His achievements made him a national hero, and his huge popularity ensured him a landslide victory in the 1952 U.S. presidential elections. He was reelected for a second term in 1956.

Commander of Allied forces on D day 1944; 34th U.S. president 1952–1960

Ho Chi Minh

1890–1969

Ho Chi Minh was born in Vietnam, then part of the French colony of Indochina. After cofounding the Communist party of France, he returned to Vietnam in 1941 and led a liberation movement that defeated the French in 1954. Vietnam was divided in two, and Ho Chi Minh became Communist leader of the North. In the south, Communists (Viet Cong) rebelled. U.S. troops arrived in 1961 to support the government. This led to the Vietnam War (1963–1975). Ho Chi Minh led the fight against the South Vietnamese government. Six years after his death Vietnam was reunified.

President of North Vietnam 1954–1969

Charles de Gaulle

1890–1970

A French tank commander, De Gaulle escaped to England after the Germans invaded France in 1940. He founded the Free French Army and led resistance against the Germans from London. In 1944 he returned to Paris acclaimed as a war hero and was made head of the new French government. He became president in 1958 and reestablished France as a major world power.

Leader of Free French Army 1940–1944; president of France 1958–1969; granted independence to French African colonies 1959–1960

POL POT 1926–1998
During the 1960s and 1970s Pol Pot led the Communist Khmer Rouge in a guerrilla war against the Cambodian government. In 1976 he became prime minister and introduced a brutal regime of executions, forced labor, and other atrocities against civilians. At least three million people were killed. Pol Pot was overthrown in 1979.

SADDAM HUSSEIN b. 1937
Iraqi president since 1979, Saddam Hussein made Iraq a major military power, fighting a bitter war with Iran from 1980 to 1988. In 1990 his troops annexed Kuwait but were driven out during the Gulf War. UN sanctions and American bombing raids have weakened the country. Inside Iraq, Saddam Hussein has waged war on the Kurds.

MU'AMMAR AL-GADHAFI b. 1942
In 1969 Libyan army officer Mu'ammar al-Gadhafi led a successful military coup against King Idris I, the then ruler of Libya. As head of state he expelled foreigners, closed British and American military bases, and encouraged Islamic fundamentalism. He declared himself president in 1977 and has since supported international terrorism.

Josip Tito

1892–1980

Josip Broz was born in Croatia, and during World War I he was held prisoner by the Russians. He became a Communist and fought for the Red Army during the Russian Civil War (1918–1920). He returned to Yugoslavia and became an active Communist, adopting the name Tito. During World War II he led resistance against the German occupation. In 1945 he forced the abdication of Yugoslav King Peter II (1923–1970), and with Soviet help he made Yugoslavia a new Communist state. He broke from the U.S.S.R. in 1948 and made Yugoslavia one of the most liberal Communist nations in Europe.

Led Yugoslav resistance against Germans 1941–1945; president of Yugoslavia 1953–1980

Che Guevara

1928–1967

Born in Argentina, Ernesto "Che" Guevara was a revolutionary and political activist. He trained as a doctor but left Argentina in 1953 because of the oppressive regime there. In Mexico he met Cuban revolutionary Fidel Castro (below) and joined with him to invade Cuba in 1956. Following their success in 1959, Guevara worked closely with Castro. He was in charge of the National Bank and organized land reform. In 1965 Guevara left Cuba for the Congo in Africa, where he fought against white mercenaries. He finally arrived in Bolivia, where he organized peasants to fight the government revolt. He was killed by Bolivian soldiers.

One of the leaders of the Cuban revolution 1956–1959; South American guerrilla leader 1965–1967

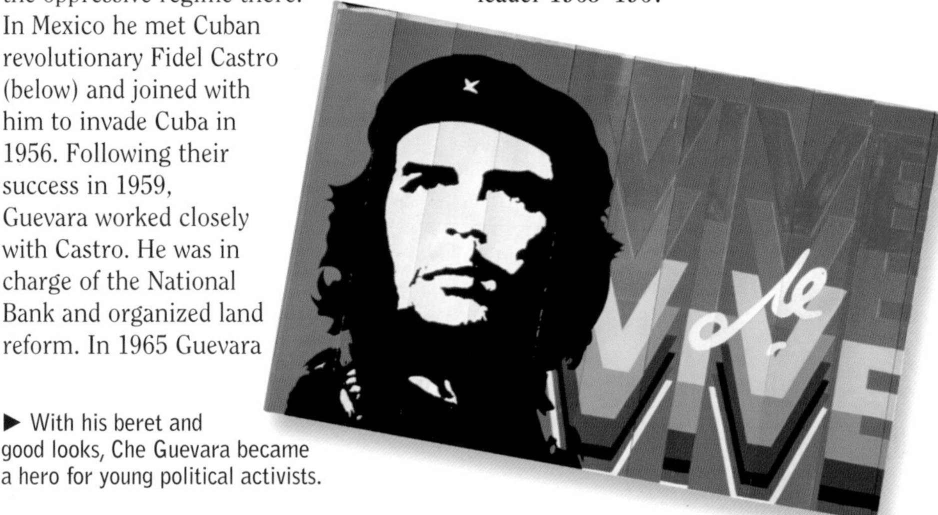

▶ With his beret and good looks, Che Guevara became a hero for young political activists.

Fidel Castro

b. 1927

In 1953 Cuban lawyer Fidel Castro led an unsuccessful uprising against the corrupt, right-wing dictatorship of the then president, Fulgencio Batista y Zaldivar (1901–1973). Castro fled to Mexico, where he organized a Cuban revolutionary movement. In 1956 he landed in Cuba with a band of revolutionaries but was forced to hide in the Sierra Madre Mountains. From there he and his followers fought a guerrilla campaign that toppled Batista in 1959. As premier of Cuba, the only Communist state in the Caribbean, and with Soviet help, Castro introduced reforms that improved the living standards of Cubans. The U.S. tried unsuccessfully to depose him in 1961. In 1962 the Soviet Union installed nuclear missiles in Cuba, and the world came close to war. Cuba's almost total dependence on Soviet aid has caused major financial problems for Castro since the collapse of communism in the U.S.S.R.

Communist leader of Cuban revolution 1956–1959; prime minister of Cuba 1959–1976; president of Cuba since 1976

◀ When Castro seized power in 1959, he nationalized American companies in Cuba. The U.S. retaliated by halting all trade with Cuba.

CHAPTER TWO

EXPLORERS

Explorers before A.D. 1000

A Greek trading mission arrives on the African coast. Once these early traders had made contact with Africa, the area became a valuable source of grain for the Greeks. Soon boatloads of settlers arrived to set up colonies on the North African coast.

For many ancient people exploration was a way of life. Early hunters in search of food often traveled to new lands in pursuit of their hunt. Later the desire to find new places to colonize, the need for better land to farm, the search for wealth from trade, and the desire for conquest led people to explore unfamiliar lands and seas.

EGYPTIAN BEGINNINGS

The ancient Egyptians had created an advanced civilization by around 2000 B.C., but they were exploring long before that. By around 4000 B.C. they had developed boats that took them across the Red Sea, where they made contact with the peoples on the African shores. By the time of the great Egyptian queen **Hatshepsut**, who reigned in around 1500 B.C., they were mounting organized expeditions. Hatshepsut sent one expedition on a voyage of exploration to the land of Punt. It is not known exactly where Punt was, but it was probably a local name for part of East Africa, perhaps somewhere in Somalia. The queen was pleased with her navigators because they brought back all kinds of exotic goods from Punt—luxurious materials like ivory, ebony, and gold, together with animals such as monkeys and dogs.

PHOENICIAN VOYAGERS

Some of the most famous early navigators were the Phoenicians, a coastal group who came from cities such as Sidon and Tyre in the eastern Mediterranean. The Phoenicians became skilled shipbuilders and soon were sending trading vessels out into the Mediterranean Sea. By the 600s B.C. they had established colonies around the Mediterranean, and one of these colonies, Carthage, in North Africa, was the base of the greatest Phoenician explorer, **Hanno**. Hanno set off down the coast of West Africa around 500 B.C. He reached Senegal and reported seeing hippos and "people" covered with hair, which were probably apes. Other Phoenician explorers sailed north up the coast of Portugal and may have even reached Great Britain.

THE ANCIENT GREEKS AND ROMANS

By the 300s B.C. the Greeks had also established Mediterranean colonies and were exploring farther afield. Their greatest explorer was named **Pytheas**. He was born in Marseilles, which is now in France but was a Greek colony at that time. He became a trader and hoped to take over some of the business that had been started by the Phoenicians. Setting off along the Atlantic coast of western

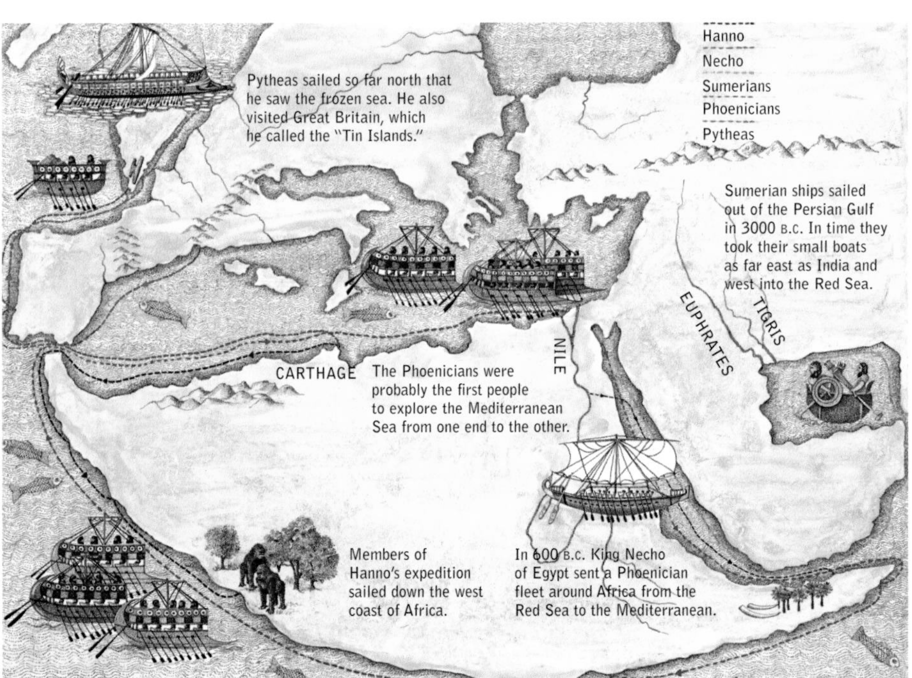

Phoenician explorers were among the greatest navigators in the ancient world. They were helped by their sturdy, broad ships, which were powered by both oars and a sail and made from cedarwood from Lebanon. From their bases in the eastern Mediterranean and North African cities, such as Carthage, Phoenician sailors traveled far down Africa's west coast. This early map shows Africa as ancient geographers believed it to be. It shows the Phoenicians traveling all around Africa, although it is unlikely that they actually went that far.

Europe around 325 B.C., Pytheas found Great Britain and sailed all around the island. He met some of the British people and saw tin being mined in Cornwall. He hoped to make money trading with the Cornish, but he also wanted to explore farther. So he sailed north again, eventually arriving at a place he called Thule. From his descriptions it is not clear exactly where Thule was, but Pytheas did say that the sun never set there, so it must have been very far north in the summer, perhaps part of Iceland or Norway. The Romans, who became powerful in 0–100 B.C., benefited from the knowledge of geography gathered by Pytheas. They sent their trading ships along similar routes to those pioneered by Greek ships. As they began conquering their neighbors and creating an empire they started to march inland through Europe. As they traveled they carried out the first surveys of the land.

CHINESE EXPLORERS

The ancient Chinese were also noteworthy explorers, making some of the ancient world's longest and most amazing journeys over land. The first explorations began as a result of warfare. Around 150 B.C. the emperor **Wu Ti** was wondering how to protect his borders from attacks by the Huns, a nomadic group from the north. So in 138 B.C. he sent his servant **Chang Ch'ien** on a long journey west to find allies. Chang Ch'ien was not very successful in finding people who would fight for China, but he did achieve an epic land journey, covering thousands of miles. He finally reached Bactria (now part of Iran) before returning on a similar route across central Asia. His journey took over 20 years, including ten years when he was held prisoner by the Huns. Later, Chinese explorers traveled for different reasons. Two of the greatest made their journeys for religious reasons. **Fa Hsien** was a Buddhist monk whose religious quest took place in the early part of the A.D. 400s. He traveled overland west, across central Asia, before traveling south into India and reaching Calcutta. Then he sailed even farther south to Sri Lanka before returning home to China by sea. During his 15-year journey he collected many relics connected with Buddhism, and he also vastly improved Chinese knowledge of India. The other great Buddhist traveler was **Hsüan Tsang**. He lived in the A.D. 600s and was inspired by the stories of Fa Hsien's travels to set out on his own religious quest. Like Fa Hsien he traveled overland across central Asia before traveling all around India, visiting cities such as Allahabad, Calcutta, and Poona. He brought around 700 religious books and other relics back home with him to China.

NAVIGATORS OF POLYNESIA

The original inhabitants of the Polynesian islands in the Pacific Ocean must have traveled thousands of miles to find their homes. No one knows where they came from, but the most likely explanation is that they originated in Southeast Asia, perhaps as long as 3,000 years ago. They traveled in large canoes and probably settled the western islands, such as Vanuata and New Caledonia, first before working their way east to Fiji, Tonga, and beyond. As they did so they developed their navigation skills, using the positions of the stars in the sky to work out their latitude. Later they created charts by joining thin sticks of palm to make a frame and attaching shells to indicate the positions of the different islands. We do not know the names of these early navigators nor the exact routes they took because they developed no writing systems, and so they produced no history of their travels.

▼ Polynesian explorers used large, double-hulled canoes to sail across the Pacific Ocean.

BY LAND

Marco Polo was appointed as a government employee by the the Mongol emperor, Kublai Khan. He was sent on diplomatic missions around China and Burma. After returning to Venice in 1295 Marco Polo dictated an important account of the Mongol Empire.

Marco Polo

1254–1324

Born in Venice, Italy, to a rich merchant family, Marco Polo set out in 1271 with his father and uncle to travel to China. The journey across central Asia took four years. In China they met Kublai Khan, a Mongol emperor, who employed Marco as a regional governor and ambassador. After 17 years of traveling around the region Polo returned with his father and uncle to Venice. He brought back a fortune in precious jewels and became a merchant in Venice, where he spent the next 30 years.

Traveled to central Asia and China 1271–1295

Ibn Battuta

1304–1368

Born in Morocco, Ibn Battuta was a devout Muslim. At the age of 21 he began a pilgrimage to Mecca that turned out to be an epic journey; he saw more of the world than any other man had at that time. His travels took him to all of the Muslim countries: Mecca, Mesopotamia, Asia Minor, India, China, Sumatra, Spain, and Timbuktu. He returned home in 1354 and dictated an account of his journeys, the *Rihlah*, one of the most famous travel books in history.

Traveled 75,000 mi. around Middle East, Far East, and Africa 1325–1354

Francisco Pizarro

c. 1478–1541

A Spanish soldier, Pizarro was serving under Vasco Balboa (1475–1519) when he discovered the Pacific Ocean in 1511. In 1526 he sailed with Diego de Almagro (1475–1538) to Peru in search of the Incas. Having found them, Pizarro received permission from King Charles V of Spain to conquer these people. Setting out for Peru in 1531, Pizarro's small force of 159 men marched inland to Cajamarca, where in 1532 they captured the Incan emperor, Atahuallpa (c. 1502–1533). After receiving an enormous ransom for him Pizarro had Atahuallpa executed. Pizarro was killed by rival Spaniards led by his former partner, Diego de Almagro.

Discovered the Incan civilization 1532

The Incan emperor was killed by Pizarro.

HERNANDO DE SOTO c. 1500–1542
A Spaniard, de Soto assisted Pizarro in his conquest of the Incas. He was appointed governor of Cuba and Florida by the king of Spain, Charles V, in 1536. Searching for gold, he explored much of the southern part of what is now the U.S. In 1541 he became the first European to reach the Mississippi River, but he died of fever one year later.

FRANCISCO CORONADO 1510–1554
Born in Salamanca, Spain, Coronado led an expedition from the Gulf of California to New Mexico in 1540. They traveled to Arizona in search of gold and saw the Grand Canyon, Texas, Oklahoma, and Kansas on their journey. They encountered hostile Native Americans and had to fight their way back to Mexico without discovering any gold.

At first Hernán Cortés and his small army were welcomed by Aztec emperor, Montezuma.

Hernán Cortés

1485–1547

After studying law in Spain, Hernán Cortés joined the expedition of Diego Velázquez de Cuellar (1465–1524) to Cuba in 1511. In 1518 Cortés led an expedition to Mexico and landed in Yucatán. At San Juan de Ulua he had his first contact with the emperor of the Aztecs, Montezuma II (p. 14). After founding Veracruz he left for Tiaxcala. Here he fought the Tiaxcalans, but they soon changed sides and became allies. In 1519 Cortés' army and his new allies reached the Aztec capital, Tenochtitlán, where he took Montezuma prisoner. The Spanish treated the Aztecs harshly, and they rebelled. Many battles were fought, and in one Montezuma was killed. Cortés retreated from the capital in 1520, but he returned with stronger armed forces and destroyed it. The Aztecs were annihilated by modern military forces and European diseases. Poor health made Cortés return to Spain.

Explored Central America 1518–1540; discovered the Aztec civilization 1518

Jacques Cartier

1491–1557

An experienced navigator, Cartier was sent by Francis I of France (1494–1547) to find gold in the New World. In 1534 Cartier sailed with a crew, mainly from Brittany, to Newfoundland. After spending time exploring its coastline he sailed up the Gulf of St. Lawrence to the Gaspé Peninsula and claimed the land for France. Owing to strong currents, he was unable to explore farther, and he sailed home. He returned in 1535 and was able to sail up a wide river, guided by two young Huron Indians. He named it the St. Lawrence River. Reaching the island he named Île d'Orléans, he and his crew then rowed upstream to Stadacona, later to become the city of Quebec, and reached Hochelaga, the site of modern Montreal. He then returned downstream to Quebec, where he spent the winter, and in May 1536 he returned to France. A third voyage in 1541 was not a success, and he retired to St. Malo.

Explored the St. Lawrence River and claimed Canada for France 1534–1536

Samuel de Champlain

1567–1635

Samuel de Champlain was a French navigator who in 1603 was sent by his king, Henry IV, to explore the St. Lawrence River in Canada. On this voyage he reached the St. Louis Falls, but he failed to ride the rapids, and he returned to France. He made two more voyages to Canada in 1604 and 1605 to explore the coastline and settle small French colonies. In 1608 he again set out from France to the St. Lawrence River. He built a small colony at a location where the river was narrow. This became the site of Quebec and a great fur-trading center. He made allies among the local Huron Indians and set out with them to raid Iroquois territory. At the Iroquois stronghold of Syracuse, Champlain was wounded in battle. In 1628 an English fleet captured Quebec, and Champlain was captured and taken as a prisoner to England. In 1633 he was released and returned to Canada.

Voyages of exploration to Canada 1603, 1604, 1605, 1608; founded Quebec 1608

SAMUEL DE CHAMPLAIN

JACQUES MARQUETTE 1637–1675
Marquette was sent to North America in 1666 as a French Jesuit missionary. He converted Native Americans around Lake Superior to Christianity and studied their languages. In 1673 he joined Louis Jolliet on his expedition that proved that the Mississippi River flowed into the Gulf of Mexico and not into the Pacific Ocean.

RENÉ LA SALLE 1643–1687
Born in Rouen, France, René La Salle traveled to Canada, where he became a trader in Montreal. In 1681 he traveled south, following the Mississippi River and claiming lands for Louis XIV of France (p. 16). He finally reached the Gulf of Mexico, where a French settlement was established. He was murdered by his own mutinous men.

LOUIS JOLLIET 1645–1700
Jolliet was a French explorer who, with James Marquette, canoed down part of the Mississippi River, at the time believed to flow into the Pacific Ocean. However, Native Americans proved to them that it flowed into the Gulf of Mexico, so Jolliet and Marquette returned along the Illinois River to Lake Michigan.

Alexander Mackenzie

1764–1820

Scottish-born explorer Alexander Mackenzie went to Canada and joined the Northwest Fur Company in 1779. In 1788 he set up a fur-trading base at Fort Chipewayan on Lake Athabasca. From here he and his party set out in canoes along a river with the intention of reaching the Pacific Ocean. However, he emerged into the Arctic Ocean and named the river River of Disappointment (now the Mackenzie River). Determined to discover a passage to the Pacific Ocean, Mackenzie set out again in October of 1792, finally reaching the Pacific at Queen Charlotte Sound in July 1793.

Discovered Mackenzie River 1789; first European to cross Rocky Mountains to the Pacific Ocean 1792–1793

Alexander von Humboldt

1769–1859

German scientific explorer Humboldt and French naturalist Aimé Bonpland (1773–1858) sailed to South America from Spain in 1799. They landed in Cumana (now northeastern Venezuela), and for five years they made scientific studies in the rain forests along the Amazon and Orinoco rivers. After crossing the Andes, Humboldt also studied the sea currents off the Peruvian coast. The Humboldt Current is named after him. Humboldt returned to Europe with thousands of geological and botanical specimens. In 1829 Humboldt explored Siberia with naturalist Christian Ehrenberg and mineralogist Gustav Rose.

Explored Amazon and Orinoco rivers, 1799–1804; explored Siberia 1829

ALEXANDER VON HUMBOLDT

Mungo Park

1771–1806

Scottish explorer Mungo Park studied medicine in Edinburgh, Scotland. In 1795 he was sent by the African Association to explore the Niger River. He sailed to the Gambia River and traveled to Segou where in June 1796 he reached the Niger River. Owing to the lack of provisions, he had to return home, where he began working as a doctor. Park returned to Gambia in 1805 and set out for the Niger River with a group of poorly equipped men, many of whom died on the journey. Battling against many dangers, Park and the survivors paddled 1,000 mi. (1,600km) to Bussa, where they were either drowned or killed by local tribespeople.

Explored Niger River 1796 and 1805

◀ Mungo Park's exploration of the Niger River was badly prepared and ill equipped.

JOSEPH BANKS 1744–1820
Born in London, England, Joseph Banks trained as a botanist. In 1766 he equipped and joined James Cook's (p. 49) round-the-world voyage in *Endeavour*, returning with many plants and specimens. He was elected president of the Royal Society, founded the African Association, and established the Australian colony of New South Wales.

ZEBULON PIKE 1779–1813
Zebulon Pike led an unsuccessful expedition in 1805 to find the source of the Mississippi River. In 1806 he explored the Arkansas River and the Rocky Mountains. He failed to scale the peak that bears his name—Pike's Peak. In 1807 he was arrested by the Spanish. His reports of the Southwest encouraged Americans to settle there. He was killed in the War of 1812.

Lewis and Clark

William Clark 1770–1838
Meriwether Lewis 1774–1809

U.S. Army sergeant Meriwether Lewis was made personal secretary to President Thomas Jefferson (p. 19) in 1801. Lewis and his friend Lieutenant William Clark were selected to explore the Missouri River, cross the Rockies, and find a direct route to the Pacific Ocean.

Lewis and Clark and a small group of soldiers set out from St. Louis in 1804. After traveling by boat and canoe up the Missouri River they crossed the Rocky Mountains with the help of local Native Americans. They finally reached the Pacific Ocean in November 1805. The knowledge gained from this epic journey encouraged the westward movement of settlers in the years that followed.

First American settlers to cross the North American continent, 1804–1805

Lewis and Clark had many adventures as they crossed the Rocky Mountains to reach the Pacific Ocean in 1805.

George Everest

1790–1866

Born in Wales, George Everest became a military engineer in India for the British. He was appointed Surveyor-General of India, and with a small group of assistants completed the Great Trigonometrical Survey of the subcontinent over a period of 11 years. He accurately calculated the heights of the Himalaya mountains, including Mount Everest, which is named after him.

Surveyor-General of India 1830–1841

Richard Lander

1804–1834

Born in Cornwall, England, Lander traveled with African explorer Hugh Clapperton in 1825 along the Niger River to Sokoto, where Clapperton died. In 1830 Lander was sent back to Africa with his brother by the British Colonial Office with instructions to follow the Niger River. They reached the sea at the Bight of Benin and established the course of the river. Lander died on his third expedition to the Niger.

Explored the Niger River 1825, 1830, and 1834

HUGH CLAPPERTON 1788–1827

Scottish explorer Hugh Clapperton was sent by the British Colonial Office in 1821 to find the source of the Niger River. He crossed the Sahara Desert from Tripoli to Lake Chad but failed to find the Niger. In 1825 he set out with Richard Lander from Benin in another attempt to find the Niger's source, but he died of fever.

CHARLES STURT 1795–1869

Sturt was a British soldier who was sent to Australia to guard convicts. Between 1828 and 1830 he crossed the Blue Mountains and explored the Darling and Murrumbidgee rivers. Suffering from blindness, he returned to England. His epic journeys were a major contribution to the exploration of southwestern Australia.

RENÉ CAILLIÉ 1799–1838

In 1827 French explorer René Caillié set out from the West African coast for Timbuktu. After walking over 1,000 mi. (1,600km) he arrived at his destination and traveled to Tangier with a camel caravan across the eastern Sahara Desert. Caillié was awarded 10,000 francs by the Geographical Society of Paris for his achievement.

Friedrich Leichhardt

1813–1848

Born in Prussia, Leichhardt emigrated to Australia in 1841. In 1844 he set out from Brisbane with aboriginal guides for Arnhem Land in the Northwest. Over a year later he reached the Gulf of Carpentaria. Following his return to Sydney in 1846, he attempted to cross northern Australia, but he had to turn back. In 1848 he set out on a third expedition, but he was never seen again.

Expedition to Arnhem Land 1844–1846; failed east–west crossing of northern Australia 1846–1847; disappeared on transAustralia expedition 1848

Peter Warburton

1813–1889

Born in England, Warburton settled in Australia in 1853 and became a police chief. With his son he set out in 1873 to cross Australia from the south coast up north to Alice Springs and across the Great Sandy Desert to the west coast. They succeeded, having traveled 2,000 mi. (3,200km) across some of the most inhospitable terrain in the world.

First man to travel across Australia from the south to the west coast 1873

John Frémont

1813–1890

During the 1840s American surveyor John Frémont was commissioned by the U.S. government to explore and map routes across the Rocky Mountains. He also led four other expeditions out West. The maps he produced were used by the pioneer wagon trains. He later ran for U.S. president and became governor of Arizona.

Expeditions to: Rocky Mountains 1842; Great Salt Lake 1843; upper Rio Grande 1848; governor of Arizona 1878–1882

When Henry Morton Stanley found David Livingstone at Ujiji on November 10, 1871, he greeted him with the immortal words, "Dr. Livingstone, I presume."

David Livingstone

1813–1873

Born in Scotland, Livingstone left work in a cotton factory at the age of 24 to study medicine in London, England. In 1840 the London Missionary Society sent him to Africa. Livingstone arrived in Cape Town in 1841 and traveled 1,000 mi. (1,600km) to Robert Moffat's missionary station in modern-day Botswana, marrying Moffat's daughter in 1844. He began his first expedition in 1853, searching for possible trade routes through Africa. Livingstone set off to the Atlantic coast, turned east, and kept walking until he reached the Indian Ocean. On this journey he discovered Victoria Falls and became the first European to travel across Africa from the west to the east coast. In 1856 Livingstone returned to a hero's welcome in Great Britain and wrote a book, *Missionary Travels*, about his journeys.

Livingstone's second expedition, which he started in 1858 by steamboat up the Zambezi River, was not as successful. The Portuguese authorities restricted his movements, and his wife, Mary, died of fever. His third expedition, to explore the central African watershed and find the source of the Nile River, was sponsored by the Royal Geographical Society in 1866. He failed to find the Nile, became ill, and disappeared. Welsh-born American journalist Henry Morton Stanley (1841–1904) was sent by the *New York Herald* to look for him. In November 1871 Stanley found Livingstone at Ujiji, Lake Tanganyika.

Livingstone led a second expedition to find the source of the Nile in 1872, but he died the following year without achieving his goal. He kept detailed maps and records of all his expeditions, thus vastly increasing European knowledge of the African interior.

First European to cross Africa from west to east 1852–1856; discovered Victoria Falls 1853; led expedition to Zambezi River and Lake Nyasa 1858–1863; led two expeditions to find source of Nile River 1866–1871 and 1872–1873

Burke and Wills

Robert O'Hara Burke 1820–1861
William Wills 1834–1861

Robert O'Hara Burke was born in Galway, Ireland. After serving in the Austrian Army and the Irish police, he emigrated to Australia. He became a police inspector and was asked to lead an expedition across the continent from south to north.

William Wills was born in Devon, England, and became a surveyor. In 1852 he emigrated to Australia and joined Burke's expedition. They set off with two other men from Melbourne in 1860 and set up a supply station halfway at Cooper's Creek in modern-day Queensland. Burke and Wills pushed on with John King (1838–1872) and eventually reached the mouth of the Flinders River in the Gulf of Carpentaria. They became the first European settlers to cross from the south to the north of Australia. On their return journey their supplies ran out, and they both died of starvation.

First European settlers to cross Australia from south to north 1860

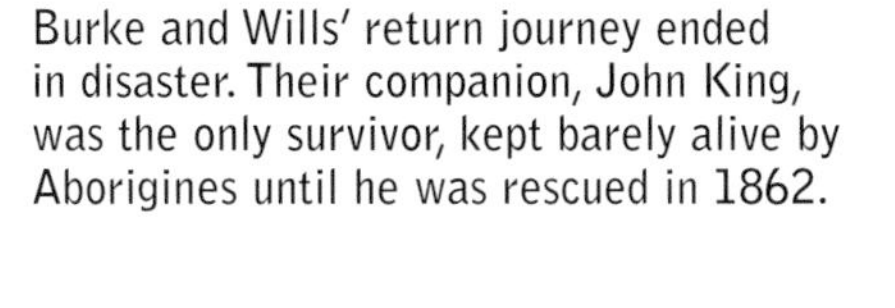
Burke and Wills' return journey ended in disaster. Their companion, John King, was the only survivor, kept barely alive by Aborigines until he was rescued in 1862.

Richard Burton

1821–1890

On his visit to Mecca, Richard Burton disguised himself as an Arab.

Born in Torquay, England, Richard Burton learned to speak many languages, including Arabic. In 1842 he joined the Indian army and developed a taste for travel. He made a pilgrimage to the holy city of Mecca in 1853, disguised as an Arab. In 1856 the British Royal Geographical Society invited Burton and fellow officer John Hanning Speke (1827–1864) to lead an expedition to Africa to find the source of the Nile River. They discovered Lake Tanganyika in 1857, but they both became ill and could not continue. After his recovery Speke set out again and discovered a large lake, which he named Victoria and declared to be the source of the Nile. However, Burton had decided that Lake Tanganyika was the source and so began their famous disagreement. Burton went on to travel in South America before entering the Foreign Office. Between 1861–1872 he held consular posts in Brazil, Syria, and Italy. Burton also wrote many travel books, but he is best known for his translation of *The Arabian Nights*.

Visited Mecca 1853; expedition to find source of the Nile River 1856–1857; discovered Lake Tanganyika 1857

Isabella Bird

1832–1904

Suffering from spinal problems, Isabella Bird was sent in 1854 on a convalescent sea voyage from her home in England to North America. The journey gave her a taste for traveling, but it was 20 years before she set out again. In 1872 she traveled to Australia, New Zealand, Hawaii, and the Rocky Mountains, and in 1877 she traveled throughout Japan and Malaya. In 1889 Bird took an intensive course in nursing and set out for India and Tibet. In the following year she extended her travels to include Persia, Kurdistan, and Armenia. Bird returned to the Far East in 1894. She traveled 8,100 mi. (13,000km) around China and established hospitals in Korea and China and an orphanage in Japan.

Traveled to: Australia, New Zealand, Hawaii, and U.S. 1872–1873; Japan and Malaya 1877–1879; India, Tibet, Persia, Kurdistan, and Armenia 1889–1890; China, Korea and Japan, 1894–1897

Ernest Giles

1835–1897

Born in England, Giles emigrated to Australia in 1850. In 1872 he set out to cross the continent from the Overland Telegraph Line to the Murchison River, 1,000 mi. (1,600km) to the west. He failed but discovered Lake Amedeus instead. In 1874, with Albert Gibson, he set out again but got lost in the Gibson Desert—named after his companion who died there. Giles tried again in 1875, and in five months he traveled 2,500 mi. (4,000km) from Port Augusta to Perth. His journey ended in 1876 when he returned a different way.

First man to cross the Australian continent in both directions 1875–1876

Robert Peary

1856–1920

U.S. Naval Captain Robert Peary led many expeditions to the Arctic between 1886 and 1909, proving that Greenland was an island. Peary's ambition was to be the first man to reach the North Pole. On April 6, 1909, accompanied by Inuits, Peary reached the area of the North Pole, but his account was not believed by many. U.S. explorer Frederick Cook (1865–1940) claimed to have reached the Pole first in 1908. At that time scientific opinion was on Peary's side and upheld his claim.

Claimed to be the first man to reach the North Pole 1909

Mary Kingsley

1862–1900

Born in London, England, Mary Kingsley was an avid reader of her father's scientific library. After her parents' deaths in 1893, she traveled to West Africa, where she lived with the native people, returning home with valuable information about their cultures. She returned to Africa in 1895 and explored previously unknown parts of the Congo River in a canoe. She was also consulted by British administrators for her knowledge of West Africans. Kingsley served as a nurse in the Boer War, but she died of enteric fever.

Traveled to West Africa 1893; explored Congo River 1895

Fridtjof Nansen

1861–1930

Norwegian explorer Fridtjof Nansen sailed aboard the *Viking* in 1882 to explore the Arctic region. In 1888 his six-man team was the first to cross Greenland. Five years later Nansen set out in the *Fram*, which was specifically designed for strength, in an attempt to reach the North Pole. Frozen in the ice, his ship drifted north from the New Siberian islands until 1895, when he was able to travel on foot to the Pole, accompanied by his husky teams and sleds. In April of that year he reached the most northerly latitude then attained by anyone, but he turned back without achieving his goal. He subsequently became a professor of zoology and oceanography and was the first Norwegian ambassador to London, England. In 1922 Nansen was awarded the Nobel Peace Prize for his work with the League of Nations to supply relief to post-Revolution Russian refugees.

In his attempt to reach the North Pole, Nansen set out on foot from his icebound ship, the *Fram*.

Made first crossing of Greenland 1888; expedition to highest latitude (86° 14'N) reached at that time 1895

Antarctic Explorers

Amundsen raised the Norwegian flag at the South Pole on December 14, 1911.

In 1773 **Captain James Cook** (p. 49) was the first man to cross the Antarctic Circle, but it was not until 1820 that American and British seal hunters actually found the edges of the frozen continent of Antarctica. Between 1837 and 1843 there were three expeditions to chart the coast of Antarctica. They were led by **Jules d'Urville** (1790–1842) for France, **Charles Wilkes** (1798–1877) for the United States, and **James Clark Ross** (1800–1862) for Great Britain.

RACE FOR THE SOUTH POLE

The real goal for explorers now became the South Pole. In 1910 **Robert Falcon Scott** (1868–1912) left Great Britain in the *Terra Nova,* reaching McMurdo Sound at the start of 1911. Seven days later Norwegian explorer **Roald Amundsen** (1872–1928) arrived at the Bay of Whales in his successful attempt to reach the Pole. Scott and his men began to drop off supplies along the way and set off on November 1. Reaching the Pole on January 18, 1912, they found a small tent with a Norwegian flag on it and realized Amundsen had already reached the Pole. Scott and his party began the return journey, but they all perished.

AGAINST THE ODDS

Two men, Irishman **Ernest Shackleton** (1874–1922) and Australian **Douglas Mawson** (1882–1958), earned well-deserved reputations as survivors in the harsh Antarctic climate. Mawson was on the scientific staff of Shackleton's 1907 Antarctic expedition and was one of the party that discovered the Magnetic South Pole. On an expedition begun in 1914, Shackleton watched his boat, *Endurance,* being crushed by pack ice before successfully guiding all of his crew 800 mi. (1,280km) across the ice and sea to safety.

Today, Antarctica is mainly explored by scientists, although some expeditions do take place, for example the 1990 crossing by dog sled from west to east.

In 1993 Liv Arnesen and Ann Bancroft (p. 44) became the first women to ski across Antarctica.

Tenzing Norgay

1914–1986

Born in Nepal, Tenzing Norgay was a mountain porter, or sherpa. As a sherpa he made his first climb on Mt. Everest in 1935. In 1953 he was a member of the British Everest Expedition led by John Hunt (b. 1910). Tenzing and Edmund Hillary (right) were the first men to reach the 29,035-ft. (8,850-m) -high summit.

Everest expeditions 1938 and 1952; one of the first men to climb Mt. Everest 1953

Edmund Hillary

b. 1919

Born in New Zealand, Edmund Hillary was a beekeeper by profession. But his first love was climbing, and he joined the British Everest Expedition led by John Hunt in 1953. On May 29 Hillary and Tenzing Norgay were the first men to reach the summit of Mt. Everest—the world's highest mountain. In 1957 Hillary became deputy leader of the British Commonwealth Antarctic Expedition. Led by Vivian Fuchs (1908–1999), they were the first to reach the South Pole using tracked vehicles. Hillary continued to climb, and in 1967 he made the first ascent of 10.940-ft. (3,335-m) -high Mt. Herschel while on an Antarctic expedition.

One of the first men to climb Mt. Everest 1953; first man to climb Mt. Herschel 1967

In 1953 Hillary and Tenzing became the first men to ascend Mt. Everest.

Ranulph Fiennes

b. 1945

English explorer Ranulph Fiennes served in the British army and was the leader of several Arctic expeditions between 1971 and 1978. Between 1979 and 1982 he led the Transglobe Expedition, which followed the Greenwich Meridian across both the North and South poles. Since then he has made several attempts to walk unaided to the North Pole. In 1993 Fiennes and his companion, Michael Stroud, walked without support across the Antarctic continent.

First man to reach the South Pole twice 1980 and 1993; one of the first men to walk without support across Antarctic continent 1993

Ann Bancroft

b. 1955

Born in Minnesota, Ann Bancroft loved the outdoors and adventure from an early age. She studied physical education at the University of Oregon. In 1986 she dog-sledded 1,000 mi. (1,600km) from the Northwest Territories in Canada to the North Pole as the only female member of the Steger International Polar Expedition. In 1993 she led the American Women's Expedition to the South Pole, a 67-day expedition of 650 mi. (1,050km) across Antarctica on skis.

First woman to cross the ice to North Pole 1986 and South Pole 1993

OTTO NORDENSKJÖLD 1869–1928
Nordenskjöld led the Swedish Antarctic Expedition of 1901–1904. His exploration of Graham Land added much to the knowledge of the area. His ship, *Antarctic,* was crushed by ice and sank. The party divided into three, and each made their way to Snow Hill Island. They were rescued one year later by an Argentinian ship.

WALLY HERBERT b. 1934
British explorer Wally Herbert joined the New Zealand Antarctic Expedition in 1960. In 1968–1969 he made the first surface crossing of the frozen Arctic Ocean across the North Pole—a journey of 3,730 mi. (6,000km), lasting 464 days. It was the longest sled journey ever made.

BY SEA

Henry the Navigator

1394–1460

Henry's father was King John I of Portugal (1327-1433). In 1415 Henry took a leading role in the capture of Ceuta in North Africa. He was made governor of the province of Algarve, Portugal, and built an observatory, school of navigation, and shipyard. Henry supplied the ships and financial backing for secret voyages of discovery. His school developed the caravel, a sailing ship that was well equipped for voyages of exploration. Henry's sailors discovered the Madeira Islands, Azores, Cape Verde Islands, and sailed down the west coast of Africa as far as Sierra Leone and up the Gambia River. In 1441 one of his ships returned with the first slaves from Africa.

Sponsored voyages of discovery to west coast of Africa 1418–1460

▲ Henry brought together navigators and shipbuilders from all over Europe to help him carry out his plans for exploration.

Zheng He

Active 1405–1433

In 1405 Chinese admiral Zheng He was commissioned by the Ming emperor Yongle (1360–1424), to undertake sea voyages to develop trade and diplomatic relations with other nations. Over a period of 28 years his large fleet of ships traveled throughout the Far East to India, the east coast of Africa, and the Red Sea. The last expedition was in 1433, when the Chinese decided to stop trading with other nations.

Sailed to: Indochina, Java, Ceylon 1405–1407; Siam, Cochin, west coast of India 1407–1409; Zanzibar and east coast of Africa 1421–1422; Red Sea 1431–1433

Zheng He returned to China with a giraffe.

John Cabot

c. 1450–1498

Originally Giovanni Caboto, John Cabot was an Italian navigator born in Genoa. Around 1490 he arrived in England and settled in Bristol. In 1497 he was sent by Henry VII (1457–1509) on a voyage of discovery across the Atlantic Ocean. Cabot, his three sons, and only 18 members of crew set sail from Bristol in a tiny ship, the *Matthew*. After 54 days at sea they saw land. They thought that they had reached Asia, but it was North America. Cabot and his crew became the first Europeans to reach the North American mainland. He made another voyage in search of a westerly route to India, but he disappeared without trace.

First European to reach the North American mainland 1497; expedition to find Northwest Passage to India 1498

PEDRO ALVARES CABRAL 1467–1520
In 1500 Portuguese navigator Pedro Cabral sailed west from Lisbon in search of the East Indies. His fleet of 13 ships finally landed on the coast of Brazil, which Cabral claimed for Portugal. He set sail for India, but he lost half of his fleet and finally landed in Mozambique. From here he sailed to Calicut on the west coast of India.

AMERIGO VESPUCCI 1451–1512
Born in Florence, Italy, Amerigo Vespucci supplied provisions and food to Christopher Columbus' ships. Between 1499 and 1502 he made several voyages to the South American coast. All of his journeys are in doubt because his records were poorly kept and sometimes completely altered. The continent of America was named after him.

Christopher Columbus

1451–1506

Born in Genoa, Italy, Columbus was an experienced sailor and navigator. In 1477 he is believed to have sailed as far north as Iceland and also to have visited Sierra Leone. Believing the world was round, he sought patrons to fund a voyage to India by sailing west.

King Ferdinand and Queen Isabella of Spain eventually agreed to back his expedition, and Columbus set sail from Palos in August 1492 on the ship *Santa María* with two caravels and 120 men. In October he saw land and believed it to be the East Indies. In fact it was an island in the Bahamas. He continued to Cuba and Hispaniola, where the *Santa María* was wrecked.

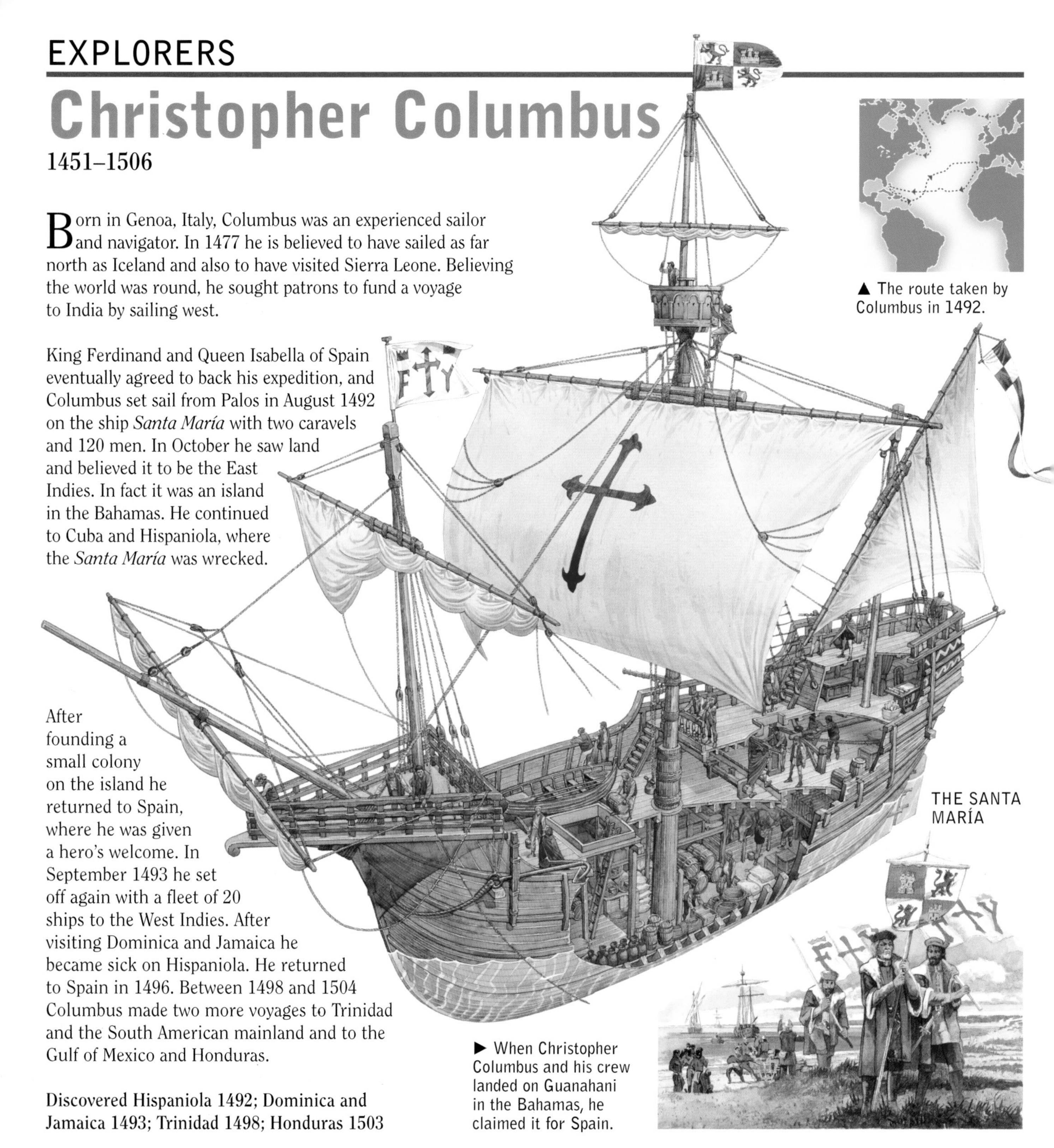

▲ The route taken by Columbus in 1492.

After founding a small colony on the island he returned to Spain, where he was given a hero's welcome. In September 1493 he set off again with a fleet of 20 ships to the West Indies. After visiting Dominica and Jamaica he became sick on Hispaniola. He returned to Spain in 1496. Between 1498 and 1504 Columbus made two more voyages to Trinidad and the South American mainland and to the Gulf of Mexico and Honduras.

Discovered Hispaniola 1492; Dominica and Jamaica 1493; Trinidad 1498; Honduras 1503

► When Christopher Columbus and his crew landed on Guanahani in the Bahamas, he claimed it for Spain.

JUAN PONCE DE LEÓN 1460–1521
Spanish explorer Juan Ponce de León sailed with Christopher Columbus on his second voyage to the New World in 1493. He became governor of Hispaniola, and in 1510 he was appointed governor of Puerto Rico. In 1512 he sailed to Florida, where he became governor. He failed to subdue the local people, retired to Cuba, and died.

SEBASTIAN CABOT 1474–1557
Born in Venice, Italy, the son of John Cabot (p. 45), Sebastian was a cartographer. In 1526 he was sent by the Holy Roman Emperor Charles V to explore the coast of Brazil, but his attempts at colonization failed. In 1544 Cabot published a map of the world. In 1548 he settled in England, where he was appointed inspector of the British navy.

VASCO DA GAMA
c. 1469–1525

After Christopher Columbus failed to reach India by sailing west Portuguese navigator Vasco da Gama was asked by the king of Portugal to find a route to India via the Cape of Good Hope. His ships left Lisbon in 1497 and reached Malindi in East Africa. With the help of an Indian pilot, da Gama sailed across the Indian Ocean and arrived at Calicut in May 1498. He sailed back to Lisbon in 1499. In 1502 he returned to India, where he established Portuguese colonies.

First European to sail around the Cape of Good Hope to India 1498

MARTIN FROBISHER
1535–1594

In 1576 English sailor Martin Frobisher sailed with two ships to Greenland in search of the Northwest Passage. One of his ships was lost, but Frobisher sailed on to the coasts of Labrador and Baffin Island. Inuits gave him what he thought was gold, but it was pyrites (fool's gold). Between 1577–1578 he returned twice to the region, sailing back to England with tons of worthless "gold." In 1585 Frobisher sailed with Drake to the West Indies and also commanded a ship against the Spanish Armada in 1588.

Voyages to find Northwest Passage 1576, 1577, and 1578; discovered Baffin Island 1576

FRANCIS DRAKE
1543–1596

After several expeditions to the West Indies, English sea captain Francis Drake was commissioned by Queen Elizabeth I (p. 15) to attack Spanish interests in Central America. When he returned to Plymouth in 1573, he was hailed a national hero. In 1577 Drake sailed from Plymouth to circumnavigate the world. His expedition faced storms, loss of men and ships, and mutiny, but he returned to England in 1580 with valuable prizes. Drake also played an important part in the destruction of the Spanish Armada in 1588.

Expeditions to Central America 1567 and 1572; first Englishman to circumnavigate the world 1577–1580

▼ Magellan encountered terrible storms when he sailed through the Magellan Straits.

FERDINAND MAGELLAN
c. 1480–1521

As a young man, Portuguese navigator Magellan sailed with merchants to the East Indies by going around Africa. Convinced that he could reach them by sailing west, and with the backing of the Spanish king, Charles V, he set sail from Seville, Spain, with five ships in 1509. He sailed down the east coast of South America, through the Magellan Straits (named after him), and across the Pacific to the Philippines. Here Magellan was killed by tribespeople. His ship, *Victoria,* and its crew completed the first round-the-world voyage when they arrived back in Spain in 1522.

Organized first circumnavigation of the world 1519–1522

WILLIAM BARENTS d. 1597
Barents was a Dutch navigator and pilot who led several expeditions in search of the Northeast Passage around the northern coast of Russia. The Barents Sea is named after him. He died on a voyage in 1597 close to the Novaya Zemlya Islands off the Siberian coast. His records, hidden in a hut on Cape Novaya, were found in 1875.

HUGH WILLOUGHBY d. 1554
In 1533 Willoughby sailed from London, England, in search of the Northeast Passage to China. In a storm Willoughby's ships were separated, and he sought safety off the Kola Peninsula. The following year Russian fishermen found his ships frozen in the ice. All on board had either frozen to death or died from scurvy.

HENRY HUDSON 1550–1611
English navigator Hudson was employed by the English Muscovy Company to search for the Northeast Passage. In 1610 he led an expedition to find the Northwest Passage. His ship became trapped in ice in Hudson Bay, his men mutinied, and with his son and seven other men Hudson was set adrift in a small boat. They were never seen again.

Walter Raleigh

1552–1618

While studying at Oxford University in 1569 English soldier, navigator, and courtier Walter Raleigh volunteered to fight for the Huguenots in France. In 1580 he was sent to Ireland to stop a rebellion, and he soon became a popular courtier at the court of Queen Elizabeth I (p. 15). Between 1584 and 1589 he sent three fleets to explore the North American east coast. He took possession of land north of Florida, which Elizabeth named Virginia. Attempts to set up an English colony in Virginia failed, but his ships returned to England carrying tobacco and potatoes. In 1587 he fell out of favor with the Queen and was imprisoned in the Tower of London for having an affair with one of her maids. On his release he led an expedition to Trinidad and Veneuzela and took part in raids against the Spanish. When James I became the king of England in 1603, Raleigh was again imprisoned in the Tower of London. He was released on parole in 1616 in order to lead an expedition to find gold in South America. He failed, and against orders he destroyed a Spanish colony. As a result the king ordered Raleigh's execution on his return in 1618.

Organized expeditions to east coast of North America 1584–1589; expedition to Trinidad and Venezuela 1595; expedition to Orinoco River 1616–1618

► In 1584 Walter Raleigh was knighted by the English Queen Elizabeth I.

George Bass

1771–c. 1812

In 1792 English naval surgeon George Bass sailed on the *Reliance* with Matthew Flinders (below) to Port Jackson, Australia. In 1795 the two young men began to explore the Australian southeast coast in a small boat called the *Tom Thumb*. In 1798 they sailed around Tasmania, proving that it was an island. The stretch of water between Tasmania and Australia is named after Bass. Not much is known about his later life, but it is thought he died in South America.

Discovered the Bass Strait between Tasmania and Australia 1798

Matthew Flinders

1774–1814

An officer and surveyor in the British navy, Flinders sailed to Australia with George Bass (above) in 1792. After their discovery of the Bass Strait in 1798 Flinders returned to England. Backed by Sir Joseph Banks (p. 38), he was commissioned to sail around Australia. Between 1801 and 1803 he explored the unknown coastline in his ship, the *Investigator*. The ship became unseaworthy, and he set off to return to England in the *Porpoise,* but it was wrecked on the Great Barrier Reef. He left again in the *Cumberland* but was imprisoned on the island of Mauritius for six years by the French. He finally returned to England in 1810.

Explored coastline of Australia 1801–1803

ABEL TASMAN 1603–c. 1659
Dutch navigator Abel Tasman was sent by Antony van Diemen (1593–1645) to find "The Great South Land" (modern-day Australia). In 1642 he sailed across the Southern Indian Ocean and saw Tasmania, which he named Van Diemen's Land. He returned in 1644 and discovered the Gulf of Carpentaria and the north coast of Australia.

VITUS BERING 1681–1741
Danish navigator Vitus Bering was sent by Peter the Great of Russia to find out if Asia was joined to North America. His voyages in 1728 and 1733 failed. In 1741 he sailed east from Okhotsk in Russia, and sighting the North American coastline he followed it north to the Bering Strait. He died of scurvy on the island of Avatcha.

JEAN LA PÉROUSE 1741–1788
French navigator Jean La Pérouse was sent by Louis XVI to explore the Pacific. In 1785 he sailed around Cape Horn and explored the coast of North America. He crossed the Pacific to the island of Sakhalin, sailed south to the Philippines, reaching Australia in 1788. His ships were wrecked near the Solomon Islands.

James Cook

1728–1779

Born in Yorkshire, England, James Cook became an apprentice to shipbuilders. In 1755 he joined the British navy and was soon promoted to captain. As a lieutenant, he was sent to Canada to survey the St. Lawrence River and Newfoundland in 1768.

In 1768 Cook was commissioned by the British Royal Society to sail on a round-the-world scientific voyage to Tahiti to observe the passage of Venus in front of the Sun. After this he was secretly sent south to New Zealand and Australia. In his ship, the *Endeavour*, Cook sailed around New Zealand, proving that it was two islands. He then sailed to Botany Bay in Australia, claiming it for Great Britain. On his second voyage to the Pacific (1772–1775), he was the first explorer to visit the Antarctic, but he was driven back by pack ice. Cook discovered the value of carrying vegetables and fruit for his sailors in order to prevent scurvy (caused by a lack of vitamin C). He also took well-trained artists with him because he was determined that any findings should be scientifically recorded. During his third voyage to the Pacific (1776–1779), Cook charted the west coast of North America as far north as Alaska. While visiting Hawaii, he was killed in an argument with local people over the theft of a boat.

Voyages of discovery to the Pacific: 1768–1771, 1772–1775, and 1776–1779

▲ Map showing the route taken by Captain Cook on his first voyage (1768–1771).

▼ When Cook arrived in New Zealand, he was met by the intricately decorated canoes of the Maori people.

JOHN ROSS 1777–1856
Scottish Naval Officer John Ross served in the Napoleonic Wars, and from 1812 he led expeditions to the Arctic. In 1818, with his nephew James Ross (p. 50), he led an expedition to find the Northwest Passage. Between 1829 and 1833 he led a privately financed expedition that discovered lands in the Arctic region of northern Canada.

FABIAN BELLINGSHAUSEN 1778–1852
In 1819 Russian Naval Officer Fabian Bellingshausen was sent to explore the South Pacific and Antarctica by the emperor, Alexander I. He reached his farthest point south in what is now called the Bellingshausen Sea. In 1821 he became the first man to discover land within the Antarctic Circle.

JAMES WEDDELL 1787–1834
During 1822 English seal captain James Weddell was looking for new hunting grounds south of the South Sandwich Islands. Because of the excellent weather conditions, he was able to sail beyond the Antarctic Circle into an unknown Antarctic sea, which he named King George IV Sea. In 1900 it was renamed the Weddell Sea.

James Ross

1800–1862

Scottish Naval Officer James Ross was a nephew of John Ross (p. 49). At a young age he traveled with his uncle on two expeditions to the Arctic. Between these voyages he sailed with Sir William Parry (1790–1855) in search of the Northwest Passage, and in 1831 he was the first person to discover the position of the Magnetic North Pole. In 1839 he was chosen by the British government to undertake an expedition to the Antarctic to find the Magnetic South Pole. The Admiralty provided him with two ships, *H.M.S. Erebus* and *H.M.S. Terror*. In 1841 his ships were the first to venture through a belt of ice into what was later named the Ross Sea after him. He discovered Mount Erebus and the Ross Ice Shelf.

Discovered: Magnetic North Pole 1831; Ross Sea, Ross Ice Shelf, Mt. Terror, and Mt. Erebus 1841

Thor Heyerdahl

1914–2002

Norwegian scientist Thor Heyerdahl believed that the Polynesian people of the Pacific had originally traveled there from South America. To prove his theory, Heyerdahl built a boat from balsa wood, and in 1947 he sailed it across the Pacific from Peru to the French Polynesian island of Tuamotu. In 1970, to prove that the ancient people of North Africa could have traveled to Central America, he sailed from Morocco to the Caribbean in the *Ra*—a boat built from papyrus reeds.

Led the *Kon-Tiki* expedition across the Pacific 1947; *Ra* expedition across the Atlantic 1970

Heyerdahl's balsa wood boat, *Kon-Tiki*, successfully tested the theory that the Polynesians originally traveled from Peru.

Jacques Cousteau

1910–1997

As a French naval officer in 1942 Jacques Cousteau developed the Aqua-Lung with engineer Emile Gagnan. This apparatus was an enormous step forward for underwater exploration.

Cousteau became commander of the underwater research ship *Calypso* in 1950. He converted it into a floating laboratory with modern equipment and underwater television cameras. From this ship he made the first underwater color movie in the Red Sea in 1952. In 1962, to encourage research into undersea living, Cousteau started his Conshelf projects, in which men lived and worked in an underwater settlement for weeks at a time. Among his many exploits was the first offshore oil survey by divers. In his later years he focused mainly on environmental issues.

Codeveloped the Aqua-Lung 1942; made first underwater color movie 1952; organized underwater Conshelf projects 1962–1965

▼ Cousteau (right) with his son Jean Michel. Jacques Cousteau made many underwater television shows about marine life. The longest running and most popular series was *The Undersea World of Jacques Cousteau* (1968–1976).

BY AIR

Lincoln Ellsworth

1880–1951

Born in Chicago, Lincoln Ellsworth came from a very wealthy family. He was a surveyor, railroad engineer, prospector, and mining engineer. In 1925 Ellsworth financed and took part in an unsuccessful flight to the North Pole with Roald Amundsen (p. 43). The following year Ellsworth and Amundsen flew with Italian pilot Umberto Nobile (below) in the airship Norge from Spitzbergen over the North Pole to Alaska. In 1931 Ellsworth provided financial backing for George Wilkins' (below) unsuccessful attempt to reach the North Pole in the submarine *Nautilus*. He succeeded in flying over Antarctica from the Weddell Sea to the Ross Sea in his monoplane *Polar Star* in 1935. During this flight and another in 1939 he claimed land for the U.S. Ellsworth Land in Antarctica is named after him.

First man to fly over both poles: North Pole 1926, South Pole 1935; explored Antarctica 1935 and 1939

Lincoln Ellsworth's plane *Polar Star*.

At the end of their epic flight across the Atlantic Ocean, Alcock and Brown's plane landed in an Irish swamp.

Alcock and Brown

Arthur Brown 1886–1948
John Alcock 1892–1919

After the end of World War I the British aircraft company Vickers recruited John Alcock and Arthur Brown to fly one of their aircraft nonstop over the Atlantic Ocean.

Arthur Whitten Brown was born in Scotland of American parents, and he became an engineer in the British army and air force during World War I. John William Alcock was born in England and trained as a mechanic. He witnessed action in the Royal Naval Air Service during the war and won an award for bravery. At the end of the war he was appointed chief test pilot for Vickers. The company wanted to be the first to fly an aircraft nonstop across the Atlantic Ocean, and they chose Alcock as pilot with Brown as his navigator. On June 14, 1919, their specifically designed Vickers Vimy bomber took off from St. John's, Newfoundland. Almost at once they flew into a gale and lost the use of their radio. Then they ran into fog, and the aircraft went into a spin. Disaster was avoided by pilot Alcock, who managed to pull the plane up just a few feet above the sea. During the flight Brown was forced to crawl onto the wings to break off ice, which threatened to make the plane too heavy. With basic navigational equipment Alcock piloted the plane to Ireland, where he landed it in a swamp near Galway. They had flown a distance of 1,884 mi. (3,032km) in just over 16 hours at an average speed of 190 mph (306km/h). Both men were granted knighthoods by the queen of England and shared the large cash prize that an English newspaper had offered the first men to fly nonstop across the Atlantic. Six months after their epic journey Alcock was killed in a flying accident. Brown subsequently became a manager of the Vickers aircraft company.

First men to fly nonstop across the Atlantic Ocean 1919

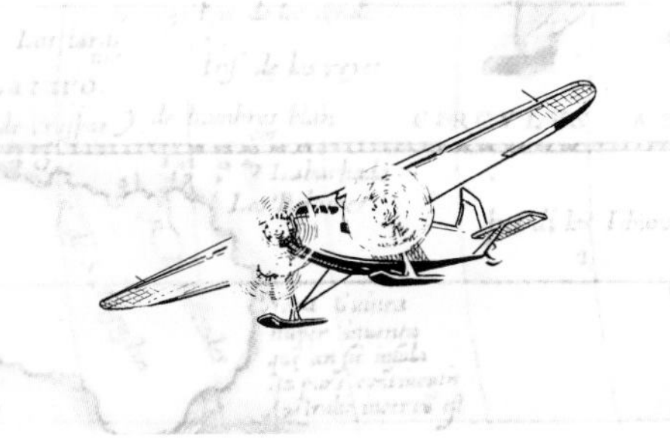

UMBERTO NOBILE 1885–1978
Born in Italy, Umberto Nobile trained as an aeronautical engineer and joined the Italian Military Aeronautic Corps. In his airship *Norge* he flew across the North Pole with Roald Amundsen (p. 43) and Lincoln Ellsworth (above) in 1926. His second flight to the Pole in 1928 ended when his airship *Italia* crashed on the return journey.

GEORGE WILKINS 1888–1958
Australian explorer George Wilkins first visited the Arctic in 1913, and in 1919 he flew from England to Australia. In 1928 he made pioneering flights over the Arctic and Antarctic. He led the expedition, financed by Lincoln Ellsworth (above), in the *Nautilus* in 1931 in an unsuccessful attempt to reach the North Pole under the ice.

Richard Byrd

1888–1957

American admiral and explorer Richard Byrd joined the U.S. Navy's air force in 1912. During an Arctic expedition in 1925 Byrd flew over Ellesmere Island and Greenland several times. With Floyd Bennett (1890–1928) he flew from Spitzbergen over the North Pole in 1926. In 1928 Byrd led the first U.S. expedition to the Antarctic since 1840. He set up his base camp, Little America, near the Bay of Whales on the Ross Ice Shelf. Byrd and his team explored the area to the east of Edward VII Land using sleds and planes, and they named it Marie Byrd Island. In 1929 he became the first man to fly over the South Pole. Byrd's scientific expedition made use of radio transmitters and aerial photography. Between 1933 and 1956 he led four more expeditions to Antarctica. In 1933 Byrd almost died of poisonous fumes when the chimney of his hut became blocked.

One of first men to fly over North Pole 1926 and South Pole 1929

Charles Kingsford Smith

1897–1935

Australian pilot Kingsford Smith went to England and flew in the British Royal Flying Corps during World War I. He teamed up with Australian pilot Charles Ulm (1898–1934) in 1927. In 1930 they made the first flight across the Pacific from the U.S. to Australia and then flew from Sydney to London in just under 13 days. In 1933 Kingsford Smith flew from England to Australia in 7 days, 4 hours. A year later he flew from Australia to the U.S., the first west–east flight across the Pacific. In 1935 he set out in his plane, *Lady Southern Cross*, from England in an attempt to break the England to Australia record. On the leg between India and Singapore his plane disappeared over the Bay of Bengal, and he was never seen again.

First flight across Pacific 1928; first flight around the world 1929–1930; broke England to Australia flying record 1933; first west–east crossing of Pacific 1934

Amelia Earhart

1898–1937

In 1932 American pilot Amelia Earhart flew from Newfoundland to Wales in a Lockhead Vega—the first woman to fly solo across the Atlantic. Three years later she flew solo across the Pacific from Honolulu, Hawaii, to Oakland, California in 18 hours. During her attempt to become the first woman to fly around the world in 1937, her plane came down in the Pacific. Despite many searches, she was never found.

First female solo flight across Atlantic Ocean 1932; across Pacific Ocean 1935

Amelia Earhart after making her first solo flight across the Atlantic in 1932,

Charles Lindbergh

1902–1974

Born in Detroit, Lindbergh was a stunt pilot before attending a U.S. Army flying school in Texas. He then worked as a pilot carrying airmail between St. Louis and Chicago.

In 1926 a $25,000 prize was offered for the first New York City to Paris, France, nonstop flight. A group of St. Louis businessmen backed his attempt, and on May 20, 1927 he took off from Roosevelt Field, New York, in his plane, the *Spirit of St. Louis*. He flew via Newfoundland, Ireland, and England to Le Bourget Airfield in Paris—a journey of 3,610 mi. (5,809km) covered in 33 ½ hours. He returned home to a hero's welcome and was awarded the Congressional Medal of Honor. Lindbergh suffered personal tragedy in 1932 when his son was kidnapped and murdered. To escape the publicity he retired to Europe. His autobiography, *The Spirit of St. Louis*, won him a Pulitzer Prize in 1954.

First solo crossing of the Atlantic Ocean 1927

Lindbergh made the first solo flight across the Atlantic in his single-engined Ryan monoplane, *Spirit of St. Louis.*

Amy Johnson

1903–1941

English aviator Amy Johnson trained to become a qualified ground engineer to maintain planes and qualified as a pilot in 1923. In her Gipsy Moth aircraft, *Jason,* she flew solo from England to Australia in 1930. She won a reward worth $6,000 from an English newspaper but just failed to beat the record set up by James Mollison (1905– 1959), who she later married. In 1931 she flew to Japan and back, and in 1932 she made a record solo flight to Cape Town and back. With her husband she made a record flight in 1933 across the Atlantic Ocean in 39 hours. In 1934 they flew to India in only 22 hours, and in 1936 she again set a new solo record for flying from London to Cape Town. She died when her plane crashed over the Thames River, in England, during World War II.

First woman to fly solo from England to: Australia 1930; Japan 1931; Cape Town 1932. Record-breaking flights with husband: Atlantic 1933; India 1934

Amy Johnson qualified as a pilot in 1923 and joined the London Airplane Club.

Jean Batten

1909–1982

Jean Batten began training as a musician, but in 1929 she gave up her studies in New Zealand to train as a pilot in England. She obtained her pilot's and ground engineer's licenses in 1930. An excellent pilot with ambitions to fly solo and break existing records, Jean Batten found sponsors, and in 1934 she beat Amy Johnson's record flight from England to Australia by five days. In 1935 she set another speed record by flying solo from England to Brazil, becoming the first woman to fly across the South Atlantic. During the next few years she set new solo records between England, New Zealand, and Australia, earning the title of England's top woman pilot. She gave up flying at the outbreak of World War II in 1939.

Broke speed records for female solo flights: England to Australia 1934; England to Brazil 1935; England to New Zealand 1936; Australia to England 1937

Ballooning

Auguste Piccard 1884–1962

Swiss physicist Auguste Piccard became one of Europe's leading authorities on cosmic rays. To learn more about these rays, Auguste planned to fly into earth's stratosphere in a balloon. His 500,050-ft. ($14,160\text{-m}^3$) balloon with a pressurized gondola lifted off from Augsburg, Germany, in 1931. Breathing purified air, Auguste and his assistant, Paul Kipfer, reached a height of 9.8 mi. (15.78km).

Altitude record for balloon flight 1931

Steve Fossett b. 1944

In 1995 American Steve Fossett became the first person to fly a balloon solo across the Pacific Ocean. An attempt to circle the world nonstop with Richard Branson (p. 236) in 1997 failed when their craft dropped into the Pacific.

First solo transpacific balloon flight 1995

Bertrand Piccard b. 1958

Grandson of Auguste Piccard (left), psychiatrist Bertrand Piccard and English copilot Brian Jones (1947–) became the first men to fly nonstop around the world in a hot-air balloon. Lifting off from Switzerland on March 1, 1999, their balloon, *Breitling Orbiter 3,* traveled 28,444 mi. (45,755km) before landing in Egypt 19 days, 21 hours, and 47 minutes later.

One of the first men to fly nonstop around the world in a hot-air balloon 1999

Auguste Piccard and Brian Jones became the first men to circle the world in a hot-air balloon in 1999.

IN SPACE

John Glenn

b. 1921

Born in Ohio, John Glenn joined the U.S. Marine Corps as a fighter pilot in 1943. He served in the Pacific during World War II and later in the Korean War, winning many medals and honors. While in charge of the U.S. Navy F8U Crusader jet project in 1957, he made a record-breaking supersonic flight from Los Angeles to New York. Glenn joined the North American Space Agency (NASA) in 1959 and was assigned to the Space Task Group, where he specialized in the design and development of spacecraft. On February 20, 1962, Glenn piloted the Mercury–Atlas 6 *Friendship 7* spacecraft on the first United States manned orbital mission. In 1974 he began a career in politics and was elected Democratic senator for Ohio.

First supersonic flight across U.S. 1957; First American to orbit Earth 1962

In 1962 John Glenn climbed into the *Friendship 7* spacecraft and became the first American to orbit Earth.

Ed White

1930–1967

Ed White was born in Texas and served in Germany as a jet fighter pilot with the U.S. Air Force. He returned to the U.S., where he became a test pilot. In 1962 he was selected for astronaut training by NASA. With James McDivitt (b. 1929) as his commander, White was the pilot aboard the Gemini IV mission that began on June 3, 1965. On the first day he made a 21-minute space walk with the aid of a "jet gun" and a special suit. Sadly, White and fellow astronauts Virgil Grissom (1926–1967) and Roger Chaffee (1935–1967) died in a spacecraft fire during a launchpad test for the Apollo I mission on January 27, 1967.

First American to "walk" in space 1965; killed in fire aboard Apollo I 1967

◀ Ed White became the first American astronaut to leave his capsule in space.

Alan Shepard

1923–1998

Alan Shepard graduated from the U.S. Naval Academy in 1944 and served aboard a destroyer in the Pacific. He won his wings in 1947 and became a U.S. Navy test pilot. In 1959 he was selected by NASA as one of the original seven U.S. astronauts. On May 5,1961 he became the first American to fly into space, making a 15-minute suborbital flight in the *Freedom 7* capsule. He controlled the entire 15-minute flight manually. Because of a medical problem with his ear, Shepard was kept from spaceflights for ten years. However, in 1971 he was given command of the Apollo 14 mission to the Moon. He and Ed Mitchell (b. 1930) landed their lunar module in the moon's highlands, where they made two scientific excursions on the lunar surface. Shepard retired from NASA and the navy in 1974.

First American in space 1961; fifth man to walk on the moon 1971

"Buzz" Aldrin

b. 1930

Born in New Jersey, Edwin Eugene Aldrin served as a U.S. Air Force pilot during the Korean War. While studying at the Massachusetts Institute of Technology, Aldrin developed rendevous techniques for orbital spacecraft. These were selected by NASA for all of their rendezvous missions. Aldrin was selected as an astronaut by NASA in 1963. On his first space mission in 1966 in Gemini XII, Aldrin made a record-breaking 5½-hour space walk. On July 20, 1969, Aldrin and Neil Armstrong (p. 55) landed their Apollo 11 lunar module on the Moon's Sea of Tranquillity. They were the first men to land on the Moon. After two hours they rejoined Michael Collins (p. 55) in the orbiting command module and returned safely to Earth.

Developed space rendezvous techniques 1963; record-breaking spacewalk 1966; second man to walk on the Moon 1969

In 1969 "Buzz" Aldrin (above) and Neil Armstrong became the first men to walk on the Moon.

Neil Armstrong

b. 1930

Born in Ohio, Neil Armstrong joined the U.S. Navy and became a fighter pilot in 1949. He later became a civilian test pilot for NASA, flying the *X-15* rocket plane. In 1962 he was selected as an astronaut, and in 1966 Armstrong commanded the Gemini VIII spacecraft and conducted the first docking in space with an Agena target satellite. In July 1969, with "Buzz" Aldrin (p. 54) and Michael Collins (right), he traveled in Apollo 11 on the first expedition to land men on the Moon. On July 20, 1969 Armstrong became the first man to set foot on the Moon. Armstrong's words, "That's one small step for man, one giant leap for mankind," were heard around the world. He retired from NASA in 1971 and became a professor of Aeronautical Engineering at Cincinnati University.

Conducted first docking in space 1966; first man to walk on the Moon 1969

Michael Collins

b. 1930

Born in Italy, Michael Collins served as an experimental flight test officer at the Air Force Test Center in California. He joined NASA as an astronaut in 1963. Collins was pilot of the Gemini X mission in July 1966, when he and commander John Young successfully docked with an Agena satellite. During this spaceflight, Collins "walked" in space to retrieve a scientific instrument attached to the satellite. During the historic Apollo 11 flight to the moon in July 1969 Collins stayed aboard the lunar orbiter while Armstrong (left) and Aldrin (left) made their famous Moon walk. Collins retired from NASA in 1970, and he became the first director of the Smithsonian Institution's National Air and Space Museum.

Pilot of Gemini X that docked with satellite 1966; third member of crew of Apollo 11 mission to the Moon 1969

Yuri Gagarin

1934–1968

Russian cosmonaut Yuri Gagarin joined the Soviet air force in 1955 and was selected to train as a cosmonaut in 1959. On April 12, 1961 he became the first man to orbit Earth in the Vostok I spacecraft. The flight lasted 108 minutes, with his craft circling Earth at a speed of 17,026 mph (27,400km/h). After reentering Earth's atmosphere Gagarin ejected from the Vostok spacecraft and landed by parachute. In 1968 he was killed in a plane crash in the Soviet Union.

First man in space 1961

Cosmonaut Yuri Gagarin in the Vostok I spacecraft before being launched into space.

Valentina Tereshkova

b. 1937

Russian cosmonaut Valentina Tereshkova became interested in parachute jumping at an early age, and she qualified as a parachutist. In 1962 she was picked to train in the Soviet cosmonaut program. She made her first and only space flight aboard the Vostok 6 spacecraft in 1963, becoming the first woman to travel into space. During the three-day flight Vostok 6 orbited Earth 48 times. In 1963 she married cosmonaut Andrian Nikolayev (b. 1929).

First woman in space 1963

Claude Nicollier

b. 1944

Born in Switzerland, Claude Nicollier joined the Swiss air force and became a pilot in 1966. In 1978 he was selected as a member of the first group of European astronauts. He joined NASA in 1980, and he was sent to Houston for training as a mission specialist in the retrieval techniques for the Tethered Satellite System and the International Space Station. Nicollier has flown as the mission specialist on four shuttle flights. In 1998 he became the senior astronaut of the European Astronaut Corps in Germany. During the 1999 mission of the space shuttle *Discovery*, Nicollier carried out his first space walk to install a new computer and guidance sensor on the Hubble Space Telescope—becoming the first European with Extra Vehicular Activity (EVA) experience on a shuttle flight.

Mission specialist on four shuttle flights 1992, 1993, 1996, and 1999; first European to "walk" in space 1999

Eileen Collins

b. 1956

Eileen Collins graduated as a U.S. air force pilot instructor in 1979. Between 1986 and 1989 she was assigned to the U.S. Air Force Academy and was selected by NASA as an astronaut in 1990. Collins served at Mission Control in Houston in many roles, and in February 1995 she made her first spaceflight on the joint Russian-American Space Program. In addition to piloting the shuttle, she deployed and retrieved a satellite, made a space walk, and rendezvoused with the Russian space station *Mir*. On her third flight in 1999, deploying the Chandra X-ray Observatory, she became the first woman to command a shuttle mission.

First female pilot of space shuttle 1995; first female commander of space shuttle 1999

Eileen Collins and the crew of space shuttle *Columbia* on completion of their flight in 1999.

Sally Ride

b. 1951

After studying at Stanford University in California, Sally Ride applied to the U.S. Astronaut Program after seeing a newspaper ad. Her training with NASA was completed in 1979, and her first spaceflight was made on June 18, 1983 in the space shuttle *Challenger*. As a mission specialist she took part in the launching of two communication satellites and in the launching and retrieval of a test satellite. She became the first American woman to orbit Earth. Sally Ride made a second trip in *Challenger* in 1984. She resigned from the NASA Astronaut Corps in 1987 and became director of the California Space Institute in San Diego.

Mission specialist on shuttle flight 1983; first U.S. woman to orbit Earth 1983; took part in shuttle flight 1984

Sally Ride became the first American woman to orbit Earth in 1983.

Helen Sharman

b. 1963

Born in Sheffield, England, Helen Sharman trained to be a pharmacist. While driving home from work in 1989, she heard a radio broadcast, "Astronauts wanted—no experience necessary." She applied and was accepted—only one of four candidates from the original 13,000 applications for the position of U.K. cosmonaut on the Soviet space mission Project Juno. After weeks of exhaustive psychological and physical tests she was one of the two final candidates. Further intensive training followed at the Yuri Gagarin Cosmonaut training center in Moscow's Star City. Finally in May 1991 Sharman flew on the *Soyuz TM-12* spacecraft to the *Mir* space station, where she spent eight days conducting scientific experiments.

First British astronaut 1991

CHAPTER THREE

SCIENTISTS

Scientists before 1000

▲ Using early scientific principles of the lever, the shadoof was used by the ancient Egyptians to irrigate their crops in the Nile Valley.

Science is knowledge about the world that people obtain by studying and testing ideas about the way things work. What we know today about ancient science and scientists comes from the writings, pictures, and artifacts left behind by ancient civilizations.

ORIGINS OF SCIENCE

Science is the systematic study of the natural world around us. Scientists observe and measure effects and try to find their causes. Today science is divided into many different areas such as geophysics, biochemistry, and oceanography. In the past science was a part of everyday life or mixed with religion and magic.

Many consider that the first area of science that developed was astronomy. Around 9,000 years ago people started growing crops, raising animals, and living in settlements. They had to study nature and the seasons closely in order to take care of their crops.

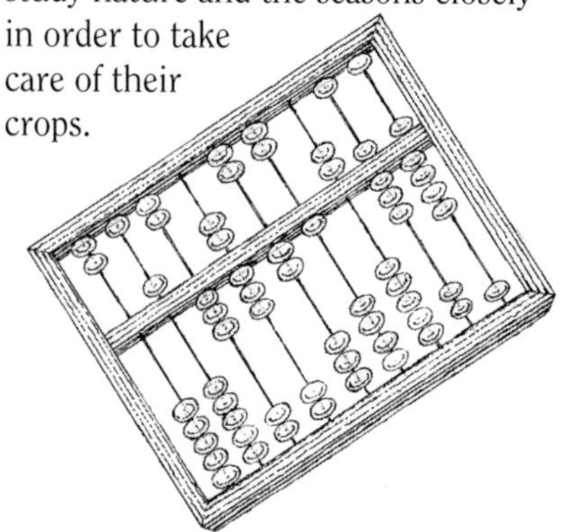

▲ The abacus is an early form of calculator. It was used in China from around 5000 B.C.

The first scientists may have been those that observed the movements of the stars, the moon, and the sun to make calendars to measure the passing of time.

Around 4,500 years ago ancient people started building astronomical observatories such as Stonehenge in England. These used carefully positioned stones to mark the positions of the sun and moon at certain points in the day or year. Ancient astronomers learned that the stars changed their positions regularly and used them as a guide to the seasons. The leading astronomer in ancient Greek times, **Hipparchus** (c. 190–120 B.C.), made a catalog of 850 stars, generated the concept of a star's brightness, called magnitude, and took some very precise measurements of star positions using only his eye as a guide.

ANCIENT GREEKS

At the height of the ancient Greek civilization, around 2,600 years ago, people started trying to give reasons and explanations for the way the world around them worked. The Greeks believed that their gods behaved logically and could not be the cause of everything that happened in nature. By thinking independently, the Greeks founded the study of natural philosophy, which ultimately led to the modern sciences.

The first-known natural philosopher was **Thales of Miletus** (624–c. 550 B.C.). He is alleged to have predicted a solar eclipse in 585 B.C. and introduced geometry—the study of shapes. Thales also developed the idea that the universe is ordered with each of the parts depending on the others. He established the idea of each effect having a natural and repeatable cause. This idea is the basis of working in a logical manner to establish scientific facts. Thales left no writings behind, but what is known about him comes from other Greeks, particularly **Aristotle** (384–322 B.C.).

The son of a physician, Aristotle questioned the world around him and investigated effects, seeking their causes. Aristotle and his followers wrote widely and in detail about a wide range of subjects, including physics, biology, medicine, and the earth sciences. Although many of his conclusions, such as how species never change, have been proven incorrect, Aristotle and his followers greatly influenced science for centuries after.

Pythagoras of Samos (c. 569–475 B.C.) is often described as the first pure mathematician. He was interested in using reason to prove mathematical principles. Today he is best known for the Pythagorean theorem, which connects the lengths of the sides of right-angle triangles. Pythagoras also discovered

▲ Sundials, used for many centuries, show the time by plotting the changing position of the sun's shadow during the day.

CELTIC BRONZE SHIELD AND SWORD

▲ Bronze is an alloy of copper and tin and was first used in around 3200 B.C. by the Mesopotamians.

that the note of a plucked string depends on its length, and so he was the first person to use mathematics to describe something that happens in nature.

The Greek mathematical genius **Archimedes** (c. 287–212 B.C.) was born in Syracuse on the eastern coast of Sicily. His many important discoveries include how to calculate the volumes of spheres and cylinders, a rough value for pi (π), and how forces work with levers. Archimedes applied math to solve many practical problems, discovering how objects float in water and building war machines to protect his native city from the Roman invasion. He was killed when Syracuse fell to the Romans.

SCIENCE IN ASIA

Science also progressed in other great civilizations. We owe the symbols 0, 1, 2, 3, 4, 5, 6, 7, 8, and 9 to Indian mathematicians from around 1,500 years ago. The ancient Egyptians divided the week into seven days, and the Mesopotamians divided each hour into 60 minutes and each minute into 60 seconds. The Maya of Central America controlled their whole society according to a complex but accurate calendar based on detailed astronomical observations.

The ancient Chinese thought that the universe was a huge living system in which everything was connected. They investigated nature in a practical way, making progress in chemistry, medicine, geology, geography, and technology.

ZHANG HENG (A.D. 78–139)

Born in Nan-yang, China, Zhang Heng was a mathematician, astronomer, and geographer who became head astrologer to the Chinese emperor An'ti. Heng corrected the Chinese calendar to bring it in line with the seasons and proposed that earth was a sphere and not flat as previously thought. He also invented a simple seismograph—a device that measures tremors and earthquakes.

SCIENCE THROUGH THE AGES

The Romans conquered Greece around 2,100 years ago. They used science to solve practical tasks in medicine and engineering. After the fall of the Roman Empire in the A.D. 400s, the writings of Aristotle and other ancient Greeks were preserved and copied by monks in Christian monasteries. Islamic scholars also made great advances in chemistry and astronomy and used Hindu math from India to create algebra. This knowledge was the basis for European science after A.D. 1000.

▲ The ancient Greek physician Hippocrates (c. 460–377 B.C.) taught a diagnostic approach to medicine based on observation.

PLINY THE ELDER

Pliny the Elder (A.D. 23–79) was a Roman scholar who served in the military for 12 years. His most famous work was the *Historia Naturalis*, published in A.D. 77. It consisted of 37 separate volumes that together documented all the Romans knew about science and the natural world and is regarded as the first detailed scientific encyclopedia.

► Archimedes was so engrossed in his mathematics that he did not even look up when a Roman soldier came to kill him.

THINKERS AND MATHEMATICIANS

Roger Bacon

c. 1214–1292

English scholar and scientist Roger Bacon became a Franciscan monk in 1247. He carried out experiments in alchemy, astronomy, and optics using mirrors and lenses, and he was the first European to describe how to make gunpowder. Bacon wrote three works: *Opus Majus*, *Opus Minus*, and *Opus Tertium*, which called for science to be based on experiment and observation. He was prevented by his religious order from publishing his work, and in 1277 he was imprisoned.

Notable achievement: first European to insist on a scientific approach to investigation 1266–1267

▲ In his writings Bacon predicted eyeglasses, flying machines, and motorized transportation.

John Locke

1632–1704

English philosopher John Locke was born into a strict Puritan family who wanted him to become a religious minister. Instead he studied medicine at Oxford University and became a secretary and doctor to the first Earl of Shaftesbury. Locke's main interest was philosophy, and he founded the idea of empiricism, which states that most of our knowledge is gained from experience. His ideas about building descriptions and explanations form the basis of modern scientific investigation.

Notable achievement: developed the philosophy of empiricism 1670–1690

René Descartes

1596–1650

Born in the French region of Touraine, Descartes was christened René, meaning "reborn," after narrowly surviving an outbreak of tuberculosis that killed his mother. He studied to be a lawyer and served in several armies. From 1620 to 1628 Descartes traveled throughout Europe before settling in the Netherlands. Although he invented Cartesian coordinates—a method of mapping shapes and equations—and investigated inertia, he was best known for his philosophies. Descartes started from the point of doubting everything, stating "I think, therefore I am." He urged people to use their own senses to build up an understanding of the world around them and not simply to rely on past teachings. This was a radical notion and led to the period known as the Enlightenment in which science made great advances. In 1649 Descartes moved to Sweden where he died.

Notable achievement: developed modern philosophy in the 1600s

Blaise Pascal

1623–1662

At the age of 16 French mathematician Blaise Pascal made new discoveries in geometry now known as Pascal's theorem. He later developed Pascal's Law, which explains that fluids transmit pressure equally and in all directions. His work with fluids led to important advances in understanding atmospheric pressure and his invention of the hydraulic press and the syringe. At the age of 21 Pascal developed the theory of probability with the mathematician Pierre de Fermat (1601–1665). This is used today to make predictions in many fields from genetics to insurance.

Notable achievement: codeveloped the theory of probability 1654

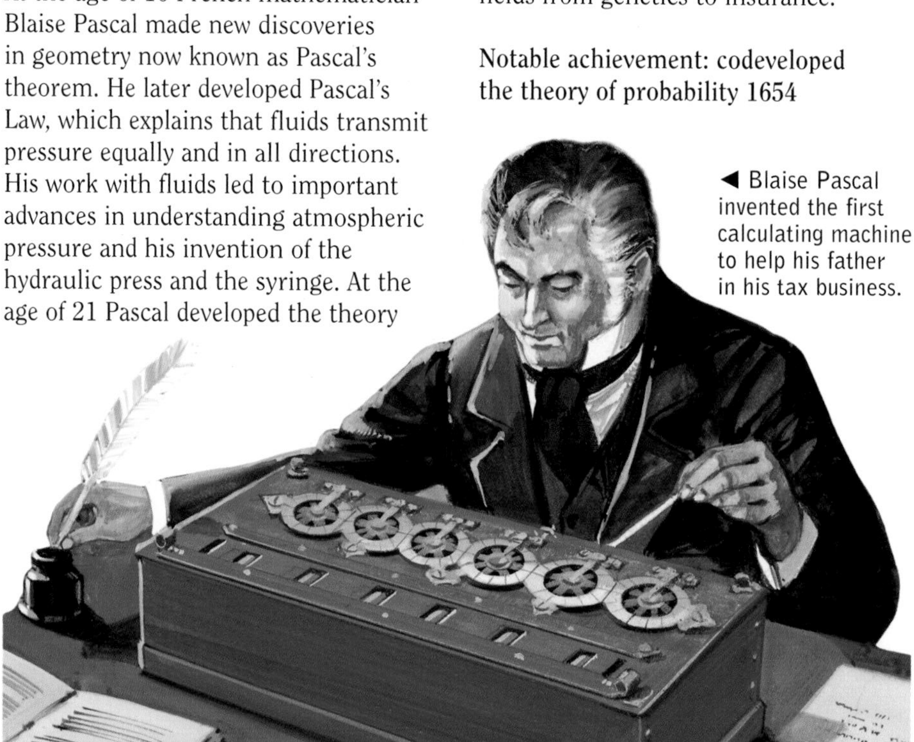

◄ Blaise Pascal invented the first calculating machine to help his father in his tax business.

Isaac Newton

1642–1727

Isaac Newton developed fundamental ideas in the fields of mathematics, mechanics, and optics. His work formed the basis of much scientific thinking up until the beginning of the 1900s.

Born in England, Newton studied and then taught at Cambridge University. He started his most important work at home in Lincolnshire in 1664 when the university was closed because of the Great Plague. Newton invented the reflecting telescope in 1668. About 30 years later he carried out experiments that used a glass prism to split white light into a spectrum of colors. Between these two periods came Newton's most fundamental work on the law of gravity and three laws of motion, which describe the effects of forces on objects. He delayed publishing his findings until 1687 when his book, *Principia Mathematica*, was published. His work revolutionized scientific thinking in physics and made it possible, for example, to accurately predict the movements of the planets, moons, and comets. Despite great fame, Newton lived modestly, yet when he died he was buried with high honors at Westminster Abbey in London.

Notable achievements: developed the Law of Universal Gravitation and the Three Laws of Motion 1684–1687

GOTTFRIED LEIBNIZ 1646–1716
German mathematician and philosopher Gottfried Leibniz became highly educated in—and wrote about—a great variety of subjects including philosophy, international law, psychology, languages, and geology. Leibniz is best known for his work in mathematics. He developed a new form of calculation called infinitesimal calculus, which is now used in all branches of science.

LEONHARD EULER 1707–1783
Swiss-born mathematician and physicist Leonhard Euler worked at the St. Petersburg Academy in Russia and the Berlin Academy of Science in Germany. He married Katharina Gsell in 1734, with whom he had 13 children. Euler wrote the first complete description of logic that laid the foundations for modern pure mathematics. He wrote over 800 papers and books, almost half of which were produced by dictation after 1766, the year he went blind.

CARL GAUSS 1777–1855
German mathematician Carl Gauss was a child prodigy, teaching himself to read and spotting errors in his father's payroll calculations. Gauss applied mathematical analysis to many branches of science, using equations to represent actual processes and making many important discoveries in algebra, geometry, and probability theory. Gauss also performed vital work in electricity, magnetism, and astronomy.

GEORGE BOOLE 1815–1864
Born in England, Boole was appointed Professor of Mathematics at Queen's College in Cork, Ireland, in 1849. He stayed there for the rest of his life, marrying Mary Everest in 1855 and raising five daughters. Boole developed a branch of mathematics that uses symbols to represent logical statements. Called Boolean algebra, it features logical operators such as "IF" and "THEN," which are as important to logic as "+" and "–" are to arithmetic. Today this is used to control the way data changes as it travels through computer circuits.

James Clerk Maxwell

1831–1879

Scottish physicist James Clerk Maxwell taught at various British universities throughout his life. He also carried out research into electricity and magnetism. Clerk Maxwell introduced the concept of the electromagnetic field and showed how light is a form of electromagnetic radiation. He also investigated the rings around the planet Saturn—his belief that they were made up of millions of small particles was proved by the 1970s *Voyager* space mission.

Notable achievement: developed equations that predicted the existence of electromagnetic radiation c. 1870

JAMES CLERK MAXWELL

Max Planck

1858–1947

Max Planck was a German theoretical physicist who developed the quantum theory. This explains how radiation, such as light waves, exists as packets of energy called quanta, and it has become a cornerstone of modern physics. Planck taught at the University of Berlin and outlived his first wife and their four children. His eldest son died in World War I, his youngest son was executed for his part in the plot to kill Hitler (p. 22), and his two daughters died in childbirth.

Notable achievement: developed the quantum theory c. 1900

Albert Einstein

1879–1955

Considered by many to be the most important scientist from the 1900s, Albert Einstein grew up in Munich, Germany, where he enjoyed playing the violin but found school boring and taught himself physics.

In 1905, while working at the Swiss patent office, he rocked the scientific world by publishing four revolutionary papers. These included an explanation of how light can behave as a stream of particles (work that won him a Nobel Prize in 1921) and his special theory of relativity that enabled later scientists to create nuclear energy.

In 1916 Einstein published his general theory of relativity, which developed a new theory of gravity and described how objects bend space and time. It led to many advances in astronomy, including the discovery of black holes. Emigrating to the United States in 1933, Einstein spoke out strongly against war and called for international disarmament. A strong supporter of a homeland for Jews, Einstein turned down the offer of becoming Israel's president in 1952.

Notable achievements: developed special and general theories of relativity 1905–1916

Niels Bohr

1885–1962

Born in Denmark, Niels Bohr was a promising student who excelled at soccer along with his younger brother, Harald. After studying under Ernest Rutherford (p. 69) in Manchester, England, Bohr gave the first modern description of the structure of the atom, in 1913. His research into hydrogen atoms showed how electrons give out and take in energy and paved the way for an understanding of how the outermost electrons determine an atom's chemical properties. Because of Jewish relations on his mother's side, life in Denmark under the Nazis during World War II became difficult, and Bohr escaped to Sweden on a fishing boat in 1943. He worked on the atomic bomb project in Great Britain and the U.S with his physicist son, also named Niels (b. 1922), but he became concerned about the dangers of nuclear weapons and urged peaceful international cooperation.

Notable achievement: described first modern model of the atom 1913

► Niels Bohr suggested that atoms are like the Sun and planets in the solar system: tiny electrons orbiting around a central nucleus.

NIELS BOHR

Timothy Berners-Lee

b. 1955

▲ By 2000 the World Wide Web linked over one billion web pages around the world.

British-born communication expert Berners-Lee graduated from Oxford University in 1976. Joining CERN, the European Particle Physics Laboratory in Switzerland, Berners-Lee wrote Enquire, a program for his own use that stored information using links called hypertext. In the late 1980s he proposed and started work on a system of global links—now known as the World Wide Web—that would allow people to combine their knowledge in a web of documents over the Internet.

Notable achievement: invented World Wide Web 1989–1990

WERNER HEISENBERG 1901–1976
German philosopher and physicist Werner Heisenberg's life was marked by both world wars. During World War I he was forced to give up his schooling to farm fields in Bavaria. In World War II he was the head of Germany's scientific research into atomic weapons. Between the wars Heisenberg made major contributions to atomic theory, developing his theories in the field of physics called quantum mechanics. He also formulated the uncertainty principle, which states that the more accurately an atomic particle is measured, the less can be known about its speed and direction.

ALAN TURING 1912–1954
The son of a British civil servant, Alan Turing is considered to be a founder of modern computing. His research work laid out the principles of artificial intelligence and the structure of computers. During World War II he played a major part in deciphering the Enigma code, used by the Germans to send top-secret messages. After the war he worked on the development of some of the world's first computers. In 1952 Turing stood trial for having had a homosexual relationship, then a crime in Great Britain. In 1954 he apparently committed suicide by cyanide poisoning.

BENOIT MANDELBROT b. 1924
Born in Warsaw, Poland, Mandelbrot was introduced to mathematics at a young age by his two uncles and attended universities in France and the U.S. He made a major contribution to chaos theory—a branch of mathematics that describes complicated, chaotic systems like the weather that do not obey the usual laws of physics and mechanics. The chaos theory has applications in many branches of science, and Mandelbrot's teaching career reflected this. He taught economics at Harvard University, engineering at Yale, physiology at a medical college, and mathematics at institutions in Paris and Geneva.

ASTRONOMERS

Nicolaus Copernicus

1473–1543

The son of Polish merchants, Copernicus studied law, art, and medicine before becoming a monk. At that time people believed that the Sun and planets orbited around Earth—the geocentric theory that stemmed back to the ancient Greeks. Copernicus did not agree with this, and in 1530 he completed his great work, *De Revolutionibus*. This explained how Earth rotated on its axis once a day and traveled around the Sun once every year. At the time this was a fantastic concept and one considered dangerous by the Church. Copernicus' book was published shortly after his death, but powerful church authorities banned it for over 300 years.

Notable achievement: first person to advance the modern view of the structure of the solar system

Tycho Brahe

1546–1601

This Danish astronomer led a colorful life that saw him lose part of his nose in a dueling accident and construct a new one out of gold, silver, and wax. Brahe studied law and philosophy at the universities in Copenhagen and Leipzig, Germany. He became fascinated by the night sky after seeing a solar eclipse in 1560. In 1576, with support from the Danish king, he set up an observatory on an island near Copenhagen, and for two decades he kept detailed observation records of the positions of over 700 stars. Without a telescope to assist him, Brahe developed astronomical instruments and also recorded a comet seen in 1577, proving that its orbit was centered around the Sun.

Notable achievement: made the first accurate star measurements 1576–1596

Galileo Galilei

1564–1642

The son of an Italian musician, Galileo first studied medicine at the University of Pisa before becoming Professor of Mathematics at Padua University in 1592. By that time he had already produced important work in physics, studying the pendulum, and in 1585–1586 inventing a hydrostatic balance that weighed objects in water. In 1609, after hearing of the invention of the telescope in the Netherlands, Galileo built his own telescope capable of magnifying objects 20 times. It enabled him to study the Moon and observe an exploding star called a supernova, as well as discover sunspots and four of Jupiter's moons. Galileo's discoveries supported Copernicus' theories of the planets orbiting the Sun and not Earth. This led to trouble with the Church, and in 1624 he was warned against Copernicus. In 1633 Galileo published a book that supported Copernicus' theories. Found guilty of heresy, he spent the final years of his life imprisoned in his own home. Galileo did not get married, although he had a relationship with Marina Gamba, who bore him two daughters and a son.

Galileo and his telescope.

Notable achievement: first person to observe the Sun, Moon, and planets through a telescope 1609

▼ Galileo also proved that objects of different weights fall at the same rate.

Johannes Kepler

1571–1630

Born into a poor family, Kepler was forced to move many times in his adult life as the Thirty Years' War raged in Europe. Once he had to leave his post and return home to Germany to defend his mother against charges of witchcraft. When Tycho Brahe (p. 64) died, Kepler, as his assistant, inherited his records. From these and his own observations he formulated the mathematical laws defining how the planets orbit the Sun. Kepler was the first to describe why telescopes work and how humans see.

Notable achievement: first person to formulate laws of planetary motion 1619

Edmond Halley

1656–1742

Born in London, England, Halley was intrigued by astronomy as a young man and was the first to establish an observatory in the Southern Hemisphere on the island of St. Helena. Studying a comet in 1682, Halley compared it with records of previous comets in 1607 and 1531. He deduced that it was the same one, plotted its path around the Sun, and accurately predicted its return in 1758.

Notable achievement: first person to calculate the orbit of a comet 1682

▲ Halley's comet returns every 76 years.

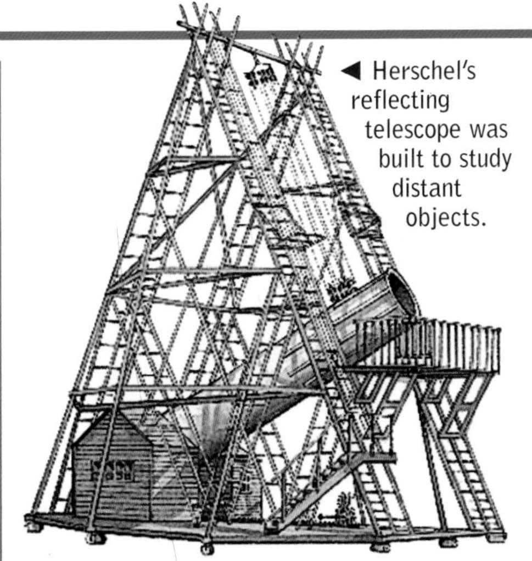

◀ Herschel's reflecting telescope was built to study distant objects.

William Herschel

1738–1822

In 1757 Herschel moved from his native Germany to England to work as a music teacher and organist. His spare time was devoted to astronomy, and in 1781 with his sister, Caroline (1750–1848), he discovered a new planet. He named it Georgium Sidus after George III (1738–1820), but it became known as Uranus. Herschel became the astronomer for the king and discovered a number of moons around Uranus and Saturn. He was also the first to suggest that the Milky Way was a vast collection of stars.

Notable achievement: first person to discover a planet, Uranus, by using a telescope 1781

George Ellery Hale

1868–1938

Born to a wealthy American family, Hale invented the spectroheliograph, which led to the discovery of magnetic fields in sunspots. Despite episodes of insanity, Hale raised enough funds from tycoons and big businesses to build a number of important observatories, including Yerkes, Mt. Wilson, and Mt. Palomar.

Notable achievements: invented the spectroheliograph 1890; founded Mt. Wilson Observatory 1904

PIERRE LAPLACE 1749–1827

Born into a French farming family, Laplace studied theology at Caen University before discovering a great interest and ability in mathematics and astronomy. Using Newton's theories of gravity, he managed to explain the attraction between the Sun and the planets. Laplace took a number of administrative positions throughout his career and sat on many science and government committees. In 1784 he was appointed examiner at the French Royal Artillery Corps, and the following year he passed a 16-year-old cadet, Napoléon Bonaparte (p. 28).

URBAIN LE VERRIER 1811–1877

Born in France, Le Verrier first taught chemistry until appointed as director of the Paris Observatory in 1854. In the 1840s Le Verrier became interested in the way that the gravity of planets appeared to pull another planet slightly off the path of its orbit. In 1845 he used mathematics to study the orbit of Uranus, and he predicted the position of a new, undiscovered planet. In the following year Neptune was discovered by the German astronomer, Johann Galle (1812–1910), exactly where Le Verrier had predicted.

ARTHUR EDDINGTON 1882–1944

Born in northern England, Arthur Eddington was one of the first astronomers to suggest that stars make energy by destroying some of their own matter. He first worked at the Royal Observatory in Greenwich, England, before becoming director of Cambridge University's observatory for 31 years. Eddington produced models of the inside of stars and researched their life cycle, publishing his findings in 1926. An excellent writer, his books—*Stars and Atoms* (1927) and *The Nature of the Physical World* (1928)—were widely read and helped popularize science.

▼ Edwin Hubble used this 8-ft. (2.4-m) reflecting telescope to study the expansion of the universe.

Edwin Hubble

1889–1953

While at college, American astronomer Edwin Hubble was an excellent athlete, but he instead turned to astronomy. He made the discovery that the Milky Way was just one of many galaxies, each containing millions of stars, and that the galaxies were all moving away from each other. This knowledge fundamentally altered the way that people viewed the structure of the universe.

Notable achievement: proved that the universe is expanding 1929

Georges Lemaître

1894–1966

Belgian astronomer Georges Lemaître entered the priesthood in 1923. His interest in astronomy led him to study at Cambridge University and at the Massachusetts Institute of Technology. In the 1930 she introduced his ideas about how the universe originated from one giant explosion. Lemaître's ideas were developed by others into what is now called the big bang theory.

Notable achievement: described elements of the big bang theory 1933

Stephen Hawking

b. 1942

Born in England, Stephen Hawking was diagnosed as having motor-neurone disease in the early 1960s and given only a few months to live. Confined to a wheelchair and reliant on computers and speech synthesis to communicate, he continues to work as a theoretical physicist. His most famous work has been in quantum theory and in seeking to explain how black holes work.

Notable achievement: wrote best-selling book *A Brief History of Time* 1988

▲ Stephen Hawking is the best-known modern expert on the subject of black holes.

CLYDE TOMBAUGH 1906–1997
U.S. astronomer Clyde Tombaugh grew up on his parents' farm. At the age of 19 he built his first reflecting telescope that included old car parts. Hired to work at Lowell Observatory in 1929, Tombaugh started a thorough search for the solar system's ninth planet. In February 1930 he discovered a planet orbiting beyond Neptune and named it Pluto. By 1946 he had cataloged 29,548 galaxies, 3,969 asteroids, and two comets during his time at Lowell.

FRED HOYLE 1915–2001
Hoyle was born in Yorkshire, England, to parents in the wool trade, and he studied at Cambridge University, where he met his wife, Barbara Clark. After working on radar during the war Hoyle returned to Cambridge, where he detailed how elements are made inside stars and developed the steady-state theory of the universe. This maintains that the universe is expanding steadily by creating more matter. He also wrote 14 popular science-fiction novels.

MARTIN RYLE 1918–1984
The son of an English doctor, Martin Ryle worked on radio and radar systems for the British government during World War II. Within two years of the war's end he was married to Rowena Palmer, with whom he had three children, and he was working at Cambridge University. He advanced radio astronomy by building more sensitive and accurate radio telescopes that were used to discover quasars.

JOCELYN BELL b. 1943
The daughter of an architect, Jocelyn Bell was born in Belfast, Northern Ireland. She failed her middle school entrance exams, but this spurred her on to study physics at Glasgow University before working in radio astronomy at Cambridge University. In 1967 she discovered unusual radio signals from space that pulsed on and off at regular intervals. These came from massive collapsed stars called pulsars.

PHYSICISTS

William Gilbert

1544–1603

While working as a doctor in London, England, William Gilbert carried out many scientific experiments. After years of work he published *De Magnete* in 1600. In it he put forward the theory that compass needles point north–south because earth acts as a magnet. He was the first person to use terms such as magnetic pole, electric force, and electric attraction. In 1601 Gilbert became physician to Elizabeth I (p. 15) but died from the plague two years later.

Notable achievement: first to carry out systematic research into magnetism 1600

Anders Celsius

1701–1744

Between 1732–1736 Swedish astronomer Anders Celsius went on a tour of all the important observatories in Europe and was part of an expedition to Lapland that proved that earth was flattened at the Poles. In 1742 he devised a temperature scale in Celcius, where water boils at 100° (212°F) and ice melts at 0° (32°F).

Notable achievement: invented Celsius temperature scale 1742

Thomas Young

1773–1829

Englishman Thomas Young was a precocious child who could read at the age of two. As an adult he practiced medicine, researched areas of physics, and helped decipher ancient Egyptian hieroglyphics. In physics Young studied elasticity, and in 1800 he proved that light existed in waves of energy. In 1801 he showed that all of the colors we see are made up of just red, green, and blue.

Notable achievement: proved that light has the properties of energy waves 1800

Benjamin Franklin

1706–1790

At the age of 10 American scientist Benjamin Franklin left school and entered the printing trade. A successful journalist and businessman, Franklin also made large numbers of discoveries that promoted science in the 1700s.

After starting a publishing business in 1726 Franklin became the postmaster of Philadelphia in 1737. Around 1744 he turned his restless intellect to science. His first invention, the Franklin stove, was a great success and encouraged more scientific research. Receiving some electrical devices from England in 1747, Franklin suggested how an apparatus called a Leyden jar stores electricity. He also introduced the idea of electricity as a flow of particles bearing negative and positive charges. Franklin is best known for his theory that lightning is a form of electricity. To prove this, in 1752 he flew a kite on a metal wire into a thunderstorm and produced electrical sparks between the wire and his fingers. These results led him to invent the lightning conductor. In later years he turned to politics, and in 1787 he helped write the Declaration of Independence and the U.S. Constitution.

Notable achievement: proved the electrical nature of lightning 1752

◀ In 1752 U.S. scientist and statesman Benjamin Franklin risked his life by flying a kite on a metal wire in a thunderstorm.

Michael Faraday

1791–1867

The son of an English blacksmith, Faraday became an errand boy for a bookbinding shop at the age of 13 and read every book that passed through his workplace.

▼ Michael Faraday demonstrates the principles of electricity at London's Royal Institution.

At the age of 21 he attended a lecture by chemist Humphrey Davy (p. 72), and after sending Davy his notes he was appointed as his assistant. Faraday discovered benzene in 1825 and then switched his research to electricity and magnetism. By 1831 he had built a simple electric motor and had discovered that moving a magnet inside a coil of wire produces an electric current. Known as induction, this vital principle allows transformers and generators to produce electricity. He published the laws that govern electrolysis in the 1830s and showed in 1845 how strong magnetic fields can affect light.

Notable achievements: discovered electromagnetic induction 1831; established principles of electrolysis 1834

James Joule

1818–1889

As a child English scientist James Joule was too sick to attend school. Instead he was educated at home before entering the family brewing business. Building a home laboratory and funding much of his research himself, Joule made many important discoveries, including the principles behind the law of conservation of energy. This states that energy cannot be created or destroyed, only changed from one form to another. Joule worked with William Thomson (right) and discovered that compressed gases cool when they expand. Joule also invented an early form of arc welding before sickness stopped his work.

Notable achievements: advanced research in theories of heat and energy 1843–1878; first scientist to measure speed of gas molecules 1848

William Thomson

1824–1907

British physician William Thomson entered the University of Glasgow at the age of 10, and he was only 16 when he published the first of his 661 scientific papers. Thomson made many advances in the study of heat—called thermodynamics—and explained how heat only flows from hot places to cooler ones. He invented many devices, including a tide predictor, a depth gauge for seas, and a new form of the nautical compass. In 1866 he was responsible for the laying of the first successful telegraph cable under the Atlantic Ocean.

Notable achievements: helped found the subject of thermodynamics 1840s; developed Absolute or Kelvin temperature scale 1840s

Joseph Thomson

1856–1940

Born in England, Joseph Thomson studied at Cambridge University, where he became a popular and influential professor. In 1897, when experimenting with cathode rays, Thomson became the first person to identify the existence of subatomic particles. He discovered particles around 2,000 times smaller than the smallest atom, which he first called corpuscles but were later known as electrons. Awarded the 1906 Nobel Prize for Physics, Thomson was a highly gifted teacher who lived to see his son, George (1892–1975), and seven of his research assistants, including Ernest Rutherford (p. 69), also win this prize.

Notable achievement: discovered subatomic particles (electrons) 1897

Heinrich Hertz

1857–1894

German scientist Heinrich Hertz was born in Hamburg, Germany, to a lawyer. After studying in Berlin, Hertz became a physics and math teacher in 1883. He married the daughter of a professor in 1886. The following year he invented a crude radio transmitter that passed sparks between the ends of a bent piece of wire. Hertz showed that radio waves are similar to light and heat rays—all forms of electromagnetic energy. A modest man, Hertz saw little practical use for his invention. He died of blood poisoning at the young age of 37.

Notable achievement: first person to transmit and receive radio waves 1887

Ernest Rutherford

1871–1937

New Zealand scientist Ernest Rutherford studied in his home country and in England. In 1898 he became a professor in Canada before settling in Cambridge, England. He discovered how radiation came in three main forms and named them alpha, beta, and gamma rays. He was the first to describe the atom as a dense nucleus surrounded by electrons. In 1919 Rutherford managed to bombard nitrogen atoms with alpha rays to produce the first manufactured nuclear reaction.

Notable achievement: Developed modern theory of atomic structure 1895–1930

Marie Curie

1867–1934

The fifth and youngest child of a physics professor, Maria Sklodowska was an excellent student who moved from her native Poland to France in 1891. In 1895 she married Pierre Curie (1859–1906), a professor of physics, and the pair embarked on research into radioactivity. They discovered two elements—radium and polonium—for which they were jointly awarded a Nobel Prize in 1903 with the French physicist Henry Becquerel (1852–1908). In 1906 Pierre was killed in a road accident, but Marie Curie continued working on the chemistry of radioactive substances and their use in medicine.

Notable achievements: discovered the radioactive elements radium and polonium 1898

▼ Marie Curie in her laboratory.

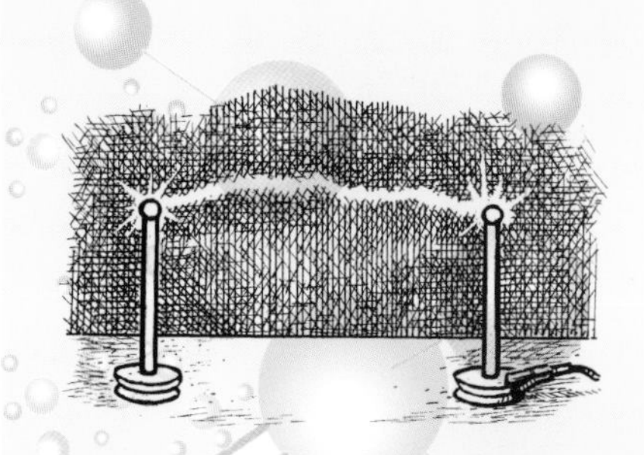

ANDRÉ AMPÈRE 1775–1836
The founder of the field of electromagnetism, French scientist André Ampère saw his father executed during the French Revolution and lost his sister and wife to illness, both at a young age. He demonstrated that electric currents produce magnetic fields and how the direction of the magnetic field depended on the direction of the current. Ampère also invented a unit of measurement of electric current, which is now known as the ampere, or amp.

WILHELM RÖNTGEN 1845–1923
Wilhelm Röntgen was the only child of a wealthy merchant family in Lennep, Prussia. He taught chemistry at a technical school and studied at Zurich University, marrying Anna Ludwig in 1872. In 1895, after many years of experimentation, Röntgen discovered X rays. He passed electricity through gases in a glass tube and worked out that invisible radiation was emitted as a result. Röntgen found that X rays passed through materials, such as skin and some metals, and would leave an image on photographic film. Röntgen became famous for his discovery, and it has had a major impact on modern medicine. He was shy and modest about his work, preferring to make regular mountain-climbing trips to the Alps than be in the public eye.

LISE MEITNER 1878–1968
Meitner was an Austrian Jew who had to battle against prejudice to become an important physicist. As a woman she was unable to finish her schooling and had to wait until restrictions on female students were relaxed to enter Vienna University in 1901. She worked with the German chemist Otto Hahn (1879–1968) to discover the element protactinum in 1918 and to learn how the nucleus of atoms could be split. This is called nuclear fission and is vital to nuclear power. Forced to leave Nazi Germany in 1938, she moved to a research center in Sweden and finally retired in England in 1958.

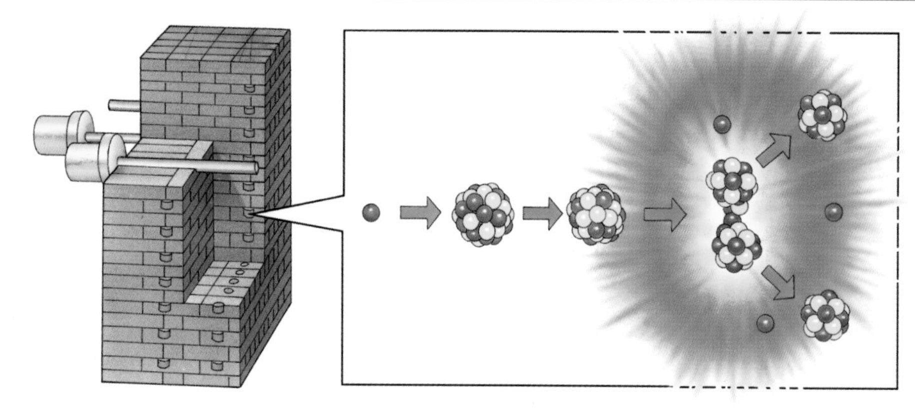

▲ Enormous energy was released when Enrico Fermi split the uranium atom in 1934.

John Cockcroft

1897–1967

English scientist John Cockcroft served in the artillery during World War I. After the war he studied electrical engineering at Manchester University and moved to Cambridge in 1924. Cockcroft and his colleague, Irish physicist Ernest Walton (1903–1995), became world famous in 1932 when they built the first machine capable of splitting atoms. Their "atom smasher" opened up a whole new field of science called nuclear physics, which studies the structure of atomic nuclei.

Notable achievement: built the first machine for splitting atoms 1932

EDWARD TELLER

Enrico Fermi

1901–1954

As a student Italian-born U.S. nuclear physicist Enrico Fermi studied theoretical physics. In 1929 he married a Jewish woman, but fearing persecution from Mussolini's (p. 30) Fascist government, they left Italy for the U.S. in 1938. In 1942 Fermi and his team produced the first controlled nuclear chain reaction—an important step toward nuclear energy and weapons. Fermi worked on the U.S. atomic bomb project for a while before later opposing its development.

Notable achievement: built the first controlled nuclear reactor 1942

Edward Teller

b. 1908

Born to an educated Jewish family living in Hungary, Teller did not talk until he was three, and his parents feared he might be mentally slow. He turned out to be an excellent student, moving to Germany first to study chemical engineering and then physics. In 1928 he lost his foot in a road accident, and the rise of the Nazis forced him to leave Germany for the U.S. in 1934. There he played a major part in developing both the atomic bomb and the hydrogen bomb. Unlike many nuclear scientists, he remained a firm believer in the need for nuclear weapons.

Notable achievement: developed the hydrogen bomb 1952

LOUIS DE BROGLIE 1892–1987
Born to a noble French family, De Broglie studied history at the Sorbonne in Paris. He developed an interest in science and went on to study theoretical physics. During World War I he served in the French Army as a radio operator on the Eiffel Tower. In 1924 he used mathematics to prove that particles of matter can behave like light and other energy waves—an important principle in physics. De Broglie received a Nobel Prize for Physics in 1929 and went on to teach in the science department of the Sorbonne from 1932 to 1962.

KARL JANSKY 1905–1950
American scientist Karl Jansky studied at the University of Wisconsin, where he was the star player in the university's hockey team. As an engineer at Bell Telephone Laboratories, Jansky's job was to track down sources of radio waves that interfered with telephone communications. During 1931 to 1932 he found that one source of radio waves did not come from earth but from the stars. Unheralded at the time, it was only after World War II and the start of radio astronomy that Jansky's discovery was fully appreciated.

RICHARD FEYNMAN 1918–1988
The son of a New York salesman, Richard Feynman made many advances in theoretical physics and won a Nobel Prize in 1965 for his work on quantum electrodynamics. He invented simple pictures called Feynman diagrams that showed how complex mathematics worked; he was involved with one of the first parallel processing computers; and in the late 1980s he solved the mystery of why the *Challenger* space shuttle had exploded in 1986. Feynman considered physics fun and was an inspiring teacher and lecturer who wrote several best-selling books.

THEODORE MAIMAN b. 1927
The son of an electrical engineer who invented an early version of the electric stethoscope, Theodore Maiman was born in Los Angeles. In his teens he earned money for his education by repairing radios and other electrical appliances. He joined the Hughes Electronics Research Laboratories in 1955. During the late 1950s there was a race between scientists to build the first optical laser—a concentrated beam of light energy. In 1960 Maiman won the race, and lasers are now widely used in manufacturing and medicine.

CHEMISTS

Hennig Brand

1600s

Little is known of the life of this German alchemist other than that he worked in the city of Hamburg and was the first known person to discover an element. Brand was trying to create gold from urine when he managed to isolate the element that he called phosphorus—named after the Greek word for "light bearing." Phosphorus is reactive and glows in the dark. It is used in manufacturing and to make fertilizers.

Notable achievement: produced phosphorus c. 1670

Joseph Priestley

1733–1804

A church minister, Englishman Joseph Priestley showed little interest in science until he met Benjamin Franklin (p. 67) in 1766. Inspired by him, Priestley made his first discovery—that graphite conducts electricity. He went on to discover and describe the properties of a number of gases including oxygen, nitrous oxide, and carbon dioxide. He showed how oxygen is important to animal life and that plants release it in sunlight. Priestley supported the French Revolution and American independence. In 1791 his church and home were burned to the ground, and in 1794 Priestley escaped further persecution by emigrating to the U.S.

Notable achievement: discovered oxygen 1774

Luigi Galvani

1737–1798

Born in the Italian city of Bologna, Luigi Galvani studied literature and philosophy before pursuing a career in medicine. He married Lucia Galleazzi, the daughter of a Bologna science professor, in 1762 and studied and then became a professor of anatomy at the University of Bologna for almost all of his adult life. In experiments with static electricity from 1780 on, Galvani established that the nervous systems of frogs and other animals use a form of electrical signal to make muscles contract. His work inspired scientists such as Alessandro Volta (p. 86) to investigate links between chemistry, biology, and electricity. The last decade of Galvani's life was unhappy. His wife died in 1790, he had no children, and his home city of Bologna was invaded by Napoléon's army in 1796. When Galvani refused to pledge allegiance to the invaders, he was dismissed from his university position and died shortly after. The galvanometer, used to detect electric currents, is named after him.

Notable achievements: simple electric cell 1780; established link between electricity and nervous systems 1791

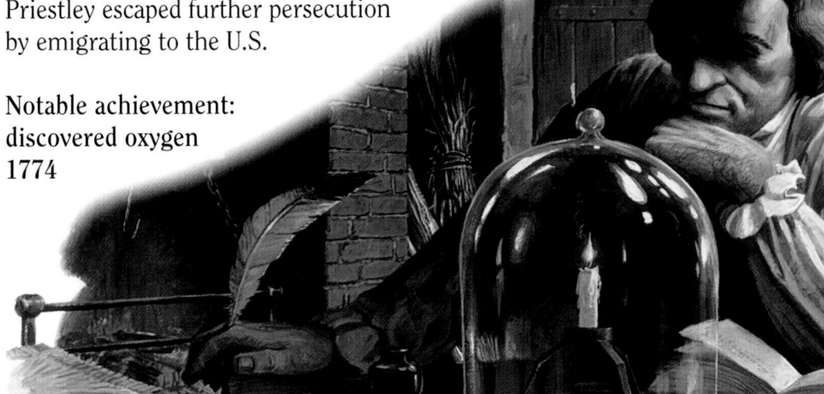
JOSEPH PRIESTLEY

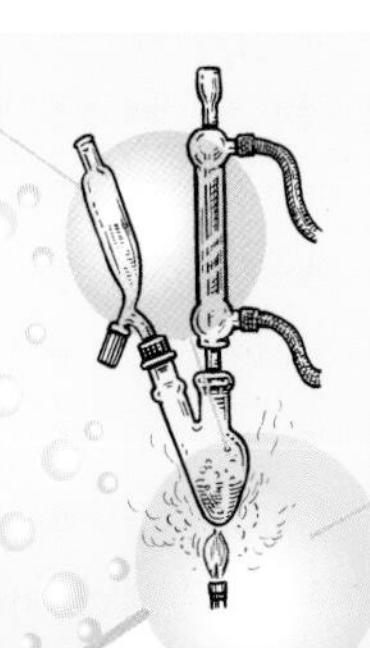

ROBERT BOYLE 1627–1691
Boyle was the youngest son of the first Earl of Cork, in Ireland, and had a privileged upbringing. In 1649 he set up a laboratory in his home in Dorset, England, and shortly after he developed the air pump. His experiments enabled him to discover the physical properties of air and how they were necessary for combustion (burning), respiration, and for sound to travel. He also discovered Boyle's Law of gas pressure.

CARL SCHEELE 1742–1786
Born into a poor Swedish family, Scheele had little formal education. His knowledge of chemistry came from practical experiments mostly conducted in his own pharmacy in his hometown of Koping. The first to discover oxygen in 1774, Scheele did not publish his results, so the credit went to Joseph Priestley (left). Scheele also discovered the poisonous gas chlorine, used to make plastic and disinfect water.

ANTOINE LAVOISIER 1743–1794
Considered the founder of modern chemistry, French scientist Antoine Lavoisier invented a new naming system for chemicals, established a number of elements that could not be broken down, and discovered that oxygen in the air was required for combustion or burning to take place. Lavoisier worked as an administrator and attempted to introduce reforms in the French tax system but fell on the wrong side of the French Revolution and was executed.

JOHN DALTON 1766–1844
The son of a weaver from northeast England, Dalton was put in charge of a Quaker school at the age of 12 and worked for most of his life as a teacher. He formed an atomic theory that states that matter is made up of tiny particles called atoms. Dalton devised a system of chemical symbols, and in 1803 he arranged them into a table based on their relative weights. He also kept a detailed weather log that by his death contained 200,000 entries.

Humphry Davy

1778–1829

Born in Cornwall, England, Humphry Davy became apprenticed to a surgeon at 16 when his father died. He experimented with many gases and discovered how nitrous oxide (laughing gas) could be used as an anesthetic. Davy also discovered that diamonds are composed of carbon. Working at the Royal Institution in England and inspired by Alessandro Volta (p. 86), Davy built his own electric batteries and pioneered electrolysis to discover a number of new metals including sodium, barium, and magnesium. In 1813 he toured Europe for three years and invented a safety lamp for miners on his return.

Notable achievements: first to use electricity to discover new elements 1807–1808

Julius von Meyer

1830–1895

German scientist Julius von Meyer earned a degree as a physician in 1854. However, he moved into chemistry, publishing an important textbook in 1864 and becoming professor of chemistry at Karlsruhe University four years later. By the mid-1860s Meyer had noted that the properties of the different chemical elements appeared to depend on their atomic weight. He developed a periodic table of the elements, but he lacked the courage to publish it until 1870, a year after Mendeleyev (above right) had published his version. In 1876 Meyer became the first professor of chemistry at the University of Tubingen.

Notable achievement: discovered a pattern to the properties of the elements 1868

Dmitri Mendeleyev

1834–1907

One of 14 children, Mendeleyev owed much of his education to his mother. The pair walked over 1,000 mi. (1,600km) from his hometown in Siberia to Moscow and then on to St. Petersburg, where Mendeleyev was admitted to the university at the age of 16. In 1869 he arranged the 62 known elements of his time into a periodic table based on their properties and in ascending order of their atomic weight. He left gaps in his table where he felt elements should be, and when three elements he predicted had to exist—gallium, germanium, and scandium—were discovered, his fame was assured.

Notable achievement: inventor of the periodic table of elements 1868–1871

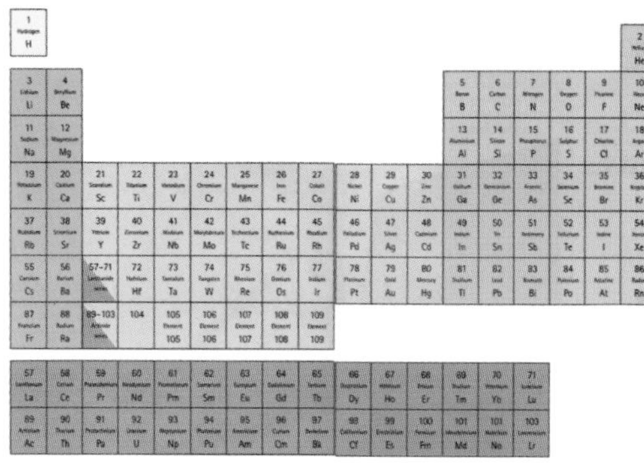

▲ Dmitri Mendeleyev's periodic table.

▲ Mendeleyev wrote over 250 scientific papers and produced a pair of important chemistry textbooks that became widely used.

James Dewar

1842–1923

Born in Scotland, James Dewar lost both his parents at 15. Studying how substances act at very low temperatures was his lifetime's work. He was the first person to cool hydrogen gas enough to turn it into a liquid, and in 1891 he built a machine capable of producing large quantities of liquid oxygen. In 1892 he invented the "vacuum flask" to store liquid oxygen. In 1904 it was manufactured in Germany—under the name Thermos. In 1905 Dewar found that cold charcoal could produce a vacuum—a technique important for experiments in atomic physics.

Notable achievements: inventor of the Thermos 1892; first person to liquefy hydrogen 1898

Fritz Haber

1868–1934

Although he made many advances in chemistry, including new ways of testing for acidity and the development of fuel cells, German chemist Fritz Haber is best known for finding a method of producing ammonia.

► In 1918 Haber won the Nobel Prize for Chemistry.

Ammonia is an essential raw material for many substances, including dyes, fertilizers, and explosives. In 1908 Haber developed a process that produced ammonia directly from hydrogen and nitrogen. In 1915 during World War I he organized and directed the first large-scale release of poisonous chlorine gas in Ypres, France. Gas warfare did not affect the outcome of the war, but it left Haber isolated from many scientists who disapproved of its use. His later years were spent trying—but failing—to extract gold from seawater.

Notable achievement: invented the modern process for the synthesis of ammonia 1908

Linus Pauling

1901–1994

U.S. scientist Linus Pauling paid his way through college by teaching the courses he had taken the previous year. Over 70 years of research, he mastered X ray crystallography techniques to learn more about the structure of chemicals and how they bond. He investigated the structure of complicated proteins and discovered that sickle cell anemia is caused by a genetic defect. A fierce critic of nuclear weapons, he received the Nobel Peace Prize in 1962.

Notable achievements: theories of chemical bonding 1939; discovered cause of sickle cell anemia 1948

Dorothy Hodgkin

1910–1994

On her 16th birthday English scientist Dorothy Hodgkin received a book that would change her life. It was about the use of X rays to analyze crystals and was by the Nobel Prize-winning scientist William Bragg (1862–1942). Although she was diagnosed with rheumatoid arthritis at the age of 24, Hodgkin went on to become a renowned crystallographer. She used X-ray technology to uncover the structure of a number of complex molecules, including vitamin B^{12}, penicillin, and insulin. In 1964 Hodgkin became only the third woman ever to receive the Nobel Prize for Chemistry.

Notable achievement: discovered the structure of complex molecules 1942–1964

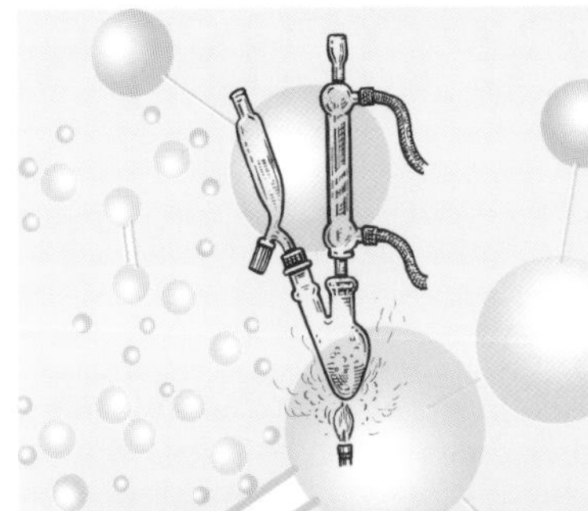

WILLIAM PERKIN 1838–1907

Englishman William Perkin was on his spring break from the Royal College of Chemistry in England when he made a startling, accidental discovery. The 18-year-old was trying to make quinine, at the time the only known treatment for malaria. What he managed to make was the world's first synthetic dye. Perkin set up a factory near London in 1857, starting the artificial dye industry. In 1874 he sold the factory, retired a wealthy man, and devoted the rest of his life to scientific research, discovering ways of producing artificial perfumes and flavorings.

JOSIAH GIBBS 1839–1903

Josiah Gibbs' father, an American professor, had become famous for helping the mutineers of the *Amistad* slave ship tell their story. Josiah Gibbs courted little publicity through his life in science, never got married, and only published his work in obscure journals. As a result it took time for his work in chemistry, physics, and mathematics to be fully appreciated. He provided many explanations for how and why chemical reactions occur, examined thermodynamics, and made advances in crystallography—the study and production of crystals. He became Yale University's first professor of mathematical physics and held that position for nine years without pay.

ERNST CHAIN 1906–1979

Ernst Chain was born in Germany to a Russian father and German mother. He considered a career as a concert pianist before studying chemistry and moving to England in 1933. Working with the British pathologist Howard Florey (1898–1968), Chain managed to isolate and purify penicillin and use it as an antibiotic to kill sickness-causing bacteria. As a result the pair won the 1945 Nobel Prize for Medicine. In 1948 he moved to Italy with his wife, the biochemist Anne Beloff, where he became the head of the first center devoted to studying antibiotics.

BIOLOGISTS

William Harvey

1578–1657

The eldest of seven children, physician William Harvey studied at Cambridge University in his native England. In 1597 he went to Italy to continue his studies at the leading medical school in Padua. Returning to England in 1602, Harvey married Elizabeth Browne, the daughter of one of Queen Elizabeth I's (p. 15) physicians. In 1618 Harvey became physician to James I (1566–1625) and later Charles I (p. 16). He studied the flow of blood through animals and humans and was the first person to map out how the heart works and how blood travels, or circulates, through the body. Harvey also correctly speculated on how humans and other mammals must reproduce through the joining of an egg and sperm.

Notable achievement: discovered circulation of blood 1628

Marcello Malpighi

1628–1694

Born to an Italian family who owned an estate near Bologna, Malpighi became a pioneer in the scientific use of the microscope. He proved that William Harvey's (above) theory of blood circulation was correct and examined and described the structure of the skin, lungs, kidneys, nerves, and taste buds on the tongue. Malpighi's findings were rejected by many scientists of his time, and this caused him to get involved in bitter disputes. Despite the controversy, he was appointed the head physician to Pope Innocent XII (1615–1700) in 1691. A number of parts of the body, including a layer of skin, are named after him.

Notable achievement: first person to use a microscope to carry out a systematic study of living things 1600s

Antoni van Leeuwenhoek

1632–1723

In an age when most scientists were wealthy, educated, and could read Latin—the language in which scientific works were published—this son of a Dutch basketmaker was at a disadvantage. Van Leeuwenhoek could not read Latin, was largely uneducated, and worked as a shopkeeper, yet he revolutionized biological science. He ground very high-quality lenses to build his own microscopes (ten of which still survive) and used these to discover bacteria and protozoa in pond water and in human saliva. In 1677 he discovered sperm in human beings. At a time when many thought that small insects came from wheat grains and sand, Van Leeuwenhoek was able to prove that they came from tiny eggs. He also described the life cycle of ants, showing how the egg, pupae, and larvae stages occur.

▼ Antoni van Leeuwenhoek made simple microscopes through which he observed tiny objects.

Notable achievement: first person to observe microscopic organisms 1674–1717

Carolus Linnaeus

1707–1778

The son of a Swedish pastor, scientist Carolus Linnaeus mounted the first of many plant studying and collecting expeditions in 1731. Appointed professor at Uppsala University in Sweden in 1741, Linnaeus started work on a comprehensive system for classifying and naming living things in the mid-1730s. Over the years his *Systema Naturae* grew from a slim pamphlet to a multivolumed work that made him the founder of modern biological classification.

Notable achievement: published the first modern system for classifying and naming living organisms 1735

Charles Darwin

1809–1892

The son of wealthy English parents, Charles Darwin studied medicine and then theology. He became interested in geology and in the study of marine animals, and at the age of 22 he obtained a post as an unpaid naturalist on board *HMS Beagle*, a ship surveying the coast of South America.

Returning to Great Britain in 1836, Darwin married his cousin, Emma Wedgwood, in 1839, moved from London to a small estate in Kent, and published accounts of his lengthy journey and other works about plants and animals. His first major account of evolution, *On the Origins of Species*, was published in 1858. Darwin believed that species were not created individually but over a long period of time from other species. This was a struggle for existence that created the conditions for the survival of the fittest. His book laid the foundations for evolutionary theory.

Notable achievements: developed the theory of the evolution of species by natural selection 1837; published *The Descent of Man* 1871

▼ When Charles Darwin's book *On the Origin of Species* was published in 1859, it caused great controversy because it went against the teachings of the Church.

Theodor Schwann

1810–1882

Born in Germany, where he attended the universities in Bonn, Warzburg, and Berlin, Theodor Schwann studied medicine and then became particularly interested in digestion. In 1836 he analyzed stomach acids and isolated a substance he called pepsin, which helps digest proteins in food. Schwann had discovered the first digestive enzyme. From 1838 to 1848 he was an anatomy professor at the University of Leuven in Belgium. He demonstrated that yeast was made up of tiny, plantlike organisms and developed the idea that animal life begins as a single cell.

Notable achievement: established the idea of cells as the smallest parts of all living things 1839

Gregor Mendel

1822–1884

Born in Austria to a poor family, Johann Mendel took the name Gregor when he entered a monastery in Brünn (now in the Czech Republic) in 1843. In 1850 he failed the exam to become a teacher, but he went on to study at the University of Vienna. Mendel returned to the Brünn monastery in 1854 and remained there for the rest of his life, becoming the abbot in 1868. From 1856 to 1863 he grew, studied, and tested nearly 28,000 pea plants. From this mass of research he formulated many of the basic principles of genetics, such as how traits are inherited independently of each other. Mendel is considered one of the founding fathers of the science of genetics.

Notable achievement: discovered the laws of heredity 1866

Louis Pasteur

1822–1895

French chemist and microbiologist Louis Pasteur was an unexceptional student, as a child he preferred fishing and drawing over more academic subjects. However, his genius for research became apparent.

Pasteur's major breakthroughs began in the 1850s at the University of Lille in France, when he established that microscopic organisms, or germs, cause decay, souring, and infections. By boiling and cooling liquids, such as wine and milk, Pasteur invented pasteurization, a way of removing germs. He also proved how germs were the cause of many infectious diseases, and by isolating the germs he managed to develop vaccines that saved lives. Despite failing health, Pasteur, who was married and had five children, also developed vaccines for chicken pox, anthrax, and rabies.

Notable achievements: proved that microorganisms cause diseases 1865; produced vaccine against rabies 1885

▼ Louis Pasteur found that microscopic organisms called bacteria spread diseases from person to person.

Joseph Lister

1827–1912

English doctor Joseph Lister proved to be an excellent surgeon as a young man. He was appointed as assistant to James Syme (1799–1870), one of the leading surgeons at that time, and Lister married Syme's daughter in 1856. At this time around half of all surgical operations resulted in the patient dying, usually because of infection. Determined to end this, in 1865 Lister read Pasteur's (above) theories of germs spreading disease, and he decided to put a germ-killing chemical barrier around the wound as well as on the surgeon's hands and instruments. Within months patient deaths had fallen by two-thirds.

Notable achievement: founder of antiseptic, germ-free conditions for surgical operations 1865

Robert Koch

1843–1910

Five-year-old Robert Koch astounded his parents by announcing that he had used newspapers to teach himself to read. The son of a German mining engineer, Koch passed his medical exams and worked at Hamburg General Hospital before opening a private practice. He managed to identify many of the microscopic organisms called bacteria that cause various diseases. In 1870 he identified the bacteria that causes anthrax. Six years later he successfully grew anthrax, and later he grew other bacteria outside of animals' bodies so that he could study them more easily.

Notable achievements: identified and grew bacteria outside of animals' bodies 1870s; identified the bacteria that causes tuberculosis 1881

Ronald Ross

1857–1932

Ronald Ross' father was an English soldier in India who rose to the rank of general. Born in Nepal, Ross scraped through his medical exams, and in 1881 he joined the British–Indian army medical services. In the 1890s he started investigating malaria—a disease that was killing millions of people every year. In the mid-1890s Ross proved that malaria is transmitted by mosquitoes and identified the malarial parasite. Ross' work led to the development of antimalarial drugs and won him a Nobel Prize for Medicine in 1902. By this time he had returned to England. He went on to teach at the Liverpool School of Tropical Medicine until 1912.

Notable achievement: discovered the cause of malaria 1895–1897

Frederick Hopkins

1861–1947

Born the son of a London bookseller, English scientist Frederick Hopkins became a pioneer of biochemistry and studied how chemistry makes muscle fibers contract when they do work. Following lengthy experiments with the diets of rats, he realized that animals needed more than pure carbohydrates, proteins, and fats to live. Hopkins named these additional elements of a healthy diet "accessory food factors"—they are now known as vitamins. In 1929 he won the Nobel Prize for Medicine.

Notable achievement: discovered the importance of vitamins 1906

Alexander Fleming

1881–1955

Scottish scientist Alexander Fleming studied medicine in London and worked at St. Mary's Hospital Medical School. Fleming researched ways of fighting bacteria, and it was in his messy laboratory in 1928 that he made the lucky discovery of a mold that released an antibiotic substance that killed bacteria. Fleming named it penicillin, but it was not until 1941, through the work of Ernst Chain (p. 73) and others, that penicillin could be produced in large enough batches to treat patients.

Notable achievement: discovered the antibiotic effects of penicillin 1928

Christiaan Barnard

1922–2001

South African surgeon Christiaan Barnard trained as a heart surgeon in the U.S. and then returned to work in his home country. In 1967 he transplanted the heart of a road accident victim into a man dying from heart failure. The replacement heart worked well, but the man died 18 days later from pneumonia. A second operation in 1968 saw the patient live for 563 days. In the 1970s drugs were developed to stop rejection and prevent infection, thus enabling successful heart transplants.

Notable achievement: performed the first human heart transplant 1967

DNA

Francis Crick b. 1916
Rosalind Franklin 1920–1958
James Watson b. 1928

DNA, or deoxyribonucleic acid, is the substance that controls the behavior of living cells and carries information from one generation to the next. The work of Crick, Watson, and Franklin has helped other scientists learn how DNA works.

American scientist **James Watson** was only 23 when he met the English scientist **Francis Crick** at Cambridge University. In 1951 the pair teamed up to work on DNA and built physical models to explore what it might look like. English scientist **Rosalind Franklin** was also working on the same puzzle at Cambridge using a technique called X-ray crystallography. Franklin's discoveries and data were made available to Crick and Watson before they published their findings in 1953. They explained how DNA was a double helix, or spiral, like two long springs wound around each other. Franklin received little credit for her efforts and died of cancer at the age of 37. Five years later Crick, Watson, and a colleague of Franklin's, **Maurice Wilkins** (b. 1916), received a Nobel Prize for their work.

Notable achievement: discovered the structure of DNA 1953

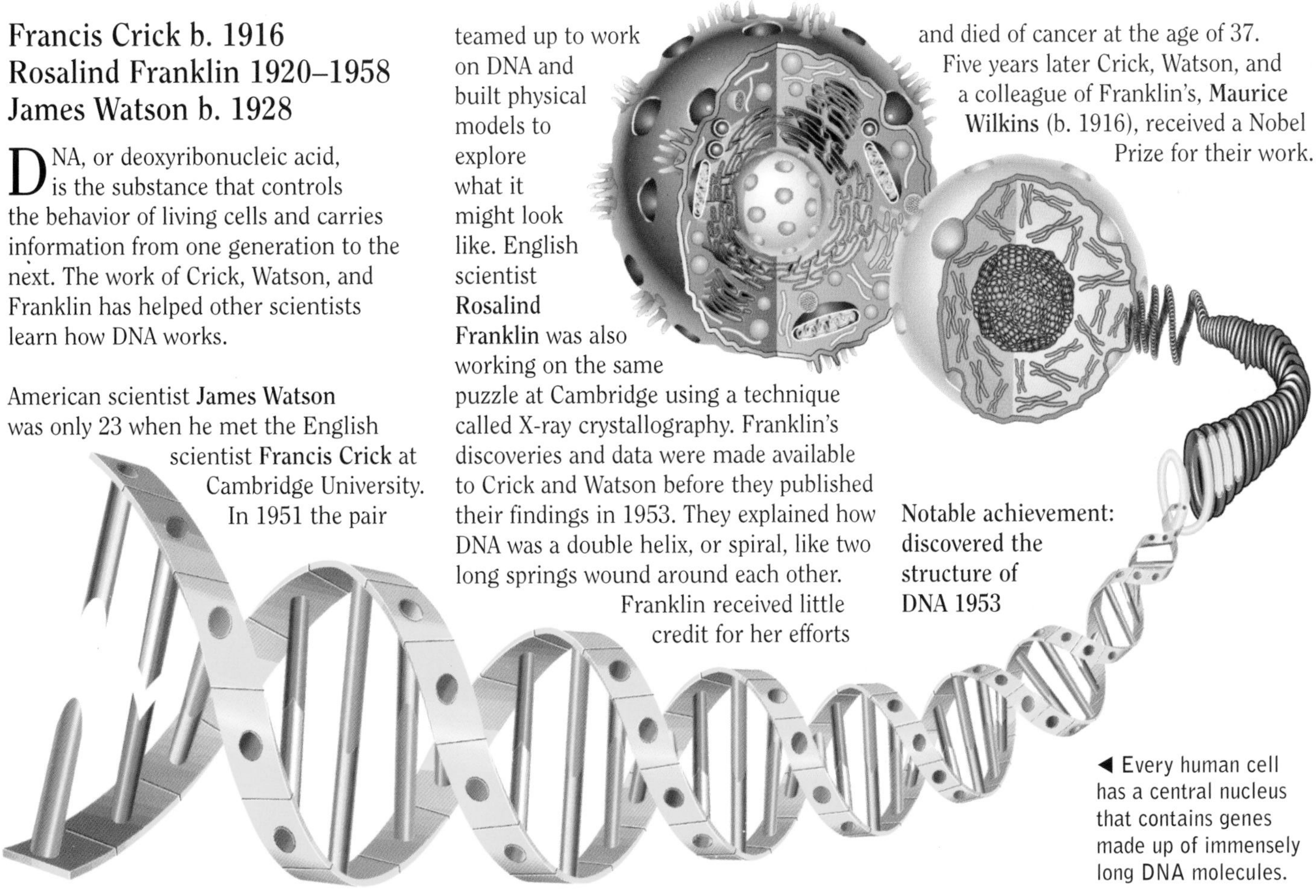

◀ Every human cell has a central nucleus that contains genes made up of immensely long DNA molecules.

EARTH SCIENTISTS

Georgius Agricola

1494–1555

German mineralogist Georgius Agricola studied medicine in Italy and became the doctor for the German mining towns of Joachimsthal and, in 1534, Chemitz. He also studied and classified minerals and rocks. As a result he became the founder of the science of mineralogy. Agricola published seven books about geology, mining, and how to smelt ores. His most famous work, *De Re Metallica* (Concerning Metal Things), was translated into English 350 years later by U.S. President Herbert Hoover (1874–1964).

Notable achievement: founded the science of mineralogy 1500s

Gerardus Mercator

1512–1594

Flemish cartographer Mercator traveled widely and became an engraver and instrument maker. From 1535 he started producing maps of countries, and in 1538 he made a map of the world. In 1544 the Church authorities charged Mercator with heresy, and he spent seven months in prison before moving to Duisberg in Germany. There he invented a new, more accurate method of making maps called the Mercator projection. First published in 1569, his maps enabled sailors to navigate the oceans more accurately.

Notable achievement: invented the Mercator map projection 1569

Charles Lyell

1797–1875

Born in Scotland, Charles Lyell trained and worked as a lawyer before becoming a geologist. He traveled on foot throughout Great Britain and Europe, taking careful notes on the types of rocks he saw and the shapes of their layers. Lyell explained his observations by claiming that the world is very ancient, shaped by the slow process of erosion and from the buildup of sediments. His book, *Principles of Geology* (1830), had a great influence on Darwin (p. 75). Lyell also investigated fossils and proposed the idea of reference fossils that indicate certain geological periods.

Notable achievement: introduced the idea of slow geological change shaping earth's surface early-1800s

◀ In 1585 Gerardus Mercator produced the first part of an atlas of the world. It was completed by his son and includes this map of North and South America.

Mary Anning

1799–1847

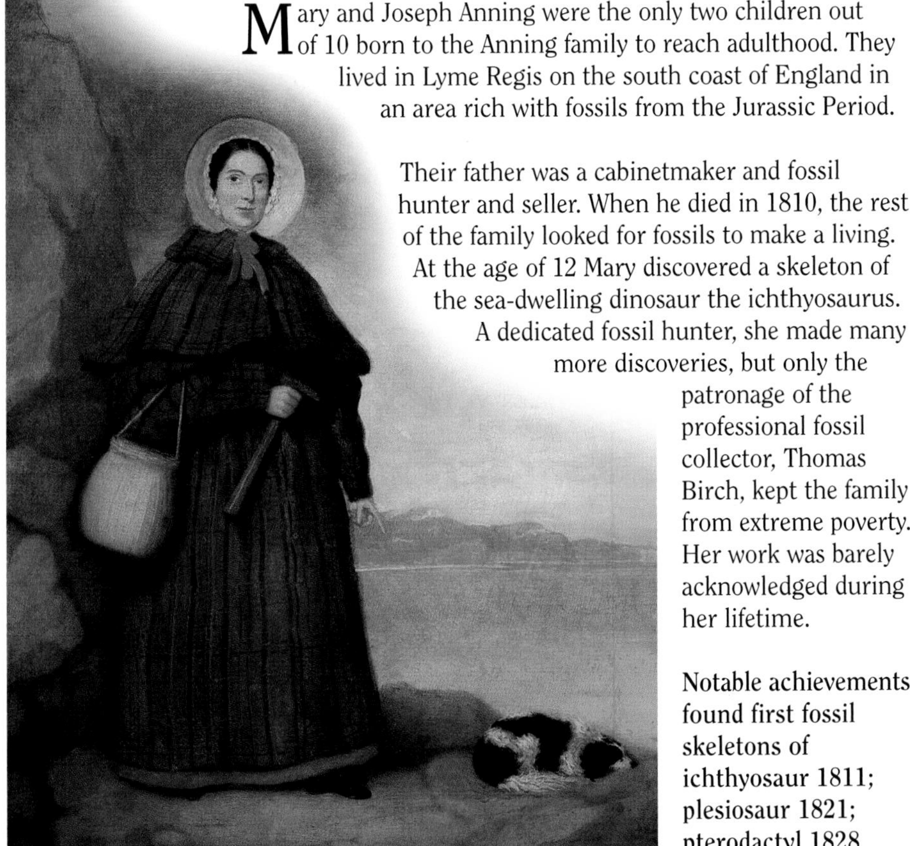

Mary and Joseph Anning were the only two children out of 10 born to the Anning family to reach adulthood. They lived in Lyme Regis on the south coast of England in an area rich with fossils from the Jurassic Period.

Their father was a cabinetmaker and fossil hunter and seller. When he died in 1810, the rest of the family looked for fossils to make a living. At the age of 12 Mary discovered a skeleton of the sea-dwelling dinosaur the ichthyosaurus. A dedicated fossil hunter, she made many more discoveries, but only the patronage of the professional fossil collector, Thomas Birch, kept the family from extreme poverty. Her work was barely acknowledged during her lifetime.

Notable achievements: found first fossil skeletons of ichthyosaur 1811; plesiosaur 1821; pterodactyl 1828

Edwin Drake

1819–1880

American Edwin Drake worked as a railroad conductor before becoming a pioneer of the oil-drilling industry. During the mid-1800s oil was collected from where it seeped to the surface. After many failed attempts to dig holes for oil Drake came upon the idea of drilling down inside a cast iron pipe that would keep the hole open. At Oil Creek in Pennsylvania, in 1859, he used an old steam engine to propel a drill bit through 65 ft. (20m) of rock, and he soon had a well producing 1,050 gal. (4,000*l*) of oil per day. Unfortunately Drake did not patent his oil-drilling device, and it was copied by others. He died in poverty.

Notable achievement: drilled the first commercial oil well 1859

Vilhelm Bjerknes

1862–1951

The son of a Norwegian math professor, Bjerknes studied in Germany with the physicist Heinrich Hertz (p. 69) before returning to Norway in 1892. The following year he became a university professor in Stockholm, Sweden. There he applied mathematics to describe the movements in the atmosphere. Bjerknes showed how areas of low pressure—called depressions—form where cold and warm air masses meet. He also described how the circling winds inside depressions affect the weather.

Notable achievement: founder of the science of weather forecasting (or meteorology) early-1900s

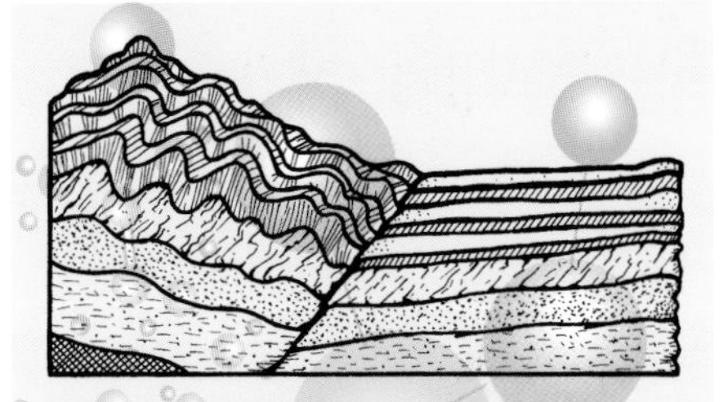

WILLIAM SMITH 1769–1839
Born on a small farm in Oxfordshire, England, Smith spent much of his childhood collecting fossils. While working as an assistant surveyor to canal engineering projects throughout England, Smith examined fossils that he found in rock strata. In 1815 he published the first geological map of England that showed how the layers of different types of rocks are arranged on the surface and underground.

MATTHEW MAURY 1806–1873
Between 1825 and 1834 U.S. Navy officer Matthew Maury made three extended voyages to Europe, to the Pacific coast of South America, and around the world. A serious stagecoach accident forced him from active service in 1839, and he turned his attention to hydrography—mapping the parts of earth's surface covered by sea. Maury published many maps showing wind fields, which helped sailing ships find the quickest routes. He also mapped the bed of the Atlantic Ocean, showing that it was possible to link the U.S. and Europe with undersea telegraph cables.

LOUIS AGASSIZ 1807–1873
The son of a Swiss minister, Agassiz studied zoology in Germany and Switzerland. In 1846 he visited the U.S. on a lecture tour and settled there. As a naturalist Agassiz made great advances in the study of extinct and living fish. As a geologist he proposed that an ice age had once gripped earth, and he revolutionized the study of glaciers and their movement. He became a founding member of the National Academy of Sciences (NAS) and was a major campaigner for more funds for scientific research.

RICHARD OLDHAM 1858–1936
While working for the Geological Survey of India, Irish geologist and seismologist Richard Oldham studied a major earthquake that happened in 1897. He showed that it was the result of three different kinds of earthquake waves. From his research in India, Oldham proved in 1906 that earth must have a dense core.

Charles Richter

1900–1985

Born on a farm in Ohio, Charles Richter moved to Los Angeles in 1916, where he studied physics. In 1935 he developed a ten-point scale that measures the energy released by an earthquake. The Richter Scale measures a mild earth tremor at two points and a major destructive earthquake at eight points. Richter stayed in California, where he mapped the earthquake-prone areas of the U.S.

Notable achievement: devised the Richter Scale to measure the strength of earthquakes 1935

Tuzo Wilson

1908–1993

The son of a Scottish engineer who had emigrated to Canada, Tuzo Wilson served in the Canadian Army for seven years. While teaching as a professor at the University of Toronto in the 1950s and 1960s he developed the theory of continental drift. Wilson showed that earth's crust consists of solid plates floating on the molten interior. These plates slowly move, or drift, a few centimeters every year. Earthquake zones and volcanoes mark the places where plates collide, move apart, or grind past each other.

Notable achievement: established the science of plate tectonics to explain continental drift 1963

John Edmond

1944–2001

Born in Scotland, Edmond studied in Glasgow and California before joining the Massachusetts Institute of Technology in 1970. A specialist in the field of chemical oceanography, he studied the chemical cycles in the world's rivers and oceans. In 1977 Edmond led a team that discovered hydrothermal vents—openings in the seabed that send out minerals into the seawater. On this expedition he discovered a range of unique and previously unknown marine life that thrive in the waters around the vents.

Notable achievement: discovered entirely new life-forms living around hydrothermal vents 1977

The Leakey Family

Louis Leakey 1903–1972
Mary Leakey 1913–1996
Richard Leakey b. 1944

The Leakey family discovered fossils in East Africa that traced the evolution of modern humans from early apelike ancestors called hominids.

Born in Kenya and the son of British missionaries, Louis Leakey started working as an archaeologist in 1931 in Tanzania. He met English archaeologist Mary Nicol in 1933, and they got married in 1936. In 1963, while excavating in Olduvai Gorge, Tanzania, Louis discovered the fossilized remains of *Homo habilis*, which he suggested was our true ancestor. Around 1.5 million years ago *Homo habilis* is thought to have evolved into *Homo erectus*, which then evolved into two species, one of which, *Homo sapiens*, is the first modern human. In 1978 Mary Leakey uncovered fossilized footprints in Laetoli, Tanzania. They were made 3.5 million years ago by hominids who walked upright.

The Leakeys' son, Richard, made his first fossil find—part of an extinct giant pig—at the age of six. During the 1970s, while working in northern Kenya, he found the fossilized remains of 230 hominids as well as stone tools, which showed that these creatures were more intelligent than previously thought. These findings proved that human ancestors lived in Africa over three million years ago.

Notable achievements: discovered oldest fossil remains of human ancestors 1959–1978

▼ Louis Leakey excavating early human artifacts in California.

CHAPTER FOUR

ENGINEERS AND INVENTORS

Engineers and Inventors before 1000

From the first experiments with tools and weapons tens of thousands of years ago, human invention and engineering had generated huge advances in materials, tools, construction, and transportation by A.D. 1000.

▲ Around 3000 B.C. the Sumerians were the first people to build wheeled vehicles. This four-wheeled cart was pulled by either an ox or by onagers, a type of wild ass.

Curiosity in the world and how to alter it to improve life has driven people to become engineers and inventors for thousands of years. Some of the earliest inventions, such as the bow and arrow (around 30,000 years ago), were used for survival, while others, such as the sewing needle (22,000 years ago), made life easier and allowed tasks to be performed better or more quickly.

EARLY ENGINEERS AND INVENTORS

People started to settle down and farm the land over 9,000 years ago. Staying in one place, they began experimenting with the natural resources around them, learning how to make beer as early as 6000 B.C., to weave fibers into clothes using a loom (4400 B.C.), and to produce soap (2000 B.C.). As small settlements grew into towns and cities engineers started producing larger and more complex buildings and structures. The first-known building engineer was the ancient Egyptian **Imhotep** (2600s B.C.), who constructed the first Egyptian pyramid in Saqqara. Another engineer from the ancient world, **Sostratus of Cnidus** (200s B.C.), designed the Pharos of Alexandria. Completed in around 280 B.C., this giant lighthouse stood over 430 ft. (130m) tall and was over 3,230 sq. ft. (300 sq m) at its base. The Romans built thousands of miles of roads throughout their empire and developed advanced construction systems and machines, including winches and cranes. These were described in *De architectura*, written by the Roman architect and engineer **Vitruvius** c. 90–20 B.C.

▲ The Romans constructed hard-wearing roads throughout their empire.

WAR AND INVENTION

Conflict has often spurred engineers and inventors to create new, more powerful weapons. Ironmaking allowed swords, axes, and daggers to be created, while transportation engineering saw the horse-drawn chariot used in battles by the Egyptians and Assyrians from 2000 B.C. Building engineers protected cities with strong outer walls. This resulted in attackers laying siege to towns and developing weapons known as siege engines. In 306 B.C. **Demetrius Poliorcetes** (c. 337–283 B.C.) developed a number of advanced siege engines while attacking the city of Rhodes. These included catapults capable of hurling rocks weighing 175 lbs (80kg) and large, portable drills 82 ft. (25m) long that were used to bore through city walls.

Callinicus of Heliopolis (A.D. 600s), a Syrian refugee who settled in Constantinople, developed the first-known chemical weapon. Called Greek fire, it was a highly flammable liquid that was fired from tubes onto enemy ships and was used from 673 until the fall of the Byzantine Empire in 1453.

MACHINES AND TOOLS

Prehistoric people used simple tools such as a tree branch that could help lift a large boulder or a sharp stone that could scrape an animal skin clean. Many machines are made up of a combination of five simple machines—levers, pulleys, wedges, wheels, and screws. The wedge and lever have existed since prehistoric times, while the first-known examples of wheels were found in Mesopotamia (now Iraq) and are over 5,000 years old.

▲ Around A.D. 100 the Chinese made paper with fibers pressed on screens and dried in the sun.

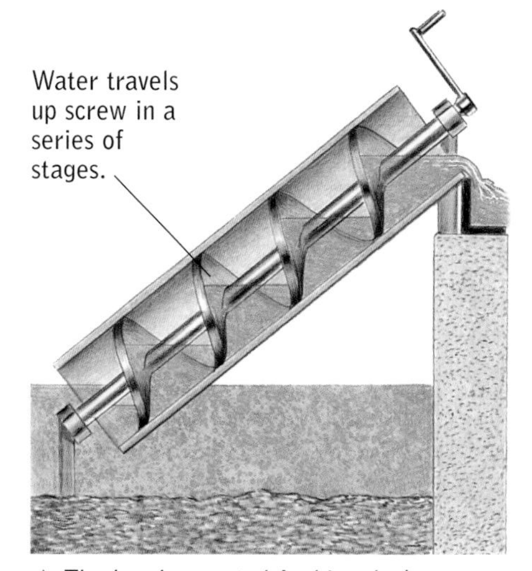

▲ The hand-operated Archimedes' screw draws water up from a river for irrigation.

Archytas of Tarentum (c. 400–350 B.C.) was a mathematician from Italy. It is believed that he invented the pulley, making the pulling and lifting of objects an easier task. No one is certain who invented the screw, but it is known that the Greek scientist and inventor **Archimedes** (c. 287–212 B.C.) built a large screw that lifted water up.

MACHINES AND POWER

Machines before A.D. 1000 were powered by humans or animals. The energy in falling water was first used to power waterwheels and water mills in around 100 B.C. Wind power was used to propel sailing ships and boats, and in A.D. 650 in Iraq the first windmills were built to grind grain or raise water. Engineers such as **Ctesibius** (100s B.C.) and **Philo of Byzantium** (c. 260–180 B.C.) experimented with air and water power. Philo invented a type of air pump and described a missile launcher powered by compressed air. Only one device using steam power is known of before A.D. 1000, and it was from Egyptian-born inventor **Hero of Alexandria** (c. A.D. 20–62). His eolopile, or "wind ball," was a sealed cauldron of boiling water that sent steam into a metal ball. The metal ball had two curved exhaust tubes that released the steam, causing the ball to spin around.

NEW MATERIALS

Engineering and invention depends on materials that are available. During prehistoric times people had to use materials found in nature such as stones, wood, and plant fibers. Through experimentation people discovered how to create, form, and use different materials, which then made other inventions possible. Around 2000 B.C. glass was first manufactured in the Middle East. It was first used for beads and then by 1500 B.C. used for jars and bottles in ancient Egypt. The ability to smelt metals from rocky ores started with copper in around 4500 B.C.

The use of bronze (from 3000 B.C.) and iron (c. 1500 B.C.) proved vital to the development of buildings, machines, and weapons. The ancient Chinese learned how to produce iron by 600 B.C., and by 450 B.C. they had started making cast iron by adding carbon. Paper was also invented in China. In A.D. 105 the inventor **Cai Lun** (c. A.D. 66–125) presented the Eastern Han Emperor Ho-Ti with a batch of paper made from tree bark, rags, pieces of rope, and worn-out fishnets.

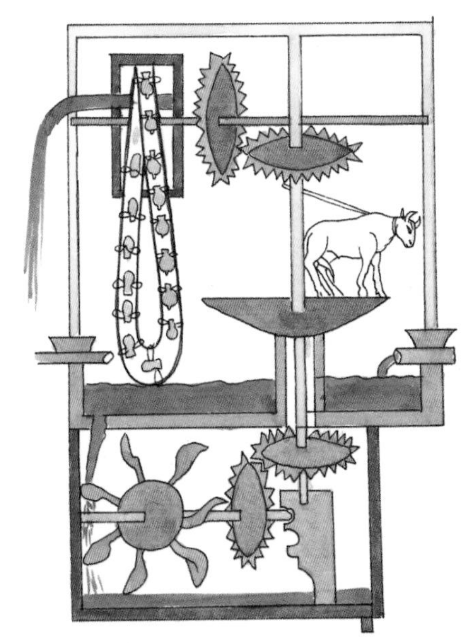

▲ This drawing from around 1,500 years ago shows an Arab machine for raising water.

ENGINEERS
Construction

James Brindley
1716–1762

Born in Derbyshire, England, James Brindley was a self-taught engineer who built his canals without drawings or written calculations. He was hired in 1759 by the Duke of Bridgewater to build a 10-mi. (16-km) canal to carry coal from pits into Manchester. Brindley engineered 360 mi. (580km) of canals.

Notable achievement: built Bridgewater Canal in England 1765

John McAdam
1756–1836

Born in Scotland, John McAdam moved to New York City at the age of 16, where he made his fortune as an "agent for prizes," handling goods that were stolen or taken in war. Returning to Scotland in 1783, he bought a Scottish estate and while repairing its roads developed new road-building methods. These quickly caught on, allowing cheaper and more reliable road systems to be built.

Notable achievement: developed modern road construction 1783–1816

Thomas Telford
1757–1834

The son of a Scottish shepherd who died when he was just one year old, Telford served as a stonemason's apprentice and taught himself architecture. He built over 900 mi. (1,450km) of roads and, in 1826, the world's first major steel suspension bridge, linking the island of Anglesey to Wales. He also built canals in Great Britain and Sweden.

Notable structures: Caledonian Canal 1822; Menai Strait Bridge 1826

Joseph Paxton
1801–1865

The son of an English farmer, Joseph Paxton began working as a gardener at the age of 15. In 1826 he was appointed head gardener at Chatsworth House in Derbyshire, England, where he built large greenhouses and the most powerful water fountain in the world. Paxton also designed the Crystal Palace, a giant iron and glass building, for the 1851 Great Exhibition in London. His design meant that the building could be taken apart later and moved. Paxton went into politics and became a Member of the British Parliament in 1854.

Notable structure: Crystal Palace 1851

Isambard Kingdom Brunel
1806–1859

Born in Portsmouth, England, the only son of French civil engineer Marc Brunel (p. 85), Isambard Kingdom Brunel became the most famous English engineer of his era.

Developing a passion for railroads, Brunel built over 1,000 mi. (1,600km) of tracks in Great Britain and Italy, as well as becoming a consultant on railroads in Australia and India. He designed a number of advanced bridges, including the Clifton Suspension Bridge (completed 1864) and the Royal Albert Bridge (completed 1859). In 1838 he designed the *SS Great Western*, the first steamship to offer a regular service across the Atlantic Ocean. Brunel also designed the *SS Great Eastern*, which was the largest ship ever built when it was launched in 1858. Despite enjoying music and performing magic, Brunel was a workaholic who thought nothing of working an 18-hour day.

Notable achievements: Clifton Suspension Bridge, Bristol, England, 1829–1864; *SS Great Western* 1837; broad gauge Great Western Railway (London to Bristol) 1841; *SS Great Eastern* 1855

Gustave Eiffel

1832–1923

French engineer Gustave Eiffel first studied chemistry before becoming a notable civil engineer renowned for his light but strong steel bridges. Eiffel's company, formed in 1866, cast thegiant Statue of Liberty in 1884, and he designed the interior frame and workings. In 1887, the year his wife of 15 years died of pneumonia, Eiffel's design for a Paris landmark to celebrate 100 years since the French Revolution was chosen from some 700 entries.

Completed in 1889, the Eiffel Tower was the world's tallest building for 40 years. After involvement in the failed French attempt to build the Panama Canal, Eiffel turned to science in the 1890s and added an aerodynamics laboratory and telegraph system to his beloved tower.

Notable structures: Statue of Liberty 1875–1885; Eiffel Tower 1887–1889

▶ Despite criticism about its impact on Paris, the Eiffel Tower was a great success in the 1889 Paris Exhibition.

◀ Paddington Station, the London terminus of Brunel's Great Western Railway.

William Le Baron Jenney

1832–1907

Born into a family of American shipowners, Jenney served in the Civil War (1861–1865) before opening an architectural firm in Chicago in 1868. He developed new techniques for building tall buildings known as skyscrapers. Jenney was the first person to use an internal steel skeleton with outer walls made of brick and stone. His structures were lighter and stronger than tall buildings made completely out of stone.

Notable structures: world's first modern skyscraper 1885; first 16-story building, the Manhattan Building 1891

JOHN SMEATON 1724–1794
Born in Yorkshire, England, John Smeaton worked first making scientific instruments before building large structures, including a canal (1790) linking the Forth and Clyde rivers in Scotland. Smeaton also developed hydraulic cement, which he used to build the fourth Eddystone lighthouse in the English Channel (1756–1759). It stood for 127 years.

WILLIAM JESSOP 1745–1814
Born in Devon, England, William Jessop started working with John Smeaton (above) and remained his assistant until 1772. In 1790 Jessop founded the Butterley Iron Works in Derbyshire, which produced improved cast-iron rails for railroad tracks. Also a canal and dock builder, Jessop worked with Telford (p. 84) and was appointed chief engineer for the Grand Union Canal that links London and the English Midlands.

JOHN RENNIE 1761–1821
Scottish civil engineer John Rennie started working at the age of 12 making gears and equipment for cotton and water mills. Studying at Edinburgh University, Rennie set up a civil engineering business in London, England, in 1791 and is known for his three bridges over the Thames River—Waterloo, New London, and Southwark.

MARC BRUNEL 1769–1849
The son of a prosperous French farmer, Brunel served in the French navy for six years. To escape the French Revolution he fled to the U.S. in 1793. There he became the chief engineer of New York City. Brunel settled in England at the turn of the century and solved many of the problems of tunneling underwater. He designed a tunnel under the Thames River (1843) used by one million pedestrians in its first four months.

FERDINAND DE LESSEPS 1805–1894
French engineer Ferdinand de Lesseps first studied law before becoming a diplomat. After a period as French ambassador to Spain De Lesseps served in Egypt, where he oversaw the building of the Suez Canal (1860–1869). In 1880 he started his next great project—the Panama Canal. Work was abandoned in 1888. The canal was completed by American engineers in 1914.

Benjamin Baker

1840–1907

Born in Somerset, England, Baker worked at an iron foundry in South Wales before becoming the assistant to an English civil engineer, John Fowler (1817–1898), in 1861. In 1875 Baker became Fowler's business partner following their success in building London's first subway system. Baker also designed the 1,700-ft. (518-m) -long Forth Railroad Bridge—at that time the longest in the world. He also worked on a number of projects in Egypt, the most notable being the Aswan Dam.

Notable structures: Forth Railroad Bridge 1890; Aswan Dam 1902

George Goethals

1858–1928

Born to Belgian immigrants in the U.S., George Goethals was an outstanding student who won a place at West Point. He began a rapid rise through the ranks, and in 1907 he was appointed as the chief engineer of the Panama Canal by President Theodore Roosevelt (1858–1919). A shy but determined man, Goethals had to overcome huge obstacles in engineering and availability of workers in order to complete the canal by 1914. He was made governor of the Panama Canal Zone from 1914 to 1916. After the end of World War I he became a civil engineering consultant in New York City.

Notable achievement: built Panama Canal 1907–1914

▲ The *SS Ancon* became the first ship to use the Panama Canal when it opened in 1914.

Electricity

Alessandro Volta

1745–1827

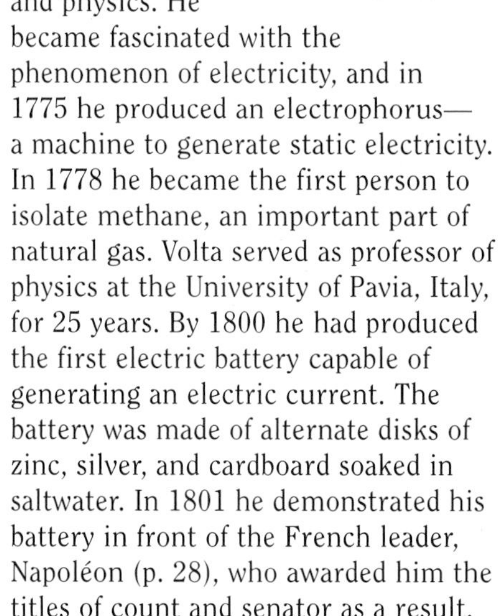

Volta was an Italian nobleman who resisted his family's insistence that he become a priest and instead studied chemistry and physics. He became fascinated with the phenomenon of electricity, and in 1775 he produced an electrophorus—a machine to generate static electricity. In 1778 he became the first person to isolate methane, an important part of natural gas. Volta served as professor of physics at the University of Pavia, Italy, for 25 years. By 1800 he had produced the first electric battery capable of generating an electric current. The battery was made of alternate disks of zinc, silver, and cardboard soaked in saltwater. In 1801 he demonstrated his battery in front of the French leader, Napoléon (p. 28), who awarded him the titles of count and senator as a result.

Notable inventions: electrophorus 1778; electric battery 1800

Samuel Morse

1791–1872

Born in Massachusetts, Morse was first an artist and then an inventor. He studied art in Europe and became a well-known portrait painter. In 1832 he started working on an electric telegraph. Using electromagnets that could be turned on and off, Morse developed a practical telegraph system that could send messages as electrical signals along wires. Morse's system caught on, leading to a communication boom in the U.S. and making him a wealthy man. Morse also served as the first president of the National Academy of Design but failed in his attempts to become a congressman or the mayor of New York City.

Notable inventions: electric telegraph 1835; Morse code 1838; first city-to-city telegraph line 1844

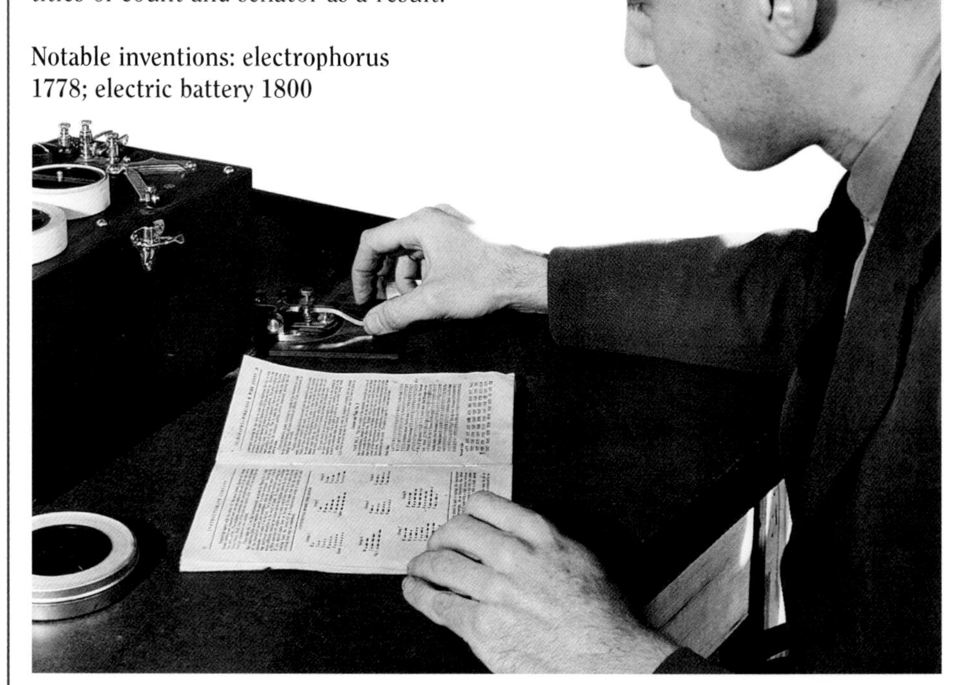

▲ Before the telephone the Morse code was the main form of world communication.

Alexander Graham Bell

1847–1922

Born in Scotland, electrical engineer Alexander Graham Bell, like his father, became an educator of deaf people.

Bell emigrated to Canada in 1870 and then moved to the U.S., where he worked at Boston University. He was fascinated by the possibilities of transmitting speech over telegraph, and in 1876 he uttered the first spoken sentence on his prototype telephone. Soon a wealthy man, Bell founded the National Geographic Society and the journal *Science*. He also invented the photophone, which transmits speech by light rays.

Notable inventions: telephone 1875; photophone 1880

► Alexander Graham Bell using one of his early telephones.

Thomas Edison

1847–1931

Edison was only 10 years old when he built his first laboratory in the basement of his home in Milan, Ohio. A self-taught engineer, he made his fortune from improving telegraph systems and from a ticker-tape machine that sent stock market prices around the U.S. Opening a research center in 1876, Edison went on to invent the first practical electric lamp, the sound recording and playing phonograph, and improved Bell's telephone by inventing a carbon microphone. He patented over 1,000 inventions during his lifetime.

Notable inventions: ticker-tape machine 1876; electric lamp 1879; phonograph 1887; first commercial power plant 1882

◄ Edison's first recording on his phonograph was of himself reciting "Mary Had a Little Lamb."

CHARLES WHEATSTONE 1802–1875
Englishman Charles Wheatstone took over his uncle's musical instrument store in London, England, at the age of 21, having already invented the flute harmonique—a type of wind instrument with keys—when he was only 16. In 1837 he invented an early kind of electrical telegraph, and in 1843 the Wheatstone bridge, a device used to measure electrical resistance.

ERNST VON SIEMENS 1816–1892
At the age of 17 Ernst von Siemens joined the Prussian artillery so that he could gain engineering training. During this time he spent a short spell in prison for his part in a duel among officers. During the 1840s Siemens improved Wheatstone's (above) electric telegraph and went on to lay telegraph cables both above and under the ground throughout Germany. In 1880 in Berlin, Germany, he built the first electrically operated railroad in Germany.

JOSEPH SWAN 1828–1914
Born in England, Joseph Swan started his working life as an assistant to a pharmacist. In 1860, two decades before Edison (left), he invented the first electric lightbulb, but his version proved to be impractical. While working on how to make carbon filaments for lights, Swan discovered how to make artificial fibers. In 1885 he exhibited the first clothes to be made completely from artificial fibers.

JOHN FLEMING 1849–1945
English physicist and electrical engineer John Fleming worked as a schoolteacher, professor, and a consultant for the companies formed by both Edison (left) and Marconi (p. 88). In 1885 Fleming became the first professor of electrical engineering at University College in London, England, a position he held for over 40 years. In 1904 Fleming invented the thermionic electron tube or "valve"—an electrical component vital for converting radio waves into sound waves.

Sebastian de Ferranti

1864–1930

At the age of 13 Sebastian de Ferranti invented an arc light for street lighting. Four years later he joined the London division of the German company, Siemens Brothers. Forming his first company in 1882, Ferranti went on to predict the use of a national grid system for electricity generation and supply and found ways of making it easier and safer to use. Between 1888 and 1891 he worked on the generator for Deptford Power Station in London, England, the world's most powerful at that time.

Notable invention: laid foundations for a national electricity grid 1887

Lee De Forest

1873–1961

After designing a number of early radio and telegraph transmitters, U.S. engineer Lee De Forest worked on improving the valve invented by John Fleming (p. 87). By 1906 he had added a grid to control and amplify signals from the valve and called it an Audion. Better known as a triode valve, his invention became a key component in almost all radio, radar, television, and computer systems until the transistor arrived in the 1950s. De Forest pioneered public radio broadcasts, and in later years he moved to Hollywood, where he invented the Phonofilm process, which added a sound track to moving pictures.

Notable invention: triode valve 1906

John Logie Baird

1888–1946

Because of poor health Scotsman John Logie Baird had to retire from his job as an electrical engineer at the age of 34. During his "retirement" Baird began working on what, in 1926, would become the very first television system. His first flickering television pictures were black and white and made up of only 50 lines—a modern television has at least 500. In 1936 the British Broadcasting Corporation (BBC) used Baird's system for the world's first-ever public television broadcast service.

Notable inventions: first working television 1926; first TV broadcasts 1929

Guglielmo Marconi

1874–1937

Born to a wealthy Italian family, Guglielmo Marconi was fascinated by electricity as a young man. He built a laboratory on his father's country estate near Bologna, Italy, and began experimenting.

In 1895 he succeeded in sending wireless signals over a distance of 1.5 mi. (2.5km), the first time such a feat had been achieved. In 1899 Marconi established wireless communication between France and England across the English Channel. In 1901 he transmitted Morse code signals across the Atlantic Ocean between Cornwall, England, and Newfoundland, Canada. This not only proved that radio waves were unaffected by earth's curvature but also acted as a starting point for global radio communication. Awarded the Nobel Prize for Physics in 1909, Marconi served as an officer in both the Italian army and navy during World War I. He experimented with radar and microwaves in the 1920s–1930s, showing that they could travel great distances.

Notable achievements: first radio signal across the English Channel 1898; first radio signal across Atlantic Ocean 1901

► Guglielmo Marconi at work on his early radio transmitter.

Vladimir Zworykin

1889–1982

Born in Russia, Zworykin began his career in electrical engineering at the age of nine, repairing equipment on his father's riverboats. He emigrated to the U.S. in 1919. There he invented the iconoscope, or television transmission tube, which forms the basis of modern TV cameras. He also invented an early version of the TV picture tube called the kinescope.

Notable inventions: electronic TV camera 1923; electronic picture tube 1924

Walter Brattain

1902–1987

Walter Brattain's American parents were in China teaching math and science when he was born. Brattain joined Bell Laboratories in 1929, and apart from a spell during World War II working on new ways of detecting submarines, he stayed there all of his working life. In 1947, with Bardeen and Shockley (right), Brattain invented the transistor, a device that was more reliable, much faster, and much smaller than the valves used in electronics at the time.

Notable invention: transistor 1947

▶ A soldier uses the modern, mobile version of Robert Watson-Watt's radar.

Robert Watson-Watt

1892–1973

A direct descendent of James Watt (p. 90), Scottish-born Robert Watson-Watt worked as a meteorologist during World War I using radio waves to locate thunderstorms and warn pilots. In the 1930s he developed this system to produce a system of radio detection and ranging—known as radar—capable of providing Allied forces with early warning of German attacks from the air.

Notable invention: radar 1935

Clive Sinclair

b. 1940

English inventor Clive Sinclair left school at the age of 17 and became an editor of electronics publications. In 1958 he set up a company to make electronic goods. He found ways of combining low-cost components into smaller and cheaper devices that he sold by mail order. His successes included the first pocket calculators, miniature TVs, and home computers.

Notable inventions: pocket calculator 1972; ZX home computers 1979–1988; C5 electric tricycle 1985

JOHN BARDEEN 1908–1991
U.S. electrical engineer John Bardeen was a member of the Bell Laboratories team that invented the transistor in 1947. In the late 1960s he worked as part of a team that developed the theory of superconductivity—how materials at very low temperatures can conduct electricity without any energy loss. Bardeen became the first American to win the Nobel Prize twice in the same category—for physics in 1956 and again in 1972.

WILLIAM SHOCKLEY 1910–1989
William Shockley was born in England to American parents, both of whom worked in the mining industry. Returning to the U.S. in 1913, Shockley studied at the Massachusetts Institute of Technology before joining Bell Laboratories in 1936. He was the head of the team that produced the first transistor in 1947. Shockley foresaw the huge impact the transistor would have and set up his own transistor-making company in the late 1950s.

JAY FORRESTER b. 1918
Born in Nebraska, Forrester was still in high school when he built a wind-driven electrical generator for his parents' cattle ranch. During World War II he was part of a team developing a flight simulator to train pilots. This grew into the Whirlwind project of the 1940s and 1950s—the largest digital computer project of its time. While working on this project Forrester invented the forerunner of Random Access Memory (RAM)—the memory now found on small chips in all personal computers.

DOUGLAS ENGLEBART b. 1925
U.S. electrical engineer Douglas Englebart joined Stanford Research Institute in the 1950s. There he researched ways of making computers more efficient and friendly to use. In the 1960s he produced a computer system that used pictures, icons, and different-sized windows on the screen—all controlled by a pointing device—the world's first computer mouse.

Machines

Thomas Newcomen

1663–1729

Born in England, Thomas Newcomen was as a metalworker in southwest England. There he learned how expensive and time-consuming it was to pump water out of mines to keep them from flooding. For 10 years he experimented with steam-driven pumps before finally building a working version in the English Midlands. Newcomen's engines were exported first to Europe and in 1755 to the U.S. for use in mines and to lift water to power waterwheels.

Notable achievement: developed first practical steam-pumping engine 1712

Joseph Marie Jacquard

1752–1834

The son of French silk weavers, Jacquard inherited a hand loom when his father died in 1772. He started improving its design, but his work was cut short in 1790 by the French Revolution. In 1801 Jacquard publicly demonstrated his automatic loom in Paris, France. It used cards with holes punched into them to instruct the loom to weave different patterns and fabrics. Jacquard's machine impressed the authorities, and in 1806 the loom was declared public property. This meant that Jacquard received a payment for each machine built. His loom proved popular, and over 10,000 were in use by 1812.

Notable invention: automatic loom 1801

Samuel Crompton

1753–1827

The son of a farmer from Lancashire, England, Samuel Crompton combined James Hargreaves' (p. 91) and Richard Arkwright's (p. 91) spinning machines to create the spinning mule in 1779. This machine produced better-quality yarn at high speeds and was a huge success. However, Crompton was too poor to patent his invention and sold the rights to his device cheaply. In 1812, with the spinning mule being used throughout the textile industry, British Prime Minister Robert Peel (1788–1850) arranged for the British government to grant Crompton an award of £5,000 (about $8,000) for his invention.

Notable invention: spinning mule 1779

James Watt

1736–1819

The son of a Scottish carpenter, Watt was a bright but frail child prone to sickness. As a teenager he became skilled at making scientific instruments and found work at Glasgow University.

In 1863 Watt was asked to repair a working model of a Newcomen (above) steam pump. He repaired it, and within two years he made great improvements to steam engines—cutting fuel costs by 75 percent. Between 1766 and 1774 Watt worked as a surveyor and civil engineer before going into partnership with Matthew Boulton (p. 91). Watt continued making improvements to his steam engines and invented a more efficient model, called the double-acting steam engine, in 1782. He also created a flyball governor, which automatically regulated the speed of a steam engine and was one of the first industrial-automated controls.

Notable inventions: condensing steam engine 1765; double-acting steam engine 1782; flyball governor 1788

▼ James Watt, the Scottish engineer, with his first wife, Margaret, and son, James.

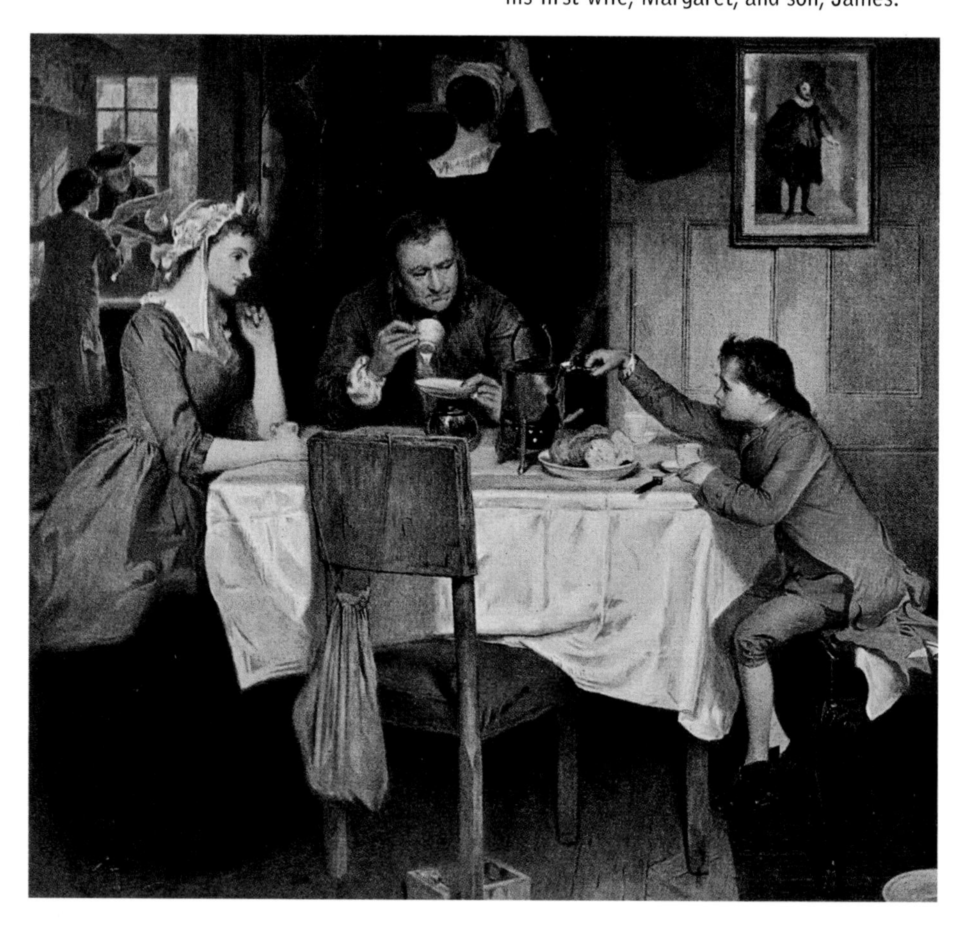

Eli Whitney

1765–1825

In 1793 U.S. inventor Eli Whitney developed the cotton gin—a machine capable of producing 50 lbs (23kg) of cotton a day. In 1798 he was hired to make muskets for the U.S. government and invented a standardized system of parts for the guns—the first use of mass production.

Notable inventions: cotton gin 1793; mass production process 1801

Joseph Henry

1797–1878

An American watchmaker's apprentice, Joseph Henry started experimenting with electromagnetism as a young man. By 1829 he had built electromagnets capable of lifting over 2,200 lbs (1,000kg). Around the same time he also developed the first practical electric motor and helped Samuel Morse (p. 86) develop his telegraph system. Henry used the telegraph to collect weather data across large areas of the U.S.

Notable invention: first practical electric motor 1829

▲ McCormick's reaper revolutionized farming, saving hours of manual labor.

Henry Maudslay

1771–1831

Englishman Henry Maudslay's first job was filling cartridges with gunpowder at an arsenal in London, England. He went on to work for a locksmith, Joseph Bramah (1748–1814). In 1797, when Bramah refused to give him a raise, Maudslay set up his own workshop. He invented a number of parts-making machines, including the metal-cutting lathe that allowed large pieces of metal to be turned and shaped with great accuracy for the first time.

Notable invention: lathe c. 1800

Cyrus McCormick

1809–1884

McCormick's father was a farmer who tried but failed to build a mechanical reaper to harvest grains. Cyrus took up his father's work, and by the end of 1831 he had built a successful version. It sold in large numbers, especially after McCormick moved to Chicago in 1847 to sell to farmers in the Great Plains.

Notable invention: reaping machine 1831

JAMES HARGREAVES
c. 1720–1778

Born in Lancashire, England, James Hargreaves never learned to read or write but was very interested in mechanics all his life. In the late 1750s he invented a device called the spinning jenny that sped up the production of spun cotton. Hargreaves' successful system bred fear and jealousy in Lancashire, and in 1768 a group of neighboring workers smashed 20 machines in his barn. Hargreaves moved to Nottingham, England, and started up again, but others had already developed—and improved—his device. He died in poverty in a poorhouse.

MATTHEW BOULTON
1728–1809

The son of an English metalsmith, Matthew Boulton bought a barren piece of land near Birmingham, England, and opened a factory in 1762 making small metal items such as buckles and buttons. Interested in using steam engines to power his machinery, Boulton entered into a partnership with James Watt (p. 90). Boulton's business sense coupled with Watt's ingenuity led to a huge and profitable steam-engine business, with Watt's power-generating machines being built in Boulton's factory. In 1786 Boulton applied steam power to machines, producing coins for the British government and the British East India Company.

RICHARD ARKWRIGHT
1732–1792

The youngest of 13 children born in Lancashire, England, to a poor family, Richard Arkwright was taught how to read and write by his cousin. He became a barber's apprentice and then started a wigmaking company before inventing the water-frame spinning machine. Highly ambitious, Arkwright started building factories to produce cotton using his machines. Two thirds of his workforce were children, some as young as six years old.

Elisha Otis

1811–1861

In 1854 Elisha Otis stood in an open-sided elevator in New York City with a large crowd below him and asked for the ropes holding the elevator to be cut. The elevator fell no more than a few centimeters because of Otis' invention—automatic safety brakes. The combination of showmanship and the invention itself effectively launched the elevator industry, as well as enabling much taller buildings to be built. Otis, the youngest of six children born to an American farmer, was familiar with factory elevators from his time working as a mechanic in bedframe factories. His company built thousands of elevators and was expanded by his sons after their father's death.

Notable invention: safety elevator 1853

▲ Otis demonstrates his new safety elevator in 1854.

Nikolaus Otto

1832–1891

At the age of 16 German engineer Nikolaus Otto dropped out of school and started working first in a grocery store and then as a traveling salesman. On his travels he learned about engines running on gases that were being built by Jean Lenoir (p. 93). Otto thought they would be more useful if they ran on liquid fuel, and from 1861 he began working on building an engine that ran on gasoline. He formed a company, N. A. Otto & Cie, with German industrialist Eugen Langen (1833–1895). The company was the first to manufacture internal-combustion engines. In 1876 Otto built a greatly improved internal-combustion engine known as the four-stroke engine. Over 30,000 were sold in the first ten years. The patent for Otto's engine was removed in 1886 when it transpired that Alphonse Beau de Rochas (1815–1893) had described and patented the principle in 1862.

Notable inventions: first practical gasoline-fueled engine 1876

Gottlieb Daimler

1834–1900

German-born Gottlieb Daimler trained first as a gunsmith before working as an engineer in Great Britain, France, and Belgium. Throughout the 1870s, he worked with Nikolaus Otto (left), helping to improve Otto's internal combustion engine. Daimler was a perfectionist and not easy to get along with and after a dispute with Otto left and formed his own company in 1882 with Wilhelm Maybach (1846–1929). The pair made lightweight, high-speed engines suitable for transportation and in 1885 created the first motorbike. Four years later Daimler produced a four-wheeled car powered by their engine. The Daimler engine became known for its reliability. In the 1894 Paris to Rouen road race in France, 102 cars started but only 15 finished. All 15 were powered by Daimler engines.

Notable inventions: spark plug 1883; high-speed, internal-combustion engine 1885; first four-wheeled car 1889

Rudolf Diesel

1858–1913

The inventor of the engine that is used in submarines, ships, trains, and electricity-generating plants was born in Paris, France, to German parents. As a boy Diesel spent many hours studying and drawing the machines in the Paris Museum of Arts and Crafts. He went on to study at Munich Polytechnic in Germany and became a refrigerator engineer. Diesel spent over ten years working on different types of power systems, including a solar-powered engine, before publishing a paper on his diesel engine in 1893. His engine squeezed air inside a cylinder, making it extremely hot before fuel was added. The first working versions of the diesel engine ran in 1897 and used less fuel than regular gasoline engines. Within two years Diesel became a millionaire. He died in mysterious circumstances, vanishing during an overnight crossing of the English Channel on the mail steamship *Dresden*.

Notable invention: diesel engine 1893

▲ Rudolf Diesel (right) works with one of his engineers on his prototype engine.

Robert Goddard

1882–1945

The only child in his family to reach adulthood, Goddard survived serious tuberculosis to become a physicist and one of the founders of rocket engineering. In 1926 Goddard watched his invention blast off and land just 185 ft. (56m) away in a cabbage patch. This short journey was nevertheless a major event in rocketry, as it was the first undertaken by a liquid-fueled rocket. Four years later Goddard launched a rocket that reached a speed of over 500 mph (800km/h) and rose to an altitude of 2,300 ft. (700m). Goddard was the first person to put instruments, such as cameras and barometers, into rockets. His experiments led him to develop many of the devices used in modern space rockets, such as high-pressure fuel pumps, stabilizers, and steering systems.

▼ Robert Goddard with his first liquid-fueled rocket in 1926.

Notable invention: first liquid-fueled rocket 1926

Frank Whittle

1907–1996

The son of an English engineer, Frank Whittle joined the British Royal Air Force as an apprentice aircraft builder in 1923. After studying at Cranwell and Cambridge universities he was selected for pilot training and was posted to a fighter squadron in 1928 before becoming a test pilot in 1931. Whittle had suggested the idea of a jet engine to power aircraft in the late 1920s, but he had been ignored by the British authorities. He continued working on the idea and left the air force in 1936. The following year Whittle successfully tested the world's first working jet engine, and in May 1941 one of his engines powered the first British jet aircraft, the Gloster E28/39.

▼ Frank Whittle explains the features of the jet engine using a model of his turbo-jet engine.

Notable invention: first successful jet engine 1937

JEAN LENOIR 1822–1900
Jean Lenoir was born in Luxembourg to Belgian parents and moved to France at the age of 16. He was a self-taught engineer, and in 1855 he invented an electric brake for trains. Lenoir's interest in power technology saw him produce the first practical internal-combustion engine, which he patented in 1860. Lenoir's engine was reliable and sold in its hundreds, but it was overtaken by other, more efficient designs. In 1883 he produced a four-stroke engine similar to Nikolaus Otto's (p. 92) model. It was not a success, and Lenoir died a poor man.

CHARLES PARSONS 1854–1931
The youngest son of a British earl, Parsons studied at Cambridge University before becoming an apprentice engineer. In 1884 he invented the first working steam turbine engine. To publicize his invention, in 1894 Parsons built the *Turbinia*, a 100-ft. (30-m) -long boat powered by turbine engines. Paraded in front of Queen Victoria (p. 18) in 1897, *Turbinia* could reach 40 mph (64km/h), making it the fastest boat in the world. Within two years the first of many British Royal Navy warships to be powered by Parsons' engines was built.

FELIX WANKEL 1902–1988
Born in Germany, Felix Wankel worked for a publisher of scientific books while tinkering with machines in his spare time. He had the idea of a different kind of internal-combustion engine as early as 1924, but it was more than 30 years before he could realize his dream. In between he was imprisoned by the Nazis in the 1930s and then worked on valves for the German military aircraft industry, only to have his workshop destroyed by the French army and be imprisoned again. In 1957 he finally developed the first practical Wankel engine—a design that used fewer moving parts and was smaller than a regular engine.

J.C. BAMFORD 1916–2001
Joseph Bamford was a British engineer who started up his own engineering company from a rented garage, and in 1954 he invented the first of the digging and construction vehicles that bear his initials, JCB. By the time of his death, JCB was Great Britain's largest privately owned engineering firm, building 30,000 machines every year.

By Land

Nicolas Cugnot

1725–1804

French engineer Nicolas Cugnot served in the Austro–Hungarian army before returning to Paris in 1763. He built a steam engine and in 1769 used it to power the first steam-driven road vehicle. Cugnot's tractor, designed to tow guns, was a heavy machine with a top speed of 3.5 mph (6km/h). His second machine, built in 1771, had the first recorded motor accident when it ran into a wall.

Notable invention: first steam-propelled vehicle 1769

John Dunlop

1840–1921

Scottish inventor John Dunlop qualified as a vet at the age of 19. In his late 20s he moved to Ireland, where he started experimenting with air-filled tubes to make riding bicycles more comfortable. In 1888 he patented his pneumatic bicycle tire and formed a company with W. H. Du Cros (1846–1918) to manufacture tires for bicycles and, from 1906, for the new car industry.

Notable inventions: air-filled bicycle tire 1888; car tire 1906

Karl Benz

1844–1929

Born in Karlsruhe, Germany, Karl Benz started his first company in 1871, supplying building materials. The following year he married Bertha Ringer, who kept Benz motivated through years of experimentation. In 1885 he unveiled the world's first car—a three-wheeled vehicle powered by his own internal-combustion engine. On sale from 1888, the car did not attract orders until his wife drove herself and two of their five children on a trip of 60 mi. (100km), drawing a lot of public attention.

Notable invention: first vehicle powered by an internal-combustion engine 1885

George Stephenson

1781–1848

First working as a cowherd, English engineer George Stephenson started taking evening classes at the age of 18 to learn how to read and write.

In 1812 he became an engine operator at a mining colliery in the northeast of England, where he learned all he could about the Newcomen (p. 90) steam engines that were used there. Stephenson convinced his employers to let him build a locomotive, and in 1814 he created the *Blucher*, which could pull 30 tons up a hill at 3.5 mph (6km/h). Over the next six years he built 16 steam locomotives and an 8-mi. (13-km) -long railroad track carrying goods to Sunderland, England. In 1825 he built the world's first public railroad. In 1829, with his son Robert, he designed the prize-winning *Rocket* for the new Liverpool & Manchester Railway.

Notable achievements: built the *Blucher* 1814; built world's first public railroad 1825; built the *Rocket* 1829

◀ The *Rocket* was designed and built in 1829 by George Stephenson and his son, Robert (1803–1859). It reached a speed of 30 mph (47km/h) and paved the way for rail travel.

▼ Henry Ford poses in one of his early Model Ts.

Henry Ford

1863–1947

Born to Irish emigrants in the U.S., Henry Ford showed an aptitude for working with machines as a child. Growing up on his parents' farm in Michigan, he repaired watches, built a small waterwheel, and tinkered with the farm machinery. He moved to Detroit at the age of 16 to become a machinist and engineer, and by 1893 he was chief engineer of the Edison Illuminating Company. Encouraged by the company's owner, Thomas Edison (p. 87), Ford developed his first car, the Quadricycle Runabout, in 1896. In 1903 he started the Ford Motor Company. Ford was the founder of the modern assembly line, where a car travels along a conveyor belt as workers attach its parts. This enabled cars to be built quickly and at lower costs. In 1908 Ford started to build and sell the Model T. Available only in black, the Model T was a basic but reliable car. At $825 it was the first affordable motor vehicle and made cars available to the general public for the first time. Over 15 million Model Ts were produced in the U.S. between 1908 and 1927, making Henry Ford a multimillionaire.

Notable invention: Model T 1908

Ferdinand Porsche

1875–1951

German car engineer and designer Ferdinand Porsche produced his first vehicle, an electric carriage, in 1900. After working for a number of aircraft and car manufacturers he started his own firm in 1931, and with his son, Ferry Porsche (1909–1998), he designed Hitler's (p. 22) "people's car"—the rear-engined, air-cooled Volkswagen Beetle.

▲ Nazi officials inspect an early VW Beetle.

Since 1934 over 22 million Beetles have been built worldwide. Designing German military vehicles during World War II, Porsche was imprisoned as a war criminal but was freed in 1947.

Notable design: Volkswagen Beetle 1934

GEORGE PULLMAN 1831–1897
Training to be a cabinetmaker, George Pullman became a store owner in Chicago, Illinois, before starting the Pullman Palace Car Company in 1867. He designed the first sleeping car for railroad passengers in 1865 and in 1868 the first dining car. His invention proved to be very popular, his company grew, and in 1880 he built the town of Pullman near 111th Street in Chicago for his employees. He was, however, a tough and disliked employer who cut wages and fired striking workers in the 1890s.

GEORGE WESTINGHOUSE 1846–1914
After serving in the Union Army during the Civil War (1861–1865) George Westinghouse joined his father's machinemaking business. He began a prolific career as an engineer, credited with over 300 inventions. The majority of his work was in improving railroad technology. He invented better signaling and in 1868 a powerful air brake that greatly increased railroad safety. In the 1880s his work in electricity generation would prove vital in establishing alternating current (AC) power systems across the world.

HENRY ROYCE 1863–1933
CHARLES ROLLS 1877–1910
In 1884 English engineer Henry Royce started his own business building dynamos, cranes, and motors. In 1904 he built three experimental cars. Their high quality came to the attention of the son of a British lord, Charles Rolls, who was selling imported French cars. Rolls' love of speed led him to become a bicycle racer and then a pioneer car racer. The two men's companies merged in 1906 to form the world-famous luxury car manufacturers, Rolls Royce. Charles Rolls became the first aviator to fly across the English Channel and back nonstop in 1910. Later the same year he died in a flying accident.

NILS BOHLIN b. 1920
As an engineer for the aircraft manufacturers SAAB, Swedish-born Nils Bohlin worked on ejector-seat designs before joining the car manufacturers Volvo. In 1959 he invented the modern, three-point, car seatbelt, considered to be one of the most important safety improvements in vehicle design.

Alec Issigonis

1906–1988

Born in Smyrna, Turkey, Alec Issigonis was taken to England by his mother in 1922 to study. He struggled in some courses, failing math three times, but he eventually became a project engineer at the Morris car company. In 1948 Issigonis designed the Morris Minor, and over a 23-year period more than 1.5 million were produced. In 1959 his radical, small, front-wheel-drive car, the Mini, was launched. By 2000 over five million had been sold.

Notable designs: Morris Minor 1948; BMC Mini 1959

THE MINI

Mike Burrows

b. 1952

British engineer Mike Burrows started developing radical new designs for bicycles in the 1980s. His most-famous design featured a frame built in one piece and made from resin and carbon fibers instead of traditional metal tubing. Lightweight and more aerodynamic than regular racing bicycles, Burrows' design was ignored by manufacturers until the car company Lotus became involved in the early 1990s. In 1992 English bicyclist Chris Boardman (b. 1968, above) won the Olympic 4,000m gold medal and broke the world 3-mi. (5-km) pursuit record riding Burrows' Lotus Superbike.

Notable invention: Lotus Superbike 1992

By Sea

Cornelis Drebbel

c. 1572–1633

A Dutch farmer's son, Cornelis Drebbel trained to be an engraver but worked as an alchemist and engineer. He discovered how to make oxygen from saltpeter and built a clock that used changes in atmospheric pressure to rewind itself. Drebbel built the first people-carrying submarine in the 1620s. His craft, a rowboat encased in leather with tubes carrying air from the surface, made a number of test journeys under the Thames River in London, England.

Notable invention: first working submarine 1620s

John Hadley

1682–1744

Born in England, John Hadley was a mathematician and inventor who in 1716 was elected a fellow of the Royal Society—Britain's independent national academy of science. In 1731 Hadley invented a device called an octant. This could accurately measure the altitude of the sun or a star above the horizon and helped sailors navigate at sea. Hadley's octant was the forerunner to the sextant, which is still used in navigation today. From 1721Hadley also worked in optics, building the most powerful reflecting telescopes of his day. For his achievements in astronomy a long valley on the moon's surface—Hadley Rille—is named after him.

Notable invention: the octant, used to find a ship's position at sea 1731

William Symington

1763–1831

Born in Scotland, Symington trained as a minister but instead became a mechanic in a lead mine. In 1784 he thought of applying steam power to propel carriages into the mines and built a working scale model. From 1787 to 1789 he built small steam-powered boats, but it was not until 1801—when he developed a more efficient engine and paddling system—that they became practical. Symington placed his engine in the canal tugboat *Charlotte Dundas*. It could tow 70-ton barges and was named after the daughter of Lord Dundas (1741–1820), who financed the work.

Notable invention: first successful steam-powered boat 1802

Robert Fulton

1765–1815

U.S. engineer Robert Fulton first earned his living in Philadelphia producing technical drawings of machinery and working as a landscape painter. Fulton traveled to England in 1786 and moved to Paris, France, in 1797, where he earned a living as an artist and pursued his interest in machinery. He engineered canals and designed a marble-cutting machine, a flax loom, and a mechanical dredger. In 1806 he returned to the U.S., where he became known for his work in France. In the following year his first steamboat, the *Clermont*, was launched. Its maiden voyage from New York City to Albany, New York, was completed in one third of the time it took to sail ships. In 1812 Fulton designed the first steam-powered warship, the *Demologos*, which contained 44 guns and was almost 330 ft. (100m) long.

Notable achievements: built first successful commercial steamboat 1807; designed first steam warship 1812

John Holland

1840–1914

John Holland was a schoolteacher in Ireland who became interested in submarines while reading about the American Civil War. Holland joined his parents and younger brother in the U.S. in 1874, and three years later he had built his first test submarine in a New York ironworks. He gave up teaching and became a draftsman, building another four experimental submarines before the *Holland VI* was launched in 1897. This cigar-shaped submarine was 52 ft. (16m) long, carried a crew of seven, and was armed with guns and torpedoes. After more than two years of sea trials the submarine was bought by the U.S. Navy, who named her *USS Holland* and kept her in service for ten years. Its inventor, who got married in 1887 and had seven children, died of pneumonia in 1914, just before the first major submarine attack of World War I.

Notable invention: first modern submarine 1897

▲ John Holland demonstrates his submarine, the *Holland VI*. All modern, nonnuclear, submarines are based on his design.

► Fulton's ship, the *Clermont*, on its record-breaking journey up the Hudson River from New York City to Albany in 1807.

By Air

Montgolfier brothers

Joseph 1740–1810
Jacques 1745–1799

In 1783, in front of the French king Louis XVI (p. 17), a sheep, a duck, and a hen became the first-ever passengers in a hot-air balloon. The craft was built by the Montgolfier brothers, two of 16 children born into a French papermaking family. The first piloted flight in their hot-air balloon, a distance of 5.5 mi. (9km), took place above Paris later the same year.

Notable invention: first passenger-carrying, hot-air balloon 1783

▲ The Montgolfier brothers' first hot-air balloon flew empty on June 4, 1783.

Ferdinand von Zeppelin

1838–1917

Born in Germany, Zeppelin served in the Prussian army for 33 years. He also took an interest in airship design, and after retiring from military service he built his first airship in 1900. It featured a rigid steel skeleton containing large bags of hydrogen gas with a passenger cabin suspended beneath it. Zeppelin's airships were successful in peacetime as passenger carriers and for making air raids in World War I. In the late 1930s airship disasters ended passenger services.

Notable achievements: built first rigid airship 1900; introduced first commercial air service 1910

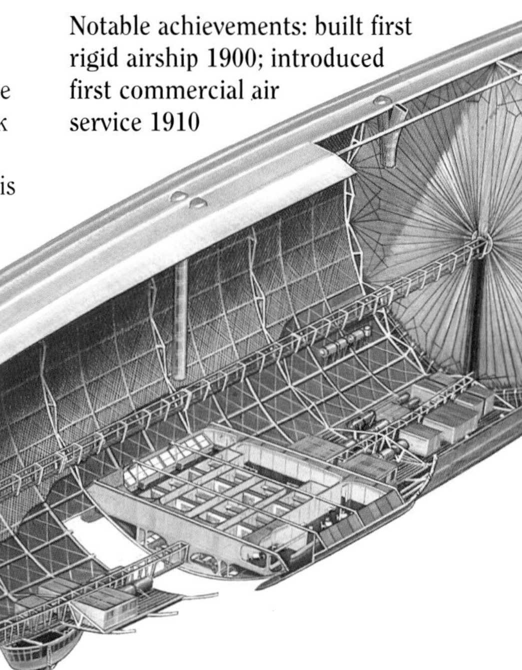

Otto Lilienthal

1849–1896

Born in Germany, Otto Lilienthal and his brother, Gustav (1849–1900), experimented as children with wings made of sewn-together bird feathers. Later they designed and built gliders, in which Otto made over 2,500 flights. In 1899 he published a book on aerodynamics that greatly influenced the Wright brothers (p. 99) and other early aviation pioneers. He died near Berlin after a flying accident in his glider.

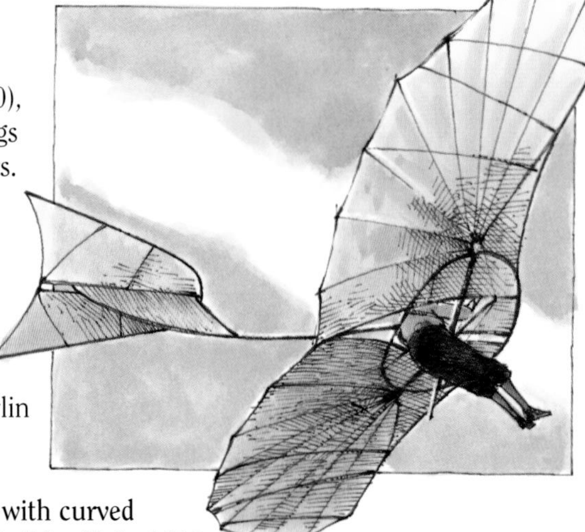

Notable achievements: built glider with curved wings 1877; first controlled piloted glider flight 1891

GEORGE CAYLEY 1773–1857
Born in England, George Cayley devoted much of his life to studying flight. He was the first to identify the forces of lift and drag, and he made scale models to measure these forces. In 1849 the ten-year-old son of one of his servants flew Cayley's first full-size glider. His coachman became the first adult glider pilot in 1853.

JOHN STRINGFELLOW 1799–1883
English inventor John Stringfellow worked in the lace industry before becoming a steam engineer. With William Henson (1805–1888) he started building a steam-powered aircraft. In 1848 Stringfellow's 10-ft. (3-m) wingspan craft, powered by a small steam engine, flew 30–33 ft. (9–10m)—the first-ever flight by a heavier-than-air machine.

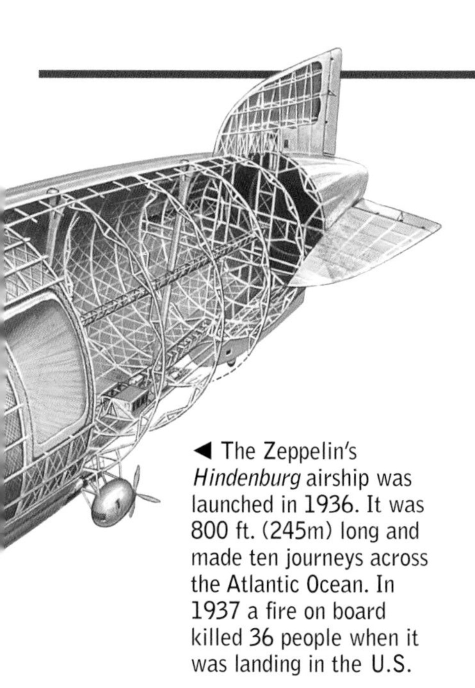

◀ The Zeppelin's *Hindenburg* airship was launched in 1936. It was 800 ft. (245m) long and made ten journeys across the Atlantic Ocean. In 1937 a fire on board killed 36 people when it was landing in the U.S.

Louis Blériot

1872–1936

Having become wealthy through his car headlight business, Frenchman Louis Blériot made his first aircraft flight in 1907 and designed a series of gliders and powered aircraft. On July 25, 1909, he flew his Model XI aircraft on a 40-minute flight across the English Channel and won a £1,000 ($1,500) prize for the feat. Orders for his aircraft designs flooded in, and Blériot went on to build 10,000 fighter planes during World War I.

Notable achievement: first flight across the English Channel 1909

▲ Blériot crossing the English Channel in 1909.

The Wright brothers

Wilbur Wright 1867–1912
Orville Wright 1871–1948

On December 17, 1903, in Kitty Hawk, North Carolina, a significant journey was made. It was only 130 ft. (40m) long and lasted just 12 seconds, but it was the first powered and piloted flight by a heavier-than-air vehicle.

The pilot was Orville Wright, the younger of two brothers who owned a newspaper and had opened a bicycle showroom and repair shop in 1892. Orville and Wilbur Wright were fascinated by the possibilities of powered flight and experimented from the 1890s on. In 1901 they built the first wind tunnel to test wing and glider designs and then made over 1,000 piloted glider flights before building their powered aircraft. Between 1908 and 1909 the Wright brothers toured Europe with their aircraft, inspiring others to build more practical flying machines.

Notable achievement: first powered and piloted heavier-than-air flight 1903

▼ The Wright brothers' *Flyer* takes off for the first time in 1903 with Orville behind the controls. His brother, Wilbur, looks on.

HENRI GIFFARD 1825–1882
In 1852 Frenchman Henri Giffard built the world's first powered and steerable airship. The 140-ft. (43-m) -long, hydrogen-filled craft was powered by a steam engine and flew 17 mi. (27km) at 5 mph (8km/h). Giffard went on to build giant, tethered balloons. Around 35,000 people took trips in his balloon at the 1878 World's Fair in Paris.

GLEN CURTISS 1878–1930
U.S. motorcycle enthusiast Glen Curtiss broke the motorcycle world speed record in 1905 before turning to aviation. He began building his own aircraft, and in 1908 he made the first 0.6 mi. (1km) flight in the U.S. In 1911 he built the first seaplane with floats instead of wheels, and in 1912 he invented flying boats—aircraft with boat-shaped hulls.

WILLIAM BOEING 1881–1956
U.S.-born William Boeing crashed his first plane on its maiden flight. Parts took a long time to be delivered, so he started designing his own aircraft. In 1917 the Boeing Airplane Company received its first military aircraft contract. It went on to build the first pressurized airliner, the *Stratoliner* (1938), and the largest airliner, the 747 (1970).

Andrei Tupolev

1888–1972

Aircraft designer Andrei Tupolev designed the first aircraft wind tunnel in his native Russia and was the first person to produce all-metal aircraft. In 1937 he was arrested, imprisoned, and forced to work on military aircraft designs until his release in 1943. In the 1950s he designed the TU104, the first Russian jet airliner. Tupolev was responsible for over 90 aircraft designs during his career. His son, Alexei (1926–2001), designed the TU144, the first supersonic airliner to fly.

Notable achievement: built first Russian jet airliner to enter regular service 1955

Igor Sikorsky

1889–1972

Russian aircraft designer Igor Sikorsky's first attempts at flying helicopters failed in 1910. Instead he built fixed-wing aircraft, including *Le Grande*—the world's first four-engined plane (1913). To escape the Russian Revolution, Sikorsky emigrated to the U.S. in 1919. There he worked as an aircraft designer and engineer before returning to helicopters. In 1941 his VS-300 helicopter flew for over an hour, and Sikorsky soon began building helicopters for the U.S. military.

Notable achievements: built first four-engined aircraft 1913; built first modern helicopter 1939–1941

▲ Igor Sikorsky flies one of his early helicopters.

Christopher Cockerell

1910–1999

Born in England, Christopher Cockerell was running a boat rental business in eastern England when he invented and developed the first air-cushioned vehicle —the hovercraft—in the 1950s. The first commercial passenger-carrying service using his invention started across the English Channel in 1959. Cockerell, who had worked as a radio engineer in the 1930s and 1940s, died on the 40th anniversary of his SRN1 hovercraft's first passenger-carrying trip.

Notable invention: hovercraft 1955

◀ The Sopwith Camel fighter aircraft of World War I.

Thomas Sopwith

1888–1989

English aviation designer Thomas Sopwith learned to fly at the age of 22 and then went on to win a major prize for the longest flight from Great Britain to the European mainland. His company, formed in 1912, built over 18,000 aircraft during World War I, including the Sopwith Camel and the Sopwith Pup—the first aircraft to fly from an aircraft carrier. Sopwith was also a yachtsman and competed for the Americas' Cup.

Notable design: Sopwith Camel 1917

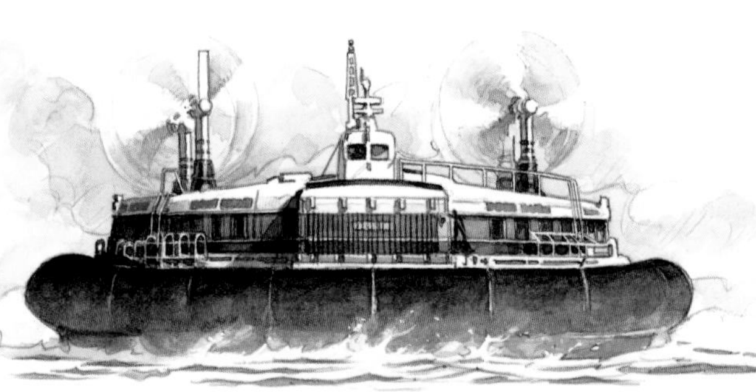

▶ The hovercraft was invented by Christopher Cockerell in 1959. He discovered that trapping a cushion of air beneath a boat lifted it up above the waves, allowing it to travel much faster.

BARNES WALLIS 1887–1979
Born in England, Barnes Wallis first designed airships. In the 1930s he invented a new, strong method of fuselage construction, first used in the Wellington bomber aircraft. During World War II, Wallis designed the bouncing bombs used to destroy the Möhne and Eder dams in Germany. After the war he developed the concept of swing-wing aircraft.

JUAN DE LA CIERVA 1895–1936
Born in Spain, Cierva designed gliders and powered aircraft between 1912 and 1919. In 1923 he invented the autogiro, a cross between a helicopter and a fixed-wing aircraft. It became popular in the 1920s and early 1930s. In 1925 Cierva opened a factory in England and licensed autogiro building in France, Germany, and the U.S.

INVENTORS

Johannes Gutenberg

1400–1468

Gutenberg is believed to have been born in Mainz in Germany. He worked as a goldsmith there until war forced him to move to Strasbourg in France, where he first experimented with printing. By 1450 he had returned to Mainz, formed a partnership with a German moneylender, and built the first printing press in Europe. Gutenberg revolutionized printing by using small pieces of cast-metal letters that could be reused to print different text. As a result books could be produced faster and cheaper, and they became more widely available.

Notable inventions: printing press c. 1450; movable metal letters c. 1450

▲ Developed in the 1440s, Gutenberg's printing press with movable letters made books available to people throughout Europe for the first time.

Hans Lippershey

c. 1570–c. 1619

Born in Wesel in Germany, Hans Lippershey settled in the Netherlands, where he made eyeglasses. He is traditionally credited with the invention of the telescope by using two glass lenses placed in a metal tube. Others may have also created versions around the same time, but Lippershey was the first to describe what he called a *kijker* (a "looker") in 1608. He offered his invention to the Dutch government for use in warfare and received a cash award as a result. However, the telescope was easy to make and was quickly reproduced in France and Italy.

Notable invention: first to describe a telescope 1608

Christiaan Huygens

1629–1695

Huygens was born in the Netherlands. The son of a diplomat, he made advances in geometry, mechanics, and astronomy. Huygens invented a new way of grinding telescope lenses and used a telescope he made to discover a moon orbiting the planet Saturn in 1655. The following year Huygens invented the pendulum clock, which offered the most accurate method of timekeeping available at the time. Watches had been invented early in the 1500s, but they were large and unreliable. In 1687 Huygens created a more accurate watch that he presented to Louis XIV of France (p. 16).

Notable invention: pendulum clock 1856

John Harrison

1693–1776

Born in Lincolnshire, England, John Harrison had little formal education and followed his father's trade, working as a carpenter. In 1713 he made his first clock—all of its parts were made out of wood. Harrison soon became known for the reliability and accuracy of his clocks. In 1763 he created the first accurate chronometer to measure how far east or west a ship lay. For this he won a £20,000 ($30,000) prize from the British government.

Notable invention: first accurate marine chronometer 1763

JOHN HARINGTON 1561–1612
Harington was an English nobleman and a godson of Elizabeth I (p. 15). He was considered an accomplished and risqué poet. In the 1590s he built the first flushing toilet, complete with a valve that would release water from a water closet when pulled. He is believed to have installed a version in Elizabeth's Richmond Palace.

ENVANGELISTA TORRICELLI 1608–1647
Italian-born Envangelista Torricelli studied in Rome, and in 1641 he was appointed secretary to the scientist and astronomer Galileo (p. 64). From 1642 he held the post of court mathematician to the Grand Duke of Tuscany. Torricelli is famous for inventing the first-known barometer in 1644.

Charles Babbage

1791–1871

Charles Babbage was the son of an English banker and was fascinated by numbers, statistics, and machinery. He invented the blinking lighthouse light, the dynamometer, and the first adhesive postage stamps, but he is best known for his work in mechanical calculating.

In the 1820s Babbage received funding from the British government to build a machine capable of calculating up to 20 decimal places. His principles were sound, as proved by a recreation of his machine in 1991 that worked perfectly—but the precision engineering required for the machine's parts was lacking, and his device remained incomplete. Undeterred, Babbage started working on a far more ambitious machine in the 1830s. Called the Analytical Engine, it was to feature input via punched cards and a separate processing mill and memory storage area. Babbage had anticipated the modern computer by over a century but was largely unheralded in his lifetime.

Notable inventions: Difference Engine 1820; Analytical Engine 1834

▼ Charles Babbage with his prototype Difference Engine No. 1.

William Talbot

1800–1877

In 1833 English mathematician and scientist William Talbot and his wife, Constance, were on their honeymoon at Lake Como in Italy. Talbot tried but failed to sketch the scenery there and dreamed of a machine using light-sensitive paper that could capture scenes. By 1841 Talbot had invented his calotype process that produced a negative image from the film in a camera. This negative image could be used to produce a limitless number of positive photographic prints.

Notable inventions: modern photographic method 1841; flash photography 1851

Samuel Colt

1814–1862

Guns played a major part in the history of America during the 1800s, and one man over all others revolutionized the types of weapons used. Born in Connecticut, Samuel Colt opened a factory in 1836 to produce his invention—the first handgun that could fire a number of shots without needing to be reloaded. When the U.S. Army started ordering his revolvers, Colt's business took off, making him the wealthiest businessman in America.

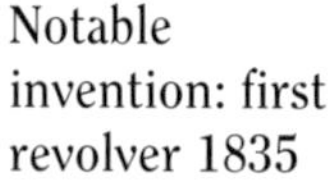

Notable invention: first revolver 1835

NICOLAS APPERT 1749–1841
French inventor Nicolas Appert first worked as a confectioner, chef, and baker. In 1795 the French government offered a prize for a way of preserving food for armies and navies. After ten years of experimenting Appert won the 12,000 francs prize in 1810. His method was to seal food in bottles and then submerge it in boiling water to kill off any bacteria.

JOSEPHINE COCHRANE 1839–1913
The wife of a U.S. politician, Josephine Cochrane was so upset with servants damaging her 17th-century crockery that she invented the dishwasher. Developed between 1886 and 1893, Cochrane's dishwashers sold to large canteens and restaurants, but it was not until the 1950s that dishwashers started selling to homes in large numbers.

ÉMILE BERLINER 1851–1929
German-born Émile Berliner emigrated to the U.S. in 1870, and eight years later he earned $50,000 for inventing a microphone to be used in early telephones. Berliner set up a research laboratory, and in 1888 he patented his gramophone sound recorder and player. Rather than cylinders, he used flat disks—the first modern records.

Elias Howe

1819–1867

Born in Massachusetts, inventor Elias Howe worked on his parents' farm before becoming an apprentice in a cotton factory at the age of 16. In 1837, while working in a watchmaker's shop, Howe conceived of the idea of a machine replacing the sewing of clothing by hand. It took him nine years before he patented his working machine, but at 250 stitches per minute it was far faster than sewing by hand. Struggling to find a financial backer in the U.S., Howe visited England with little success, and on his return he found others making sewing machines. After a long court battle Howe won a royalty on every sewing machine sold, earning $2 million by the time of his death.

Notable invention: sewing machine 1837–1846

Levi Strauss

c. 1829–1902

Levi Strauss was born in Bavaria in Germany. At the age of 16 he became an orphan and joined his five brothers and sisters in the U.S. In 1853 Strauss headed to San Francisco to sell clothing during the Gold Rush. Learning that miners needed hard-wearing trousers, Strauss started making clothes from tent canvas and then from a tough cotton material called *serge de Nîmes*, which became known as denim. In 1873 Levi patented his famous design of denim jeans with copper rivets to strengthen the pockets and seams.

Notable invention: denim jeans 1850s

Alfred Nobel

1833–1896

The son of a Swedish engineer, Alfred Nobel moved to Russia as a child, studying chemistry in France and the U.S. before returning to Sweden in 1859. There he set up a laboratory with his younger brother, Emil (1843–1864), where they worked on producing a safe and useful form of the explosive nitroglycerine. An explosion killed Emil Nobel, but Alfred persevered, and in 1867 he introduced dynamite. This sold quickly to the mining and construction industries as well as to the military. Nobel, who also invented a synthetic form of rubber and wrote plays and poems, left most of his wealth to establish the annual Nobel prizes awarded in Sweden.

Notable invention: dynamite 1867

Lumière brothers

Auguste 1862–1954
Louis 1865–1948

In 1895 people sitting in the Grand Café in Paris, France, watched in amazement as two French brothers projected the world's first moving picture, showing workers leaving their factory. The Lumière brothers were the sons of a painter who had become a photographer. The family had built up a business making 15 million photographic plates a year. The brothers' invention of a camera that took 16 pictures a second allowed movement to be captured on film and replayed for the first time ever.

Notable invention: motion picture camera and projector 1895

GEORGE EASTMAN 1854–1932
U.S. inventor George Eastman was working as a bank teller when he began experimenting with photography in 1877. He produced the first rolls of photographic film in 1885, and three years later he produced the first box camera under his new company name, Kodak. Eastman became so wealthy that he gave away millions of dollars to charities.

KING GILLETTE 1855–1932
Working as a salesman, U.S. inventor King Gillette learned that disposable items led to repeat sales. In 1895 he hit upon the idea of making the first disposable safety razor blades. Gillette found a way of making cheap, sharp, steel blades that would fit into a razor handle, and in 1903 his invention went on sale. Gillette became a millionaire.

FRANK HORNBY 1868–1936
Englishman Frank Hornby first developed bolt-together construction kits in 1901. Initially called Mechanics Made Easy, his kits became known as Meccano. In 1915 Hornby started producing model trains. At its peak in the 1930s, Hornby's factory in Liverpool, England, was producing over 70 tons of toys and one million nuts and bolts each week.

Clarence Birdseye

1886–1956

After studying to become a biologist American Clarence Birdseye set out for the Arctic to work as a field naturalist for the U.S. government. There he noted how by freezing freshly caught seafood it maintained its taste and texture when thawed and eaten weeks later. Setting up his first company in a New York City fishmarket in 1922, he developed a quick-freeze method and first produced packs of frozen foods for the public in 1929–1930. In the 1940s Birdseye developed frozen food compartments for stores and insulated railroad cars to distribute his products.

Notable invention: first commercial frozen foods 1929

George de Mestral

1907–1990

Swiss-born George de Mestral trained as an electrical engineer. In 1948, after returning from a hunting trip, he became fascinated by burrs—a type of plant seed—that were stuck to his pants. Under a microscope he saw that they were made up of hundreds of tiny hooks and wondered if this principle could be used to make a new kind of fastener. After years of trials De Mestral's Velcro® fastener, made of nylon, was introduced in 1955.

Notable invention: Velcro® nylon fastener 1955

Lazlo Biro

1900–1985

During World War II Hungarian journalist Lazlo Biro was forced to flee the invading Nazis twice—first leaving his home country for Paris, France, and then traveling from France to Argentina in 1940. His brother Georg, who was a chemist, accompanied him, and together they developed Lazlo's idea, patented two years earlier, of a ballpoint pen using smudge-free ink. The Biro pen was licensed by Great Britain's Royal Air Force during World War II because the pens worked well without leaking at high altitudes. They proved to be the inspiration for cheap, mass-produced ballpoint pens from the 1950s on.

Notable invention: ballpoint pen 1938

Akio Morita

1921–1999

Born in Nagoya, Japan, Akio Morita was expected to work in his family's brewing business that had operated for 13 generations. Instead he studied physics in Osaka and formed an electronics company in 1946. Changing its name to Sony in 1958, Morita's company pioneered many of today's electronic entertainment devices, building the first transistor radios in the 1950s and the first all-transistor televisions and color home video recorders in the 1960s. In 1979 Sony introduced the highly successful Walkman portable cassette player and in 1991 the 3.5 floppy disk.

Notable inventions: pocket transistor radio 1957; color video recorder 1966; Walkman portable cassette player 1979

Gunpei Yokoi

1941–1997

The son of the head of a Japanese pharmaceutical company, Gunpei Yokoi studied electronics in college. In 1970 he designed his first toy, an extendable gripping device called the Ultrahand, and ten years later he produced a popular series of portable computer games called Game and Watch. In 1989 Yokoi was the head of a team at the Japanese company Nintendo, which produced the Gameboy portable electronic game. By the time Yokoi left Nintendo in 1996 to pursue other inventions, over 60 million Gameboys had been sold worldwide. He died in a car accident.

Notable invention: first Gameboy machine 1989

▲ Akio Morita's Walkman allows people to listen to tapes anywhere they want.

OLE CHRISTIANSEN 1891–1958
Christiansen was a Danish carpenter who made stepladders, ironing boards, and wooden toys. The toys started outselling his other products, and in 1934 he formed a company called LEGO® from the Danish *Leg Godt* ("play well"). Their first plastic bricks were sold in Denmark in 1949, and in 1958 the modern LEGO® brick was introduced.

EDWIN LAND 1909–1991
In 1947 American inventor Edwin Land demonstrated a one-step photographic process that allowed pictures to develop in 60 seconds. His first Polaroid instant camera went on sale in 1949, and a color version was invented in 1963. In the 1950s Land designed high-altitude observation systems for spy planes and surveillance satellites.

NOLAN BUSHNELL b. 1943
U.S. computer programmer Nolan Bushnell produced his first computer arcade game in 1971. It failed, but its 1972 successor, called Pong, was a huge hit both in arcades and on the first home computer game consoles. In 1972 Bushnell founded the Atari company and created many famous games, including Pac-Man and Asteroids.

CHAPTER FIVE

WRITERS AND REFORMERS

Writers & Reformers before 1000

The first writing systems were developed around 5,000 years ago in Egypt and Sumer. The Egyptians and Sumerians left behind some interesting writings, including the first story, the Sumerian Epic of Gilgamesh. But we know little about the people who wrote these texts. The first writers that we know more about came from ancient Greece.

▲ The ancient Egyptians used hieroglyphs, a form of picture writing.

The most famous Greek poet was **Homer**, who probably lived in the 700s B.C. He is believed to have written two great epic poems: the *Iliad*, which tells the story of the Trojan War, and the *Odyssey*, which describes the adventures of the Greek hero Odysseus on his way home from Troy. Experts now believe that Homer put together the poems by combining stories that already existed and stories that had been handed down by word of mouth. Other ancient Greek poets include **Sappho** (c. 610–c. 580 B.C.), the first great female poet, and **Pindar** (c. 518–c. 438 B.C.), a famous writer of odes and songs.

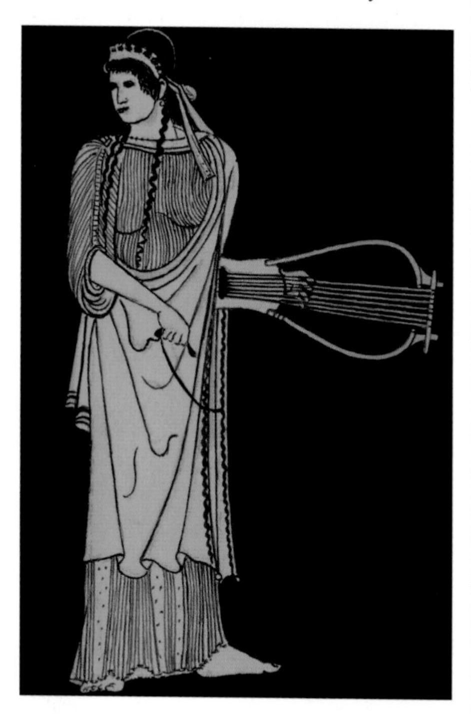

▲ Sappho, the first female poet, was born on the Greek island of Lesbos.

The Greeks loved the theater, and several of their dramatists wrote plays that are still performed today. **Aeschylus** (c. 525–c. 456 B.C.) and **Euripides** (c. 480–406 B.C.) are well known for their tragedies about characters from Greek mythology, while **Aristophanes** (c. 448–c. 385 B.C.) wrote comedies that still entertain modern audiences.

The first of the great Western philosophers also lived in ancient Greece. One of the first Greek philosophers to have a lasting influence was **Socrates** (469–399 B.C.). Socrates wrote no books, but he was known for his skills in discussions and debates. He was made even more famous by his follower, **Plato** (c. 428–c. 348 B.C.). Plato produced a series of books, or dialogues, written in the form of conversations between philosophers about important issues such as love, courage, and politics. The third great Greek philosopher was **Aristotle** (384–322 B.C.), who wrote books on a vast range of subjects, from poetry to politics and psychology to zoology.

ROMAN WRITERS

Following in the footsteps of the Greeks, the ancient Romans produced a number of notable writers. The poet **Virgil** (70–19 B.C.) wrote the *Aeneid*, an epic that tells the story of Aeneas, the legendary founder of Rome. **Ovid**

▲ Socrates was a powerful debater and one of the most outstanding Greek philosophers.

▲ Pliny the Elder died when he got too close to Mount Vesuvius as it was erupting.

(43 B.C.–A.D. 17) was another poet who used mythological material. His book *Metamorphoses* is a collection of mythological stories, all of which involve some kind of magical transformation. **Juvenal** (c. A.D. 55–c. 140) was a more down-to-earth writer. He produced a series of satirical poems attacking the manners and lifestyles of his fellow Romans.

The writer who tells us most about the Roman world is probably **Pliny the Elder** (A.D. 23–79). Pliny's most famous work was his *Natural History* in 37 volumes. This work covers everything—fact and fiction—that Pliny observed. In spite of its title it includes information about arts and inventions, as well as descriptions of the natural world.

THE DARK AGES

During the A.D. 400s the Roman Empire broke up. The following centuries became known in Europe as the Dark Ages because a lot of the skills and knowledge of the Romans were lost. But this is in many ways an incorrect name for the period because in fact a number of reformers were changing European culture. One of the most influential reformers was **St. Benedict** (c. A.D. 480–c. 547). Benedict was a monk who did a lot to change the way of life in European monasteries. He was concerned that discipline was too relaxed in many of the abbeys, so he founded a group of highly disciplined monasteries, including the famous abbey of Monte Cassino in Italy. He wrote down a new monastic rule that insisted that monks live a stricter, more regulated life than before. Soon abbeys throughout Europe were adopting the new rule. They became known as Benedictine monasteries after Benedict.

As a result of Benedict's work, monasteries became places of piety, hard work, and learning. Scholars such as **Bede** (c. A.D. 673–735), a monk from northern England, flourished in this atmosphere. Bede wrote many books about religious and historical subjects. His most well known is the *Ecclesiastical History of the English People* (731). Historians still read this book because it tells us more about the early history of England than any other work. Most European writers at this time were monks because monasteries provided the only available education. Some became famous in other areas too. For example **Alcuin** (c. A.D. 737–804) was a monk born in York, England. He became the abbot at the monastery in Tours, France, and he wrote widely on many subjects. He also met the great Frankish emperor, Charlemagne (A.D. 747–814), and became his adviser.

▲ Bede, portrayed on an illuminated manuscript made by a fellow monk.

EASTERN WRITERS

The greatest writer of early Indian literature, **Kalidasa**, probably lived in around A.D. 450, although some scholars believe he was alive in an earlier century. He wrote in the ancient language of Sanskrit and produced poems and plays.

A.D. 700 and 800 defined a golden age in Chinese writing. It was the time of the T'ang Dynasty, when a number of great poets such as the lyric writer **Du Fu** (also known as Tu Fu, A.D. 712–770) and **Li Shangyin** (c. A.D. 812–858), the first Chinese love poet, were active. **Li Bo** (also known as Li Po, A.D. 701–762) is believed by many to be the greatest of them all. He wrote beautiful short poems about subjects such as love and nature and was said to have died by drowning as he tried to grasp the moon's reflection in a lake.

At the very end of this period there was a flowering of literature in Japan. In c. 1000 **Sei Shonagon**, a lady at the royal court, wrote *The Pillow Book*, a series of short prose pieces that vividly bring the people and manners of the Japanese upper classes to life. Another lady at the court, **Murasaki Shikibu**, produced *The Tale of Genji* at around the same time. Telling the adventures of a Japanese prince, the tale is said by many to be the first novel ever written.

▲ Genji, the hero of *The Tale of Genji*, the first novel.

AUTHORS

Samuel Pepys

1633–1703

During his life the highly educated Englishman, Samuel Pepys, was the Secretary of the Admiralty (1672), imprisoned for alleged involvement in the Popish Plot (1679), and became president of the Royal Society (1684). However, he is best known for a diary he kept between 1660 and 1669. The diary gives valuable insights into contemporary England and includes details of the three great disasters of those times—the Plague, the Fire of London, and the Dutch fleet sailing up the Thames River. Written in shorthand, the diary was not deciphered until 1825.

Notable book: *Pepys' Diary* 1660–1669

Voltaire

1694–1778

Born François Marie Arouet, Voltaire was a successful French satirical writer and philosopher but was persecuted for his beliefs. In 1717 he was imprisoned in the Bastille in Paris for satirizing the Duc d'Orléans. In prison he assumed the name Voltaire and rewrote his tragedy *Oedipe*. In 1726 he insulted the Chevalier de Rohan-Chabot and was again put in the Bastille, but he was released on the condition that he left France. He spent four years in England, but on his return to Paris he offended the French government and had to leave Paris again. He moved to Switzerland, where he wrote his best-known work, *Candide*.

Notable books: *Letters Concerning the English Nation* 1734; *Zadig* 1748; *Candide* 1759

▲ Voltaire was imprisoned in the Bastille for criticizing the French monarchy and church.

Jonathan Swift

1667–1745

Born in Ireland, Jonathan Swift was ordained into the Anglican Church of Ireland in 1695. For 30 years he was the Dean of St. Patrick's Cathedral in Dublin. Swift was also a satirical writer and poet. He wrote for the *Bickerstaff Papers* and *Tatler* magazine and cofounded the Scriblerus Club. Swift's most famous book, *Gulliver's Travels*, is a savage satire of politicians, religion, inventors, and humanity.

Notable books: *On the Conduct of the Allies* 1713; *Gulliver's Travels* 1726; *A Modest Proposal* 1729

▶ Gulliver is tied down by the people of Lilliput in Swift's satire *Gulliver's Travels*.

J. W. von Goethe

1749–1832

German-born Johann Wolfgang von Goethe studied law in Leipzig, Germany, and is considered to be the greatest figure in German literature. He was a newspaper critic, playwright, novelist, poet, songwriter, and essayist on all branches of natural history and papers on subjects from law to religion. Goethe was also a court official to the Duke of Weimar, an actor, and a manager of a theater.

Notable books: *The Sorrows of Young Werther* 1774; *Wilhelm Meister* 1796–1829
Notable plays: *Faust* 1775–1832; *Egmont* 1788; *Iphigenie* 1789

DESIDERIUS ERASMUS c. 1466–1536
Dutch scholar Desiderius Erasmus was educated by monks. He traveled throughout Europe teaching in universities. Erasmus also criticized the Catholic Church and Protestant reformers such as Martin Luther. He wrote many books, including *In Praise of Folly* (1509), and he edited a new Latin translation of the New Testament (1516).

MIGUEL DE CERVANTES 1547–1616
Spanish-born Miguel de Cervantes became a soldier in Italy in 1570. He was captured by Algerian pirates and spent five years in prison. After a ransom was paid he was released and moved to Madrid, Spain. He had little success as a writer until 1605 when he published the first part of *Don Quixote*, and it became an immediate success.

Mary Shelley

1797–1851

Born Mary Godwin in London, England, she eloped with English poet and writer Percy Shelley (1792–1822) in 1814. After marrying in 1816 the Shelleys lived abroad, and while they were on vacation in Lake Geneva, Switzerland, Mary began writing her best-known novel, *Frankenstein*. It is believed that Lord Byron (p. 119), who was with them at the time, challenged the group to write a ghost story. The book took two years to write and was published in 1818. Percy Shelley died in 1822, and Mary returned to England with their son, Percy. Her novel, *The Last Man* (1826), tells of a world ravaged by disease. She also wrote travel books and pieces of verse, of which "The Choice" is the most well known.

Notable books: *Frankenstein*, or *The Modern Prometheus*, 1818; *Valperga* 1823; *Lodore* 1835; *Falkner* 1837

▲ Mary Shelley, author of *Frankenstein*, and her husband, poet and writer Percy Shelley.

◀ Alexandre Dumas' famous stories, *The Three Musketeers*, are about the adventures of D'Artagnan and his friends during the reign of French King Louis XIII.

Alexander Pushkin

1799–1837

Russian writer Alexander Pushkin held a government post in Moscow, but he was exiled to Pskov in 1824 because of his political poems. It was during this time that he worked on his greatest novel, *Eugene Onegin*. He returned to Moscow after Nicholas I came to the throne in 1825. In 1832 Pushkin married the beautiful Natalia Goncharova. However, a Frenchman, Baron D'Anthès, fell in love with her. Pushkin challenged him to a duel and was killed.

Notable play: *Boris Godunov* 1825
Notable novel: *Eugene Onegin* 1832

Alexandre Dumas

1802–1870

French playwright and novelist Alexandre Dumas was a prolific writer and produced around 300 works of historical fiction. He first became popular in 1829 for his historical drama *Henri III*. While recovering from cholera in Switzerland in 1832 he wrote his first travelogue, *Impressions de Voyage*. Between 1855 and 1864 he lived in exile in Belgium and Italy.

Notable novels: *The Three Musketeers* 1844; *Twenty Years After* 1845; *Ten Years Later* 1848–1850; *The Count of Monte Cristo* 1844–1845

SAMUEL JOHNSON 1709–1784
English writer Samuel Johnson first worked in London writing for *The Gentleman's Magazine*. His most famous work was the *Dictionary of the English Language* (1747–1755). After a visit to the Hebrides in Scotland with his biographer, James Boswell (1740–1795), Johnson wrote *A Journey to the Western Isles in Scotland* (1775).

JEAN-JACQUES ROUSSEAU 1712–1778
Swiss-born, Rousseau worked in Paris as a secretary and copying music. There he met Voltaire (p. 108) and Diderot (1713–1784). Rousseau is best known for writing *Discourse on the Origin and Foundations of Inequality Among Men* (1754) and *A Treatise on the Social Contract* (1762).

HONORÉ DE BALZAC 1799–1850
French novelist Honoré de Balzac left his law studies to become an author in Paris. He spent many years in debt, but he worked long hours and produced 85 novels in 20 years. He is best known for his observations on French society in the series of novels, *The Human Comedy* (1842–1853). The last one was finished by his wife after his death.

The Brontë sisters

Charlotte 1816–1855
Emily 1818–1848
Anne 1820–1849

The Brontë sisters were born in Yorkshire, England. Their father, Patrick Brontë, was a clergyman, and in 1820 the family moved to Haworth, England, where he became the rector.

Their mother died in 1821, and the sisters were brought up by their father and an aunt. They and their brother Branwell had a lonely childhood and were all sickly. After working as teachers and governesses the girls began writing. They published a volume of poems in 1846 under the male pseudonyms of Currer Bell (Charlotte), Ellis Bell (Emily), and Acton Bell (Anne). Anne wrote two novels, *Agnes Gray* and *The Tenant of Wildfell Hall* (1848). Emily wrote one very successful novel, *Wuthering Heights*. Charlotte's second book, *Jane Eyre,* established her as a writer and was a great success.

Notable novels: *Agnes Gray* (Anne) 1845; *Jane Eyre* (Charlotte) 1847; *Wuthering Heights* (Emily) 1847

▲ The only surviving portrait of the Brontë sisters was painted by their brother, Branwell, c. 1834.

Victor Hugo

1802–1885

As a teenager French writer Victor Hugo won many prizes for his poems and plays. In 1830 *Hernani* established him as one of the great writers of the Romantic movement. His novel *Notre Dame de Paris* sealed his reputation. In 1848 he was elected to the French Assembly but was sent into exile to the island of Guernsey (1851–1870) because of his opposition to Napoléon III. Here he wrote his masterpiece *Les Misérables*.

Notable novels: *Notre Dame de Paris* 1830; *Les Misérables* 1862

► Victor Hugo's novel *Notre Dame de Paris* was made into the movie *The Hunchback of Notre Dame* in 1924.

Hans Christian Andersen

1805–1875

At the age of 14 Danish writer Hans Christian Andersen ran away from his home in Odense to Copenhagen. His talent for poetry led him to receive a special education. In 1829 Hans wrote a satirical narrative of his travels, and in 1833 he received money to travel from the king, Frederick VI. Andersen visited many European countries, writing plays, travel books, novels, poetry, and fairy tales.

Notable stories: *The Little Mermaid* 1837; *The Emperor's New Clothes* 1837; *The Ugly Duckling* 1843; *The Red Shoes* 1845

▲ ► Charles Dickens and an illustration from one of his most popular books, *David Copperfield*.

Charles Dickens

1812–1870

After a difficult childhood English writer Charles Dickens joined the London *Morning Chronicle* in 1828 as a reporter of debates in the House of Commons. In 1836 *Sketches by Boz* was published in serial format and was soon followed by *Pickwick Papers*, an immediate success. Dickens' stories of social life and injustices in Victorian England made him the most popular writer of his day. He traveled widely in Europe and the U.S.

Notable books: *Oliver Twist* 1837–1839; *Nicholas Nickleby* 1838–1839; *A Christmas Carol* 1843; *David Copperfield* 1849–1850; *Great Expectations* 1860–1861

Karl Marx

1818–1883

German philosopher and political theorist Karl Marx became a newspaper journalist in Cologne in 1842. The following year he moved to Paris, where he formed a lifelong friendship with German philosopher Friedrich Engels (1820–1895). In Paris, Marx became a Communist and was the first to express the idea that "the people" must make revolutionary changes to society. In 1849 Marx and Engels moved to London, England, where they continued developing their Communist ideas.

Notable books: *Communist Manifesto* 1848; *Das Kapital* (Volume I) 1867

Leo Tolstoy

1828–1910

Russian aristocrat and novelist Leo Tolstoy fought in the Crimean War at the siege of Sebastopol (1854–1855). The war inspired him to write *Tales of Army Life*. After the war he joined the literary circle in St. Petersburg. In 1862 he got married and went to live on his Volga estate. It was there that he wrote his most famous novel, *War and Peace*. It tells of the lives of two families over a period of 12 years and describes domestic and military life during the Napoleonic War. His second great novel, *Anna Karenina,* is the story of a married woman's sad love affair with a soldier. In around 1883 Tolstoy gave up all his material possessions to live as a peasant.

Notable novels: *War and Peace* 1863–1869; *Anna Karenina* 1874–1876

▲ In later years Tolstoy rejected his own work as having no value, living a simple life.

EDGAR ALLAN POE 1809–1849
American poet and author Edgar Allan Poe was orphaned at the age of three. With his adopted parents he moved to England, where he was educated in London. He returned to America in 1826, and his first book of poems was published one year later. After a brief spell in the army Poe began working as a journalist and writing short stories. Between 1835 and 1847 he was the editor of various magazines for which he wrote his most famous stories, *The Fall of the House of Usher* and *The Murders in the Rue Morgue,* and his famous poem, *The Raven.*

FYODOR DOSTOEVSKY 1821–1881
Born in Moscow, Russia, Fyodor Dostoevsky held a government post before he became a writer. His first published short story, *Poor Folk,* was an immediate success. In 1849 he was arrested for his part in a Socialist plot. He escaped a death sentence but was sent to a prison camp in Siberia until 1854. In 1860 he published his novel *The House of the Dead* based on his experiences in prison. Like Charles Dickens (left), Dostoevsky's novels are about social injustice and poverty. His most famous novels are *Crime and Punishment* (1866), *The Idiot* (1868), and *The Brothers Karamazov* (1880).

JULES VERNE 1828–1905
French novelist Jules Verne studied law and from 1848 to 1862 wrote the text for operas. He also collaborated with Alexandre (Fils) Dumas (1824–1895) in writing for the theater. In 1863 Verne's novel *Five Weeks in a Balloon* was published and was a great success. Jules had discovered his true gift for writing futuristic adventure stories. Among his best-known novels are *A Journey to the Center of the Earth* (1864), *From the Earth to the Moon* (1865), *Twenty Thousand Leagues Under the Sea* (1869), and *Around the World in Eighty Days* (1873).

Louisa May Alcott

1832–1888

U.S. writer Louisa May Alcott was born in Philadelphia and worked as a nurse in a Union hospital during the Civil War (1861–1865). She first wrote romantic novels for magazines, and her first book, *Flower Fables*, was published in 1855. Her greatest success was *Little Women*, published in 1868. This was followed by *Good Wives* a year later. Both books were about family life in a New England town during the Civil War.

Notable book: *Little Women* 1868

Mark Twain

1835–1910

Born Samuel Langhorne Clemens, U.S. writer Mark Twain became a steamboat pilot on the Mississippi River at the age of 17. After a series of other jobs he became a journalist. His first book, *The Celebrated Jumping Frog* (1857), was an immediate success. He then traveled to Europe to collect material for his novel *Innocents Abroad* (1869). Although often in debt, Twain went on to write many successful books, including *Tom Sawyer* and *Huckleberry Finn*, both based on his childhood experiences.

Notable books: *Tom Sawyer* 1876; *Huckleberry Finn* 1884; *A Connecticut Yankee in King Arthur's Court* 1889

MARK TWAIN

◀ Alice and the Cheshire Cat in *Alice's Adventures in Wonderland.*

Lewis Carroll

1832–1898

Born Charles Dodgson, English writer Lewis Carroll was educated at Oxford University, where he studied mathematics. He took a teaching post at the university and wrote several textbooks on mathematics and also completed some comic writing. He became an Anglican deacon in 1861, but because he was a shy man with a stutter, he seldom preached. His first children's book, *Alice's Adventures In Wonderland*, was an immediate success. *Alice Through The Looking Glass* and collections of nonsense poems were equally successful and are still read and loved by children and adults all over the world.

Notable books: *Alice's Adventures in Wonderland* 1865; *Alice Through the Looking Glass* 1872

Émile Zola

1840–1902

French novelist Émile Zola began working in a Paris publishing house before becoming a journalist. His first short stories, *Stories For Ninon*, were published in 1864. Zola formed a literary society with other like-minded writers and from this grew the Naturalist school of novel writing. Zola's novels are very detailed stories of French contemporary life. His first, *Thérèse Raquin*, was published in 1867. Zola also fought against social injustice. In 1898 he wrote "J'accuse" ("I accuse"), a letter to a newspaper in defense of Frenchman Alfred Dreyfus (1859–1935), who had been unfairly imprisoned for spying. Zola was sent to prison for libel, but he escaped and lived in England for a year.

Notable novels: *Nana* 1880; *Earth* 1887; *The Dream* 1888; *The Beast in Man* 1890

Thomas Hardy

1840–1928

English novelist and poet Thomas Hardy first worked for a London architect for five years. He was so determined to become a writer that he returned home to Dorset in 1867. Hardy's fourth novel, *Far From The Madding Crowd* (1874), was his first great success. He continued to write many novels, but in 1895 *Jude the Obscure* was attacked by critics and, Hardy turned to his first love—poetry. By his death he had written over 900 poems.

Notable novels: *The Return of the Native* 1878; *The Mayor of Casterbridge* 1886; *Tess of the D'Urbervilles* 1891

Robert Louis Stevenson

1850–1894

Scottish writer Robert Louis Stevenson qualified as a lawyer in 1875, but he soon turned to writing. His first book, *Inland Voyage* (1876), described a canoe journey in Belgium. However, *Treasure Island* (1883) gave him a name as a writer of adventure stories. Some of his best works were short stories, articles, and essays that appeared in magazines. His poems in *A Child's Garden of Verses* are ranked among the finest. In 1891 he settled on the Pacific island of Samoa, where he spent his last years.

Notable books: *Kidnapped* 1886; *The Strange Case of Dr. Jekyll and Mr. Hyde* 1886; *The Master of Ballantrae* 1889

Oscar Wilde

1854–1900

Dublin-born Oscar Wilde won a prize in 1878 for his poem *Ravenna*. A collection of poetry published in 1881 was followed by children's fairy tales in 1888. His novel *The Picture of Dorian Gray* was published in *Lippincott's Magazine* and caused a scandal. Wilde went on to become a successful playwright.

Notable novel: *The Picture of Dorian Gray* 1891Notable play: *The Importance of Being Earnest* 1895

◄ In 1895 Oscar Wilde was sent to prison for two years for being a homosexual.

HENRY JAMES 1843–1916
Born in New York, Henry James was contributing to the *Atlantic Monthly* magazine as well as writing literary reviews and short stories by the age of 22. In 1876 James settled in England, where he lived for the rest of his life. In all he wrote 20 long novels, many on the theme of American–European relationships. They include *Daisy Miller* (1879), *The Bostonians* (1886), and *The Golden Bowl* (1904). James is also well known for his many short stories. His ghost story, *Turn Of The Screw* (1898), showed him to be a master of the supernatural. He also wrote critical studies and travelogues.

GUY DE MAUPASSANT 1850–1893
French novelist Guy de Maupassant spent his whole life in Normandy, France. He worked as a government clerk but was encouraged to take up writing by the novelist Gustave Flaubert (1821–1880). Maupassant only wrote six novels, of which the first, *Ball of Tallow*, was published in 1880. However, he is more well known for his short stories, of which he wrote nearly 300. He went insane in 1892. His novel *The Fear* predicted his own insanity.

EMILIA PARDO BAZÁN 1852–1921
Spanish feminist, novelist, and critic Emilia Pardo Bazán wrote her first novel, *Pascual Lopez*, in 1879. Bazán is best known for *The Manors of Ulloa* (1886) and *Mother Nature* (1887), written in the French Naturalist style. Her later, more modernist novels include *The Chimera* (1905). Bazán also wrote over 500 short stories, critical works about French authors, poems, and ran a library for women.

JOSEPH CONRAD 1857–1924
Born in Poland as Józef Korzeniowski, Conrad moved to England in 1877, where he joined the British Merchant Navy. He earned his sailing certificate and became a British citizen in 1884. He spent the next ten years at sea and in 1895 settled down to a life of writing. Many of his novels, including *Lord Jim* (1900) and *Shadow Line* (1917), are based on his own seafaring experiences. His work earned him little money but much praise from critics. Conrad also wrote many short stories, including *Tales of Unrest* (1898) and *Heart of Darkness* (1902).

Arthur Conan Doyle

1859–1930

Born in Scotland to Irish parents, Arthur Conan Doyle became a doctor and began writing to supplement his meager income. His Sherlock Holmes detective novels were begun in 1887 with *A Study in Scarlet*, which introduced Dr. Watson as Holmes' assistant. First published in the *Strand Magazine* as a series of stories, they became immensely popular. Later published as books, the Sherlock Holmes stories still have a worldwide following. Doyle also wrote historical romances and novels.

Notable books: *The Sign of Four* 1890; *Rodney Stone* 1896; *The Hound of the Baskervilles* 1902; *The Lost World* 1912

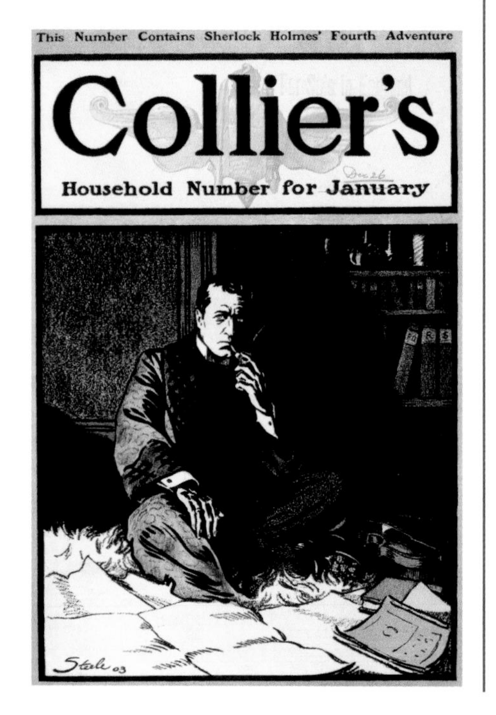

Beatrix Potter

1866–1943

As a child English children's author and illustrator Beatrix Potter taught herself how to draw and paint. To amuse younger children, she drew animals dressed in human clothes. She developed this style and wrote stories to go with her drawings. *The Tale of Peter Rabbit* was first sent to the child of one of her nannies in 1893 and was privately published by Potter in 1901.

Notable books: *The Tailor of Gloucester* 1902; *The Tale of Squirrel Nutkin* 1903; *The Tale of Benjamin Bunny* 1904; *The Tale of Jeremy Fisher* 1906

Marcel Proust

1871–1922

French novelist Marcel Proust suffered from poor health all of his life, and when his mother died in 1905 he became a recluse. He published his first collection of short stories, *Pleasures and Regret*, in 1896. After being rejected by many publishers Proust also had to pay for the publication in 1914 of his 13 volumes of autobiographical novels, *Remembrance of Times Past*. His writing is often long and drawn out—"six pages to analyze a woman's smile." At other times he captures the essence of a human emotion in three lines. Four of his books were published posthumously.

Notable novels: *Remembrance of Times Past* 1914; *Within a Budding Grove* 1919; *The Cities of the Plain* 1922; *The Captive* 1923; *Time Regained* 1927

Colette

1873–1954

French novelist Colette's first series of novels, *Claudine*, were published by her first husband under his own pen name, Willy. When their relationship ended, she wrote under the name Colette Willy. They got divorced in 1906, and for a while she earned her living on the stage with mime and dance routines. Colette's novel *Music Hall Sidelights* (1913) tells of her life at that time. Considered one of France's leading writers from the 1900s, Colette wrote over 50 books. A recurring theme in them was a woman's struggle for independence. *Gigi* in particular has remained popular as a movie and play.

Notable novels: *The Vagabond* 1910; *Music Hall Sidelights* 1913; *Cheri* 1920; *Sido* 1929; *The Cat* 1933; *Gigi* 1944

RUDYARD KIPLING 1865–1936

Kipling was born in India but spent part of his childhood in England. At the age of 16 he returned to India to work as a journalist and started to write verse and short stories about Indian life. In 1889 he returned to London, where he wrote many successful books including *The Jungle Book* (1894), *Kim* (1901), and the *Just So Stories* (1902).

H.G. WELLS 1866–1946

English novelist H.G. Wells became a college professor until the success of his short stories led to a writing career. In 1895 he wrote the popular science-fiction novel *The Time Machine*. Wells followed this with *The Invisible Man* (1897) and *War of the Worlds* (1898). His *Outline of History* (1920) also achieved great success.

James Joyce

1882–1941

Born in Dublin, the influential Irish writer James Joyce first studied modern languages. In 1902 he settled in Paris, France, where he taught and wrote. There he wrote his well-received collection of short stories, *The Dubliners* (1914). Joyce's *A Portrait of the Artist as a Young Man* was then serialized in the *Egotist* magazine. His novel *Ulysses* caused a scandal when it was published and was banned in Great Britain and the U.S. for its sexual explicitness for many years.

Notable books: *Portrait of the Artist as a Young Man* 1914–1915; *Ulysses* 1922; *Finnegan's Wake* 1939

J.R.R. Tolkien

1892–1973

Born in South Africa to English parents, novelist J.R.R. Tolkien was an English professor at Oxford University from 1925 to 1959. His interest in the history of languages and folklore led him to write fantasy stories for his children. The first of these, *The Hobbit*, was an immediate success. The three-volume sequel, *The Lord of the Rings,* took 12 years to write and has recently been made into a highly successful movie.

Notable books: *The Hobbit* 1937; *The Lord of the Rings* 1954–1955

Graham Greene

1904–1991

English writer Graham Greene was educated at Balliol College in Oxford. He became a Roman Catholic at the age of 22 and worked as a journalist for the London newspaper *The Times*. Greene did not achieve success as a writer until his fourth novel, *Stamboul Train*, was published in 1932. He traveled widely, and many of his novels are set in tropical countries. A recurring theme is a belief in God and the fight against evil, oppression, and corruption. Many of his books, for example *Brighton Rock*, have also been made into highly successful movies.

Notable books: *Brighton Rock* 1938; *The Power and the Glory* 1940; *The Third Man* 1950; *Our Man in Havana* 1958; *The Honorary Consul* 1973

◀ J.R.R. Tolkien's *The Hobbit* is a children's fantasy story set in a place called Middle Earth. This early edition of the book was also illustrated by the author.

GERTRUDE STEIN 1874–1946
U.S. writer Gertrude Stein studied medicine and psychology and then settled in Paris, France. She was interested in abstract art and tried using its theories in her writing. Her first book, *Three Lives,* was published in 1908. Stein also wrote two operas. She left Paris during World War II to live in Germany and wrote *Wars I Have Seen* (1945).

D. H. LAWRENCE 1885–1930
During his short life English writer D. H. Lawrence produced an enormous quantity of novels, short stories, poems, plays, essays, and travelogues. His first major novel was *Sons and Lovers* (1913). *Lady Chatterley's Lover* was thought obscene when it was privately published in Florence, Italy, in 1928. It was banned in Great Britain until 1961.

JORGE LUIS BORGES 1899–1986
Argentinian poet and short-story writer Jorge Luis Borges was educated in Switzerland and England. His first work was published in Spanish avant-garde magazines. In 1921 he returned to Buenos Aires, where he wrote several collections of fantasy short stories. Most notable are *Fictions* (1944) and *El Aleph* (1949).

George Orwell

1903–1950

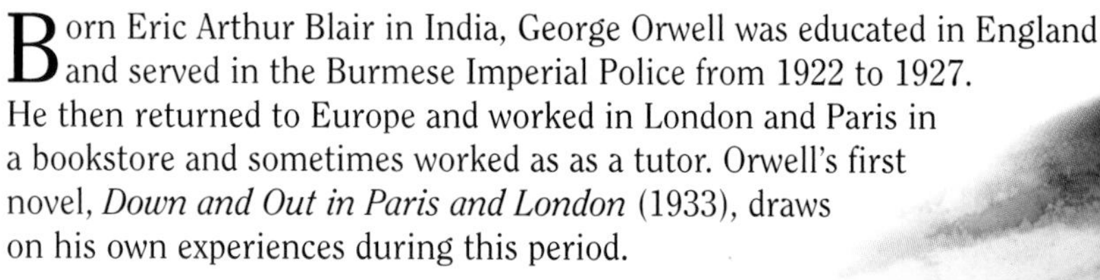

Born Eric Arthur Blair in India, George Orwell was educated in England and served in the Burmese Imperial Police from 1922 to 1927. He then returned to Europe and worked in London and Paris in a bookstore and sometimes worked as as a tutor. Orwell's first novel, *Down and Out in Paris and London* (1933), draws on his own experiences during this period.

Orwell was a Socialist, and during the Spanish Civil War (1936–1939) he fought on the Republican side and was wounded. In World War II he was the war correspondent for the BBC and the London newspaper *The Observer*. After the war Orwell's novels *Animal Farm*, a satirical attack on the Russian Revolution, and *1984*, a futuristic story of the dangers of dictatorships, brought him worldwide fame.

Notable novels: *Keep the Aspidistra Flying* 1936; *Coming Up For Air* 1939; *Animal Farm* 1945; *1984* 1949

▼ Orwell's biting satirical attack on communism and human greed, *Animal Farm*, was also made into a classic animated movie.

Roald Dahl

1916–1990

Born in Wales to Norwegian parents, Roald Dahl served as a pilot in the British Royal Air Force during World War II. He served in Africa, the Middle East, and the U.S. and was badly injured in an air crash. After the war he began writing adult short stories. *Someone Like You* (1954) and *Kiss, Kiss* (1960) both brought him success. However, it is for his fantasy children's books that he is famous. The first of these, *James and the Giant Peach*, was published in 1961. Many others followed but brought with them the criticism of teachers and librarians who felt that they were too rude and cruel for children. Despite—or because of—this Dahl's books have sold in the millions all over the world.

Notable children's books: *Charlie and the Chocolate Factory* 1964; *Revolting Rhymes* 1982; *The BFG* 1982; *The Witches* 1983; *Dirty Beasts* 1984

Arthur C. Clarke

► Arthur C. Clarke, seen here with his latest book, *3001: Odyssey Four*, has lived in Sri Lanka since the 1950s.

b. 1917

English science-fiction author Arthur C. Clarke worked as a radar instructor during World War II. In 1945 he predicted worldwide communication through the use of satellites. His first work of science fiction was *Prelude to Space* (1951). Clarke aims for technological realism in his novels about exploration in space. The novel for which he is most famous, *2001: A Space Odyssey*, was made into a classic movie by the U.S. director Stanley Kubrick (p. 151) in 1968. The book series continued with *2010: Odyssey Two* (1982), *2061: Odyssey Three* (1988), and *3001: Odyssey Four* (2001).

Notable books: *Childhood's End* 1953; *The City and the Stars* 1956; *2001: A Space Odyssey* 1968; *Rendezvous with Rama* 1973; *The Fountains of Paradise* 1979

Alexander Solzhenitsyn

b. 1918

Russian writer Alexander Solzhenitsyn was sent to a prison camp for eight years in 1945 after criticizing the Soviet dictator Stalin (p. 21). Solzhenitsyn's first novel, *One Day in the Life of Ivan Denisovich* (1956), described the terrible conditions that he experienced in prison. His later works were banned in Russia, and he was deported to West Germany in 1974.

Notable books: *The Cancer Ward* 1968; *The Gulag Archipelago* 1974–1978

Anne Frank

1929–1945

Born in Germany, Anne Frank was four years old when her father, a Jewish banker, moved his family to the Netherlands to escape Nazi persecution. When the Germans occupied the Netherlands during World War II, Anne moved with her family into hidden rooms in her father's office building. They lived there between 1942 and 1944, and during this time Anne kept a detailed diary. The family were betrayed and sent to concentration camps. Only her father, Otto, survived.

Notable book: *The Diary of Anne Frank* 1947

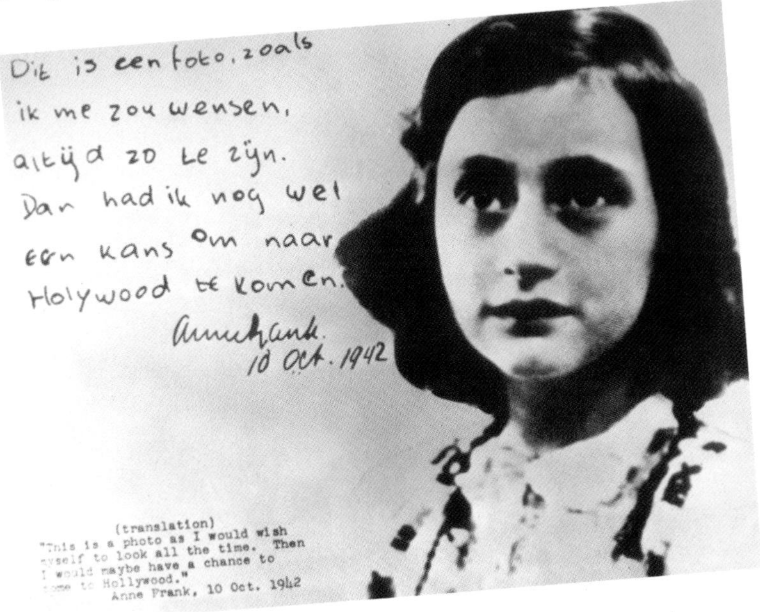

► For two years, Anne Frank hid from the Germans in a small room at the top of her father's office in Amsterdam. During this period she kept a daily diary of her life.

Isaac Asimov

1920–1992

U.S. novelist Isaac Asimov was born in Russia and emigrated with his family to America in 1923. There he studied chemistry and became a well-known biochemist. Asimov also wrote many science-fiction novels. His collection of short stories, *I, Robot*, introduced the term "robotics" to the English language.

Notable books: *I, Robot* 1950; *Foundation* 1951; *Foundation and Empire* 1952; *Second Foundation* 1953; *The Caves of Steel* 1954; *The Naked Sun* 1957

J.K. Rowling

b. 1965

While working as an English teacher in Portugal, English children's writer J.K. Rowling began writing a story about wizards. She moved to Scotland, and with the aid of a grant she completed the story. When *Harry Potter and the Philosopher's Stone* was published, it became an immediate success. It was also made into a highly successful movie that has broken all box-office records.

Notable book: *Harry Potter and the Philosopher's Stone* 1997

ISAAC SINGER 1904–1991
Polish-born writer Isaac Singer emigrated to the U.S. in 1935, where he worked as a journalist on the *Jewish Daily Forward* newspaper. His first novel, *Satan in Gray*, was published in Poland. His short stories and novels are based on Jewish life in his native country and in the U.S. Notable novels include *The Family Moskat* (1950), *The Manor* (1967), and *The Estate* (1970). Singer also wrote a play, *Schlemiel the First* (1974), and was awarded the Nobel Prize for Literature in 1978.

JEAN-PAUL SARTRE 1905–1980
French writer and philosopher Jean-Paul Sartre was born in Paris, educated at the Sorbonne, and then taught philosophy. He was imprisoned during World War II, and on his release he joined the Resistance in Paris. In 1946 he founded the monthly magazine *Modern Times* with his lover, Simone de Beauvoir (below). Sartre was one of the founders of the Existentialist movement in France. His book, *Being and Nothingness* (1943), expanded on his theory that human beings are nothing until they make conscious decisions. Other notable books include *Nausea* (1938) and *The Roads to Freedom* (1945–1949). Sartre also wrote several notable plays, including *The Flies* (1943) and *In Camera* (1944).

SIMONE DE BEAUVOIR 1908–1986
Born in Paris, France, Simone de Beauvoir was a Socialist and feminist and is probably best known for her book *The Second Sex* (1949). In 1954 she won the Prix Goncourt for her autobiographical novel, *Les Mandarins*. For most of her life De Beauvoir was the partner and lover of Existentialist author and philosopher Jean-Paul Sartre (above).

J.D. SALINGER b. 1919
Born in New York, Jerome David Salinger had a burning ambition to become a writer. After fighting in World War II he held journalistic posts on various magazines, finally working on the *New Yorker*. Salinger is best known for his first novel, *The Catcher in the Rye* (1951), which became a cult book for young people and still sells thousands of copies a year. He now lives in seclusion in New Hampshire, avoiding all publicity.

POETS

Dante Alighieri

1265–1321

Born in Florence, Italy, Dante was only nine when he fell in love with a young girl, Beatrice Portinari. His love for her had a profound influence on his work as a poet. The story of Dante's love is told in his book of sonnets, *La Vita Nuova*. He became involved in Florentine politics, and in 1301 he fell out with the Pope's supporters. He was banished from Florence and finally settled in Ravenna. His greatest book, *Divina Commedia* (The Divine Comedy), tells of his journey through the afterworld guided by his childhood love, Beatrice.

Notable books: *La Vita Nuova* c. 1292; *Divina Commedia* c. 1307

Geoffrey Chaucer

c. 1345–1400

English poet and author Geoffrey Chaucer served in the Hundred Years' War between England and France. He was taken prisoner in 1359 and released after a ransom was paid by Edward III. Chaucer then became a diplomat and Controller of Customs in London. His most famous work is *The Canterbury Tales*. Written in verse and prose, it contains the tales told by a group of pilgrims traveling from London to Canterbury in England.

Notable books: *Troilus and Cressida* c. 1380; *The Canterbury Tales* c. 1387–1400

William Blake

1757–1827

Born in London, England, William Blake trained as an engraver and studied art at the Royal Academy. He also wrote poems and combined this with his talent for engraving illustrations. He produced many illuminated books where the text is an integral part of the illustrations. Blake's poetry was not widely appreciated during his lifetime, and much of it was discarded. As a poet he is most well known for "Milton" and "Jerusalem." As an artist Blake produced many book illustrations, notably for the *Book of Job* (1826), and paintings such as *Job and his Daughters* (1799–1800).

Notable collections of poems: *Songs of Innocence* 1789; *Songs of Experience* 1794. Notable poems: "Milton" 1804–1808; "Jerusalem" 1804–1820

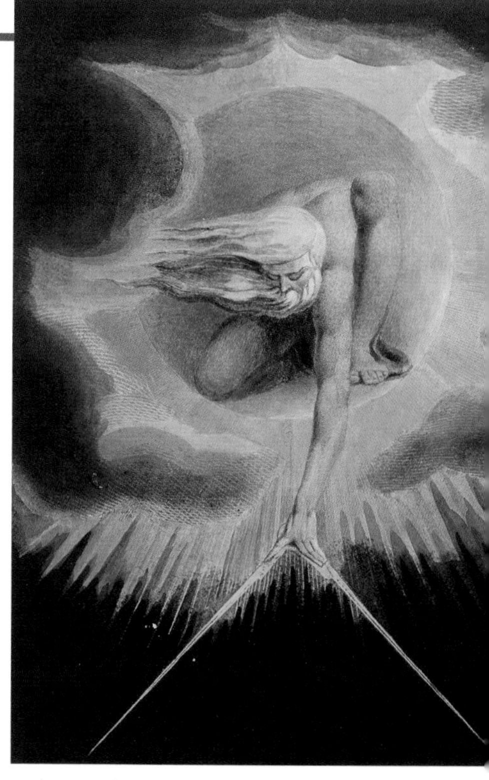

▲ William Blake's illustration from his book *The Ancient of Days* (1794).

William Wordsworth

1770–1850

English poet William Wordsworth was born in northwest England and studied at Cambridge University. After a brief visit to France and Switzerland, he settled down in southwest England with his sister, Dorothy, and friend, the poet Samuel Taylor Coleridge (p. 119). Wordsworth and Coleridge produced a collection of poems together, *Lyrical Ballads*, which included Wordsworth's famous "Tintern Abbey." Wordsworth got married in 1802 and moved with his wife, Mary, back to northwest England, where he wrote some of his finest poems, including "To Daffodils."

Notable poems: "Tintern Abbey" 1798; "Lucy" 1798–1799; "The Prelude" 1805

Wordsworth and his wife, Mary

FRANCESCO PETRARCH 1304–1374
Italian scholar and poet Petrarch settled in Avignon, France, in 1326, where he fell in love with a young woman, Laura. This romance inspired him to write his book of sonnets and songs, *Canzoniere* (1342). Petrarch also traveled widely, searching for ancient manuscripts. His famous poem, "Africa," was written during this period.

MATSUO BASHO 1644–1694
At the age of nine Japanese poet Matsuo Basho was the apprentice of a samurai and studied literature. He led a nomadic life when he wrote many of his most famous poems in *The Narrow Road to the Deep North* (1689). His greatest contribution to literature was his mastery of the Japanese 17-syllable haiku, or three-part poem.

HENRY LONGFELLOW 1807–1882
Born in New England, Longfellow was a university professor at Harvard University before he became a poet. He made several visits to Europe, where his first book of poems, *Voices of the Night* (1839), was well received. His epic poem *The Song of Hiawatha* (1855) is based on the myths and legends of Native Americans.

Samuel Taylor Coleridge

1772–1834

English poet Samuel Taylor Coleridge was educated at Cambridge University. After a brief spell as a soldier he went to the U.S., where he planned to set up a commune. Nothing came of this, and Coleridge returned to England, where he became a professor and journalist. In 1797 he moved to Somerset and met the poet Wordsworth (p. 118). Together they produced *Lyrical Ballads* (1798), which included Coleridge's masterpiece "The Rime of the Ancient Mariner." In 1800 he moved to northwest England, but poor health, drug addiction, and an unhappy marriage led him to move to London in 1810. There he wrote a play, continued to write poetry, and taught politics, education, and religion.

Notable poems: "The Rime of the Ancient Mariner" 1798; "Kubla Khan" 1816

Lord Byron

1788–1824

Born in Scotland, English poet Lord Byron was educated at Cambridge University. In 1809 he set out on a grand tour of Europe and wrote his successful poem, "Childe Harold's Pilgrimage," describing the countries that he visited. Owing to his tangled love life he left London for Venice, Italy, where he wrote some of his best poems. He died from fever in Greece while helping the Greeks gain independence from the Turks.

Notable poems: "Childe Harold's Pilgrimage" 1812; "Don Juan" 1819–1824

Emily Dickinson

1830–1886

American poet Emily Dickinson spent most of her life in her birthplace of Amherst, Massachusetts. In 1853 she retreated into almost total seclusion. Her only contact with the outside world was in letters that she exchanged with a small number of friends and the women's rights writer and preacher Thomas Higginson (1823–1911). Between 1858 and 1865 Emily wrote around 1,700 poems, but only a few were published—anonymously—during her lifetime. Her talent as a poet was not recognized until after her death when her poems were published in three volumes.

Notable poems: "Success is counted sweetest" c. 1859; "There is no frigate like a book" c. 1873

A 19th-century miniature portrait of the reclusive American poet Emily Dickinson.

▲ T. S. Eliot studying his manuscripts.

T. S. Eliot

1888–1965

U.S.-born poet Thomas Stearns Eliot spent most of his life in England. After studying at Oxford University he worked in a bank before becoming a publisher. He wrote his first book of poems, *Prufrock and Other Observations*, in 1917. Eliot's modern poetic masterpiece, "The Waste Land," received critical acclaim when it was published. Later, Eliot turned to writing religious plays, of which *Murder in the Cathedral* (1935) is the most famous. His collection of children's poetry, *Old Possum's Book of Practical Cats* (1939), was made into the hit musical *Cats* in 1981.

Notable poems: "The Waste Land" 1922; "Four Quartets" 1944

CHARLES BAUDELAIRE 1821–1867
French poet Baudelaire was a rebellious teenager. He left home to become a writer in Paris and became addicted to opium. At the age of 20 he was sent by his family to India, but he only got as far as Mauritius, where he had an affair. He returned to Paris, where he wrote several collections of poems, including the controversial *Flowers of Evil* (1857).

e. e. CUMMINGS 1894–1962
U.S. poet Edward Estlin Cummings studied art in Paris, France, and was mistakenly imprisoned during World War I. Influenced by jazz and slang, his first volumes of poetry in the 1920s were *Tulips and Chimneys*, *&*, and *Is 5*. His work is characterized by the unusual use of punctuation and typography, as shown by the use of lowercase letters in his name.

ALAN GINSBERG 1926–1997
In the late 1950s gay U.S. poet Alan Ginsberg was a member of a group of American writers called the Beats. They hated middle-class values and tried to explore their minds through the use of religious meditation, sex, drugs, and music. Ginsberg wrote many collections of poems, including the notorious *Howl and Other Poems* (1956).

PLAYWRIGHTS

Christopher Marlowe

1564–1593

English playwright Christopher Marlowe wrote his first play, *Tamburlaine the Great*, at the age of 23. As a playwright, Marlowe greatly influenced the early works of William Shakespeare (below) and is believed to have contributed to at least one of his plays. Marlowe led a controversial private life and was stabbed to death in a tavern in London, England.

Notable plays: *The Tragical History of Dr. Faustus* c. 1589; *Edward II* c. 1592

MOLIÈRE

Molière

1622–1673

Born Jean-Baptiste Poquelin, French actor and playwright Molière set up a theater company in Paris in 1643. With the support of the French king Louis XIV's brother, Philippe d'Orléans, his company toured France with considerable success. In 1658 the king gave them a permanent home in Paris. At this time Molière also started writing satirical comedy plays for his theater company. He died soon after acting in his play *Le Malade Imaginaire*.

Notable plays: *Don Juan* 1665; *Le Misanthrope* 1666; *Tartuffe* 1667; *Le Bourgeois Gentilhomme* 1671

William Shakespeare

1564–1616

Playwright, poet, and actor William Shakespeare is considered to be England's finest dramatist.

Shakespeare's early life was spent in his birthplace, Stratford-upon-Avon, in central England. He got married at the age of 18, and little is known of his life until he became an actor in London in 1592. He also wrote his first play, *The Two Gentlemen of Verona*, at this time. As a member of an acting group, the Lord Chamberlain's Men, he regularly performed at the court of the queen, Elizabeth I (p. 15). When James I came to the throne in 1603, the group became known as the King's Men. Shakespeare's early plays, such as *Romeo and Juliet* (1595), were an immediate success in London and made him a wealthy man. In total Shakespeare wrote 37 plays, including tragedies, comedies, and historical plays, as well as over 150 sonnets.

Notable plays: *Richard III* 1593; *Richard II* 1595; *A Midsummer Night's Dream* 1596; *The Merchant of Venice* 1597; *Julius Caesar* 1599; *Hamlet* 1601; *Othello* 1604; *Macbeth* 1606; *King Lear* 1606

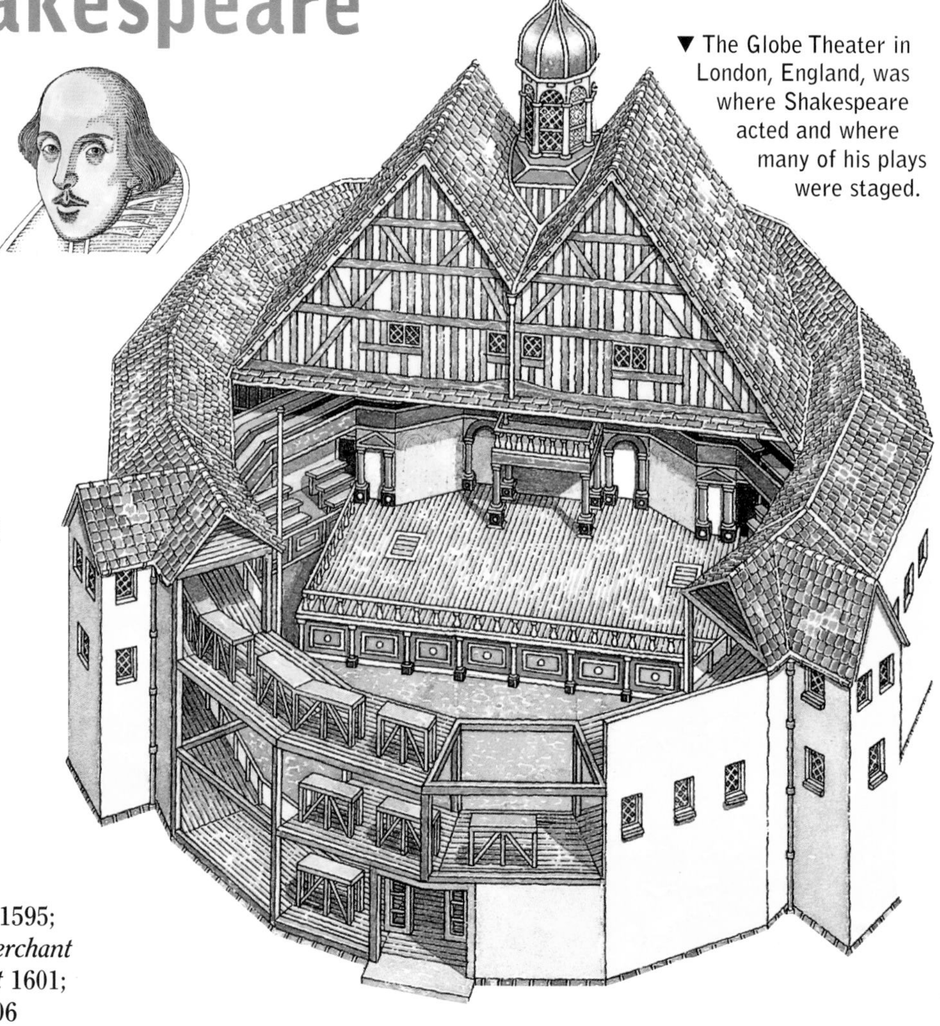

▼ The Globe Theater in London, England, was where Shakespeare acted and where many of his plays were staged.

Jean Racine

1639–1699

Playwright and poet Jean Racine is considered one of France's greatest tragic dramatists. He started writing poetry while studying philosophy in college, and in 1664 his first play, *The Fatal Legacy*, was staged by Molière's theater company in Paris. The partnership was short-lived because Racine fell out with Molière during the staging of his second play, *Alexander the Great*. Racine was very influenced by ancient Greek tragic plays, and he went on to write some of his best works between 1667 and 1677.

Notable plays: *Andromache* 1667; *Iphigenia* 1675; *Phèdre* 1677

Henrik Ibsen

1828–1906

Considered to be the first modern dramatist, Norwegian playwright Henrik Ibsen wrote his first play while working as a pharmacist's assistant. In 1851 Ibsen was appointed stage director and resident playwright at a theater in Bergen, Norway. He became director of the Norwegian Theater in 1857, where he wrote dramatic poetry and the first of his major plays. The majority of Ibsen's work was written during his stays in Italy and Germany between 1864 and 1890.

Notable plays: *A Doll's House* 1879; *Ghosts* 1881; *An Enemy of the People* 1882; *Hedda Gabler* 1890

HENRIK IBSEN

George Bernard Shaw

1856–1950

Irish dramatist George Bernard Shaw moved to London, England, in 1876. There he became a Socialist and worked as a music and drama critic for several newspapers. The first of his many plays, *Widowers' Houses,* was first staged in 1892. Shaw is also highly regarded for his book *The Intelligent Woman's Guide to Socialism and Capitalism* (1928).

Notable plays: *Man and Superman* 1902; *Pygmalion* 1913; *Saint Joan* 1923

▲ Anton Chekhov is Russia's greatest dramatist.

Anton Chekhov

1860–1904

Born into a poor Russian family, Anton Chekhov first started writing humorous short stories as a medical student. After working as a doctor Chekhov's first successful play, *The Seagull,* was performed by the Moscow Art Theater in 1898. He went on to write many more notable plays and short stories. Their recurring theme was the heroic struggle of the ordinary Russian people in czarist Russia. Chekhov's work has greatly influenced many Western writers.

Notable plays: *Uncle Vanya* 1896; *The Three Sisters* 1901; *The Cherry Orchard* 1904

BEN JONSON 1572–1637

English dramatist Ben Jonson worked as a bricklayer before enlisting in the English army to fight against the Spanish in the Low Countries. When he returned to England, he joined a London theater group as an actor. He was not a success and was imprisoned after killing a fellow actor in a duel. He then turned to writing plays. One of his earliest, *Every Man In His Humor* (1598), included Shakespeare (p. 120) in its cast. Jonson is best known for his four comedies; *Volpone* (1605), *Epicoene* (1609), *The Alchemist* (1610), and *Bartholomew Fair* (1614). He was also favored by the king, James I, for the lavish entertainment of drama, dance, and music (known as masques) that he produced with the architect and stage designer, Inigo Jones (p. 173).

PIERRE BEAUMARCHAIS 1732–1799

The son of a Parisian watchmaker, Pierre Beaumarchais followed his father's trade and then became rich through successful investments. He was also a playwright and wrote two highly successful comedies, *The Barber of Seville* (1775) and *The Marriage of Figaro* (1785). He fell out of favor with the French people during the French Revolution of 1789 and was forced to flee first to the Netherlands and then England.

AUGUST STRINDBERG 1849–1912

Swedish novelist and dramatist August Strindberg led a very colorful life. He dropped out as a student, held many jobs, had three failed marriages, suffered from a persecution complex, dabbled with the occult, and almost went crazy. However, as a writer of modern plays such as *The Father* (1887) and novels such as *The Red Room* (1879), Strindberg is regarded by many as Sweden's greatest writer.

SEAN O'CASEY 1884–1964

Irish playwright Sean O'Casey came from a poor Dublin family and first worked as a construction worker. His first plays, written about the city's poor for Dublin's Abbey Theater, were not well received by audiences. One, *The Plough and the Stars* (1926), even led to a riot. O'Casey left Dublin for London, where he continued writing plays that touched on subjects such as communism and the Irish Church.

Bertolt Brecht

1898–1956

Regarded as Germany's greatest modern dramatist, Brecht studied medicine and philosophy before writing his first play, *Drums in the Night* (1918). Brecht also wrote operas—*The Threepenny Opera* (1928) combined his interests in both music and drama. He broke away from the traditional theater by writing experimental plays such as *Puntilla* (1940). Brecht fled Nazi Germany in 1933 and settled in California. There he was accused of being a Communist, so in 1948 he went to live in East Germany, where he founded a theater.

Notable plays: ***Mother Courage and Her Children*** 1941; ***The Caucasian Chalk Circle*** 1947; ***The Resistable Rise of Arturo Ui*** 1957

Tennessee Williams

1911–1983

U.S. playwright Tennessee Williams worked various odd jobs while struggling to become a writer. His breakthrough came in 1940 when he was awarded a grant for his play *The Battle of Angels*. His first success was in 1945 when he was recognized as an important U.S. playwright by the New York Drama Critics' Circle for his play *The Glass Menagerie*. In 1948 he won the Pulitzer Prize for *A Streetcar Named Desire*. Many of his plays have been made into successful movies.

Notable plays: *Cat on a Hot Tin Roof* 1955; *Suddenly Last Summer* 1958; *The Night of the Iguana* 1961

▲ The comedy *French Without Tears* was Terrence Rattigan's first successful play.

Samuel Beckett

1906–1989

Irish novelist and playwright Samuel Beckett was a professor of languages in Paris and Dublin. From 1932 he settled in France, where he worked for a while as assistant to the Irish novelist, James Joyce (p. 115). Apart from some poetry and two novels, most of his work was first written in French. However, Beckett is more well known for his plays. *Waiting for Godot* (1953) brought him international fame and firmly placed him as a leading playwright for the Theater of the Absurd. He won the Nobel Prize for Literature in 1969.

Notable plays: *End Game* 1957; *Happy Days* 1961; *Play* 1963; *Breath* 1970

▲ Beckett's masterpiece *Waiting for Godot* is about the predicament of modern man.

Terrence Rattigan

1911–1977

Born in London, England, Terrence Rattigan was educated at Oxford University. In 1936 his comedy play *French Without Tears* took London's West End by storm and was a huge success. He followed it with more successful plays, many based on real-life incidents and people. Rattigan's plays are still popular and are regularly performed. Many have also been made into movies for which Rattigan wrote the scripts.

Notable plays: *Flare Path* 1942; *The Winslow Boy* 1946; *The Browning Version* 1948; *Separate Tables* 1954

JEAN ANOUILH 1910–1987

French dramatist Jean Anouilh studied law in Paris and was the secretary for the actor and theater director Louis Jouvet (1887–1951). Anouilh's many plays are based on classical Greek mythology brought into a modern setting. Notable among them are *Antigone* (1946), *The Lark* (1953), *Becket* (1959), and *Dear Antoine* (1969).

ARTHUR MILLER b. 1915

U.S. playwright Arthur Miller first shot to international fame in 1949 when he was awarded the Pulitzer Prize for his play *Death of a Salesman*. Miller suffered political persecution, and his famous play *The Crucible* (1953) concerns this subject. He was also married for five years to the actress Marilyn Monroe (p. 143).

EDWARD ALBEE b. 1928

U.S. playwright Edward Albee was heavily influenced by Theater of the Absurd writers such as Samuel Beckett (above left). In plays such as *Who's Afraid of Virginia Woolf* (1962) he attacks American middle-class values. Albee won Pulitzer Prizes for his plays *A Delicate Balance* (1966), *Seascape* (1975), and *Three Tall Women* (1991).

REFORMERS

Thomas à Becket

1118–1170

Born in London, England, Becket quickly rose to power. King Henry II (1133–1189) appointed him chancellor in 1155 and Archbishop of Canterbury in 1162. As chancellor Becket was a close friend and advisor to the king. However, as archbishop he renounced courtly life and opposed the king on most matters. They argued, and Becket fled to France. He returned to England in 1170 but continued to oppose the king's policies. Four knights murdered him as he prayed in Canterbury Cathedral.

English saint and martyr, murdered 1170

Francis of Assisi

c. 1181–1226

Remembered for his vows of absolute poverty and his kindliness toward animals, Francis began life as the son of a rich Italian cloth merchant. As a young man he fought in a local war and was captured and imprisoned. When he was freed, he began looking for a more spiritual way of life. In 1205 he had a vision of Christ, which inspired him to reject his father, give up all his wealth, and try to live as much like Jesus did as possible. He lived as a hermit, began preaching, rebuilt churches, and healed the sick. Many followed him, and he set up the Franciscan Order of monks. He was made a saint in 1228.

Founder of the Franciscan Order 1209

Martin Luther

1483–1546

The son of a German copper miner, Martin Luther was studying law when he had a spiritual experience in 1505 that led him to join a monastery.

Luther became a priest in 1507, and the following year he moved to Wittenberg, where he lectured and preached. He thought deeply about the relationship between God and man and what God wanted from people. His conclusions differed from those of the Roman Catholic Church. He questioned the authority of the Bible. He also disapproved of indulgences that were granted by the Church to help people atone for sins—they might be asked to make pilgrimages or give money. Luther believed this to be an insult to God's forgiveness and that the sale of indulgences to raise money for the Church was not acceptable. He wrote down his objections in 95 theses, and in 1517 he nailed them to a church door in Wittenberg in defiance of the Pope. In 1519 Luther claimed that the Pope was not infallible and was excommunicated. When called to a Diet (meeting) at Worms, Germany, in 1521 by Charles V, the Holy Roman Emperor, Luther refused to retract his statements because he could not go against his conscience. He escaped death because of the protection provided by the Elector of Saxony. Luther hoped his teachings would reform the Catholic Church; instead they were the basis of a new religious movement called Protestantism.

Founder of Protestant movement 1530

John Calvin
1509–1564

Born in France, Calvin spent most of his life in Switzerland, where he became one of the most important leaders of the Protestant Reformation. Like Luther (p. 123), he believed that faith was better than good deeds. An intellectual and an administrator, Calvin laid out Protestant beliefs and organized the way Protestant churches were run. Because he believed that the Church should be free from the State to work for social reform, he separated the Church from civil government.

Leader of the Protestant Reformation 1541–1564

John Knox
c. 1513–1572

Born in Scotland, John Knox was ordained as a Roman Catholic priest in 1540 but became a Protestant through the reforms of Martin Luther (p. 123). In 1549 he went to England to support the Protestant policies of Edward VI (1537–1553), but he fled to Europe when the Catholic Mary I (1516–1558) came to the throne in 1553. Knox met John Calvin (above) in Switzerland and was very influenced by him. In 1559 he returned to lead the Calvinist movement in Scotland. His impressive preaching and open hostility toward the Catholic Church led partly to the downfall of Mary, Queen of Scots (1542–1587).

Founded Church of Scotland 1560

William Penn
1644–1718

The son of an English admiral, William Penn was thrown out of Oxford University for refusing to accept the teachings of the Church of England. After a brief spell in France, Penn was sent to Ireland by his father to look after the family estates, and it was here that he became a Quaker. In England he preached for religious tolerance but was imprisoned on several occasions. In 1681 he was granted land in North America by the English king, James II. Penn named the land "Pensilvania" in memory of his father. A year later he sailed there with Quaker emigrants, founding the colony of Pennsylvania.

Founded Pennsylvania 1682

Samuel Adams
1722–1803

American politician Samuel Adams was born in Boston. He was a constant critic of British colonial rule and especially of the taxes imposed on the colonies. In 1773 the British imposed a tea tax and granted the East India Company a monopoly to supply tea. Adams organized a group of Boston patriots to protest when three tea-laden ships entered the Boston harbor. When the Governor of Boston refused to ask the ships to leave, a band of 60 or so Bostonians dressed as Mohawks boarded the ships at night, and at a signal from Adams they tipped the tea into the harbor. This was one of the key events that led to the American Revolutionary War (1775–1783) and the American Declaration of Independence, which Samuel Adams signed in 1776.

▲ The Boston Tea Party was organized by Samuel Adams as a symbolic protest against British taxation in the American colonies.

Organizer of the Boston Tea Party 1773

JOHN WYCLIFFE c. 1329–1384
English revolutionary philosopher and religious teacher John Wycliffe questioned the authority of the Pope and the clergy. He believed that the only authority people should obey was the word of God as it appeared in the Bible. To make this easier for poorly educated people, he organized the first English translation of the Bible.

THOMAS MORE 1478–1535
In 1529 politician and scholar Thomas More was appointed Lord Chancellor of England by Henry VIII (p. 15). He opposed the king's reformation of the Church and his break with Rome. More resigned in 1532, and two years later Henry was made head of the English Church. More's refusal to recognize this led to his execution.

ADAM SMITH 1723–1790
In 1776 Scottish philosopher Adam Smith published *The Wealth of Nations*, the first textbook of modern economics, which described how economies work and how they could develop. Smith supported the theory of Free Trade. He believed that the removal of trade restrictions would allow the world's wealth to be shared fairly.

Edmund Burke

1729–1797

Politician, philosopher, and writer Edmund Burke was born in Dublin, Ireland. He was elected to the English Parliament for the Whigs in 1765 and appointed Secretary for Ireland. An excellent orator, he argued that the American colonists should have the same rights as the English. Burke opposed the slave trade, worked for the improvement of Anglo–Irish relations, and supported religious tolerance. He opposed the French Revolution because he felt that it was too violent and ignored the rights of the individual. Burke's ideas formed the basis for the policies of the modern Conservative party in Great Britain.

Father of British Conservatism 1765–1783

William Wilberforce

1759–1833

English politician William Wilberforce combined evangelical Christianity with politics and used his position as a Member of British Parliament to push reforms ahead. He worked for better conditions for the poor but is best known for his opposition to slavery. In 1787 he began a campaign for its abolition. His abolition bill was passed in 1807, but the act only abolished the slave trade in the British West Indies. Wilberforce worked for the rest of his political life for total abolition. This was achieved in 1833.

Campaigner against the British slave trade 1787–1833

Guiseppe Mazzini

1805–1872

Italian-born Giuseppe Mazzini was a revolutionary republican and a leading figure in the *Risorgimento*, the struggle for Italian unity. As a member of the Carbonari, an illegal revolutionary group, Mazzini was arrested in 1830 and exiled to France. There he founded the Young Italy movement and traveled across Europe looking for support. In 1848 Mazzini returned to Italy to lead a revolt and became the head of a short-lived republican government in Rome. He led a number of revolts throughout the 1850s, but none succeeded.

Italian nationalist and founder of the Young Italy movement 1833

Thomas Paine

1737–1809

English political agitator Thomas Paine became a revolutionary hero and a citizen of both America and France, but he was considered a traitor in his native England. In 1774 he went to Philadelphia to support American independence and wrote *Common Sense*, a pamphlet detailing the colonists' aims. Back in England he wrote *The Rights of Man* in support of the French Revolution. He fled to Paris before he could be arrested for treason and was granted French citizenship. However, he opposed the execution of Louis XVI and was imprisoned in France. In jail he wrote *The Age of Reason*, a revolutionary view of religion and religious tolerance. Released in 1797, he returned to the U.S., where he died in poverty.

◄ A cartoon of Thomas Paine.

Wrote the revolutionary *The Rights of Man* 1791–1792

Harriet Tubman

c. 1820–1913

Born into slavery, Harriet Tubman fought for its abolition and for women's rights in America. In 1849 she escaped to Philadelphia (where slavery was illegal) and set up the Underground Railroad, a network of sympathizers to help southern slaves escape to the north and to Canada. She risked her freedom many times, helping over 300 people escape, including her own parents.

Organizer of the Underground Railroad network 1849–1863

ELIZABETH GARRETT ANDERSON 1836–1917
As a nurse Elizabeth Garrett Anderson was denied a place in a medical school because she was a woman. She studied privately, and in 1865 she became the first English woman to qualify as a doctor. She set up a hospital for women and helped create the London College of Medicine for Women.

CHARLES BOOTH 1840–1916
English shipowner Charles Booth produced the first scientific survey of poverty. *Life and Labor of the People in London* (1903) mapped the poverty of the city and showed the causes of it, one being old age. Booth introduced the idea of retirement funding for anyone over 65. The Old Age Pension Act was passed in 1908 in England.

CHARLES PARNELL 1846–1891
Anglo–Irish politician Charles Parnell devoted his political career to fight for Irish independence from Britain. He used political and violent means to support the cause. In 1881 he was imprisoned for his part in the Land League (tenants that fought eviction by English landlords). After the Home Rule Bill of 1886 failed Parnell continued his fight.

Votes for Women

Elizabeth Cady Stanton 1815–1902
Emmeline Pankhurst 1857–1928
Anita Augspurg 1857–1943

From the mid-1800s to the mid-1900s women were involved in a suffrage movement, fighting for the right to vote.

Elizabeth Cady Stanton began the fight in the U.S. when she organized the first women's rights convention with Susan B. Anthony (1820–1906) in 1848. Stanton campaigned tirelessly for the vote as well as the abolition of slavery. The vote was first granted in Wyoming in 1890. It took until 1920 before full equal suffrage (the same rights as men) was granted throughout the U.S. Black women in the southern states had to wait until 1965 before they were allowed to vote. In Germany, Anita Augspurg was the leading figure, gaining the vote for women in 1919. In England the Pankhurst family became the driving force behind the movement. Emmeline became an activist and founded the Women's Franchise League, which won the right to vote in local elections in 1894. In 1903 Emmeline and her daughters, Christabel and Sylvia, moved to London. There they formed the Women's Social and Political Union. They believed in direct action and demonstrated, paraded, broke windows, and chained themselves to railings. Along with many other supporters, they were repeatedly arrested and jailed for their actions. Many went on hunger strikes and were force-fed. At the end of World War I (1918) Prime Minister Lloyd George (1863–1945) granted the vote to women over 30. In 1928 the bill to give women equal voting rights was passed, three weeks before Emmeline's death.

◄ Emmeline Pankhurst founded the Women's Social and Political Union and campaigned for women's right to vote in Britain.

► Elizabeth Cady Stanton organized the first women's rights convention in the U.S.

► Suffragettes demonstrating for the right to vote, London, England, 1908

BOOKER T. WASHINGTON 1856–1915
Born an American slave, Booker Taliaferro Washington reformed higher education for black Americans. He believed that education led to economic independence, which in turn led to social equality. In 1881 he founded an adult education institute in Alabama to train black Americans to be teachers, farmers, and tradespeople.

MARIA MONTESSORI 1870–1952
Italian doctor and educationalist Maria Montessori developed the method of teaching young children that is named after her. She opened her first school in 1907, teaching children from the slums of Rome. The Montessori Method aims to teach children as individuals and allow them to find things out for themselves.

BERTRAND RUSSELL 1872–1970
English philosopher and mathematician Bertrand Russell taught in English and American universities and wrote many books on philosophy. He was also a pacifist and peace campaigner and was imprisoned several times for his beliefs. In 1958 he cofounded CND, the Campaign for Nuclear Disarmament, and was its first president.

Carrie Chapman Catt

1859–1947

A major campaigner for women's right to vote in America, Carrie Chapman Catt was first chairman and then president of the National American Woman Suffrage Association between 1895 and 1920. She also cofounded the International Woman Suffrage Alliance and was its president between 1904 and 1923. After American women were granted the right to vote in 1920, Catt set up the League of Women Voters in order to show women how to use their votes effectively.

Organizer of the Woman Suffrage Movement in America 1890–1920

Albert Schweitzer

1875–1965

Born in Alsace (then part of Germany), Albert Schweitzer's philosophy led him into a life of service to others. He was the Principal of St. Thomas Theological College in Strasbourg when he decided to become a medical missionary. After studying medicine from 1905 to 1913 he went to work in Lambaréné in what is now Gabon, Africa. He built a hospital there, financing his medical work by playing organ recitals and writing books. He used the money from his Nobel Prize in 1952 to fund a leper colony.

Humanitarian missionary 1913–1965

Albert Schweitzer devoted his life to providing medical aid for African people.

A reenactment of the incident that led to the arrest of Rosa Lee Parks (above) in 1955

Rosa Lee Parks

b. 1913

Born in Alabama, Rosa Lee Parks was a leading black American figure in the modern U.S. civil rights movement. In her home city of Montgomery in 1955 she refused to give up her seat on a bus to a white man, and she was arrested. This brought about a boycott of the bus company led by Martin Luther King (p. 128). A federal suit challenging segregation laws (separating black and white people) was filed with the U.S. Supreme Court. The following year the Court declared that Montgomery's segregation laws were unconstitutional. In 1999 Rosa Parks was awarded a Congressional Gold Medal.

Began the bus boycott that led to the Civil Rights Movement in America 1955

MARY BETHUNE 1875–1955
Mary McLeod Bethune was born the child of former slaves in South Carolina. She first worked as a teacher, and in 1935 she founded the National Council of Negro Women. From 1936 to 1943, as director of Negro Affairs within the National Youth Administration, she was the first black woman to be the head of a federal agency.

MARCUS GARVEY 1887–1940
Militant black activist Marcus Garvey was born in Jamaica. He founded the Universal Negro Improvement Association in 1914 and moved to New York City in 1916. There he set up the Back to Africa movement to urge black Americans to establish a black-governed country in Africa. Garvey's ideas inspired the Black Pride groups of the 1960s.

MOTHER TERESA 1910–1997
Mother Teresa was born Agnes Bojaxhiu in Skopje, Macedonia. When she was 17 she joined an Irish order of Roman Catholic nuns and was sent to India. For 20 years she taught in a convent school. In 1950 she founded the Order of the Missionaries of Charity to provide refuge to sick people who would otherwise die on the streets.

Martin Luther King, Jr.

▼ In August of 1963 Martin Luther King gave his famous "I have a dream" speech in front of 200,000 people in Washington, D.C.

1929–1968

Before the 1950s blacks in the South had to use different shops, schools, streets, and transportation. To fight this inequality, the civil rights movement began in 1951, and Martin Luther King, Jr. became its leader.

Born in Atlanta, Georgia, King became a Baptist minister. He was influenced by Mahatma Gandhi (p. 20) and encouraged nonviolent protest through boycotts, demonstrations, and freedom marches. From 1957 King began to coordinate campaigns for racial equality. In 1963 he organized a march on Washington, D.C. There, 200,000 people—black and white—heard King give a speech that outlined his aims for the integration of black and white Americans. In 1964 the Civil Rights Act ended segregation in public places. One year later King organized a march in Selma, Alabama, to claim equal voting rights. The state governor, George Wallace (1919–1998), sent the National Guard to stop the march. This outraged many Americans. As a result the government passed the Voting Rights Act. King was assassinated by James Earl Ray (p. 244) in 1968.

U.S. civil rights leader 1955–1968; founded Southern Christian Leadership Council 1957

Desmond Tutu

b. 1931

Desmond Tutu was born in Transvaal, South Africa. Although his family was poor, Tutu studied to become a teacher. In 1960 he became an Anglican priest and went to England to study theology. Returning to South Africa in 1967, he became an important leader of the nonviolent fight against apartheid. In 1984 he became the first black Archbishop of Cape Town, and in the same year he was awarded the Nobel Peace Prize for his efforts to unite people of all ethnic backgrounds in his country.

First black Secretary-General of the Council of South African Churches 1978; first black Archbishop in S. Africa 1984; chairman of S. African Truth and Reconciliation Commission 1995–1997

Lech Walesa

b. 1943

In 1980 Polish trade union leader Lech Walesa founded Solidarity to oppose Communist rule. Solidarity's popularity forced the government to make many changes. In 1981 it was made illegal, Walesa was arrested, and the military took over the country. Walesa was released in 1982, and Solidarity was legalized in 1988. As communism crumbled, the first free elections were held in Poland, and Walesa was elected president.

Founded Solidarity 1980; first elected president of Poland 1990

Steve Biko

1946–1977

An active opponent of apartheid and leader of the Black Consciousness Movement of South Africa, Steve Biko died in police custody in September 1977 after a severe beating. As a medical student at the University of Natal, Biko had founded the all-black South African Student Association in 1969 and the Black Consciousness Movement, which encouraged black South Africans to be proud of their culture. South Africa's white government regarded him as a terrorist. His murder outraged the world and led to the imposition of trade and cultural sanctions on South Africa.

Founded all-black South African Student Association and the Black Consciousness Movement 1969

CHAPTER SIX

STARS OF STAGE AND SCREEN

Entertainment before 1000

Long before motion pictures were invented, singers, dancers, and actors performed for audiences onstage and in theaters. It is believed that the origins of theater can be found in the religious rituals of primitive communities from thousands of years ago. However, activities that are considered to be direct forerunners to modern theater can be found in the 400s B.C. in ancient Greece.

By 500 B.C. the authorities in Athens had established four annual festivals to honor the Cult of Dionysus, the Greek god of wine and fertility. In around 534 B.C. a dramatic competition was set up for the City Dionysus, the most important and prestigious festival. Poets and composers had to submit three tragedies and one satyr play (comedy). The winner of the first City Dionysus was the leader of a dithyrambic chorus named **Thespis**. He is considered to be the first actor, which is why actors are called thespians and acting is known as the thespian art.

Other poets who competed in the City Dionysus are some of the earliest dramatists. **Aeschylus** (c. 525–456 B.C.), who wrote the trilogy *Oresteia*, was a key figure. Other significant writers and prizewinners of the City Dionysus include **Sophocles** (c. 496–405 B.C.), who wrote *Antigone* and *Electra*, and **Euripides** (c. 484–406 B.C.), who wrote the satyr play *Cyclops*. The satyr plays were developed into comedies in the plays of **Aristophanes** (448–380 B.C.). By the end of the 300s B.C. comedy had become more important, and one of the major writers of this genre was the comic dramatist **Menander** (c. 343–291 B.C.).

As the Roman Empire spread south the Romans witnessed Greek theater and adopted many of its characteristics. Despite this, Roman theater differed greatly from Greek theater. Similar to other Roman entertainment, such as gladiator contests, their theater became nothing more than a popular spectacle and was usually extremely cruel. Actors were often no more than slaves and were even killed in some plays.

As the Christian church became established this kind of theater fell by the wayside, and by A.D. 4 Christians were soon forbidden to attend or take part in theatrical performances. Actors, acrobats, wrestlers, jugglers, and ballad singers had to travel around as lone players, performing at special occasions such as weddings and baptisms.

▶ Greek theaters evolved into a semicircle of seats surrounding a flat circular area. By 500 B.C. this stone amphitheater became the standard arrangement for Greek theaters.

ACTORS AND ACTRESSES

▲ Nell Gwyn became the mistress of King Charles II of England.

Nell Gwyn

1650–1687

Nell Gwyn, a popular English comic actress, became involved in the theater when she began selling oranges as a teenager at the King's Theater in London, England. Spotted by the actor, Charles Hart, she entered the profession in 1665 and appeared at the Theater Royal in London and in parts written for her by the poet, John Dryden (1631–1700). English diarist Samuel Pepys (p. 108) called her "pretty, witty Nell," and she earned many admirers, including Charles II (1630–1685). Nell became one of his many mistresses and retired from acting in 1669 when she became pregnant. She bore him two sons, James and Charles Beauclerk. The king was very fond of Nell, and on his deathbed he asked his brother James to "let not poor Nellie starve."

English comic actress 1665–1669; mistress of Charles II 1669–1685

David Garrick

1717–1779

Garrick went to London in 1737 with his friend Samuel Johnson (p. 109). After playing small roles he became an overnight sensation in 1742 as Shakespeare's Richard III. Garrick introduced a refreshing, natural style of acting that made him very popular. In 1747 he bought and became the manager of Drury Lane Theater in London. Garrick's reforms, such as the notion of sets and hidden lighting—foundations of modern-day theater.

Notable plays as actor: *Richard III* 1742. Notable plays as writer: *Miss in Her Teens* 1747; *Bon Ton* 1775

Edmund Kean

1789–1833

One of England's greatest tragic actors, Kean was famous for his portrayals of villains in Shakespearean plays. As a teenager he became a strolling player and married fellow player Mary Chambers in 1808. His big break came in 1814, when he appeared at London's Drury Lane Theater as Shylock in Shakespeare's *The Merchant of Venice*. Kean excelled in roles such as Hamlet, Macbeth, and Richard III, acting in England and the U.S. English poet Samuel Taylor Coleridge (p. 119) said of Kean, "To see him act is like reading Shakespeare by flashes of lightning." However, Kean's popularity suffered when he was sued for adultery in 1825, and his audiences became hostile and violent. Othello was his final role. He collapsed during the performance and died two months later.

Notable plays: *The Merchant of Venice*, *Macbeth*, and *Richard III* 1814–1825

P.T. Barnum

1810–1891

Born in Connecticut, America's greatest showman, Phineas Taylor Barnum, became famous for his "freak shows." The public flocked to see attractions like the bearded lady, Siamese twins, or the popular dwarf General Tom Thumb at Barnum's American Museum in New York City, which opened in 1842. Tom Thumb was Charles Stratton (1838–1883), aged five. Barnum also successfully managed the American tour of a genuine talent, the Swedish soprano Jenny Lind (1820–1887), in 1850. His "Greatest Show on Earth" circus opened in Brooklyn in 1871. A decade later he joined with his rival, James A. Bailey (1847–1906), to create the Barnum and Bailey circus. A huge self-publicist, he wrote several autobiographies, and just before he died he asked the newspapers to write his obituary early so that he could read it.

Opened American Museum 1842. Notable show: "Greatest Show on Earth" 1871

► P. T. Barnum advertised his circus using colorful publicity posters.

Sarah Bernhardt

1844–1923

Sarah Bernhardt studied at the Paris Conservatoire drama school. Despite making her acting debut in 1862, her talent was not fully recognized until 1869, when she played the minstrel character Zanetto in *Le Passant*. She also won acclaim when she played the Queen of Spain in *Ruy Blas* in 1872. Sarah performed at the Comédie Française (1872–1880), where she was impressive as Racine's Phèdre. She began touring in 1880, acting in England, the U.S., and Denmark. She bought a theater in 1898, renaming it Théâtre Sarah Bernhardt. Despite having a leg amputated in 1915, she continued acting until 1922.

Notable plays: *Le Passant* 1869; *Ruy Blas* 1872; *Phèdre* 1877; *La Dame aux amélias* 1884

Lillie Langtry

1853–1929

Born in the English Channel Islands, Lillie Langtry was the daughter of the dean of the island of Jersey. Marriage to Edward Langtry in 1874 took Lillie to the English mainland. There she was painted by Sir John Millais (p. 161) and nicknamed "the Jersey Lily." She had many admirers, most notably Prince Albert Edward (later Edward VII [1841–1910]). Lillie took to the stage in 1881 to achieve independence after her husband's financial failure and became a popular actress. She opened the Imperial Theater in London in 1901 and also lived in the U.S., where she opened wineries and bred racehorses, becoming a millionaire. Her husband died in 1897, and she married Hugo de Bathe in 1899. Lillie's final stage performance was in 1917.

Notable play: *Lady Windermere's Fan* written for her by Oscar Wilde 1892

Charlie Chaplin

1889–1977

Born in London, England, comedy actor and director Charlie Chaplin was the son of vaudeville entertainers. His father died of alcohol abuse, and his mother was often in mental institutions.

Although Chaplin spent his childhood in poorhouses and orphanages, he pursued his show-business ambitions, and by the age of eight he was clog dancing with the "Eight Lancashire Lads." His ticket to fame came when he joined Fred Karno's vaudeville troupe at the age of 17. While they were touring the U.S. in 1912 he was spotted by the king of slapstick comedy, Mack Sennett (1880–1960). Sennett's Keystone Studios signed him up, and Chaplin's career on the big screen began. His silent movie debut was in the popular *Making a Living* (1914). Audiences loved Chaplin, and it was *The Tramp* (1915) that established the moustache, bowler hat, baggy trousers, swinging cane, and flat-footed walk of his famous trademark character. He made many popular comedies, including *Easy Street* and *The Immigrant,* for various movie companies. His first full-length feature was the classic *The Kid* (1921). In 1919 he founded United Artists with D. W. Griffith (1875–1948), Mary Pickford (p. 135), and Douglas Fairbanks, Sr. (right), and he went on to create some of his best comedies, such as *The Gold Rush* (1925) and *The Circus* (1928). Although sound cinema began in 1927, Chaplin continued using mime in movies such as *Modern Times* (1936).

Notable movies: *The Tramp* 1915; *Easy Street* 1917; *The Kid* 1921; *The Gold Rush* 1924; *Modern Times* 1936; *The Great Dictator* 1940

► *The Great Dictator*, a satirical movie based on Adolf Hitler (1940), was Chaplin's first "talkie."

W.C. FIELDS 1880–1946
One of America's greatest comedians, Fields developed a vaudeville juggling act, starring in the Ziegfeld Follies on Broadway between 1915 and 1921. He achieved true stardom with the advent of sound, where his nasally voice, pomposity, and stiff delivery of funny quips could truly thrive. He moved to Hollywood in 1931 and wrote, directed, and acted in most of his movies.

DOUGLAS FAIRBANKS, SR. 1883–1939
Born in Colorado, Fairbanks began acting in 1901, and by 1914 he had made a name for himself on Broadway. His first movie was *The Lamb* (1915), and by 1917 he had formed his own production company. During the 1920s he reigned as "King of Hollywood," starring in popular movies as the dynamic, dashing hero. In 1919 he cofounded United Artists.

BORIS KARLOFF 1887–1969
Born William Pratt, Karloff emigrated from England to Canada in 1909. There he began acting in plays with a touring company. Soon he headed to Hollywood, and by 1918 he was playing minor roles in movies. He achieved initial recognition as a villain in Howard Hawks' *The Criminal Code*, but his big career break was in *Frankenstein* in 1931.

EDWARD G. ROBINSON 1893–1973
At the age of 10 Edward G. Robinson emigrated to the U.S. from Romania. He attended the American Academy of Dramatic Arts and made his Broadway debut in 1915. He began appearing in movies with the advent of sound. His most famous role was playing the gangster mob boss, Rico, in *Little Caesar* (1930).

Laurel and Hardy

Stan Laurel 1890–1965
Oliver Hardy 1892–1957

Skinny guy Stan Laurel and tubby partner Oliver Hardy were movie's first great comedy team. Laurel was born in Ulverston, England, and Hardy hailed from Harlem, Georgia.

Laurel grew up around music halls and performed in vaudeville. He arrived in the U.S. at the age of 20 as a member of a musical comedy troupe, and by 1917 he was acting in movies. Hardy had been working in silent comedies since 1913, but prior to that he had also performed in vaudeville acts. Both became members of Hal Roach's Hollywood studio in 1926. *Putting Pants on Philip* (1927) was their first comedy hit, and they became a famous duo, regularly getting into "another fine mess." Together they made over 100 movies and were known as "The Boys."

Notable movies: *Putting Pants on Philip* 1927; *Sons of the Desert* 1934; *Way Out West* 1937; *The Music Box* 1932; *Blockheads* 1938

◀ Laurel and Hardy became one of the most successful comedy duos in the history of motion pictures.

Marx Brothers

Chico 1891–1961
Harpo 1893–1964
Groucho 1895–1977
Zeppo 1901–1979

The Marx Brothers were an American comedy team who began performing vaudeville acts in 1908. By 1914 they were nicknamed Chico, Harpo, Groucho, and Zeppo. Their improvisational style, wisecracks, and ridiculing of conventional society made them popular. Early stage successes included the Broadway plays *I'll Say She Is* (1924) and *Animal Crackers* (1928). By the late 1920s they began making successful movie adaptations of their many stage plays.

Notable movies: *Animal Crackers* and *Monkey Business* both 1932; *Duck Soup* 1933; *A Night at the Opera* 1935; *A Day at the Races* 1937; *Go West* 1940

Mae West

1893–1980

An actress, playwright, and scriptwriter, Brooklyn-born blond bombshell Mae West's witty one-liners are still quoted today. West performed in burlesque and vaudeville as a teenager, and by 1911 she made her Broadway debut as an entertainer. In 1926 West was imprisoned for obscenity following her scandalous Broadway show *Sex*. Her 1928 play *Diamond Lil* brought success, and Paramount studios soon snapped her up. West first wowed movie audiences with her performance in *Night after Night* (1932). Her early movies are still considered her best.

Notable movies: *She Done Him Wrong* 1933; *I'm No Angel* 1933; *Klondyke Annie* 1934; *My Little Chickadee* 1940; *Myra Breckenridge* 1970

► One of Buster Keaton's most notable movies was *The General* (1927).

Rudolph Valentino

1895–1926

Born in Italy, Valentino emigrated to the U.S. in 1913, and while in New York City he made a living as a dancer. Five years later he moved to Hollywood and achieved stardom as Julio in *The Four Horsemen of the Apocalypse* (1921). He became the handsome, exotic "great Latin lover" and was adored by many. Valentino's tragically premature death was caused by a perforated ulcer.

Notable movies: *The Sheikh* 1921; *Blood and Sand* 1922; *The Eagle* 1925; *The Son of the Sheikh* 1926

▲ Rudolph Valentino in *The Sheikh*.

Buster Keaton

1895–1966

U.S. actor Buster Keaton learned comedy and acrobatic stunts from his parents' vaudeville act. His movie debut was in *The Butcher Boy* (1917), and by 1921 he was scripting, directing, and starring in his movies. He signed to MGM Studios in 1929 and lost popularity, but he made a comeback in the 1940s. He received an Oscar in 1959 for "his unique talents."

Notable movies: *The Saphead* 1920; *The Navigator* 1924; *The General* 1927; *Steamboat Bill* 1927

Humphrey Bogart

1899–1957

Born in New York City, Bogart began acting on Broadway after World War I. His success led to movie roles, but it was not until 1941 that leading roles in *High Sierra* and *The Maltese Falcon* revealed his true talent. "Bogie" rarely appeared in a bad movie, and he played cynical tough guys with hearts of gold.

Notable movies: *Casablanca* 1942; *The Big Sleep* 1946; *Key Largo* 1948; *The African Queen* (for which he won an Oscar) 1951

MARY PICKFORD 1893–1979
Canadian-born actress Mary Pickford became one of the first Hollywood silent movie stars, appearing in almost 200 movies and earning the title "America's Sweetheart." She shot to movie stardom in 1914, wowing audiences as the angelic heroine of the silent screen. During the 1920s her popularity soared, and she won an Academy Award for the movie *Coquette* (1929).

HAROLD LLOYD 1893–1971
Born in Nebraska, Lloyd settled in San Diego, where he joined a drama school. He began taking minor roles in screen comedies, and in 1915 he joined Hal Roach's company. Doing his own stunts, Lloyd developed various popular characters—the bum Willie Work, Lonesome Luke, and in 1917 the bespectacled *The Glass Character*. He starred in over 100 short- and 11 full-length movies.

SPENCER TRACY 1900–1967
After attending the American Academy of Dramatic Arts, Spencer Tracy acted with various touring companies. While playing on Broadway in 1930 he was spotted by a Hollywood director and went on to play a wide variety of screen roles, costarring with Katharine Hepburn (p. 139) in nine movies. He was the first actor to win an Oscar two years in a row.

CLAUDETTE COLBERT 1903–1996
Claudette Colbert was born in Paris, France, and moved to New York City in 1910. She appeared in over 60 movies, most famously as the spoiled, rich runaway, Ellie Andrews, in *It Happened One Night* (1934), for which she and costar Clark Gable won Oscars. She is best remembered as a sophisticated comedienne in comedies from the 1930s and 1940s.

Fred Astaire

1899–1987

Born in Omaha, Nebraska, Fred Astaire's first dance partner was his sister, Adele. In their teens they became a popular vaudeville act and had great success on Broadway. By the 1920s they were international stage stars. Adele got married and retired in 1932, and Fred moved to Hollywood, where he partnered with Ginger Rogers (p. 139).

Flying Down to Rio (1933) was Fred Astaire and Ginger Rogers' on-screen dancing debut, their natural rapport making them an instant hit. They starred in ten movies together, taking the big screen's musical comedy to very sophisticated heights. Astaire retired in 1946, but he returned two years later to join Judy Garland in *Easter Parade*. In later years Astaire acted on television and in movies. In 1981 he received a Lifetime Achievement Award from the American Film Institute.

Notable movies: *The Gay Divorcée* 1934; *Top Hat* 1935; *Swing Time* 1936; *Easter Parade* 1948; *Funny Face* 1956; *The Towering Inferno* 1974

◀ Fred Astaire and Ginger Rogers dance their way through the smash hit movie *Flying Down to Rio* (1933).

James Cagney

1899–1986

Cagney grew up on New York City's Lower East Side and joined vaudeville in 1920 as a singer and dancer. In 1929 he made his successful Broadway debut in the musical *Penny Arcade*. Signed up to Warners, he made his name playing a ruthless gangster in the box-office hit *Public Enemy*. The true breadth of his talents were displayed in his portrayal of an entertainer in *Yankee Doodle Dandy*.

Notable movies: *Public Enemy* 1931; *Angels with Dirty Faces* 1938; *Yankee Doodle Dandy* 1942

Clark Gable

1901–1960

American actor Clark Gable began his career on the stage and took small movie roles in Hollywood in 1924. He was signed to MGM Studios in 1934 and became so popular that he was called "King of Hollywood." Gable is best remembered as Rhett Butler, the lead in *Gone with the Wind*. Gable won an Oscar for his role in *It Happened One Night*.

Notable movies: *It Happened One Night* 1934; *Gone with the Wind* 1939; *Mogambo* 1953; *The Misfits* 1961

▼ Clark Gable starred with Vivien Leigh (p. 139) in *Gone With the Wind.*

Gary Cooper

1901–1961

Gary Cooper grew up on a ranch in Montana and learned how to ride horses as a young boy. He used this skill as an actor, first as a cowboy extra in silent movies and later as the strong but silent hero in classic Westerns.

Cooper was initially spotted while playing a minor role in *The Winning of Barbara Worth* (1926). His first leading role was in Ernest Hemingway's *A Farewell to Arms* (1933). He also appeared in gangster and war movies. He won Oscars for *Sergeant York* and *High Noon*.

Notable movies: *Mr. Deeds Goes to Town* 1936; *For Whom the Bell Tolls* 1943; *Sergeant York* 1941; *High Noon* 1952

▼ Gary Cooper and Grace Kelly starred in the classic Western *High Noon*.

Marlene Dietrich

1901–1992

Born in Berlin, Germany, Marlene Dietrich was a cabaret singer and appeared in German silent movies. Her career took off in 1930 when Josef Von Sternberg (1894–1969) cast her as cabaret singer Lola in *The Blue Angel*. She moved to Hollywood and became a top movie star, often playing the bad woman. Her role in *Destry Rides Again* revealed her talent as a comedienne.

Notable movies: *The Blue Angel* 1930; *Morocco* 1930; *Shanghai Express* 1932; *Destry Rides Again* 1939

Jean Gabin

1904–1976

French actor Jean Gabin worked in construction before becoming an entertainer in music halls and theaters. *Chacun sa chance* (1930) was his big-screen debut; *Maria Chapdelaine* (1934) was his first big French success; and *Pépé le Moko* (1936) won him international fame. His career in French movies peaked during the late 1930s. He often played noble, ill-fated losers.

Notable movies: *La Grande Illusion* 1937; *La Bête Humaine* 1938; *Quai des Brumes* 1938; *Le Jour Se Lève* 1939

RALPH RICHARDSON 1902–1983

Skilled in Shakespearean and modern plays, English actor Ralph Richardson made his stage debut in 1921. He joined the Old Vic in London, England, in 1930, where fellow actors included John Gielgud (p. 138) and Laurence Olivier (p. 138). He made over 70 movies, including *Anna Karenina* (1948), *A Long Day's Journey into Night* (1962), and *A Doll's House* (1973).

BOB HOPE b. 1903

Born in England, Bob Hope moved to the United States in 1907. He started out in vaudeville as a comedian and singer, and by the late 1920s he was on Broadway. "Thanks for the Memory" became his theme tune after he sang it in his big-screen debut, *The Big Broadcast* (1938). His movie career peaked when he starred in the seven *Road to . . .* comedies with Bing Crosby (1904–1977).

HENRY FONDA 1905–1982

Nebraska-born Fonda headed to New York City in 1928 to pursue an acting career. By 1934 he was on Broadway, where his first major success was *The Farmer Takes a Wife* (1935). On the big screen Fonda was the epitome of the American hero, starring in over 100 movies, notably *Young Mr. Lincoln* (1939), *The Grapes of Wrath* (1940), *Twelve Angry Men* (1957), and *On Golden Pond* (1981).

JOHN WAYNE 1907–1979

Wayne played the all-American, tough-guy hero in Westerns and war epics. While in college in California he met director John Ford. He began acting as a movie extra under the name Duke Morrison, but it was Ford's Western *Stagecoach* (1939) that brought him stardom. Other notable movies include *Red River* (1948), *Sands of Iwo Jima* (1949), *The Searchers* (1956), and *True Grit* (1969).

▼ Cary Grant played the hero in Alfred Hitchcock's *North by Northwest.*

Cary Grant

1904–1986

Cary Grant, born Archibald Leach, left England when he joined an acrobatic comedy troupe as a teenager. After touring the U.S. in 1920 the young actor moved there. He soon appeared in a number of stage musicals before heading to Hollywood, where he changed his name. His big-screen debut was in *This Is the Night* (1932). Although he achieved success as the male lead in comedies, his more serious roles in Hitchcock's thrillers were some of his best.

Notable movies: *Bringing up Baby* 1938; *His Girl Friday* 1940; *Suspicion* 1951; *Notorious* 1946; *To Catch a Thief* 1955; *North by Northwest* 1959

John Gielgud

1904–2000

English actor John Gielgud studied at London's Royal Academy of Dramatic Art. His acting debut, a minor role at London's Old Vic Theater, was in 1921, and by 1929 he was impressing audiences with his portrayals of Shakespearean leads such as Hamlet, Richard III, and Macbeth. Recognized as a superb actor and director, he won acclaim for performances in plays such as Anton Chekhov's (p. 121) *The Seagull.* He also starred in over 80 movies.

Notable stage roles: *The Cherry Orchard* 1954; *The Chalk Garden* 1956
Notable movies: *Arthur* 1981; *Prospero's Books* 1991

Greta Garbo

1905–1990

Swedish actress Greta Garbo was discovered by director Mauritz Stiller (1883–1928) when she was working as a young store assistant. She studied drama in Stockholm, Sweden, and her first major movie role was in *The Story of Gösta Berling* (1924). She moved to Hollywood in 1925. A mysterious figure of the silent movies, she made a smooth transition to sound. She moved to New York City in 1951 and became a total recluse for the rest of her life.

Notable movies: *Flesh and the Devil* 1927; *Anna Christie* 1930; *Queen Christina* 1938; *Ninotchka* 1939

Laurence Olivier

1907–1989

One of the 20th century's finest actors, Laurence Olivier became a member of the Old Vic in London, England, from 1937. On stage he played all the major Shakespearean roles. Appearing in almost 60 movies, some of which he directed, his role in *Wuthering Heights* (1939) made him a Hollywood matinée idol.

Notable stage roles: *Othello* 1964; *The Entertainer* 1957
Notable movies: *Henry V* 1945; *Hamlet* 1948; *Richard III* 1955; *Sleuth* 1972

▲ Laurence Olivier in *The Entertainer.*

Bette Davis

1908–1989

American actress Bette Davis began on Broadway and moved into movies in 1931. She achieved stardom in *The Man Who Played God* (1932), becoming a popular movie star and excelling in melodramatic performances in a career that spanned 58 years. Nominated for ten Academy Awards, she won two Oscars for *Dangerous* (1935) and *Jezebel* (1938).

Notable movies: *Now, Voyager* 1942; *All About Eve* 1950; *Whatever Happened to Baby Jane* 1962

James Stewart

1908–1997

After studying architecture at Princeton University, James Stewart began acting on Broadway and was soon playing in small movie roles. His career took off when he starred in director Frank Capra's (1897–1991) big hit, *Mr. Smith Goes to Washington* (1939). He won an Oscar for his performance as a reporter in *The Philadelphia Story* in 1940. During the 1950s he starred in Westerns and several Alfred Hitchcock thrillers.

Notable movies: *Destry Rides Again* 1940; *It's a Wonderful Life* 1946; *Rear Window* 1954; *Vertigo* 1958

▲ James Stewart (left) in *Harvey.*

Katharine Hepburn

b. 1907

Born in Hartford, Connecticut, Katharine Hepburn began her career on stage in Baltimore, Maryland, in 1928. After acting on Broadway her big-screen career took off in 1932. She starred in many notable movies, including *Morning Glory* (1933) and *Bringing up Baby* (1938), collecting 12 Oscar nominations and four Academy Awards. She also enjoyed a 25-year partnership, on and offscreen, with the actor Spencer Tracy (p. 135).

Notable movies: *The African Queen* 1951; *On Golden Pond* 1981

▲ Errol Flynn in *The Adventures of Robin Hood.*

Errol Flynn

1909–1959

Born in Australia, Flynn was first cast as Fletcher Christian in the Australian movie *In the Wake of the Bounty* (1933). He then joined an English repertory company. Signed by Warner Bros., he hit the big time starring as a pirate in *Captain Blood* (1935). Flynn became famous for playing the dashing hero of romantic, historical, action-adventure movies.

Notable films: *The Charge of the Light Brigade* 1936; *The Adventures of Robin Hood* 1938; *The Sea Hawk* 1940

PAUL HENREID 1908–1992
Austrian-born Henreid first began a career as a book designer in Vienna, Austria. He moved on to acting school, where he was discovered by director Otto Preminger (1906–1986). In the 1930s, to escape the Nazis, Henreid moved to England, where he appeared in wartime movies. He made his Hollywood debut in 1941 and is best known for his roles in *Now, Voyager*, and *Casablanca* (both 1942).

JEAN HARLOW 1911–1937
Born in Kansas City, Kansas, Jean Harlow moved to Los Angeles at the age of 16. She first appeared as a screen siren in Hal Roach's silent comedies, including *Double Whoopie* (1929) with Laurel and Hardy. Success followed with Howard Hawkes' sound version of *Hell's Angels* (1930). A talented comedienne, she starred alongside Clark Gable in six movies. Her personal life was beset with scandal.

GINGER ROGERS 1911–1995
By the age of 14 Ginger Rogers was performing in vaudeville and made her Broadway debut in *Top Speed* in 1929. She moved to Hollywood, where in 1933 she starred in *Flying Down to Rio* with Fred Astaire (p. 136). The pair successfully went on to dance together in another nine movies. In 1940 Rogers won an Oscar for her solo performance in *Kitty Foyle*.

VIVIEN LEIGH 1913–1967
Born in India, British stage and screen actress Vivien Leigh is best remembered as southern belle Scarlett O'Hara in the romantic epic *Gone with the Wind* (1939), for which she won an Oscar. She married English actor Laurence Olivier (p. 138) in 1940. Other notable movies included *Anna Karenina* (1948) and *A Streetcar Named Desire* (1951), for which she won a second Oscar.

Gene Kelly

1912–1996

Actor, dancer, choreographer, and director, Gene Kelly began dancing in vaudeville as a boy, appearing with his siblings as "The Five Kellys."

While studying economics at the University of Pittsburgh, Kelly taught dance at the family-run dance studio he set up in 1932. He headed for Broadway in 1938, appearing in several shows. His performance in *Pal Joey* (1940) led to Hollywood movie offers, and in 1944 *For Me and My Girl* became his hit debut. The handsome and athletic Kelly became the star and choreographer in major musicals, for which he won a special Oscar in 1951. His career peaked in 1952 with the popular classic, *Singin' in the Rain*.

Notable movies: *Ziegfeld Follies* 1946; *The Three Musketeers* 1948; *On the Town* 1949; *An American in Paris* 1951; *Singin' in the Rain* 1952

◀ Gene Kelly (right) and the young Frank Sinatra (p. 189) sang and danced their way through *Anchors Aweigh* (1945).

Ingrid Bergman

1915–1982

Stockholm-born actress Ingrid Bergman made her Swedish movie debut in *Munkbrogreven* (1934). She was signed by MGM Studios in 1936 and had many successes in the 1940s, including *Casablanca*. In 1944 she won an Oscar for *Gaslight*. After living in Italy she returned to Hollywood in 1956, winning another Oscar for her role in *Anastasia*. In 1974 she earned a third Oscar for *Murder on the Orient Express*.

Notable movies: *Casablanca* 1942; *Gaslight* 1944; *Spellbound* 1945; *Notorious* 1946; *Anastasia* 1956

◀ Kirk Douglas as Spartacus.

Kirk Douglas

b. 1916

Born Issur Daniel Demsky to poverty-stricken, Russian-Jewish immigrants in the U.S., Douglas started acting on Broadway in 1941. His Hollywood big-screen debut was in *The Strange Love of Martha Ivers* (1946), and in 1949 he shot to fame playing a boxer in *Champion*. He formed his own production company in 1955 and has appeared in over 80 movies. He received an American Film Academy Life Achievement Award in 1991.

Notable movies: *Champion* 1949; *The Bad and the Beautiful* 1952; *Lust for Life* 1956; *Spartacus* 1960

Gregory Peck

b. 1916

Tall, dark, and handsome actor Gregory Peck was born in San Diego. An only child, he was raised by his grandmother. He enrolled at the University of Berkeley but left to pursue his acting ambitions at New York City's Neighborhood Playhouse. His Broadway debut was in *The Morning Star* (1942), and one year later he appeared in his first Hollywood movie. It was his second movie, *The Keys of the Kingdom* (1944), that propelled him to stardom. Peck was often cast as honest, heroic characters with integrity. His Oscar-winning portrayal of the fair lawyer, Atticus Finch, in *To Kill a Mockingbird* is his most famous role. In 1989 he received an American Film Academy Lifetime Achievement Award.

Notable movies: *Spellbound* 1945; *The Gunfighter* 1950; *To Kill a Mockingbird* 1962; *The Omen* 1976; *Cape Fear* 1991

▼ Gregory Peck in *The Gunfighter*.

Marcello Mastroianni

1923–1996

Italian Marcello Mastroianni was working as a draftsman in Rome when he was captured and imprisoned by the Nazis during World War II. He escaped and hid in Venice, Italy. After the war he became an accountant for a movie company and began acting with a drama group. Director Luchino Visconti (1906–1976) spotted him and put him in many of his stage productions. *Miserabili, I* (1947) was Mastroianni's big-screen debut, but it was Visconti's *Le Notte Bianchi* (*White Nights* 1957) that made him famous in Italy. He achieved international recognition and stardom in his leading role as a world-weary, disillusioned columnist in Fellini's classic, *La Dolce Vita*.

Notable movies: *La Dolce Vita* 1960; *Divorce—Italian Style* 1962; *8½* 1963

Robert Mitchum

1917–1997

Brawny, droopy-eyed actor Robert Mitchum's acting career spanned 50 years. He began in amateur dramatics and went on to become a major Hollywood star of the 1940s and 1950s. Mitchum was still appearing in television miniseries in the early 1980s. A drifter and a vagrant in his youth, he worked various menial jobs. Early movie roles included the *Hopalong Cassidy* Westerns. In 1945 fame beckoned when he was nominated for a Best Supporting Actor Oscar for his performance of Lt. Walker in *The Story of G.I. Joe*. Mitchum's laid-back manner was unique. He starred in romantic dramas and played the tough guy in Westerns, actions, and war movies.

Notable movies: *The Story of G.I. Joe* 1945; *River of No Return* 1954; *The Night of the Hunter* 1955; *Cape Fear* 1962, 1991; *Ryan's Daughter* 1970; *Farewell, My Lovely* 1975

Judy Garland

1922–1969

American actress and singer Judy Garland is legendary for singing "Somewhere Over the Rainbow" as the young Dorothy in the magical musical, *The Wizard of Oz*. A child actor, she first performed with her sisters in a vaudeville act. *Broadway Melody* (1938) launched her movie career, and *The Wizard of Oz*, for which she won a Juvenile Oscar, made her a fully-fledged star. She appeared in two successful musicals directed by Vincent Minnelli, whom she married. Their daughter, Liza Minnelli (b. 1946), is an actress and singer. Garland died of a drug overdose.

Notable movies: *The Wizard of Oz* 1939; *Meet Me in St. Louis* 1944; *Easter Parade* 1948; *A Star is Born* 1954

◄ Judy Garland, born Frances Gumm, became a child star as Dorothy in *The Wizard of Oz*.

Marlon Brando

b. 1924

Born in Omaha, Nebraska, Marlon Brando learned Stanislavsky's Method technique at Lee Strasberg's New York City Actors' Studio. He first won critical acclaim for his Broadway performance in *A Streetcar Named Desire* (1947). Moving to movies, Brando was the white T-shirt, leather-clad rebel in *The Wild One* and won an Oscar as he tough guy in *On the Waterfront*. Brando's career dipped during the 1960s, but he made a spectacular return to form as the Mafia don Vito Corleone in *The Godfather*, but he refused an Oscar as a protest on behalf of Native Americans.

Notable movies: *The Wild One* 1953; *On the Waterfront* 1954; *The Godfather* 1972; *Last Tango in Paris* 1973; *Apocalypse Now* 1979

◀ Marlon Brando shot to fame as the motorcycling rebel in *The Wild One* (1953).

Sidney Poitier

b. 1924

Sidney Poitier was born in Miami but was raised in the Bahamas. He studied at New York City's American Negro Theater and made his screen debut in 1950. Poitier was Oscar-nominated for *The Defiant Ones* (1958) and finally struck gold as Homer Smith in *Lilies of the Field*. He was the first African American to win an Academy Award. He often plays eloquent and intelligent characters, fighting prejudice with dignity rather than aggression.

Notable movies: *The Defiant Ones* 1958; *Lilies of the Field* 1963; *Guess Who's Coming to Dinner* 1967; *In the Heat of the Night* 1967

Richard Burton

1925–1984

Welsh actor Richard Burton was the son of a coal miner. Born Richard Jenkins, Burton was encouraged to study English by his teacher Philip Burton. He adopted the name Burton at Oxford University, where he began acting. His first leading movie role was in *My Cousin Rachel* (1952). Continuing to act onstage, he also made many successful movies. While costarring with Elizabeth Taylor (p. 145) in *Cleopatra* in 1963, they fell in love and got married twice, becoming a highly publicized movie-star couple.

Notable movies: *The Robe* 1953; *Look Back in Anger* 1959; *Becket* 1964; *Who's Afraid of Virginia Woolf* 1966

Paul Newman

b. 1925

American actor Paul Newman made his Broadway debut in the play *Picnic* (1953) and became one of the biggest movie stars of the 1960s. In 1956 he won acclaim for his performance in *Somebody Up There Likes Me*. The first of nine Oscar nominations came in 1958 for *Cat on a Hot Tin Roof*. He finally won an Oscar in 1986 for his performance in *The Color of Money*.

Notable movies: *The Hustler* 1961; *Hud* 1963; *Cool Hand Luke* 1967; *Butch Cassidy and the Sundance Kid* 1969; *The Sting* 1973; *The Color of Money* 1986

Klaus Kinski

1926–1991

After serving in the German army during World War II, Kinski toured as an actor. He appeared in over 120 German and American movies over a 40-year period and thrived on playing evil characters, starring in several movies directed by Werner Herzog (p. 151).

Notable movies: *Nosferatu* 1979; *Fitzcarraldo* 1982; *Cobra Verde* 1987

Marilyn Monroe

1926–1962

Legendary movie star Marilyn Monroe, the most famous blond of all time, shot to fame in the 1950s. The young Norma Jean Baker spent an unhappy childhood in Los Angeles' foster homes because of her mother's mental illness and hospitalization. Norma Jean was spotted by movie studios while she was modeling, and she became a blond starlet, changing her name to Marilyn Monroe.

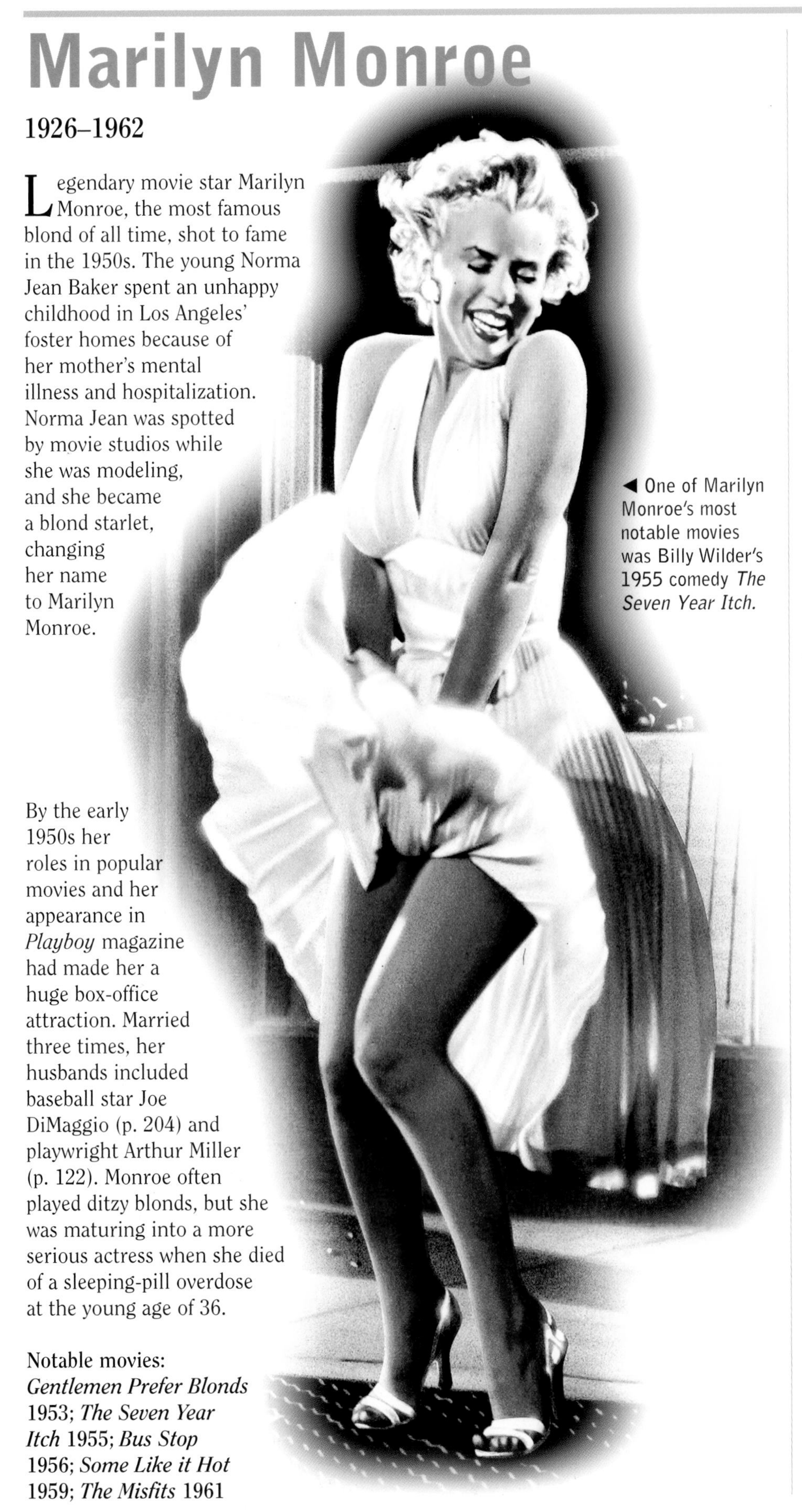

◀ One of Marilyn Monroe's most notable movies was Billy Wilder's 1955 comedy *The Seven Year Itch.*

By the early 1950s her roles in popular movies and her appearance in *Playboy* magazine had made her a huge box-office attraction. Married three times, her husbands included baseball star Joe DiMaggio (p. 204) and playwright Arthur Miller (p. 122). Monroe often played ditzy blonds, but she was maturing into a more serious actress when she died of a sleeping-pill overdose at the young age of 36.

Notable movies: *Gentlemen Prefer Blonds* 1953; *The Seven Year Itch* 1955; *Bus Stop* 1956; *Some Like it Hot* 1959; *The Misfits* 1961

Shirley Temple

b. 1928

An American child movie star of the 1930s, Shirley Temple's first movie, at the age of three, was *War Babies* (1932). By 1934 she was considered a true star as she sang and tap-danced her way through several movies, including *Little Miss Marker* and *Bright Eyes,* in which she sang the hit, "On the Good Ship Lollipop." As a teenager her movies were less popular, and she retired in 1949. She entered politics during the late 1960s, becoming an ambassador for the U.S. government.

Notable movies: *Bright Eyes* 1934; *Poor Little Rich Girl* 1936; *Heidi* 1937; *Rebecca of Sunnybrook Farm* 1938

Grace Kelly

1929–1982

Grace Kelly was born into one of Philadelphia's wealthiest families. She studied at the American Academy of Dramatic Arts in New York City and appeared on television and Broadway before her screen debut in 1951. Kelly played the elegant, enigmatic blond in three Alfred Hitchcock (p. 149) thrillers, and she won an Oscar for *Country Girl* (1954). In 1956 she married Prince Rainier and became Princess Grace of Monaco. She died in a car crash.

Notable movies: *High Noon* 1952; *Dial M for Murder* 1953; *Rear Window* 1954; *To Catch a Thief* 1955; *High Society* 1956

Audrey Hepburn

1929–1993

Actress Audrey Hepburn was the daughter of an English banker and a Dutch baroness. Born in Brussels, Belgium, she attended private schools and studied ballet in London, England. She began appearing in movies from 1948 and in 1951 was cast as the lead in the Broadway adaptation of Colette's novel, *Gigi*. Her big movie break was in *Roman Holiday*, for which she won an Oscar and critical acclaim. Audiences admired her elegance and sophistication. She was unforgettable as Holly Golightly in *Breakfast at Tiffany's* and Eliza Doolittle in *My Fair Lady*. In the 1970s she became an ambassador for UNICEF.

Notable movies: *Roman Holiday* 1953; *Sabrina* 1954; *Funny Face* 1957; *Breakfast at Tiffany's* 1961; *My Fair Lady* 1964; *Always* 1989

◀ Audrey Hepburn starred with George Peppard (1928–1994) in *Breakfast at Tiffany's* (1961).

Steve McQueen

1930–1980

Before studying acting in New York City, Steve McQueen spent time in reform schools and the U.S. Marines. *Somebody Up There Likes Me* was his screen debut in 1956, and between 1958 and 1961 he appeared in the television Western series *Wanted: Dead or Alive*. When McQueen costarred as a gunslinger in *The Magnificent Seven*, his action-hero screen persona was established. Offscreen, McQueen loved racing bikes and cars and often performed his own stunts, including the legendary car chase in *Bullitt*. He was married to *The Getaway* costar Ali McGraw (b. 1938).

Notable movies: *The Magnificent Seven* 1960; *The Great Escape* 1963; *The Cincinnati Kid* 1965; *Bullitt* 1968; *The Getaway* 1972

Sean Connery

b. 1930

Actor Sean Connery made his name playing Ian Fleming's secret agent 007, the suave, martini-sipping James Bond. The son of working-class parents from Edinburgh, Scotland, Connery left school at the age of 13 and briefly joined the British Royal Navy. He had many jobs, including as a manual laborer, lifeguard, and as a model for art classes, and he came third in a Mr. Universe contest. In 1953 his physique landed him a chorus part in the stage musical *South Pacific*. More stage and television roles followed, including *Requiem for a Heavyweight* (1956). He was cast as James Bond in *Dr. No* (1962) and achieved international success, playing Bond a total of seven times. Featuring in over 60 movies, Connery has also played many other characters with great success. He won a Best Supporting Actor Oscar for his portrayal of an Irish-American policeman in *The Untouchables* (1987). He continues to act and produce and is proudly nationalistic, supporting many Scottish causes. He is also a highly competitive golfer.

Notable movies: *From Russia with Love* 1963; *Goldfinger* 1964; *Marnie* 1964; *Thunderball* 1965; *The Hill* 1965; *You Only Live Twice* 1967; *Diamonds Are Forever* 1971; *Never Say Never Again* 1983; *Highlander* 1986; *The Name of the Rose* 1987; *Indiana Jones and the Last Crusade* 1989; *Hunt for Red October* 1990; *The Russia House* 1991

▶ Sean Connery in his most-famous screen role as James Bond, secret agent 007.

Clint Eastwood

b. 1930

Born in San Francisco, Clint Eastwood achieved acting success in the Western television series *Rawhide* (1959–1965). In the 1960s he found movie fame as the sombrero- and poncho-clad stranger in a trio of Italian-made spaghetti Westerns. He followed this up in the early 1970s by playing a violent cop in the popular *Dirty Harry* movies. He is a well-regarded movie director and made his first acting-directorial debut in *Play Misty for Me* (1971). *Bird* (1987) was particularly well received, and in 1992 *Unforgiven* won him two Oscars—one for Best Director and one for Best Picture. Between 1986 and 1988 he served as the mayor of Carmel, California.

Notable movies: ***A Fistful of Dollars* 1964; *The Good, the Bad, and the Ugly* 1966; *Play Misty for Me* 1971; *Dirty Harry* 1971; *Pale Rider* 1985; *Bird* 1988; *Unforgiven* 1992**

Elizabeth Taylor

b. 1932

Elizabeth Taylor became a child star in the 1940s, appearing in *Lassie* movies and the smash hit, *National Velvet* (1944). She successfully made the transition to a serious adult actress with *Giant* in 1956 and by gaining Oscar nominations for *Raintree County*, *Cat on a Hot Tin Roof*, and *Suddenly, Last Summer*. She finally won an Oscar for *Butterfield 8*. Taylor met her most-famous husband (out of seven) actor Richard Burton (p. 142), while filming *Cleopatra*, and they made appearances in many movies together. *Who's Afraid of Virginia Woolf* won her a second Oscar.

Notable movies: ***Raintree County* 1957; *Cat on a Hot Tin Roof* 1958; *Suddenly, Last Summer* 1959; *Butterfield 8* 1960; *Cleopatra* 1963; *Who's Afraid of Virginia Woolf?* 1966**

▼ Liz Taylor and Richard Burton fell in love while filming *Cleopatra*.

James Dean

1931–1955

Although he starred in only three movies, James Dean became a cult youth figure, his legendary status guaranteed by his tragically early death at the age of 24. He began acting at the University of California before moving to New York City. In 1951, after various bit parts, he appeared on Broadway in *See the Jaguar*. He soon moved on to television and movies. His first movie, *East of Eden* (1955), made Dean an overnight sensation. As the tormented teenager in his second movie, *Rebel Without a Cause* (1955), he captivated young moviegoers. Filming had barely finished on *Giant* (1956) when Dean collided with another car and died behind the wheel of his Porsche. He won posthumous Oscars for his last two movies.

Movies: ***East of Eden* 1955; *Rebel Without a Cause* 1955; *Giant* 1956**

◀ James Dean's third and final movie was *Giant*.

Jean-Paul Belmondo

b. 1933

Jean-Paul Belmondo is one of the major talents of French New Wave cinema of the 1960s. He studied drama at the Paris Conservatoire des Arts Dramatiques. During the 1950s he appeared in various theatrical productions and movies. He shot to fame in 1959 in Jean-Luc Godard's (b. 1930) directorial debut, *A Bout de Souffle* (*Breathless*). Apart from his starring roles in French art house movies by directors such as Louis Malle (1932–1995) and François Truffaut (1932–1984), Belmondo also appeared in mainstream movies, romances, thrillers, and action comedies, often performing his own stunts. In 1988 *Itinéraire d'un Enfant Gaté* won him a César, the French equivalent of the Oscar.

Notable movies: ***A Bout de Souffle* 1959; *Pierrot le Fou* 1965; *Le Voleur* 1967; *Casino Royale* 1967; *Borsalino* 1971**

Brigitte Bardot

b. 1934

Paris-born French actress Brigitte Bardot was modeling for *Elle* magazine when she was spotted by director Roger Vadim (1928–2000), and at the age of 18 she married him. She earned her "sex kitten" nickname after appearing in Vadim's *Et Dieu Créa la Femme*. Bardot retired from motion pictures in 1974, and she is now a fervent animal rights campaigner.

Notable movies: *Et Dieu Créa la Femme* 1956; *La Vérité* 1960; *Contempt* 1963

Alain Delon

b. 1935

Alain Delon became a French marine parachutist at the age of 17. His good looks and magnetism attracted movie offers when he visited the Cannes Film Festival in 1957. Delon's screen debut was in *Quand la femmes s'en mele* (1957). He achieved international fame in *Plein Soleil* (1960), an adaptation of a Patricia Highsmith thriller. By the 1970s he was one of France's top movie stars.

Notable movies: *Le Samorai* 1967; *Borsalino* 1971; *Monsieur Klein* 1976

Jack Nicholson

b. 1937

American actor Jack Nicholson's screen debut was in 1958, but it was not until 1969 that he impressed audiences, playing a dropout in *Easy Rider* (1969). Extremely versatile, he played an ex-musician in *Five Easy Pieces* (1970), a detective in *Chinatown* (1974), and won an Oscar for his portrayal of a psychiatric patient in *One Flew Over the Cuckoo's Nest*. He also won Oscars for *Terms of Endearment* (1983) and *As Good As It Gets* (1997).

Notable movies: *One Flew Over the Cuckoo's Nest* 1975: *The Shining* 1980; *The Postman Always Rings Twice* 1981; *Prizzi's Honor* 1985; *The Witches of Eastwick* 1987

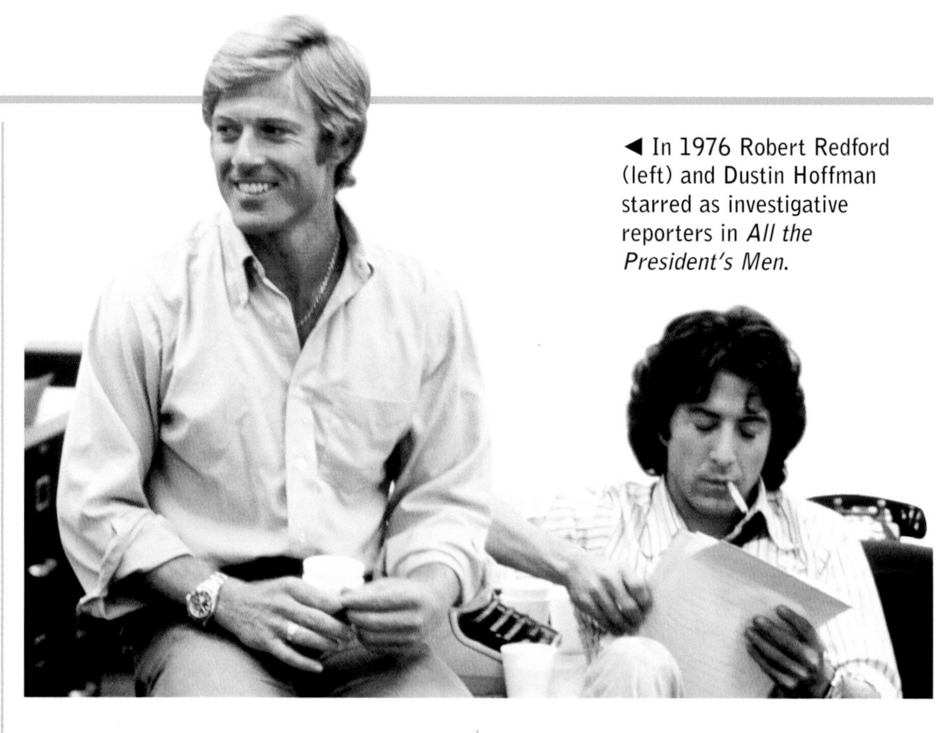

◀ In 1976 Robert Redford (left) and Dustin Hoffman starred as investigative reporters in *All the President's Men.*

Robert Redford

b. 1937

While studying art in New York City, Robert Redford turned to acting and appeared in Broadway plays and on television before going to Europe. Redford returned to star in the highly acclaimed *Barefoot in the Park* (1968). He costarred with Paul Newman in the classic *Butch Cassidy and the Sundance Kid* and again in *The Sting* (1973). His directorial debut, *Ordinary People,* won him an Oscar.

Notable movies: *Butch Cassidy and the Sundance Kid* 1969; *All the President's Men* 1976; *Ordinary People* 1980; *Out of Africa* 1985; *Indecent Proposal* 1993

Dustin Hoffman

b. 1937

American actor Dustin Hoffman worked odd jobs as he struggled to become an actor. He made his Broadway debut in 1961 and acted on stage and television before moving into movies. In 1969 he shot to fame in the classic *The Graduate*. Nominated for seven Oscars, the versatile Hoffman won Academy Awards for *Kramer vs. Kramer* and *Rain Man*.

Notable movies: *The Graduate* 1967; *Midnight Cowboy* 1969; *Little Big Man* 1970; *Kramer vs. Kramer* 1974; *Marathon Man* 1976; *All the President's Men* 1976; *Tootsie* 1982; *Rain Man* 1988; *Hook* 1991

◀ Jack Nicholson was unforgettable as the writer turned psycho in Stanley Kubrick's horror classic *The Shining.*

Arnold Schwarzenegger

b. 1947

At the age of 14 Arnold Schwarzenegger began bodybuilding in an attempt to escape his disadvantaged childhood. Born in Austria, he became the youngest Mr. Universe at the age of 20 and won Mr. Olympia seven times. Schwarzenegger went to the U.S. and acted in screen and television movies but with little success. *Pumping Iron* (1977), a documentary about bodybuilding, made him a household name. He then became an international movie star as *Conan the Barbarian* and as the indestructible robot in *Terminator*, as well as its sequel. He has broadened his appeal by appearing in comedies such as *Twins* (1988) and *Kindergarten Cop* (1990).

Notable movies: *Conan the Barbarian* 1981; *Terminator* 1984; *Predator* 1987; *Total Recall* 1990; *True Lies* 1994

▲ Arnold Schwarzenegger as Conan the Barbarian.

Gérard Dépardieu

b. 1948

Gérard Dépardieu's screen debut was in *Le Beatnik et le minet* (1965), but *Les Valseuses* (1974) brought him fame in his native France. He won Césars for his leading roles in *Le Dernier Metro* and the international hit *Cyrano de Bergerac*. Dépardieu has appeared in over 100 movies in France and Hollywood.

Notable movies: *Le Dernier Metro* 1980; *Jean de Florette* 1986; *Cyrano de Bergerac* 1990

Jackie Chan

b. 1954

Born in Hong Kong, Jackie Chan was only seven when he started learning kung fu. After performing with a traditional Chinese opera company he went on to appear as a stunt double in the Bruce Lee (1940–1973) movies *Fist of Fury* and *Enter the Dragon*. His first big movie as an actor, *Drunken Master* (1978), was a box-office hit in Hong Kong. After two brief periods in Hollywood, Jackie Chan returned to Hong Kong, where he directed and starred in many hit movies, all featuring him in fight scenes and dangerous stunts. In 1996 he finally broke into the mainstream U.S. market with *Rumble in the Bronx*.

Notable movies: *Drunken Master II* 1994; *Rumble in the Bronx* 1996

Russell Crowe

b. 1964

Born in New Zealand, Russell Crowe moved to Australia as a young child, and at the age of six he worked as a child extra in television. In 1980 he formed a rock band that became known as "30 Odd Foot of Grunts," and they went on to make several singles and albums. At the same time he continued working odd jobs and as a television and stage actor. Crowe's first screen role was in *Blood Oath* (1990), and he went on to win several awards from the Australian Film Institute. His Hollywood break was in 1995 with *The Quick and the Dead*.

Notable movies: *L.A. Confidential* 1997; *Gladiator* 2000; *A Beautiful Mind* 2001

Julia Roberts

b. 1967

Julia Roberts planned on becoming a vet but ended up pursuing an acting career. She became a major box-office star and one of Hollywood's highest-paid actresses after playing a prostitute in *Pretty Woman*. Roberts won an Oscar for her performance in the real-life environmental story *Erin Brockovich*.

Notable movies: *Pretty Woman* 1990; *The Pelican Brief* 1993; *Erin Brockovich* 2000

Nicole Kidman

b. 1967

Born in Hawaii, Australian actress Nicole Kidman studied dance, drama, and mime before making her acting debut with a street theater at the age of 14. In 1983 she started a successful career in television and made her screen debut in *Dead Calm* (1989). Kidman met her husband-to-be, Tom Cruise (b. 1962), in her second movie, *Days of Thunder* (1990). Amid much publicity, they got divorced in 2001.

Notable movies: *Eyes Wide Shut* 1999; *Moulin Rouge* 2001; *The Others* 2001

BEHIND THE SCENES

Cecil B. De Mille

1881–1959

Cecil B. De Mille made his acting debut on Broadway in 1900. With Samuel Goldwyn, he founded Paramount Studios in Hollywood in 1913. De Mille directed the first successful silent feature film, *The Squaw Man,* in 1914. He launched the careers of many stars and directed epic, spectacular pictures with lavish sets and costumes, often with Biblical themes.

Notable movies: *The Ten Commandments* 1923 and 1956; *The Volga Boatman* 1926

Samuel Goldwyn

1882–1974

Born in Poland, Goldwyn emigrated to America in 1895. After working as a glove salesman he cofounded Paramount Studios in 1913 with Cecil B. De Mille (above). In 1917 he founded Goldwyn Pictures, which in 1925 was merged to create Metro-Goldwyn-Mayer (MGM). Goldwyn produced many successful screen adaptations of books.

Notable movies: *All Quiet on the Western Front* 1930; *Wuthering Heights* 1939; *Guys and Dolls* 1955

Fritz Lang

1890–1976

Born in Vienna, Austria, Fritz Lang began writing screenplays while recovering from serving in World War I. He directed his first movie, *Halbblut* (*The Half-breed*), in 1919. Lang's early German movies of the 1920s were expressionistic and bleak in outlook. In 1934 he moved to the U.S. and directed many popular thrillers and crime melodramas for MGM.

Notable movies: *Metropolis* 1926; *Fury* 1936; *You Only Live Once* 1937; *The Big Heat* 1953; *Human Desire* 1954

Busby Berkeley

1895–1976

Busby Berkeley organized stage shows while serving as a U.S. army lieutenant in World War I. He continued his career in theater and became one of the top Broadway dance directors. In Hollywood he choreographed various movies for the producer Samuel Goldwyn (below left) and is famous for his lavish, spectacular, kaleidoscopic arrangements of chorus girls, nicknamed "Busby's Babes."

Notable movies: *42nd Street* 1933; *Gold Diggers of 1933* 1934; *Ziegfeld Girl* 1941; *Lady Be Good* 1941

Sergei Eisenstein

1898–1948

Russian movie director Sergei Eisenstein joined the Bolsheviks during the 1917 Russian Revolution. After directing at Moscow's Theater of the People he began making movies. He made only seven during his lifetime, but his contribution to motion pictures was considered revolutionary. Eisenstein's highly creative editing skills had a great influence on future movie directors.

Notable movies: *The Battleship Potemkin* 1925; *Ten Days That Shook the World* 1928; *Ivan the Terrible* 1944

▲ Busby Berkeley created stunning kaleidoscopic effects in the movie *Footlight Parade* (1933).

▼ Alfred Hitchcock with actress Tippi Hedrun on the set of *The Birds* (1963).

Alfred Hitchcock

1899–1980

Born in London, England, Hitchcock studied engineering but left to pursue his moviemaking ambitions at a movie studio. By 1922 he was an assistant director, and his directorial debut was in 1925 with *The Pleasure Garden*. He always made a cameo appearance in his movies, which often involve plots about good versus evil, people wrongly accused of murder, and an exploration of the relationship between sex and violence. His first U.S.-made movie, *Rebecca,* won him an Oscar. Hitchcock soon became known as the "Master of Suspense."

Notable movies: *The 39 Steps* 1935; *The Lady Vanishes* 1938; *Rebecca* 1940; *Suspicion* 1941; *Spellbound* 1945; *Dial M for Murder* 1954; *To Catch a Thief* 1955; *Rear Window* 1954; *North by Northwest* 1959; *Psycho* 1960; *The Birds* 1963

Luis Buñuel

1900–1983

At Madrid University Spanish surrealist movie director Luis Buñuel befriended the artist Salvador Dali (p. 166). Buñuel's directorial debut, *Un Chien Andalou* (1928), was made with Dali. Their second film, *L'Age d'Or* (1930), criticized the bourgeoisie and the Church and caused great controversy. Buñuel's daring movie about Mexican street kids, *Los Olvidados* (1950), won the Cannes Film Festival Best Director award, and *The Discreet Charm of the Bourgeoisie* (1972) won him an Oscar.

Notable movies: *Un Chien Andalou* 1928; *L'Age d'Or* 1930; *Los Olvidados* 1950; *Viridiana* 1961; *Belle de Jour* 1967

JEAN RENOIR 1894–1979
Movie director Jean Renoir was the son of the French artist Pierre Auguste Renoir (p. 161). He started his own production company in 1924 and became one of motion picture's greatest directors. He won critical acclaim for the movies he directed during the 1930s, including *La Grande Illusion* (1937), *La Bête Humaine* (1939), and *La Règle du Jeu* (1939). He moved to the U.S. in 1941.

WALT DISNEY 1901–1966
American Walt Disney was a commercial artist who set up a movie company in 1923 to make short, animated cartoons. His most famous cartoon characters are Mickey Mouse, first screened in 1928, and Donald Duck, in 1934. Disney's first full-length animated movie was *Snow White and the Seven Dwarfs* (1937). He also made movies that mixed cartoons with live action, such as *Mary Poppins* (1964).

DAVID LEAN 1908–1991
British filmmaker David Lean worked his way up from clapper boy to movie editor and then codirected with Noël Coward (1899–1973) on *In Which We Serve* (1942). He adapted many of Coward's plays for the screen, including the Oscar-nominated classic *Brief Encounter* (1945). Lean is best known for his spectacular, awe-inspiring epics, especially the Oscar-winning *Lawrence of Arabia* (1962).

ORSON WELLES 1915–1985
American movie director, writer, and actor Orson Welles' major contribution to motion pictures was *Citizen Kane* (1941), which he wrote, produced, directed, and acted in. It won the Oscar for Best Screenplay and changed moviemaking forever, pioneering new lighting, photography, and sound techniques. His most notable acting role was as Harry Lime in *The Third Man* (1949).

◀ Japanese director Akira Kurosawa became internationally famous in 1951 for the movie *Rashomon*.

Akira Kurosawa

1910–1998

Japanese director and screenwriter Akira Kurosawa's 50-year career began when he became an assistant director and scriptwriter in 1936. His first full-length movie was *Sanshiro Sugata* (1943), and *Rashomon* won him international fame and the Best Foreign Film Oscar in 1951. His movies, with grand battle scenes and noble heroes, have inspired many Hollywood movies. John Sturges' (1910–1992) Western *The Magnificent Seven* (1960) was a remake of Akira's masterpiece *The Seven Samurai*. Akira's career dipped in the late 1960s, but he went on to make more epic movies, receiving an Oscar for *Dersu Uzala* in 1976.

Notable movies: *Rashomon* 1951; *The Seven Samurai* 1954; *Dersu Uzala* 1976; *Ran* 1985; *Dreams* 1990

Federico Fellini

1920–1993

Italian movie director Federico Fellini was a journalist and cartoonist before he became a scriptwriter in the 1940s. He began making his own movies in the neorealist style in the 1950s. He won Best Foreign Film Oscars for *La Strada*, *Le Notte di Cabiria* (1957), and *Amarcord*. Fellini wrote his movies often dealing with his dislike of Roman Catholicism and contrasting fantasy with reality. His controversial movie about the high life in modern Rome, *La Dolce Vita* (1960), won the Cannes Festival Prize. Other movies include *Città delle Donne* (1980) and *Voice of the Moon* (1990).

Notable movies: *La Strada* 1954; *La Dolce Vita* 1960; *8½* 1963; *Satyricon* 1969; *Amarcord* 1973

▲ Federico Fellini (right) on the set of *La Strada*.

Satyajit Ray

1921–1992

Satyajit Ray, one of India's greatest movie directors, was a trained musician and became a scriptwriter and commercial artist before turning to movies. While illustrating a children's book he made the story into a movie, *Pather Panchali* (1955), which won a Cannes Film Festival prize. The international acclaim and success allowed Ray to make the award-winning sequels, *Aparajito* (1957) and *Apur Sansar* (1959).

Notable movies: *Devi 1960*; *Charulatha* 1964; *Ashanti Sanket* 1973

▲ Stanley Kubrick's science-fiction movie *2001: A Space Odyssey* thrilled audiences with its wide-screen special effects.

Stanley Kubrick

1928–2000

American director Stanley Kubrick received a camera for his 13th birthday and by the age of 17 was a magazine photographer. Determined to make documentaries and full-length movies, Kubrick's first movie was *Day of the Fight* in 1951. Kubrick moved to Hollywood, where he directed *Paths of Glory* (1957) and *Spartacus* (1960). He then moved to England, where he made his famous antiestablishment movie, *Dr. Strangelove*, the innovative sci-fi movie *2001: A Space Odyssey*, and the violent, controversial movie *A Clockwork Orange*.

Notable movies: *Dr. Strangelove* 1964; *2001: A Space Odyssey* 1968; *A Clockwork Orange* 1971; *The Shining* 1980; *Full Metal Jacket* 1987

Francis Ford Coppola

b. 1939

Oscar-winning screenwriter and director Francis Ford Coppola is most famous for making the *Godfather* trilogy and the Vietnam war epic *Apocalypse Now*. The son of creative Italian-American parents—a composer and an actress—he studied theater and then film in Los Angeles. Coppola learned his craft as an apprentice to the director Roger Corman. His directorial debut was with *Dementia 13* (1963). In 1970 he won his first Academy Award, the Best Adapted Screenplay Oscar for the movie *Patton* (1970). He formed the independent production company American Zoetrope with George Lucas (p. 152) in 1969. His second Oscar for a screenplay was for the phenomenally successful *The Godfather*, which he also directed. Coppola landed three more Oscars for writing, directing, and producing *The Godfather: Part II*.

Notable movies: *The Godfather* (parts 1 and 2) 1972, 1974; *The Conversation* 1974; *Apocalypse Now* 1979; *Peggy Sue Got Married* 1986; *Bram Stoker's Dracula* 1992

ROBERT ALTMAN b. 1925
American director Altman worked as a radio and magazine writer before entering the movie industry. In 1957 he wrote and directed his debut movie, *The Delinquents*. Years of directing for television followed. He finally achieved success with *M*A*S*H** (1970), a black comedy set in the Korean War, *The Long Goodbye* (1973), *The Player* (1992), and *Gosford Park* (2001).

ROMAN POLANSKI b. 1933
Polish-born movie director Roman Polanski studied film at Poland's Lodz Film School. He gained international recognition with his movie debut, the thriller *Knife in the Water* (1962). His movies are often violent, dark, and sinister; his most famous Hollywood-made movies are *Rosemary's Baby* (1968) and *Chinatown* (1974). In 1969 his wife, Sharon Tate, was murdered by Charles Manson (p. 245).

WERNER HERZOG b. 1942
Award-winning writer and director Werner Herzog was born in Munich, Germany, and briefly studied art before dropping out of college to teach himself filmmaking. In 1963 he started his a movie production company. A major figure of New German cinema, Herzog's subject matter is often philosophical. He is best known for the movies *Nosferatu the Vampyre* (1978) and *Fitzcarraldo* (1982).

RAINER FASSBINDER 1946–1982
Rainer Fassbinder's movie career lasted only 14 years, but in that time he made over 40 full-length movies and is regarded as the leading filmmaker of New German cinema. His first success in Germany was the award-winning *Katzelmacher* (1969). Many of his movies were political critiques of modern, bourgeois German society. He died of a drug overdose, aged 36.

George Lucas

b. 1944

American director and scriptwriter Lucas made the *Star Wars* movies, the first three of which broke box-office records and won seven Oscars. He studied film at the University of Southern California and won a prize in 1965 for his student movie, *THX-1138:4EB*. While working at Warner Bros. he befriended director Francis Ford Coppola (p. 151), and they briefly worked together. Coppola helped Lucas finance his first successful full-length movie, *American Graffiti* (1973). Lucas joined forces with director Stephen Spielberg (right) to produce *Raiders of the Lost Ark* (1981) and its sequels.

Notable movies: *American Graffiti* 1973; *Star Wars* 1977; *The Empire Strikes Back* 1980; *Return of the Jedi* 1983

Wim Wenders

b. 1945

German movie director Wim Wenders studied philosophy and medicine at Freiburg University and attended Munich's Cinema and Television College, both in Germany. He says of his work, "All my movies have as their underlying current the Americanization of Germany." Wenders is best known for his road movies, such as *Kings of the Road,* and particularly the haunting and highly acclaimed *Paris, Texas* (1984). In 1987 *Wings of Desire* won him the Cannes award for Best Director.

Notable movies: *Alice in the Cities* 1974; *Kings of the Road* 1976; *Paris, Texas* 1984; *Wings of Desire* 1987

Steven Spielberg

b. 1946

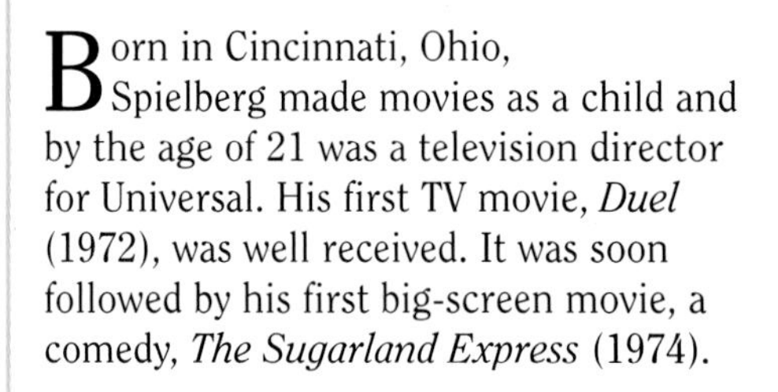

Born in Cincinnati, Ohio, Spielberg made movies as a child and by the age of 21 was a television director for Universal. His first TV movie, *Duel* (1972), was well received. It was soon followed by his first big-screen movie, a comedy, *The Sugarland Express* (1974).

The master of exploring fears and fantasies, Spielberg's first major success was *Jaws* in 1975, which broke all previous box-office records. This was followed by *Close Encounters of the Third Kind* (1977), *Raiders of the Lost Ark* (1981), and *E.T.* (1982), which again broke all box-office records. In 1982 Spielberg formed his own movie production company, making *Gremlins* (1984), *Back to the Future* (1985), *Who Framed Roger Rabbit* (1988), *Empire of the Sun* (1988), and *Hook* (1991).

Spielberg's magic touch continued in 1993 with *Jurassic Park,* notable for its computerized special effects. His next movie, about the Jewish Holocaust in World War II, was markedly different—*Schindler's List* (1994) was made in black-and-white and won six Oscars, including Best Film. In the same year he cofounded Dreamworks, the first new movie studio in Hollywood in 75 years. Spielberg's most recent box-office hits have been *Saving Private Ryan* (1998) and *AI* (2001).

Notable movies: *Jaws* 1975; *Raiders of the Lost Ark* 1981; *E.T.* 1982; *Jurassic Park* 1993; *Schindlers List* 1994; *Saving Private Ryan* 2000

▼ Steven Spielberg's sci-fi movie *E.T.* gave us one of the most familiar and enduring screen images of the late-1900s.

CHAPTER SEVEN

ARTISTS AND ARCHITECTS

Artists and architects before 1000

The earliest examples of art made by humans date back to around 40,000 years ago. At that time humans lived in caves and were hunter-gatherers, surviving by hunting and eating wild animals. They created art tied in with human survival and painted images of animals and hunting scenes on the walls of their caves.

▲ Cave artists from Lascaux, France, used pigments made from powdered ocher, hematite, and manganese. They applied it moist with brushes, pads, or blowpipes.

Some early cave paintings can still be seen today in Spain, France, and the Sahara Desert. In Lascaux in southwest France ice age people made cave paintings, possibly to honor the spirits of the animals they hunted for food and clothing. The first people who lived in Europe also made small clay models of goddesses and animals. These figures were associated with human survival and usually symbolized fertility.

ART OF THE FIRST CIVILIZATIONS

Between 10,000 and 5000 B.C. humans started farming and living in communal settlements and began making clay pottery that they decorated. As copper and bronze replaced stone for weapons and tools metalworkers became important, and the tools and objects they made were richly decorated. As towns and cities grew and states became wealthier, impressive temples, palaces, and other monumental buildings were decorated with carvings and paintings showing what life was like. From the frescoes of Mycenae to the Egyptian tomb paintings, from Olmec carvings to Chinese painted pottery, the art of these ancient people has provided us with a valuable insight into their ways of life.

EARLY ARCHITECTURE

The first buildings people made were animal-skin tents supported on wooden poles or sometimes even large animal bones. Around 6000 B.C. the people of Çatal Hüyük in Turkey began building homes using dried mud and wood. They covered the walls with fine plaster on which they painted using pigments made from plant materials.

BUILDING WITH STONE

In around 3000 B.C. people in Europe, Egypt, South America, the Middle East, and China started using stone as a building material. Not all of these early buildings were built for people to live in. Some were made for religious purposes and others as tombs for the dead. They include the pyramids and temples of Egypt and South America, the ziggurats of the Middle East, and monuments such as Stonehenge in Great Britain. Near Cairo, Egypt, the Great Pyramid of Khufu is the greatest of them all. It was built by the Egyptian

▼ From around 2630 B.C. Egyptians built many pyramids, the most famous being the Great Pyramid of Khufu. By building such great monuments the pharaohs sought to please the gods and leave a significant, permanent mark on history.

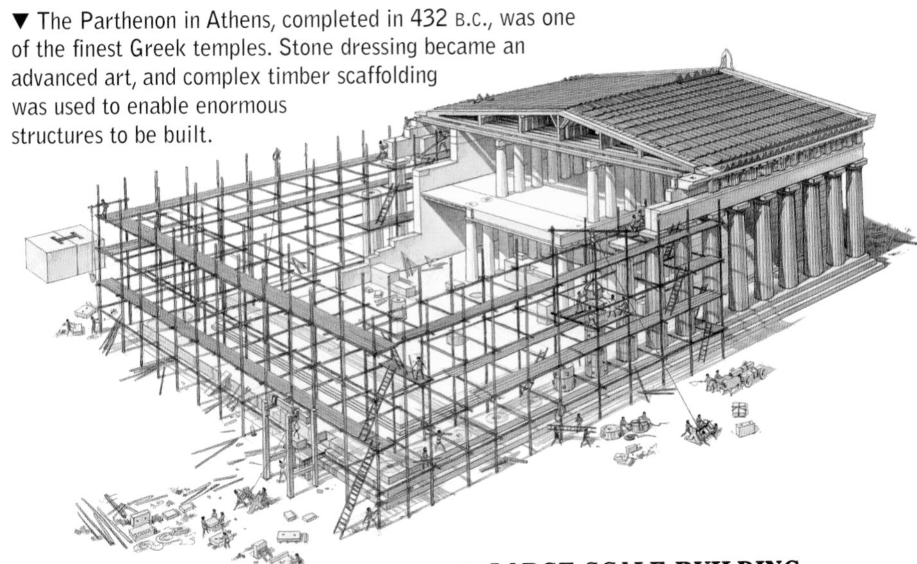

▼ The Parthenon in Athens, completed in 432 B.C., was one of the finest Greek temples. Stone dressing became an advanced art, and complex timber scaffolding was used to enable enormous structures to be built.

pharaoh **Khufu** (c. 2500s B.C.) as a tomb for his burial. One of the Great Wonders of the World, it is 478 ft. (145.75m) tall and took 20 years to build.

ART OF THE FIRST EMPIRES

From around 500 B.C. the arts were developed to express creativities and decorate houses, streets, and everyday objects. The wealth accumulated by empires and urban traders was used to sponsor and support artists and led to major advances in artistic creation. In ancient Greece the finest art was produced in the classical period, which reached its height around 400–300 B.C. Two Athenian sculptors from this period, **Praxiteles** (c. 400–330 B.C.) and **Scopas** (c. 395–350 B.C.), worked mainly with marble, producing lifelike sculptures for temples and tombs. Another Greek sculptor from the 300s B.C., **Lysippus**, produced an enormous number of figurative bronze statues.

Through the conquests of Alexander the Great, Greek ideas about art reached as far as India, and the spread of Buddhism took them farther east to China, Japan, and Southeast Asia. Roman artists often copied the work of the Greeks and developed their own, sometimes harshly realistic, styles.

China also had its own unique styles. There the artist **Gu Hong Zhong** (A.D. 910–980) was especially noted for his fine paintings of court scenes from the period known as the Five Dynasties.

LARGE-SCALE BUILDING

The Greeks were skilled architects. The study of mathematics helped them design well-proportioned buildings that fit in with their surroundings. In 447 B.C. construction started on the temple to the goddess Athena—the Parthenon—on the Acropolis above Athens. This enormous building, designed by the Greek architects **Iktinos** and **Kallikrates** (both 400s B.C.), was completed in 432 B.C. By 300 B.C. the Greeks had also developed town planning, designing whole cities in detail and arranging streets in a grid pattern. The city builders of Central America used urban planning as well.

The Romans adopted many Greek ideas, but they also discovered new techniques. One was how to make concrete in around 200 B.C., and it was soon used to build walls and huge domed roofs. They also developed arches for buildings, bridges, and aqueducts. The largest man-made structure on earth, the 3,000-mi. (4,800-km) -long Great Wall of China, was begun in 221 B.C. by the first Chinese emperor, **Shi Huangdi** (c. 259–210 B.C.), to protect China's northern borders. He also built an enormous tomb that took 700,000 laborers 34 years to complete, filling it with 7,000 terra-cotta soldiers to protect it. In Central America the Mayas built huge pyramids and other structures in impressively large religious centers.

RELIGIOUS ART

By A.D. 313 Christianity had become the dominant religion throughout much of the Roman Empire. Other religions, such as Islam and Buddhism, became important in other parts of the known world. Consequently, for the next 1,000 years or so, most artistic expression was used for religious purposes.

Churches, mosques, and temples across the world became wealthy and attracted the finest craftspeople. In England in around A.D. 698 the Bishop of Lindisfarne, **Eadfrith**, is believed to have written and illuminated a book called *The Lindisfarne Gospels*. Its rich, intricate design makes it one of Great Britain's greatest artistic treasures. Byzantine churches were decorated with wall mosaics and holy pictures called icons. Muslims designed geometrical patterns on their buildings. Buddhists in Asia painted stories of the life of Buddha. In Tang and Song China they painted and carved new kinds of landscape art and natural images. In Mexico stone carvings and murals, or wall paintings, were common.

◀ The Dome of the Rock in Jerusalem, completed in A.D. 691, was built on the site of Solomon's Temple.

ARTISTS

▼ *Virgin Mary and Child with St. John the Baptist and Others,* painted by Sandro Botticelli.

Giotto di Bondone

c. 1267–1337

Giotto di Bondone was first apprenticed to the artist Cimabue in the Italian city of Florence. He became established as a fresco painter when he decorated the church in Assisi with 28 scenes of the life of St. Francis. He worked on chapels belonging to the banking families, Bardi and Peruzzi. In 1334 Giotto became the director of works on Florence Cathedral.

Notable paintings: *Life of St. Francis* c. 1287–1299; Arena Chapel, Padua 1303–1306; Bardi and Peruzzi chapels c. 1320

Sandro Botticelli

c. 1445–1510

In 1461 Florentine artist Botticelli joined the workshop of painter Filippo Lippi (c. 1458–1504). He established his own workshop in 1470 and painted religious subjects. His patrons included the Medici family and the pope, Sixtus IV (1414–1484), who asked him to paint frescoes in Rome's Sistine Chapel.

Notable paintings: *Madonna of the Magnificat* 1480–1485; *The Birth of Venus* c. 1485; *The Annunciation* 1490

Hieronymous Bosch

1450–1516

Dutch medieval artist Hieronymous Bosch painted horrific, nightmarish visions of hell and damnation that reflected the religious and superstitious beliefs of the Middle Ages. It is believed that *The Seven Deadly Sins* is his first work (c. 1475). Bosch was a religious moralist, and most of his paintings were warnings against sin and the temptations of earthly pleasures. He drew on themes such as witchcraft and astrology to create his apocalyptic, hellish scenes that are full of medieval symbolism. His masterpiece, *The Garden of Earthly Delights*, is a triptych altarpiece.

Notable paintings: *The Garden of Earthly Delights* c. 1500–1510; *The Temptation of St. Anthony* c. 1500–1510

▲ "Hell," the right-hand panel of *The Garden of Earthly Delights* by Hieronymous Bosch.

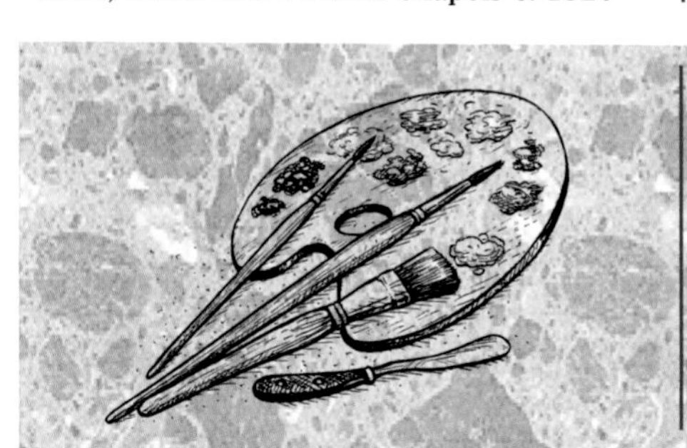

FRA ANGELICO c. 1387–1455
Italian painter Fra Angelico became a Dominican friar when he was 18. In around 1430 he began painting, and in 1436 he moved to Florence's San Marco convent, where he painted around 50 frescoes. He moved to Rome in 1445 to paint frescoes in the Vatican's Chapel of the Sacrament and the Orvieto Cathedral.

PIERO DELLA FRANCESCA c. 1415–1492
This artist and mathematician lived mostly in his Italian hometown of Borgo San Sepolcro near Florence. He decorated chapels for the Pope in Rome and rich families in Urbino, Rimini, and Arrezo. He was admired for his command of perspective and painting of natural light.

Leonardo da Vinci

1452–1510

Leonardo da Vinci was the ultimate Renaissance man. Both an artist and a scientist, he studied many different subjects—painting, aeronautics, geology, and engineering. He even dissected cadavers to study human anatomy.

Born in Vinci, Italy, Leonardo showed great talent as a boy and became an apprentice to Andrea del Verrocchio (1435–1488) in Florence. He proved his merit painting an impressive angel in Verrocchio's *The Baptism of Christ* (1472), and aged only 20 he became a Master of the Guild of Artists. In 1482 he asked the Duke of Milan, Ludovico Sforza, if he could create a "Great Horse" statue for him. He was employed by Sforza in Milan but only managed to produce a clay model in 1493—the statue itself was never started. He did paint Sforza's mistress, *Lady in Ermine*, in 1485 and a major commission, *The Virgin of the Rocks* (1508), took a year to complete. His masterpiece, *The Last Supper*, painted for a church in Milan, has deteriorated because he experimented with oil paint on plaster.

France invaded Milan, and Da Vinci left, finally returning to Florence in around 1503. He painted the enigmatic *Mona Lisa* around this time. Da Vinci ended his days in a manor in Cloux, near Amboise in France, an honored guest of Louis XII (1498–1515).

▲ *Mona Lisa* is probably Leonardo da Vinci's most famous painting —her eyes are said to follow the viewer around the room.

Notable paintings: *The Last Supper* 1497; *Mona Lisa* c. 1500–1504; *The Virgin and Child with St. Anne* c. 1510

Raphael

1483–1520

Raphael was born in Urbino, Italy, where his father was a court painter. An orphan by the age of 11, Raphael was raised by an uncle. In 1504 he moved to Florence, where inspired by Da Vinci (left), he started painting the *Madonna and Child*. His major work was in the Vatican in Rome, where he decorated three rooms for Pope Julius II and his successor, Leo X (1475–1521). Raphael was always busy painting frescoes for private villas, and in 1514 he became the Papal Architect. His final work was *Transfiguration*, but he died of a fever before he could complete the painting.

Notable paintings: *The School of Athens* 1509–1511; *Madonna Della Sedia* 1514; *Transfiguration* 1517–1520

Titian

1488–1576

Titian left his home in the Italian Alps to serve apprenticeships in Venice. Giovanni Bellini (below) taught him oil painting, and upon Bellini's death in 1516 Titian succeeded him as the official painter of the Republic. Titian painted religious altarpieces, portraits, and mythological scenes for wealthy patrons and royalty, including *Sacred and Profane Love* for the Chancellor of the Republic and the *Assumption of the Virgin* altarpiece for Venice's Sta Maria dei Frari. He was court portrait painter to Charles V (1500–1558).

Notable paintings: *Sacred and Profane Love* c. 1514; *Bacchus and Ariadne* 1520–1523; *Venus of Urbino* 1538

GIOVANNI BELLINI 1430–1516
Italian artist Bellini was influenced by the Flemish style of painting with oils. His portraits and frescoes often featured detailed landscape scenes. He painted the Doge of Venice's portraits and decorated the Doge's Palace, and in 1483 he became the head painter for the Venetian Republic. His pupils included the artist Titian (above).

ALBRECHT DÜRER 1471–1528
This German artist was greatly influenced by the Italian Renaissance artists. A master draftsman, Dürer excelled at woodcuts, copperplate engravings, and watercolors. His patrons included Emperor Maximilian I (1459–1519). Dürer's subjects ranged from religious themes, such as *Virgin and Child* (1512), to detailed studies of wildlife.

TINTORETTO 1518–1594
Venetian painter Jacopo Robusti was called "Tintoretto" because his father was a *tintore* ("cloth dyer"). Very religious, he excelled at capturing the effects of perspective and light—for example, in *The Removal of the Body of St. Mark* (1562). Three of his seven children also became painters, including Marietta (1560–1590), "La Tintoretta."

Pieter Bruegel

1520–1569

This Flemish artist is called "Peasant" Bruegel because of his many paintings of peasants feasting and dancing. He was a religious man, and his pictures tell of the sins of humankind. By 1551 he had become a Master in the Antwerp Guild of Artists. He traveled to France and Italy (c. 1552–1554) and was very impressed by the Alps. Upon his return he engraved landscapes for his printer employer and other engravings in the style of Bosch (p. 156). In 1563 Bruegel got married and settled in Brussels, Belgium, where he produced his best landscapes—*Haymaking* and *Hunters in the Snow*.

Notable paintings: *Netherlandish Proverbs* 1559; *Wedding Dance in the Open Air* 1566; *The Parable of the Blind* 1568

Peter Rubens

1577–1640

German-born Baroque painter Peter Paul Rubens lived in Antwerp, Belgium, from 1587. From 1591 he did a series of apprenticeships, becoming a Master of the Painters' Guild in 1598. Rubens was the court painter in Italy for Vincenzo I (1562–1612), and he presented Spain's Philip III (1578–1621) with paintings in 1603. Returning to Antwerp, he became court painter for Archduke Albert (1559–1621) in 1609. His many commissions include tapestries for France's Louis XIII (1601–1643) and a ceiling painting in England's Whitehall Palace for Charles I (p. 16), who knighted him in 1630.

Notable paintings: *Leda and the Swan* 1601–1602; *Fall of the Damned* c. 1620

Rembrandt van Rijn

1606–1699

By 1625, after serving apprenticeships, Dutch painter Rembrandt van Rijn became an independent artist in Leiden, Holland. He moved to Amsterdam in 1632, where he worked as the leading portrait painter. His first success was the group portrait of Amsterdam surgeons—*The Anatomy of Dr. Tulp* (1632). Rembrandt did many self-portraits (see above) and also loved to paint his wife Saskia, who died in 1642.

Notable paintings: *The Night Watch* 1642; *A Woman Bathing in a Stream* 1655

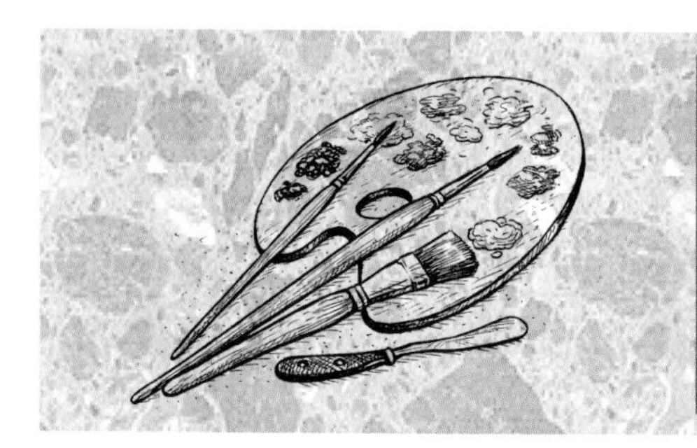

EL GRECO 1541–1614
Born Domenico Theotocopoulos on the Greek island of Crete, El Greco moved to Venice, Italy, in 1567, briefly studying with Titian (p. 157). He settled in Toledo, Spain, in 1577, completing religious commissions and altarpieces for Spanish churches. El Greco's style was very distinctive, and in his later works he painted elongated figures.

FRANS HAL 1581–1666
Frans Hal was born in Antwerp, Belgium, but from 1561 he spent his life in Haarlem. A portrait painter, he was known for his ability to capture the personality of his models. He specialized in group portraits of families, militia companies, and important men of society. His most famous portrait is *The Laughing Cavalier* (1624).

Jan Vermeer

1632–1675

Dutch artist Jan Vermeer lived in Delft, Holland, and probably took over the family inn and an art dealership after his father's death. Vermeer's paintings are of peaceful domestic scenes, with one or two figures engaged in an activity, such as sewing or playing music, lit by light from a nearby window. Only 35 of his paintings survive, and only three are dated. He died in debt and was not recognized until the 1800s.

Notable paintings: *Woman with a Water Jug* c. 1660; *Woman Reading a Letter* c. 1662; *The Lacemaker* c. 1670

Antonio Giovanni Canaletto

1697–1768

Canaletto spent his life painting views of his native city—Venice, Italy. Painted on canvas or copper, they were very popular with the English aristocracy, who bought them as souvenirs when they traveled around Europe on the "Grand Tour." Canaletto also spent 10 years in England painting views of London and the Thames River.

Notable paintings: *The Stonemason's Yard* c. 1728; *The Horses of San Marco in the Piazzaetta* 1743

Francisco de Goya

1746–1828

Spanish artist Francisco de Goya first drew cartoons (preparatory drawings) for royal tapestries in Madrid, Spain. He joined the Madrid Academy in 1780 and became Director of Painting in 1795. He began painting portraits, and in 1789 he was appointed royal painter to Charles IV (1788–1819). An illness in 1792 left Goya deaf, and his later series of etchings—*Los Caprichos* (1796–1978) and *The Disasters of War* (1810–1813) —show his growing fascination with the macabre and the horrors of humanity.

Notable paintings: *The Third of May, 1808* 1814; *Saturn Devouring One of His Sons* 1820–1823; *The Bullfight* c. 1827

◀ The Grand Canal was one of many views of Venice painted by Giovanni Canaletto. Many of his pictures were bought by wealthy European visitors to the city.

NICOLAS POUSSIN 1594–1665
French artist Nicolas Poussin left Normandy to study art in Paris in 1612. In 1624 he moved to Rome, Italy, where his first public commission—the *Martyrdom of St. Erasmus* (1629)—was unpopular. This led him to work only for private patrons. His paintings of religious stories, heroic scenes, and landscapes are complex and symbolic.

DIEGO VELASQUEZ 1599–1660
Spanish painter Diego Velasquez became an independent master painter in 1617 and painted religious pictures such as *The Adoration of the Magi.* He became Philip IV's (1605–1665) court painter in 1623, and the king refused to let anyone else paint his portrait. In 1629 Velasquez visited Italy and was inspired by Renaissance art.

THOMAS GAINSBOROUGH 1727–1788
Gainsborough was a successful British portrait painter who actually preferred painting landscapes. Most of his high-society lords and ladies and their families were painted using the landscape as a backdrop. He also painted actors, actresses, and the British royal family at Windsor Castle.

William Turner
1775–1851

At the age of 13 Turner began showing his artwork in the window of his father's barbershop in London, England. By the age of 16 he was exhibiting watercolors at London's Royal Academy. He became Professor of Perspective for the Academy in 1802. Turner painted river-, sea-, and landscapes in a vibrant and expressive style described as Romantic. He captured the warm light of the sunrise, rain showers, and dramatic ocean storms. His handling of natural light greatly influenced the Impressionist painters. He died a recluse, leaving over 20,000 paintings to Great Britain.

Notable paintings: *The Shipwreck* 1805; *Fighting Téméraire* 1839; *Rain, Steam and Speed* 1844

John Constable
1776–1837

English landscape painter John Constable studied at the Royal Academy in London. He produced so many oil paintings of his native Suffolk and the Stour Valley in England that it is now known as "Constable Country." During his lifetime he did not achieve proper recognition in England, but he was popular in France, where he won the Paris Salon gold medal for *The Hay Wain* (1821). Constable worked outside, painting the country as he saw it. He especially focused on the sky, its cloud formations, and the changing light.

Notable paintings: *Dedham Vale* 1802; *Dedham Vale: Morning* 1811; *Flatford Mill* 1817; *The White Horse* 1819; *The Cornfield* 1826; *Hadleigh Castle* 1829

▲ *Shipwreck of the Minotaure on Haack Sands* was painted by William Turner in 1805.

James McNeill Whistler
1834–1903

In 1855 U.S. artist James Whistler traveled to Paris, France, to study art before settling in London, England, in 1859. He was the first U.S. painter to be made welcome by the Paris art establishment. He believed in exploring color and art for art's sake, and he caused a stir by calling the portrait of his mother *Arrangement in Gray and Black*. Inspired by Japanese woodcuts, he did many "nocturne" (night) paintings and etchings of the Thames River in London.

Notable paintings: *At the Piano* 1859; *Arrangement in Gray and Black, No. 1* 1872; *Nocturne in Blue and Gold: Old Battersea Bridge* 1875

Edgar Degas
1834–1917

French painter Edgar Degas was taught by Jean Ingres (below left) at the École des Beaux-Art, Paris, France. To begin with Degas copied the works of Old Masters and painted historical subjects, but they were not well received. He immediately changed his focus to the human life he observed around him. He painted theaters and circuses, but he is most famous for his studies of racehorses and graceful ballet dancers. Failing eyesight led him to work with pastels and sculpture later in his career.

Notable paintings: *Race Horses* 1868; *Dancing Examination* 1874; *Dancer Lacing Her Shoe* 1878; *Jockeys in the Rain* 1879; *Four Dancers* 1899

JEAN AUGUSTE INGRES 1780–1867
French artist Ingres studied art in Toulouse and Paris, both in France. His style was classical and his drawing ability legendary. He painted portraits of the nobility, including Napoléon (p. 28). Ingres spent many years in Rome, Italy, where he drew many studies of the female nude. When he returned to Paris in 1841, he received a hero's welcome.

JOHN AUDUBON 1785–1851
Bird artist John Audubon grew up in France. In 1804 his father sent him to Philadelphia, Pennsylvania, to look after family land. He enjoyed sketching wildlife and decided to draw and record every bird in America. His *Birds of America*, published between 1827 and 1838, contains color plates of over 1,000 birds in their habitats.

CAMILLE COROT 1796–1875
French artist Camille Corot was 26 before his father would agree to fund his artistic endeavors. Corot became a successful landscape artist and a firm believer in painting directly from nature. The forest of Fontainbleu near Paris was one of his favorite locations. He lived in Paris but traveled all over Europe for inspiration.

Paul Cézanne

1839–1906

While in school French artist Paul Cézanne befriended the writer Emile Zola (p. 112). Cézanne's father wanted him to study law, but in 1861 he followed Zola to Paris to take up art. The landscape painter Pissarro (below) was an early influence, and they painted together in Pointoise, France. Cézanne took part in the first Impressionist exhibition in 1873, where his female nude—*Modern Olympia*—shocked the public. He was very versatile and worked to represent form and structure, not simply light and color. He urged artists to search out "the cylinder, the sphere, the cone" in nature. His approach paved the way for Fauvism and Cubism.

Notable paintings: *Card Players* 1890–1892; *Apples and Oranges* 1895–1900; *Mount Sainte-Victoire* 1904–1906; *Les Grandes Baigneuses* 1905

▲ An 1869 self-portrait by Paul Cézanne.

▲ Claude Monet in his studio in Giverny, France, framed by one of his water-lily masterpieces.

Claude Monet

1840–1926

French painter Claude Monet was the leading member of the Impressionist movement. While in Paris he befriended Pissarro (below) and later Renoir (right) and Manet (below). They exhibited together in 1874, and Monet's painting *Impression: Sunrise* led to the name Impressionists. Monet devoted himself to capturing shifting natural light and color. In 1916 he began his enormous, near-abstract series of paintings of water-lilies in his garden in Giverny, France.

Notable paintings: *Haystacks* 1890–1891; *Rouen Cathedral* 1891–1895; series of water-lily paintings 1916–1923

Pierre Auguste Renoir

1841–1919

Renoir was born in Limoges, France, but he grew up in Paris. From 1860 he studied art and befriended Monet (left). During the 1870s he earned a living as a successful portrait painter. He took part in the Impressionist exhibitions (1874–1879, 1882) and painted pictures of cafe scenes, dancing couples, flowers, and landscapes. From the mid-1880s the female nude was his favorite subject.

Notable paintings: *The Boating Party Lunch* 1880–1881; *Dance in the City* 1883; *The Bathers* 1884–1887

JOHN MILLAIS 1829–1896
At the age of 11 English painter Millais studied art at London's Royal Academy. With Dante Gabriel Rossetti (1828–1882) and Holman Hunt (1827–1910) he cofounded the Pre-Raphaelite Brotherhood. Millais also designed woodcuts that were used to illustrate magazines. His most famous painting is *Bubbles* (1886).

CAMILLE PISSARRO 1830–1903
Born in the West Indies, Camille Pissarro moved to Paris, France, to study art in 1855. Heavily influenced by Corot (p. 160), he is famous for his use of color to capture the effects of light in outdoor settings. Pissarro was the only artist of the French Impressionist movement to take part in all eight of its exhibitions (1874–1886).

ÉDOUARD MANET 1832–1883
Manet came from a privileged Parisian family background. He began as an artist's apprentice (1850–1856) and traveled around Europe studying the Old Masters. In his paintings Manet devoted himself to capturing the everyday modern life of the people of Paris, from barmaids to musicians. He inspired many other artists.

Paul Gauguin

1848–1903

Born in Paris, France, Paul Gauguin spent part of his childhood in Peru, his mother's country. He worked on a ship at the age of 17, and in 1871 he returned to Paris and became a stockbroker. He painted in his spare time, and by 1876 he was showing his work. In 1886 Gauguin left his wife and five children and moved to Brittany, France. In 1891 he settled in Tahiti, where he produced his brightly colored "primitive" paintings of the local people. Poverty-stricken, he visited Paris briefly in 1893 but returned to the South Sea islands in 1895, where he died.

Notable paintings: *The Vision After the Sermon* 1888; *Where Do We Come From? What Are We? Where Are We Going?* 1898

▲ A self-portrait by the French artist Henri de Toulouse-Lautrec.

Henri de Toulouse-Lautrec

1864–1901

Toulouse-Lautrec was born into an aristocratic family in Albi, France. As a child he broke both legs, and they never grew properly, so he was very short. He showed artistic talent and received private art lessons. In 1882 he moved to Paris, did several apprenticeships, and in 1885 he established a studio in the artistic quarter, Montmartre. He made his name with his lively posters of Montmartre's *demimonde*—the entertainment and nightlife of circuses, dance halls, brothels, and cabarets, such as the Moulin Rouge. He died of alcohol poisoning at the age of 36.

Notable paintings: *At the Circus Fernando* 1888; *La Goulue* 1891; *Ambassadeurs—Aristide Bruant dans Son Cabaret* 1892; *Le Divan Japonais* 1893

Vincent van Gogh

1853–1890

Although Dutch painter Vincent van Gogh lived a tragically short, poverty-stricken life, he produced an impressive body of work that influenced other artists and provided the basis for the Expressionist movement. At 16 he began working with his brother, Theo (1857–1891), for an art dealer. In 1877 he followed in his pastor father's footsteps and turned to religion.

Van Gogh was an evangelist in Belgium from 1878 to 1880, and around this time he decided to pursue an artistic career. During the early 1880s he studied and practiced drawing and painting in Belgium and Holland. In 1886 he moved to live with his brother, then the director of an art gallery in Paris, France. While there Van Gogh met Impressionist and Post-Impressionist artists, including Toulouse-Lautrec (above), Degas (p. 160), and Gauguin (above). Inspired by such artists, he developed his energetic brushwork and vibrant colors, painting Montmartre, flowers, portraits, and self-portraits. In 1888 he moved to Provence, France, and began painting the landscape in his vivid, expressive style. Gauguin stayed with him, and they painted together. However, in December 1888, Van Gogh became depressed and cut off part of his left ear. In the last two years of his life Van Gogh was committed to asylums, but he continued painting. He sold his first painting in 1890, but in July of that year he shot himself.

Notable paintings: *The Potato Eaters* 1885; *Sunflowers* 1888; *The Bridge* 1888; *The Starry Night* 1889; *Cornfields with Flight of Birds* 1890

▶ Van Gogh's painting of a church: *L'eglise d'Auvers-sur-Oise vue du chevet.*

▲ *Odalisque à la culotte rouge* (Odalisque in red trousers) by Henri Matisse.

Henri Matisse

1869–1954

French artist Henri Matisse trained as a lawyer in Paris and began painting while recovering from an illness. His early work was influenced by the Impressionists, but he developed his own distinctive style after studying "primitive art." He led a group of artists coined the Fauvists ("wild beasts") by a critic and created expressive paintings using strong forms and colors.

Notable paintings: *Green Stripe (Madam Matisse)* 1905; *La Joie de Vivre* 1906; *The Dance* 1910; *Icarus* 1943–1944

Georges Braque

1882–1963

French artist Georges Braque cofounded the revolutionary art movement Cubism with Picasso (p. 164). Their work showed people and objects painted from multiple viewpoints. In the 1920s Braque created stage set designs for ballets by Diaghilev (p. 199). His later work often featured birds, including the ceiling he painted in the Louvre Museum in Paris, France.

Notable paintings: *Violin* 1912; *Woman with Guitar* 1913; *Man with Guitar* 1914; *The Birds* (in the Louvre) 1949–1951

Paul Klee

1879–1940

This Swiss artist's work was influenced by music, children's art, dreams, and the spiritual world. He first did etchings and exhibited them in 1906. In 1911 he met avant-garde artists including Kandinsky (right) and joined the Expressionist *Der Blaue Reiter* ("Blue Rider") group of artists. After a visit to Tunisia in 1914 he began producing colorful, mosaic-like, landscape watercolors. He taught at the Bauhaus in Germany from 1920 to 1931, but he returned to Switzerland in 1933 when his work was labeled "degenerate" by the Nazis.

Notable paintings: *Red and White Domes* 1914; *Senecio* 1922; *Twittering Machine* 1922; *Still Life* 1940

JOHN SINGER SARGENT 1856–1925
John Singer Sargent was born in Italy to American parents. Although a U.S. citizen, he lived mainly in Europe and studied art in Paris, France. He made his name painting elegant portraits of high society figures, business entrepreneurs, and the artists and writers of his day. His portrait of Virginie Gautreau, *Madam X*, caused controversy at the 1884 Paris Salon exhibition. As a result he moved to England, where he became one of the most sought-after portrait painters. He was also commissioned to produce paintings for public buildings. During World War I (1914–1918) he was an offical war artist.

WALTER SICKERT 1860–1942
British Impressionist painter Walter Sickert was born in Munich, Germany, but was raised in England from 1868. His illustrator father discouraged him from becoming an artist, so he pursued an acting career. However, in 1881 he enrolled in London's Slade School of Art. He assisted the painter Whistler (p. 160) and befriended Degas (p. 160) on a visit to Paris, France, in 1883. London music halls and city life were his favorite subject matter.

GUSTAV KLIMT 1862–1918
Austrian avant-garde painter and designer Gustav Klimt was born in Vienna, Austria, and attended Vienna's School of Plastic Art from the age of 14 until he was 20. He then worked with his brother, Ernst (1864–1892), doing theater murals before setting up his own studio. In 1897 he became president of the Vienna Secession, the Austrian version of Art Nouveau. Klimt produced richly gilded portraits, such as *The Kiss*, which is now a popular poster, and fantasy scenes full of symbolism.

WASSILY KANDINSKY 1872–1944
Born in Moscow, Russia, Kandinsky studied law before moving to Germany at the age of 30. He studied art in Munich, and in 1896 he produced his first paintings. He is generally regarded as being the founder of abstract art. In 1911 he cofounded the group of artists, *Der Blaue Reiter*. Between 1914 and 1922 he lived in Russia. He returned to Germany, where he taught at the Bauhaus School, and moved to Paris, France, in 1933, where he spent the rest of his life.

Pablo Picasso

1881–1973

By the age of 16 Spanish artist Pablo Picasso was studying art in Madrid and displaying a talent at drawing and painting. In 1901 he moved to Paris.

Between 1901 and 1904 he used blue tones in his paintings—his Blue Period. From 1905 to 1906 he painted circus performers and clowns in warmer colors—his Rose Period. In 1907 he painted *Les Demoiselles d'Avignon* in a revolutionary style that marked the birth of Cubism. With the artist Georges Braque (p. 163), Picasso challenged the traditional ways of depicting people and objects by using perspective and by painting all three dimensions. He also designed sets and costumes for ballets and the theater and produced work in ceramics, lithography, and engraving. His antiwar masterpiece, *Guernica*, was a response to bombing by the Nazis.

Notable paintings: *Les Demoiselles d'Avignon* 1907; *The Three Musicians* 1921; *The Three Dancers* 1925; *Guernica* 1937

▼ Pablo Picasso was probably the most influential artist from the 1900s. Over his 75-year career he mastered every medium he used, from painting and sculpture to ceramics and printmaking.

Amedeo Modigliani

1884–1920

Italian painter and sculptor Amedeo Modigliani studied art in Florence and Venice, moving to Paris, France, in 1906. He was inspired by the sculptor Constantine Brancusi (1876–1957), and from 1910 to 1912 he carved elegant, elongated, stone heads, greatly influenced by African masks. He then returned to painting, achieving sculptural portraits of "swanlike" people and graceful nudes. He died tragically of tuberculosis at the young age of 36.

Notable paintings: *Têtes* 1912; *Jean Cocteau* 1916; *Great Nude Reclining* 1917; *Self-portrait* 1919

▲ *Sweethearts* was painted by Modigliani in around 1910. His style was strongly influenced by African carvings of elongated heads.

Marc Chagall

1887–1985

Born in Russia, Marc Chagall's art was inspired by his childhood experience of Jewish village life. After studying art in St. Petersburg in 1910 he moved to Paris, France, where he was influenced by Fauvist, Cubist, and Surrealist artists. His dreamlike paintings depict Jewish villagers, animals, lovers, and musicians, often floating in air. After returning to Russia for a brief period he traveled to the U.S. before settling in France. He also illustrated books and produced many murals, tapestries, and stained-glass windows for public buildings.

Notable paintings: *I and My Village* 1911; *Bouquet of Flying Lovers* 1947; *The Creation of Man* 1956–1958

Joan Miró

1893–1983

Spanish abstract artist Joan Miró produced quirky paintings, usually in primary or simple, bright colors. They depict odd organic shapes, stars, birds, symbols, lines, and squiggles. Although abstract, they are bursting with life. Miró also produced etchings and many other works of art, including ceramic murals.

Notable work: *Wall of the Moon and Wall of the Sun* UNESCO mural 1957

Norman Rockwell

1894–1978

U.S. illustrator and artist Norman Rockwell painted realistic "storytelling pictures" of contemporary American people. He was commissioned by popular magazines and for patriotic posters during World War II. In 1977 he was awarded the Presidential Medal of Freedom for his contribution to American society.

Notable painting: *The Four Freedoms* 1943

▲ *Boy at the Pawnbrokers* painted by Norman Rockwell for the *Saturday Evening Post*.

Maurits Escher

1898–1972

Dutch artist Maurits Escher trained as an architect but was attracted to graphic art. He traveled widely, and the decorative Moorish tilework and designs in Spain inspired him from 1937 to pursue his imaginative, unique artwork—lithographs, woodcuts, and drawings based around mathematical patterns, geometry, and optical illusions.

Notable prints: *Cycle* 1938; *Drawing Hands* 1948; *Ascending and Descending* 1960; *Waterfall* 1961

▲ The optical illusion that is *Relativity* was produced as a woodcut by Escher in 1953.

PIET MONDRIAN 1872–1944
Dutch artist Piet Mondrian cofounded the *De Stijl* ("The Style") movement in painting and architecture in 1917. He lived in Paris, France (1919–1938), where he was influenced by Matisse (p. 163) and Cubism. Mondrian's work became increasingly abstract, and his paintings in the 1920s, for example *Composition with Blue and Yellow* (1920), were a series of geometric shapes in primary colors set within black grid lines. He lived in England in 1938 and settled in New York City in 1940.

EDWARD HOPPER 1882–1967
Realist painter Edward Hopper studied at the New York School of Art (1899–1906). He made a living as a commercial illustrator and did not achieve success as a painter until the early 1920s. Hopper's focused on scenes of the U.S. He painted bleak landscapes and sparsely populated public spaces, such as bars, theaters, cinemas, railroads, and hotels, showing human loneliness and the sheer size of the American landscape.

MARCEL DUCHAMP 1887–1968
French artist Marcel Duchamp followed his artist brothers to Paris to study art. His Cubist body-in-motion painting, *Nude Descending a Staircase, No. 2,* caused a stir when it was exhibited in Paris and New York City in 1912–1913. In 1915 he pioneered the shocking "anti-art" Dada movement, introducing "ready-made" artwork constructed from everyday objects such as urinals. He made "kinetic sculptures"—artwork that moved—such as *Bicycle Wheel* (1913–1951). His avant-garde work and ideas inspired the Surrealists and the Pop Art movement.

GEORGIA O'KEEFE 1887–1986
Georgia O'Keefe studied art in Chicago and New York City before working as a commercial artist and teacher. In 1916 some of her early abstract drawings were seen by the photographer Alfred Stieglitz (p. 172). He put on shows of her work in his New York City gallery, and they got married in 1924. Her later paintings of landscapes and flowers became popular, and by 1928 she had become a huge success.

René Magritte

1898–1967

Belgian Surrealist painter René Magritte studied art in Brussels, Belgium, and moved to Paris, France, in 1927. He befriended artists like Joan Miró (p. 165) and began developing his own distinctive style, which has been called "magic realism." He painted everyday objects in a very realistic way but often in strange combinations, such as an apple instead of a head or a man wearing a bowler hat or a large rock floating in midair. The paintings are mysterious, like visual riddles with no solution.

Notable paintings: *Reckless Sleeper* 1928; *The Key of Dreams* 1930; *The Human Condition* 1934–1935

▲ René Magritte's dreamlike Surrealist painting, *L'Heureux Donateur* (The Happy Giver).

Salvador Dali

1904–1989

Spanish artist and eccentric exhibitionist Salvador Dali was the most famous of the Surrealist painters. He was greatly influenced by Sigmund Freud's (p. 232) idea of the subconscious and described his pictures—which often contained tricks of the eye—as "hand-painted dream photographs." Dali also wrote movie scripts exploring religious themes and produced sculptures and jewelry.

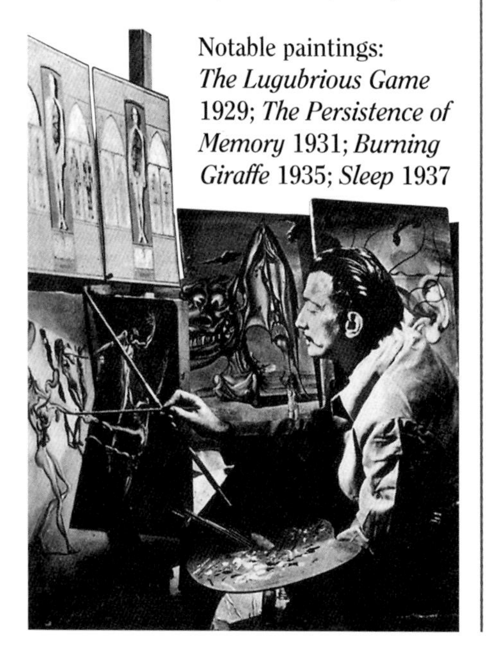

Notable paintings: *The Lugubrious Game* 1929; *The Persistence of Memory* 1931; *Burning Giraffe* 1935; *Sleep* 1937

Francis Bacon

1909–1992

Born in Dublin, Ireland, Expressionist painter Francis Bacon moved to London in 1928 and began painting in 1930. His *Three Studies for Figures at the Base of a Crucifixion* caused controversy when it was shown in 1945. For most of his paintings he focused on "the violence of life," finding inspiration for his tortured human figures in slaughterhouses.

Notable paintings: *Three Studies for Figures at the Base of a Crucifixion* 1945; *Pope Innocent X* 1950

Jackson Pollock

1912–1956

In the late 1940s American Abstract Expressionist painter Jackson Pollock abandoned the easel and dripped, splashed, and threw multicolored paints at his canvases on the floor. This energetic method was called "action painting," and Pollock's idea was that this free approach would express the artist's unconscious mind and release the power of paint for paint's sake.

Notable paintings: *Number 1* 1948; *Number 32* 1950; *Blue Poles* 1953

Roy Lichtenstein

1923–1997

New Yorker Lichtenstein used the devices of comic-strip pictures—such as speech bubbles, simple primary colors, and bold black outlines—to make his famous 1960s Pop Art paintings.

Notable paintings: *Blam* 1962; *Whaam!* 1964; *As I Opened Fire* 1964; *M-Maybe (A Girl's Picture)* 1965

▲ A major figure in the 1960s Pop Art movement, Roy Lichtenstein painted his cartoon-style *Blam* in 1962.

Andy Warhol

1926–1987

One of the most important artists of the 20th century, Andy Warhol far outlived his declaration that "everyone will be famous for 15 minutes."

Born Andrew Warhola in Pittsburg, Pennsylvania, to Czechoslovakian parents, he studied art history and design before moving to New York City, where he worked as an illustrator for *Vogue* and *Harper's Bazaar* magazines. He achieved recognition in the 1960s when he took brands such as Campbell's Soup and Coca-Cola and replicated and repeated their images using a silk-screen printing technique. In his studio, "The Factory," he began making portraits of movie stars and celebrities, such as Marilyn Monroe and Elvis, endlessly repeating their faces. Warhol's work reflected American culture of the time—the cult of celebrity and the endless sameness of a media-saturated consumer society. He also made lengthy art movies, published books, and encouraged younger artists and musicians.

Notable screenprints: *Campbell's Soup Can* 1962; *Car Crash* 1963; *Marilyn* 1964
Notable movies: *Chelsea Girls* 1967; *Flesh* 1968; *Trash* 1969

◀ One of Andy Warhol's many silkscreens of Campbell's Soup.

MARK ROTHKO 1903–1970

Abstract Expressionist painter Mark Rothko moved from Latvia to the U.S. in 1913. In 1935 he formed the group "Ten" with other artists. In the 1950s he began painting large canvases with soft-edged, floating blocks of deep colors. He was commissioned to produce paintings for New York City's Four Seasons restaurant (1958) and the Philip Johnson-designed Houston chapel, now called the Rothko Chapel (1964–1967). He committed suicide in 1970.

WILLEM DE KOONING 1904–1997

Dutch artist Willem de Kooning studied at the Rotterdam Academy of Fine Art and did various commercial art jobs before hiding away on a boat bound for the U.S. in 1926. By 1935 De Kooning was painting full-time in New York City. He achieved recognition as part of the postwar Abstract Expressionist movement. De Kooning is best known for his large, almost grotesque but vivid portraits of women, which he painted over and over in the late 1930s, early 1950s, and 1960s.

SYDNEY NOLAN 1917–1992

Sydney Nolan was born in Melbourne, Australia, and attended the National Gallery Art School in Victoria from 1934. He served in the Australian army during World War II and started to paint landscapes of the hot, desolate bush of Victoria's Wimmera District. After the war Nolan's favorite subject was Ned Kelly (p. 239), the infamous Australian bushranger, and these paintings won him recognition. Much of his work focused on specifically Australian themes, either portraits of historical characters or landscapes of remote townships and dry deserts. He also designed ballet and opera stage sets.

ROBERT RAUSCHENBERG B. 1925

U.S. painter Robert Rauschenberg studied art in Kansas City, Paris, and New York City. During the mid-1950s in New York City he began experimenting with "combine paintings"—multimedia collages that blended photos, paint, printmaking, newspaper, and magazine images. Marcel Duchamp (p. 165) and the Dada movement influenced his work. Rauschenberg's subjects (contemporary urban life) and his use of unconventional materials and everyday objects paved the way for the Pop Art movement.

Jasper Johns

b. 1930

U.S. painter, sculptor, and printmaker Jasper Johns moved to New York City from Georgia in 1949 and worked as a commercial artist. He then began making bold statements with his painting as a reaction to the emotion and politics of Abstract Expressionism—for example in the Stars and Stripes canvas, *Flag*, from 1954–1955. Johns' choice of familiar subject matter—flags, targets, numbers, alphabet letters, maps—and his simple, "minimal" style of painting paved the way for the Pop Art movement. His debut solo show of the flag series, held in 1958, won him instant recognition.

Notable paintings: *Flag* 1954–1955; *False Start* 1959; *Numbers* 1960; *Zero Through Nine* 1961; *Perilous Night* 1982

Frank Stella

b. 1936

After studying at Princeton University, U.S. painter Frank Stella moved to New York City in 1958. He soon made an impact with his simple, monochrome-striped "Black Paintings," exhibited at the Museum of Modern Art in New York. Stella is also a printmaker. In the mid-1970s his work became three-dimensional and colorful by mixing materials. He has more recently worked with aluminum, steel, and fiberglass, and he completed public commissions such as the Miami *Bandshell* sculpture.

Notable paintings: "Black Paintings" 1959–1960; *Jarama II* 1982; *Die Marquise von O...* 1998

▲ Hockney's *Le Plongeur: the board* (1971) was made from colored and pressed paper pulp.

David Hockney

b. 1937

British artist David Hockney became an established artist while studying at London's Royal College of Art. A visit to Los Angeles in 1965 inspired his blue-sky paintings of swimming pools and water spraying and splashing. His most-famous portrait is of the fashion designer Ossie Clark, his wife, and cat. Hockney's other work includes etchings and collages and murals made from faxed images and Polaroids.

We 2 Boys Together Clinging 1961; *Bigger Splash* 1967; *Mr. and Mrs. Clark and Percy* 1970–1971

Damien Hirst

b. 1965

British conceptual artist Damien Hirst studied fine art at London's Goldsmith's College. While there he organized the groundbreaking "Freeze" exhibition, which launched the careers of a new generation of artists collectively labeled "Brit Artists." Hirst uses mixed media to explore themes of life and death. He is best-known for dissected animals that he floats in large tanks of formaldehyde, for example his preserved shark *The Physical Impossibility of Death in the Mind of Someone Living* (1991).

Notable works: *God* 1989; *Hymn* 1999

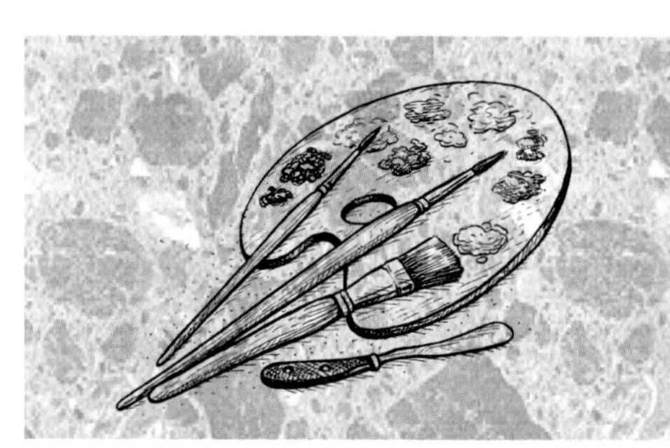

CLAES OLDENBURG b. 1929
Swedish-born Pop artist Claes Oldenburg moved to Chicago in 1937. He studied at the Art Institute of Chicago before moving to New York City in 1956. His soft sculptures of everyday consumer objects, which he sold from "The Store," made him famous in the early 1960s. In the 1970s these were developed into permanent public sculptures.

JIM DINE b. 1935
In the 1960s U.S. artist Jim Dine participated in the performance art "Happenings" with his contemporary Claes Oldenburg (left). Considered a Pop artist, Dine was also influenced by Surrealism. His mixed-media work is very autobiographical—early collages consist of large, colorful canvases with everyday household objects stuck to them.

SCULPTORS

Michelangelo

1475–1564

The Italian artist, sculptor, architect, and poet Michelangelo di Lodovico Buonarroti is considered, alongside Leonardo da Vinci (p. 157), as one of the outstanding figures of the Renaissance.

At the age of only 13 Michelangelo was learning to paint frescoes. He attended the Medici Garden sculpture school in Florence, and Lorenzo de Medici (1449–1492) became his patron. When Lorenzo died in 1492, Michelangelo moved to Bologna before being called to Rome by Cardinal San Giorgio in 1496. In Rome he studied ancient ruins and carved the marble *Pietà* (Mary holding the body of Christ) for St. Peter's Church. In Florence in 1501 he created the magnificent, larger-than-life, marble statue of *David* before returning to Rome to sculpt Pope Julius II's (1443–1513) tomb. He spent the last 30 years of his life in Rome, much of that time painting the superb ceiling of the Sistine Chapel.

Notable sculptures: *Bacchus* 1496–1498; *Pietà* 1498–1500; *David* 1501–1504; *Moses* 1515; *Rondanini Pietà* 1564

Notable paintings: Sistine Chapel 1508–1512; *The Last Judgement* 1537

▶ Michelangelo's *Moses* was originally intended to be part of Julius II's tomb.

▼ Rodin's sculpture *The Thinker* (1904).

Auguste Rodin

1840–1917

French figurative sculptor Auguste Rodin did not attend art school but instead became an apprentice in various arts, including masonry. By his mid-20s he was producing sculptures such as *The Man with the Broken Nose* (1864). His freestanding figure, *The Age of Bronze*, was so realistic that people accused Rodin of casting it from a real human body. He developed the idea that body fragments, such as a pair of hands(*The Cathedral*, 1907) could be sculptures in themselves. His marble sculptures *The Kiss* and *The Thinker* originated from his grand project "The Gates of Hell," which was inspired by Dante's (p. 118) *Inferno*.

Notable sculptures: *The Age of Bronze* 1877; *The Kiss* 1898; *The Thinker* 1904

DONATELLO 1386–1466
Italian Renaissance sculptor Donatello's real name was Donato de Betto di Bardi. Regarded as the founder of modern sculpture, he created many statues of saints and oversized heroic figures in marble and bronze, such as St. Mark and St. George at the Or San Michele (1415) and the bronze statue of David in Bargello (1430–1434).

GIOVANNI BOLOGNA 1524–1608
Flemish sculptor Giovanni Bologna was born Jean Bologne in France. He trained in Flanders before moving to Florence, Italy, where he became a great Renaissance sculptor and changed his name. He received many commissions from the wealthy Medici family, notably for *Flying Mercury* (1564) and *The Rape of the Sabines* (1580).

GIAN LORENZO BERNINI 1598–1680
This Rome-based sculptor, portrait painter, and church architect had prestigious patrons, including various popes, rich families, and France's Louis XIV (p. 16). Bernini combined colored marbles, stained glass, bronze, and stone, and he was the creator of the decorative Italian Baroque style.

Henry Moore

1898–1986

Henry Moore wanted to sculpt, but his coal-miner father encouraged him to become a teacher. Moore served in the war from 1917 to 1919, and afterward he studied sculpture in Leeds and London, England. By becoming a teacher at the Royal College of Art (1924–1931) and the Chelsea School of Art (1931–1939), both in England, he was able to continue sculpting. Moore created large, semiabstract, wood, stone, and bronze figures inspired by the natural forms around him. He achieved international recognition in the 1940s for his "Shelter Drawings"—huddled figures hiding in the London subway during the Blitz. He has been incredibly influential on the work of other artists, and his work is on display across the globe.

Notable sculptures: *Madonna and Child* 1943–1944; *Family Group* 1948–1949; *Reclining Figures* 1958 and 1965

Alberto Giacometti

1901–1966

This Swiss sculptor and painter moved to Paris, France, in 1922. In the early 1930s he was influenced by the Surrealists and produced abstract and symbolic pieces. However, in 1934 he began working on figurative sculptures. He is best known for his tall, skinny, single figures with textured surfaces that he produced starting in the late 1940s.

Notable sculptures: *Pointing Man* 1947; *Three Men Walking* 1948

▶ Henry Moore's *Reclining Figure.*

Barbara Hepworth

1903–1975

British sculptor Barbara Hepworth studied at Leeds School of Art, where she met and worked with fellow student Henry Moore (left). The pair continued their studies at London's Royal College of Art. During the 1930s she developed an abstract style inspired by the relationship between people and nature. Negative space in the form of holes, or voids, became a recurring motif in her simple, geometric, carved shapes in wood, stone, bronze, and alabaster.

Notable sculptures: *Pierced Form* 1931; *Single Form* 1963; *Four Square* 1966

Louise Bourgeois

b. 1911

In 1938 Bourgeois left her home city of Paris, France, and moved to New York City, where she still lives today. She began as a painter, but for the past 60 years she has devoted herself to sculpture. Influenced by Surrealism, she has produced sculptures and entire dreamlike room installations using plaster, wood, rubber, bronze, and found objects. She says that she often draws on childhood experiences for her work.

Notable sculptures: *Labyrinthine Tower* 1963; *Spiders* 1995

▶ In 1995 the French-born U.S. sculptor Louise Bourgeois produced a series of large, metal spiders.

JACOB EPSTEIN 1880–1959
Born in New York City, Epstein studied sculpture in Paris, France, with Rodin (p. 169) for two years until 1904. He then moved to London, England, where he spent most of his life. Epstein's bronze, stone, and aluminum public sculptures are large, bold, and abstract. He also sculpted bronze portrait heads of celebrities and children.

JEAN ARP 1887–1966
Born in Strasbourg, France, Jean Arp was a member of the *Der Blaue Reiter* group in Munich, Germany. One of the founders of the Dada movement, he produced many abstract sculptures in the 1920s but later worked more in three dimensions in his bas-reliefs and collages. Notable works include a 1958 mural for UNESCO in Paris.

ELIZABETH FRINK 1930–1993
This British sculptor studied at Guildford and Chelsea schools of art in England and also taught at various art schools, including London's Royal College of Art in the 1960s. Frink is known for her bronze sculptures of horses and riders, which she first modeled and carved in plaster. Her last commission was a Christ figure for Liverpool Cathedral.

PHOTOGRAPHERS

Louis Daguerre

1789–1851

Louis Daguerre began his career as a set painter at the Paris Opera in the early 1800s. In 1829 he teamed up with inventor Joseph Niépce (1765–1833) to work on developing a photographic process. Six years after Niepce's death Daguerre reduced the lengthy exposure time and improved the process by "fixing" the image. This meant that he was able to mass-produce positive images on silver plates. He gave his invention, the Daguerrotype, to France in 1839 and received a life pension in return.

Invented the first practical photographic process, the Daguerrotype 1839

▲ Louis Daguerre, inventor of the Daguerrotype.

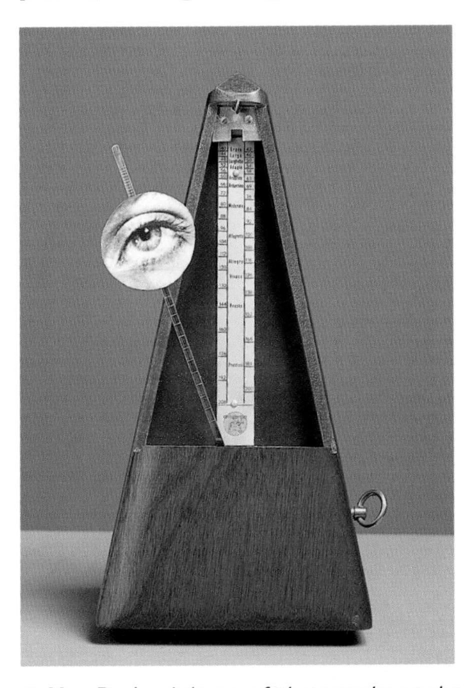

▲ Man Ray's subtle use of photography can be seen in *Metronome (Object to be destroyed).*

Man Ray

1890–1976

This avant-garde U.S. photographer, painter, and sculptor changed his name from Emmanuel Radnitzky. He won a scholarship to study architecture but instead became a painter in New York City. He took up photography at the age of 25, and his portraits began appearing in stylish magazines such as *Vogue*. With Marcel Duchamp (p. 165) he founded the Dada group. Ray moved to Paris, France, in 1921 and made Surrealist movies. He created Rayographs—cameraless photographs where an object is placed on photographic paper and exposed.

Notable work: *Aviary* 1919; *Metronome* 1923/1972; *Champs Delicieux* (Rayograph) 1922; *The Orator* 1935

Ansel Adams

1902–1984

U.S. photographer and conservationist Ansel Adams is well known for his landscape photography of the western United States, especially the National Parks such as Yosemite. He originally trained as a pianist, but in his late 20s he changed to photography. In 1932 he teamed up with photographer Edward Weston (1886–1958) to form the f/64 Group, whose aim was to achieve the highest-quality image and reproduce their subject matter as realistically as possible. Adams' photographs of craggy mountain ridges, valleys, and forests show a great depth of field but also contain fine details of nature and texture. His *Zone System* shows other photographers how to get the broadest tonal range from black-and-white film.

Notable work: photographs of western United States 1930s; *Zone System* 1941

Cecil Beaton

1904–1980

English socialite Cecil Beaton left Cambridge University to become a photographer, and by the age of 22 he had his first exhibition in London. His stylized fashion shots and portraits of aristocrats, movie stars, politicians, and royalty first made him famous in the 1930s. He also designed scenery and costumes for plays and movies, winning an Oscar for Audrey Hepburn's costumes in *My Fair Lady* in 1964.

Notable work: fashion photographs for *Vogue* and *Vanity Fair* 1920s; designed scenery and costumes for *Gigi* 1958

JULIA CAMERON 1815–1879
British photographer Julia Cameron was born and grew up in India. When her husband died, she returned to England and at the age of 48 was given a camera. She soon became known for her photographic portraits of famous Victorian people, such as Charles Darwin (p. 75) and the Pre-Raphaelite artist John Millais (p. 161).

EADWEARD MUYBRIDGE 1830–1904
Muybridge was born in England and moved to California in 1852, where he became a professional landscape photographer. He is known for his photographic studies of animals and humans in motion. They are seen as the forerunner to motion pictures, especially when viewed in sequence through his "zoopraxiscope," invented in 1880.

LENI RIEFENSTAHL b. 1902
German filmmaker Leni Riefenstahl produced documentaries of the Nuremberg rallies and the 1936 German Olympic Games. In 1945 she was briefly imprisoned for being a Nazi sympathizer, and she was blacklisted by the Allies until 1952. In the 1970s she produced two photographic books on the Nuba, a tribe in Africa.

Henri Cartier-Bresson

b. 1908

Before Henri Cartier-Bresson became a photographer, he studied painting with the Cubists and Surrealists in his native Paris. In 1930, while traveling around the Ivory Coast in Africa, he took his first photographs. He was soon selling his work to newspapers and magazines all over the world. Cartier-Bresson was one of the great pioneers of reportage photography, championing the idea that it is important to capture the most expressive and decisive visual moment in a social situation.

Cofounded Magnum Photos agency with Robert Capa (1913–1954) 1947

▲ Henri Cartier-Bresson at work in New York.

Paul Horst

1906–1999

Horst left his native Germany for Paris, France, where he became an apprentice to architect Le Corbusier (p. 175). While there he met the fashion photographer George Hoyningen-Huene and switched careers to become a photographer. Horst began working for *Vogue* in 1932. His extravagant style comes from his knowledge of classical art and Greek sculpture. His models and movie stars are dramatically lit and beautifully poised with luxurious backgrounds.

Notable work: Fashion photographs for *Vogue*, photographs of the Duchess of Windsor, Marlene Dietrich, and Coco Chanel 1930s

Richard Avedon

b. 1923

One of the most important 20th-century photographers, New Yorker Richard Avedon served in the photography department of the Merchant Marines during World War II. After the war he became the staff fashion photographer for *Harper's Bazaar* and *Vogue*. Avedon made the fashion models move and display emotion, and he often placed them in interesting outdoor locations. His reportage-style photographs include 1960s antiwar protesters and Vietnam victims, as well as the collapse of the Berlin Wall in 1989. The *New Yorker* made him staff photographer in 1992.

Notable work: *Harper's Bazaar*, *Vogue* 1945–1988; publications: *Observations* 1959; *Nothing Personal* 1964

◄ Since 1945 Richard Avedon has produced strikingly dramatic fashion photographs for *Harper's Bazaar*, *Vogue*, and *New Yorker* magazines.

ALFRED STIEGLITZ 1864–1946
Born in New York City, Stieglitz was influential in promoting photography as an art. He studied photography in Berlin, Germany, but returned to New York City in 1890. In 1902, with Edward Steichen (1879–1973), he established the American Photo-Secession Group and founded *Camera Work* magazine.

DAVID BAILEY b. 1938
British photographer David Bailey became a fashion photographer in 1959, and by 1960 he was working for *Vogue* magazine. During the "Swinging Sixties" in London, England, Bailey photographed every famous and fashionable celebrity. Since then he has also produced many books, documentaries, and television commercials.

ROBERT MAPPLETHORPE 1946–1989
New York City-born Mapplethorpe was originally a painter, but by the 1970s he was working as a photographer. Mapplethorpe's black-and-white photographs are admired for their classical beauty. His subject matter ranged from controversial male nudes to flowers and celebrity portraits.

ARCHITECTS

Filippo Brunelleschi

1377–1446

Born in Florence, Italy, Brunelleschi was one of the great architects of the Italian Renaissance.

Brunelleschi first trained as a goldsmith but was also a sculptor. In 1401 he was the joint winner in a competition to carve the bronze Baptistry doors in Florence, but he refused to work on the project with the other winner, Lorenzo Ghiberti (1378–1455). Instead he began studying classical architecture, visiting Rome to study the ruins. He also acted as an architectural consultant, and in 1418 he received the commission of a lifetime—to create the dome for the then incomplete Florence Cathedral. Inspired by classical themes, he built the huge dome—a marble octagonal—using Roman techniques such as herringbone brickwork.

Notable Florentine buildings: San Lorenzo Sacristy 1418–1428; Innocenti Hospital 1421–1444; Pazzi Chapel 1429–1461; Santo Spirito c. 1436

◀ Brunelleschi's masterpiece, the dome of Florence Cathedral, took 42 years to construct and displayed his talent for technical innovation, engineering, and geometry.

Andrea Palladio

1518–1580

This Italian architect began working as a stonemason in a guild in Vicenza, Italy. In his late 20s poet Giangiorgio Trissino (1478–1550) encouraged him to study architecture. In 1545 Palladio visited Rome and was impressed by the classical ruins. His Palladian style has greatly influenced other architects.

Notable Venetian buildings: San Giorgio Maggiore 1566; The Redentore 1577

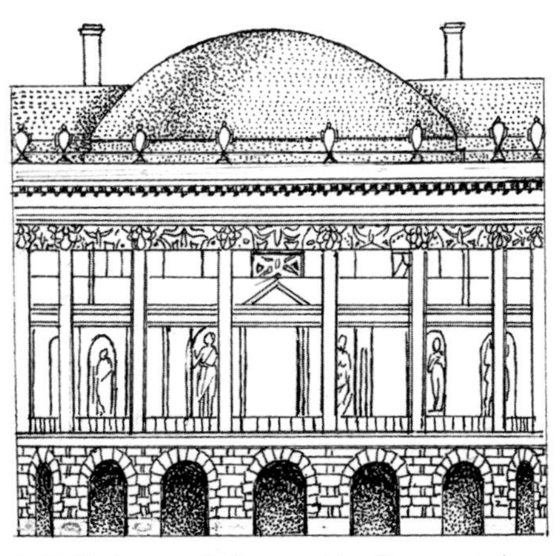

▲ Palladio was influenced by Roman styles.

Inigo Jones

1573–1652

English architect Inigo Jones was a self-taught architect. In 1615 he became Surveyor of the King's Works and championed the English Renaissance style. His buildings, inspired by Italian villas, show the influence of Palladio.

Notable London, England, buildings: Queen's House, Greenwich 1616–1618; Banqueting House, Whitehall 1619–1622; Covent Garden 1631–1638

JOHN VANBRUGH 1664–1726
Born in London, England, accomplished English Restoration comedy playwright John Vanbrugh was also a highly successful architect of Baroque-style buildings. Notable commissions included Castle Howard, Yorkshire (1702) and Blenheim Palace, Oxfordshire (1705). Vanbrugh was put in charge of the royal buildings in 1714.

JOHN NASH 1752–1835
English architect and town planner John Nash designed large country houses until he was commissioned by the king, George IV (1762–1830), to redesign a large area of central London. Between 1811 and 1825 Nash planned Regent's Park, Regent Street, Trafalgar Square, St. James' Park, Marble Arch, and Buckingham Palace.

AUGUST PUGIN 1812–1852
Born in England, Pugin learned architectural drawing from his French father, an expert in the Gothic style. He led the Gothic Revival in architecture and built many English churches and furnished them in this style. In 1840 Pugin was commissioned to design the furniture, fittings, and sculptures for the Houses of Parliament in London, England.

Christopher Wren

1632–1723

English architect Christopher Wren was an incredible scientist and scholar. At the age of only 25 he became professor of astronomy at Gresham College, London, and then at Oxford University in 1661. Wren was also a founding member of the Royal Society, a prestigious group of scientists. Early architectural projects include Pembroke College Chapel at Cambridge University (1663) and Oxford's Sheldonian Theater (1664). After the Great Fire of London in 1666 King Charles II (1630–1685) appointed him surveyor-general of royal buildings in 1669 and asked him to design 51 London churches and the new St. Paul's Cathedral. His style is Classical with Baroque influences.

Notable buildings in London: St. Stephen's, Walbrook (1672–1687); St. Paul's Cathedral (1675–1710); Chelsea Royal Hospital (1682–1692)

Robert Adam

1728–1792

Robert Adam was the son of Scottish architect William Adam (1689–1748), and he joined the family's architectural firm when his father died. In 1754 Adam visited Italy to learn about Roman architecture. He returned to London in 1758 and established an architectural firm with his brother, James Adam (1730–1794). Adam's Neoclassical style drew on French, Byzantine, Greek, and Baroque influences. He designed lavish decorative interiors down to every last detail for grand, stately homes.

Notable British buildings: Osterley Park 1761–1780; Syon House 1762–1769; Kenwood 1767–1769

Antonio Gaudí

1852–1926

Spanish architect Antonio Gaudí initially followed the Gothic Revival style, which was associated with Catalan nationalism, but he was also greatly inspired by Moorish architecture. Gaudí's style became increasingly decorative as he created fantastically ornate buildings with organic, curved forms and colorful mosaics. Gaudí was killed by a streetcar outside his unfinished masterpiece, the Sagrada Familia Church in Barcelona.

Notable Barcelona buildings: Sagrada Familia begun 1883; Palacio Güell 1886–1889; Casa Batlló 1904–1917

Charles Rennie Mackintosh

1868–1928

Influential Scottish architect and designer Charles Rennie Mackintosh was a leader of the "Glasgow group" of artists. He combined both traditional Scottish art and Art Nouveau in his work. Very few of his buildings remain.

Notable building: Glasgow School of Art 1897–1909

▲ Gaudí's masterpiece, the Sagrada Familia

Frank Lloyd Wright

1869–1959

U.S. architect, teacher, and writer Frank Lloyd Wright championed Organic Design. This movement sought to design buildings that were sympathetic to nature and the surrounding landscape. Wright had briefly studied engineering before moving to Chicago in 1887, and in 1893 he set up his own architectural firm. He is known for his Arts and Crafts style—low-built "prairie houses" with open-plan, split-level interiors.

Notable buildings: Imperial Hotel, Tokyo 1916–1920; Falling Water, Pennsylvania 1937–1939; Taliesin West, Arizona 1938; Guggenheim Museum, New York 1946–1959

◀ Wright's Guggenheim Museum of Art, New York City.

Ludwig Mies van der Rohe

1886–1969

German-born architect and designer Ludwig Mies worked with his stonemason father before moving to Berlin in 1905 to work with various architects, including Peter Behrens (1868–1940), between 1908 and 1911. Mies founded his own company in 1912 and adopted his mother's maiden name, Van der Rohe. A pioneer of Modernism and Functionalism, he championed a minimalist approach to architecture. In 1930 he became the last director of the Bauhaus Arts and Crafts movement. In 1937 he moved to Chicago, where he became a professor of architecture.

Notable buildings: German Pavilion, Barcelona 1929; Mannheim Opera House 1954; Seagram Building, New York 1958; Berlin National Gallery 1962–1968

Le Corbusier

1887–1965

French architect, painter, sculptor, and writer Le Corbusier was the most influential exponent of the modern "International Style" of architecture. Born Charles Edouard Jeanneret, he moved to Paris in 1917 and adopted the name Le Corbusier. He favored pure forms and steel-reinforced concrete. He also believed the house should be a "machine for living" and that cities should be ordered into high-rises.

Notable buildings: Unité d'Habitation, Marseilles 1946–1952; Notre-Dame-du-Haut, Ronchamp 1955

Louis Kahn

1901–1974

Born in Estonia, Louis Kahn's family emigrated to Philadelphia, Pennsylvania, in 1905. He was Professor of Architecture at Yale (1948–1957) and a dean at the University of Pennsylvania (1957–1974). Kahn was a Functionalist architect who liked using unfinished concrete and brick to create simple, geometric forms. His works were often on a monumental scale.

Notable U.S. buildings: Yale University Art Gallery 1952–1954; Richards Medical Research Building, Philadelphia 1958–1961; Salk Institute Laboratories, California 1959–1965

Jørn Utzon

b. 1918

Danish architect Jørn Utzon worked briefly for the architect Alvar Aalto (right). He set up his own company in 1950 and achieved international recognition for the Sydney Opera House in Australia. The sails of ships in Sydney harbor were the inspiration for his sculptural design. Utzon resigned before the project was completed because of the various changes that were made to his design during construction.

Notable buildings: Kingo Houses, Elsinore, Denmark 1956; Sydney Opera House 1957–1973; Bagsvaerd Church, Copenhagen 1974–1976

▼ Designed by Jørn Utzon, Sydney Opera House is constructed of curved concrete roof vaults that rise to a height of 220 ft. (67m).

EDWIN LUTYENS 1869–1944
A former London Royal College of Art student, English architect Edwin Lutyens designed furniture, churches, commercial buildings, monuments, castles, and country homes. The Arts and Crafts movement influenced him, but he also mastered Neo-Georgian and Baroque styles and later favored classical architecture. Lutyens designed the Cenotaph in London's Whitehall (1919–1920) and the Viceroy's House in New Delhi, India (1912–1930).

WALTER GROPIUS 1883–1969
Walter Gropius studied architecture in Munich and Berlin, both in Germany, and established a practice with Adolf Meyer in Berlin (1910). They designed the ultramodern glass and steel Werkbund Pavilion for the Cologne Exhibition (1914). Gropius founded the influential, German-based Bauhaus school in 1919 and was the director until 1928. He later moved to the U.S. and became Professor of Architecture at Harvard University (1937–1952). He created private residences, skyscrapers, and many public buildings.

ALVAR AALTO 1898–1976
Finnish architect Alvar Aalto was a major contributor to Scandinavia's Modernist architecture movement and an influential founding father of Organic Design. He designed the Paimio Sanitorium (1929–1932) and Otaniemi Technical University (1949–1964), both in Finland, as well as residential, religious, and public buildings in Scandinavia and Europe. Aalto believed in using natural materials, especially wood, and invented bent plywood (1932) that changed chair design forever. His company, Artek (1935), manufactured his furniture, including the classic L-legged stacking stools (1933).

MINURO YAMASAKI 1912–1986
Born in Seattle, Washington, architect Minuro Yamasaki studied architecture at the University of Washington and graduated in 1934. He moved to New York City and achieved fame in the 1950s with his sensuous, textile-like structures. Notable buildings from this period include St. Louis Airport (1951–1956) and the American Concrete Institute (1958). Yamasaki also designed the twin towers of the World Trade Center, (1966–1977), New York City, which were destroyed in a terrorist attack on September 11, 2001.

Richard Rogers

b. 1933

English architect Richard Rogers was born in Florence, Italy. He studied architecture in London, England, and at Yale University, where he met Norman Foster (below). They worked together in England as "Team 4" (1963–1966), introducing their "High Tech" style of architecture in the Reliance Controls Building in Swindon, England (1965). Rogers is famous for the brightly colored, factory like Pompidou Center in Paris, France, which he created with Italian architect Renzo Piano (b. 1937), his partner from 1971–1977. Rogers favors large, open spaces inside buildings with the plumbing pipes and elevators on the outside. He also designed the European Court of Human Rights, Strasbourg, completed in 1995.

Notable buildings: Pompidou Center, Paris, France 1972–1976; Lloyds Building, London, England 1979–1984

▲ The controversial and dramatic steel and glass Lloyds Building in London, England, was designed by Richard Rogers.

Philippe Starck

b. 1949

French designer Philippe Starck is famous for his fantastical restaurants, surreal hotel interiors, and quirky consumer products such as the tripod-shaped "Juicy Salif" lemon squeezer. His career took off in 1969 when he became the art director of Pierre Cardin's studio, producing 65 furniture designs while there. Starck moved into interior design with nightclubs like Les Bains Douche (1978) in Paris. He gained widespread recognition when he was commissioned to design French President Mitterand's (b. 1916) private suite at the Elysée Palace in 1982. His products include three-legged chairs, colanders, toothbrushes, lamps, and even a motorcycle. Since designing the Royalton Hotel in New York City in 1988 he has created many other hotels.

Notable hotels: Mondrian, Los Angeles, California 1996; Sanderson, London, England 2000

Norman Foster

b. 1936

English architect Norman Foster studied architecture at Manchester University in England and at Yale, where he met fellow student Richard Rogers (above). They formed the "Team 4" partnership after returning to England in 1963 and designed buildings with the steel structure exposed to look very industrial and technological. In 1967 Foster formed Foster Associates, and they now have offices in London, Berlin, and Singapore. Since then Foster and his team have designed the award-winning Willis Faber and Dumas Headquarters in England (1970–1974), the Hong Kong & Shanghai Bank in Hong Kong (1979–1986), Stansted Airport in London, England (1981–1991), and the London Millennium Bridge (1996–2000).

Notable buildings: Chek Lap Kok Airport, Hong Kong 1992–1998; New German Parliament at the Reichstag, Berlin 1992–1999

▲ Designed by Norman Foster, The Great Court at the British Museum, London, opened in 2000.

CHAPTER EIGHT

MUSICIANS AND DANCERS

Music and Dance before 1000

Since the Stone Age when people made pipes out of hollow bones, music and dance have played an important part in people's lives. By 3000 B.C. when the first great civilizations were established in Egypt and Mesopotamia (modern-day Iraq), music was used both in rituals and as entertainment, and many instruments—from harps and lyres to trumpets and rattles—had become well established.

▲ The Etruscans, who lived in Italy before the Romans, made rich and varied music with instruments such as lyres and double flutes.

THE GREEKS AND ROMANS
The ancient Greeks were accomplished musicians who admired the power of music to move and entertain the listener. They used many different instruments, such as panpipes, kitharas (12-stringed lyres), and *aulos* (double-reed pipes), and they played music at banquets, during ceremonies, and at plays. Many famous Greek playwrights were also musicians, and the writer **Sophocles** (495–406 B.C.) was also one of the most famous dancers of his time. **Timotheus** (446–357 B.C.) and **Philoxenus** (430–380 B.C.) were notable composers who wrote moving vocal music and explored new ways of writing for instruments. Their music was based on scales known as modes. The Etruscans and Romans were heavily influenced by ancient Greek music and dance. Perhaps the most famous dancer in the Roman world was the princess **Salome** (A.D. 100s), who was said to have performed the famous dance of the seven veils in front of Herod Antipas.

THE CHRISTIAN WORLD
With the fall of the Roman Empire the arrival of Christianity took music in new directions, and monasteries became the main places for teaching music. **St. Paul** (died c. A.D. 64) encouraged his followers to sing psalms and hymns, and by A.D. 387 **St. Ambrose** had introduced professional choirs who sang solos and choral refrains. In Rome, **Pope Gregory I** (A.D. 540–604) founded a music school and wrote a series of choral chants. Music in this style is still known as Gregorian chants. The other major change was that music was written down. Flemish monks such as **Hucbald** (A.D. 840–930) invented new forms of notation that helped music become more sophisticated.

EASTERN MUSIC
From Arabia to China, the eastern cultures created their own styles of music. The sage **Bharata**, known as the father of Indian music, wrote a book on Hindu music in around 200 B.C. The Arabs invented the lute and produced master musicians such as **Ibn Misjah** (died c. A.D. 715). In India, dance and music were used in temples and palaces.

◀ Painted by Buddhist monks between 200 B.C. and A.D. 650, these wall paintings in Ajanta, India, show musicians and dancers entertaining royalty at a banquet.

CLASSICAL MUSIC

Antonio Vivaldi

1678–1741

Born in Venice, Italian violinist and composer Antonio Vivaldi first became a priest in 1703 and then a violin teacher at a school for orphaned girls. There he wrote a number of concertos to use as teaching aids. Publication of the concertos brought him a much wider audience and fame throughout Europe. Vivaldi became one of the best-known composers of the Baroque era, writing over 40 operas and over 500 concertos, 230 of them for solo violin and over 100 for other musical instruments. He did plenty to establish the form of the concerto in three movements in its fast–slow–fast format. Vivaldi's final years were spent in relative poverty, and his music was forgotten until it was rediscovered in the 1800s.

Notable compositions: *L'Estro Armonico* 1712; *The Four Seasons* 1725

J. S. Bach

1685–1750

German composer Johann Sebastian Bach was orphaned before he was 10 and raised by his older brother, also called Johann, who was an organist. Bach showed great talent at the instrument, and in 1717 he became director of music to Prince Leopold of Cöthen (1694–1728). He moved to Leipzig, where he wrote his choral works, the *St. Matthew Passion* (1727) and *Mass in B Minor* (1733). Although Bach never left Germany, he was influenced by French and Italian styles, working in most musical forms except opera. He is one of the world's supreme composers of orchestral and choral works.

Notable compositions: Six *Brandenburg Concertos* 1721; *The Well-tempered Clavier* 1722; *St. John Passion* 1724

George Frideric Handel

1685–1759

German composer Handel became the organist at Halle Cathedral at the age of 17. He then spent several years in Italy, building up his reputation as a keyboard player. In 1710 Handel became director of music to the court in Hanover, Germany. However, he spent most of his time in London, England, which angered the Elector of Hanover, who in 1714 became George I of England. Handel's *Water Music* is thought to have been a peace offering to the king. His output included 46 operas, 32 oratorios, and other orchestral music.

Notable compositions: *Water Music* 1714; *Messiah* 1742

▼ Handel composed much of his most-popular music in London, England.

JOSQUIN DES PREZ c. 1450–1521
Composer Josquin des Prez was born in what is now Belgium. He spent much of his time in Italy as the composer for the wealthy Sforza family. Des Prez was a highly sought-after master of music, and in later life he composed music for Louis XII of France (1462–1515). His musical output was prolific and it included masses, motets (songs composed for the choir in Catholic church services), and nonreligious songs in French and Italian.

JOHN TAVERNER c. 1490–1545
English composer John Taverner was the organist in Boston, Lincolnshire, and at Christ Church College, Oxford, both in England. He is best known for his religious music, sung in Latin. Taverner's work includes eight masses and a number of motets, or short religious choral pieces. In Oxford, he was accused of heresy and briefly imprisoned. Taverner was pardoned by Cardinal Wolsey (c. 1475–1530) and released because he was considered to be "merely a musician."

GIOVANNI PALESTRINA c. 1525–1594
Italian composer Giovanni Palestrina was appointed by Pope Julius III (1487–1555) as the organist and choir master at St. Peter's Church in Rome. There he wrote a large number of masses and choral works before retiring. Palestrina is widely regarded as the most important composer of the Renaissance period, and his work greatly influenced composers such as Bach (left) and Mozart (p. 180).

ALESSANDRO SCARLATTI 1659–1725
Born in Sicily, Italian composer Alessandro Scarlatti started his career in Rome and wrote his first opera at the age of 21. This attracted the patronage of the Swedish queen, Kristina (1626–1689). In 1693 Scarlatti became the musical director to the Naples court. Over his lifetime he composed 120 operas, 200 masses, and 500 cantatas.

Wolfgang Amadeus Mozart

1756–1791

Born in Austria, Mozart was a child prodigy, playing the piano at the age of four and composing music by five. Under his father's management he played for royalty in many European countries.

By the age of 13 Mozart had written his first opera and played the violin for some of the most important European courts. In 1774 he was appointed as a court musician to the Archbishop of Salzburg, Austria, where he composed a number of symphonies, sonatas, and concertos. Unhappy with his employers, he left Salzburg and settled in Vienna, where he successfully wrote and taught music. In later years, although poor, he wrote some of the most brilliant music of his career. He worked himself into a state of total exhaustion trying to complete his great *Requiem*, and he died at the age of 35. He composed 41 symphonies, 11 operas, 27 piano concertos, and plenty of chamber, keyboard, and religious music. Mozart was one of the world's greatest musical geniuses. His music is known for its melodic beauty and richness of harmony.

Notable compositions: *The Marriage of Figaro* 1786; *Don Giovanni* 1787; *Cosi fan tutte* 1790; *The Magic Flute* 1791

◀ As a young child Mozart played the piano and violin for many European rulers, including the Austrian empress Maria Theresa (1717–1780) and the French king Louis XV (1710–1774). Mozart's serenade, *Eine Kleine Nachtmusik*, was composed at the peak of his career in 1787.

Ludwig van Beethoven

1770–1827

German composer Beethoven moved to Vienna, Austria, in 1787, where he was briefly taught by Mozart (above). In 1792 he was taught composition by Joseph Haydn (p. 181). Beethoven made his public debut as a pianist in 1795 and by 1802 had composed two symphonies and three piano concertos. Although suffering from deafness and depression, he went on to write some of his finest masterpieces.

Notable compositions: *Moonlight Sonata* 1801; "Symphony No. 3" *(Eroica)* 1804; *Für Elise* 1810

▲ Beethoven greatly influenced later composers.

Franz Schubert

1797–1828

Born in Austria, Schubert won a choral scholarship to a music school in 1808. He wrote his first symphony at the age of 16, and by 1815 he had written over 100 songs, including *Gretchen am Spinnrade* and *Erlkönig*. For a while, Schubert earned his living by teaching music but gave this up in 1817. Poverty-stricken for most of his life, Schubert wrote a total of seven operas, six masses, over 600 songs, and nine symphonies. His symphonies are emotional and inventive and display an impressive command of orchestration.

Notable compositions: *Trout Quintet in A major* 1819; *Unfinished Symphony* 1822

Frédéric Chopin

1810–1849

Polish-born musician and composer Frédéric Chopin made his public debut as a pianist at the young age of eight, and by the age of 15 he had published his first composition. Chopin moved to Paris, France, in 1831 and tried making a living as a concert pianist. However, the delicacy of his touch on the keyboard did not suit the large concert halls, and he found himself playing in smaller, more intimate salons. Chopin's many mazurkas, polonaises, études, and waltzes reflected his Polish origins.

Notable compositions: "Scherzo in B flat Minor" 1835–1837; *Fantasia* 1841

▲ Johannes Brahms in his later years.

Johannes Brahms

1833–1897

German composer Brahms was taught to play the piano at the age of seven. To earn money he played in Hamburg's dockland bars. Brahms became a close friend of both Robert Schumann (1810–1856) and Franz Liszt (1811–1886), and in 1863 he settled in Vienna, Austria. Brahms set very high standards for his own work, destroying anything that was not perfect.

Notable compositions: *Hungarian Dances* 1868–1880; *German Requiem* 1869

▲ Photograph of Tchaikovsky with a dedication to his friend, the Czech composer Antonín Dvorák (1841–1904).

Pyotr Ilich Tchaikovsky

1840–1893

Russian composer Tchaikovsky showed an early talent for music, but he studied law and became a minor civil servant. In 1862 he enrolled at St. Petersburg's music conservatory, and in 1866 he became the professor of music at the music conservatory in Moscow. In the same year Tchaikovsky wrote his first symphony. Further compositions soon followed, bringing his name to the attention of Moscow's music lovers. He got married in 1877, but only one month later he suffered a nervous breakdown and left his wife. He resigned from the music conservatory and retired to the country to devote himself to composing. He died soon after the first performance of his Sixth Symphony. It was thought that he died from cholera, but it is now believed that he may have committed suicide. Much of his richly emotional music—including ballet scores, operas, and symphonies—are still widely performed.

Notable ballet: *Swan Lake* 1877
Notable compositions: *1812 Overture* 1882; "Sixth Symphony" *(Pathétique)* 1893

JOSEPH HAYDN 1732–1809
Self-taught Austrian composer Joseph Haydn began his career playing in street orchestras. After working with Italian opera composer Niccola Porpora (1686–1766), Haydn became the musical director to the wealthy Hungarian Esterházy family in 1761. For 30 years his duties involved composing and performing orchestral and chamber music, religious music, and operas. His enormous output made him one of the most notable composers of his day.

NICCOLÒ PAGANINI 1782–1840
Urged on by his domineering father, Italian violinist Niccolò Paganini gave his first concert at the age of 11. By 1805 he was touring Italy. During the 1820s Paganini's fame had spread to Europe as audiences were dazzled by his astonishing violin playing, demonic manner, and showmanship. Paganini also wrote many pieces for the violin and for the guitar, an instrument that he also played with great skill.

HECTOR BERLIOZ 1803–1869
French composer Hector Berlioz had to overcome his family's objections and abandon a career in medicine for his love of music. After studying at the Paris Conservatoire, Berlioz wrote *Symphonie fantastique*, in which he expressed his love for the Irish actress and wife-to-be Harriet Smithson (1800–1854). His many symphonies, overtures, and operas, although hugely popular across most of Europe, were never acknowledged in his native land.

JOHANN STRAUSS 1825–1899
Born in Vienna, Austria, and one of 13 children fathered by the composer Johann Strauss (1804–1849), Johann formed his own orchestra and toured Europe and the U.S. Known as the "Waltz King," Strauss was a prolific composer of hundreds of waltzes, including *The Blue Danube* (1874) and *Tales From the Vienna Woods* (1868), as well as polkas and operettas.

Edward Elgar

1857–1934

Apart from receiving violin lessons, English composer Edward Elgar was mainly self-taught. In 1891, encouraged by his wife, Caroline, Elgar moved to the country to concentrate on his composing. His early works, including the *Enigma Variations* and *The Dream of Gerontius* (1900), won much praise in England and Germany, and he began to acquire the reputation as being one of England's leading musical figures. The *Pomp and Circumstance* marches added greatly to his fame, and after the Elgar Festival in London in 1904 he was knighted into British society. After the death of his wife in 1920 Elgar virtually gave up composing. A symphony and an opera remained unfinished at his death.

Notable compositions: *Enigma Variations* 1899; *Pomp and Circumstance* 1901; *Cockaigne* 1901; *Cello Concerto* 1919

▶ From 1924 Edward Elgar was Master of the King's Music for George V (1865–1936).

Gustav Mahler

1860–1911

Born in Czechoslovakia, Mahler entered the Vienna Music Conservatory in 1875 to study composition and conducting. He worked as a conductor in various European cities before becoming Artistic Director of the Vienna State Opera House in 1897. Mahler resigned in 1907 after attacks on his Jewish origin, and in 1908 he became the conductor of the New York Philharmonic Society Orchestra. Mahler wrote nine symphonies and is considered to be the first of the modern classical composers.

Notable compositions: Second Symphony 1895; *Das Lied von der Erde (Song of the Earth)* 1908

◀ Mahler was not fully recognized as a composer until the 1960s.

Sergei Rachmaninov

1873–1943

Russian composer and virtuoso pianist Sergei Rachmaninov studied music at the St. Petersburg and Moscow music conservatories. One of the leading concert pianists of his day, he was in great demand across Europe and became famous for his interpretations of Chopin (p. 181) and Liszt (1811–1886), as well as his own work. In 1918 Rachmaninov fled to the U.S. to escape the Russian Revolution. His piano compositions, especially the *Prelude in C Sharp Minor* (1938), and concertos fully extended the repertoire of this instrument.

Notable compositions: 2nd and 3rd Piano Concertos 1900–1909; *Rhapsody on a Theme of Paganini* 1934

Gustav Holst

1874–1934

Born to Swedish parents, English composer Holst became an orchestral trombonist in 1892. In 1903 he began teaching music at girls' schools in London, England, and went on to teach at the British Royal College of Music and in American universities. He was also a composer, working his interest in Indian mysticism and English folk songs into his music. His major work, *The Planets*—a series of sound portraits of seven planets in the solar system—became one of the most popular orchestral pieces from the 1900s. Holst also wrote four short operas, two concertos, and several shorter works for orchestra.

Notable compositions: *The Planets* 1914–1916; *The Hymn of Jesus* 1917; *Ode to Death* 1919; *The Perfect Fool* 1922

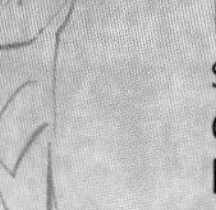

NIKOLAY RIMSKY-KORSAKOV 1844–1908
Russian composer Nikolay Rimsky-Korsakov studied music while working as a naval officer. Self-taught in musical composition, he was appointed Professor at the St. Petersburg Conservatory in 1871. His most notable works are *Scheherazade* (1888) and the opera *The Golden Cockerel* (1907).

GABRIEL FAURÉ 1845–1924
French composer Gabriel Fauré went to music school at the age of nine and became a skilled organist. He settled in Paris, France, playing the organ in churches and teaching at the Paris Conservatoire. As a composer Fauré spent most of his time writing songs, but he is best remembered for his choral work *Requiem* (1887–1890).

Pablo Casals

1876–1973

Spanish cellist, conductor, and composer Pablo Casals studied at the Madrid Conservatory before moving to the Barcelona Conservatory as Professor of the Cello. In 1895 Casals became the lead cellist in the Paris Opéra. Three years later he began his long solo career. He founded the Barcelona Orchestra in 1919, which he conducted until the start of the Spanish Civil War in 1936. In a protest against the Fascists he left Spain for France, never to return again. In 1950 he began a music festival in Prades, France, which featured classical chamber music. Casals died in Puerto Rico.

Notable compositions: Suite in D for Cello 1932; *El Cant Dels Ocells* 1950

▼ The young Pablo Casals with his cello.

▼ Andrés Segovia, the maestro of the Spanish guitar, playing at a concert in his later years.

Sergey Prokofiev

1891–1953

Russian composer Sergey Prokofiev wrote his first piano piece at the age of five, and by the age of 11 he had written two operas. From 1904–1914 he studied at the St. Petersburg Conservatory. Prokofiev was a rebellious student with radical ideas about composition. He caused a sensation among his teachers, who thought his music was ugly and discordant. In 1917 he left the Soviet Union, touring the U.S. and living in Paris, France. Prokofiev composed operas, symphonies, ballet, piano, and violin concertos, and movie scores. He returned to the Soviet Union in 1936 but was never in favor with the Communist regime.

Notable compositions: *The Fiery Angel* 1927; *Peter and the Wolf* 1936

Andrés Segovia

1893–1987

Spanish guitarist and composer Andrés Segovia was greatly influenced by Spanish nationalist composers, and he developed a guitar style that suited a wide variety of music. As a child he was discouraged from playing the guitar by his family because they felt it was not a serious musical instrument. However, he continued and made his concert debut in Paris, France, in 1924. Within a few years Segovia was world famous, and many of the top composers were writing specifically for him. Above all he was responsible for the acceptance of the acoustic guitar as a valid classical concert instrument. Segovia also transposed many classical masterpieces for the guitar.

Notable composition: "Estudio for Guitar in E Major" 1912

JOHN PHILIP SOUSA 1854–1932
U.S. composer and bandleader Sousa studied the trombone before joining the U.S Marine band in 1867. In 1880 he became the band's conductor. He formed his own band in 1892, gaining an international reputation. Sousa composed over 100 marches, including his most famous, *Stars and Stripes Forever* (1896), as well as a few comic operas.

CLAUDE DEBUSSY 1862–1918
French composer Claude Debussy entered the Paris Conservatoire at the age of 10. By the age of 18 he had perfected his skills at composition, finally winning one of the Conservatoire's most prestigious prizes. His compositions, including *La Mer* (1905), explored new avenues of musical expression and had a profound effect on French music.

ARNOLD SCHOENBERG 1874–1951
Austrian-born Schoenberg learned to play the violin as a young boy but was otherwise self-taught. An experimental composer, Schoenberg tried to express "pure emotion" in sound and developed a new style of composition known as the" twelve-note method." He was also a notable painter and friend of artist Wasily Kandinsky (p. 163).

Shinichi Suzuki
1898–1997

It is not surprising that Shinichi Suzuki became a violin player—his father made violins, and he spent his childhood in Japan surrounded by them. Suzuki learned to play as a child and then went to Germany to continue studying. In 1946 he opened his own school, where he created the Suzuki Method to teach children to play the violin. His method involves playing by ear and not by reading music. It is used worldwide to teach children many types of instruments.

Notable achievement: created the Suzuki Method of teaching the violin 1946

▲ Shinichi Suzuki demonstrates his Suzuki Method to a group of young violin students.

Aaron Copland
1900–1990

Born to Russian immigrant parents, U.S. composer Aaron Copland wrote many types of music—from concertos to movie scores. In 1921 he went to Paris, France, to study music, returning to the U.S. in 1924, where his first commissioned concerto, *Symphony for Organ and Orchestra*, was performed in 1925. Influenced by jazz and folk, Copland became the first serious composer of American music. He composed several ballets, often about American history—for example, *Appalachian Spring* (1944).

Notable compositions: *Billy the Kid* 1938; *Rodeo* 1942; *A Lincoln Portrait* 1942

◀ Indian sitar player Ravi Shankar was brought up by his poverty-stricken mother. Ravi's older brother, Uday (1900–1977), was an Indian dancer, who during the 1920s performed with ballerina Anna Pavlova (1881–1931) in London, England.

Ravi Shankar
b. 1920

Award-winning composer, teacher, and sitar player Ravi Shankar is India's most famous musician, and he has been highly influential in introducing Indian music to the West. From 1930 he lived and studied in Paris, France, and began playing in public at the age of 12. He made his name playing classical Indian music on the sitar, making his first appearance as a soloist in 1939. His many compositions include a violin–sitar piece for Yehudi Menuhin (p. 185) and himself, concertos for orchestras, and music for ballets and movies, including the scores for Satyajit Ray's (p. 150) *Apu* trilogy. Shankar has toured the world, playing at festivals such as Woodstock (1969). He has also founded Indian music schools and formed the National Orchestra of India. He has taught and worked with many western musicians, including Philip Glass (p. 185) and George Harrison (p. 191), who called him the "Godfather of World Music."

Notable albums: *East Greets East* 1978; *Tana Mana* 1987; *Passages* 1990
Notable movie scores: *Dharti Ke Lal* 1946; *Neecha Nagar* 1946; *Gandhi* 1982

Evelyn Glennie
b. 1965

Scottish-born Evelyn Glennie is the world's only percussion soloist. She was deaf by the time she was 12 but taught herself how to sense music by feeling vibrations. Glennie trained at London's Royal Academy of Music and plays many different types of music—from classical to popular. She has won many awards for her playing.

Notable composition: *Sonata for Two Pianos and Percussion* 1989

▲ Many famous composers have written works for deaf percussionist Evelyn Glennie.

Child Prodigies

Yehudi Menuhin 1916–1999
Daniel Barenboim b. 1942
Jacqueline du Pré 1945–1987
Nigel Kennedy b. 1956
Vanessa-Mae b. 1978

Many famous musicians showed talent at a very young age and were encouraged by their parents and teachers to develop their special skills.

At the age of seven New York City-born **Yehudi Menuhin** demonstrated a special talent for the violin by performing Mendelssohn's "Violin Concerto" in front of an audience in San Francisco. He went on to become a world-famous violinist, and in 1963 he founded a school of music for talented young musicians.

Born in Argentina, Israeli pianist and conductor **Daniel Barenboim** also made his first public performance at the age of seven. He later became a leading conductor and married the British cellist **Jacqueline du Pré** in 1967. Du Pré had been given her first cello by her parents at the age of five. She made her first public performance at the age of 16 and soon became the world's leading cellist. Sadly she died from multiple sclerosis at the young age of 42. English virtuoso violinist **Nigel Kennedy** studied at the Yehudi Menuhin School and made his solo debut at London's Royal Festival Hall in 1977. He went on to become an internationally acclaimed violinist.

Singapore-born **Vanessa-Mae** was also a child prodigy—at the age of 10 she became the youngest violin soloist in history to play the Bach and Mozart violin concertos, which she did with the British Royal Philarmonic Orchestra.

◀ Young Yehudi Menuhin playing his violin.

◀ At the age of eight Vanessa-Mae moved to China, where she learned to play the violin at the Central Conservatoire in Beijing. By the time she was 12 she had recorded three albums.

DMITRY SHOSTAKOVICH 1906–1975

Russian composer Dmitry Shostakovich studied music at the St. Petersburg Conservatory. The performance of his *First Symphony* in 1926 brought him worldwide fame. He composed 15 symphonies and many concertos, ballets, and operas. Shostakovich often fell out of favor because the Communist authorities disliked his experimental music, for example his opera *The Nose* (1927–1928).

JOHN CAGE 1912–1992

Avant-garde U.S. composer John Cage is known for his experimental and unusual music. He studied under the composers Henry Cowell (1897–1965) and Arnold Schoenberg (p. 183) and became interested in percussion and timing. Cage experimented, producing new musical sounds and even composing a piece of music in 1952 that was totally silent! He invented the "prepared piano"—placing objects inside a grand piano to alter its sound.

KARLHEINZ STOCKHAUSEN b. 1928

In 1951 German avant-garde composer Karlheinz Stockhausen went to Paris, France, where he spent two years working with a group of composers called "Musique Concrète." In 1954 he attended Bonn University, in Germany, where he studied acoustics, composition, and the sounds made by music. He also experimented with electronic sounds, and some of his work, such as *Kontakte* (1959–1960), contrasts the sounds of regular musical instruments with electronic noises.

PHILIP GLASS b. 1937

U.S. composer of modern music Philip Glass studied with French musician Nadia Boulanger (1887–1979) in Paris, France, from 1964. He was influenced by eastern music after working with Ravi Shankar (p. 184). Glass composes music for dance, movies, operas, and theater, including *Einstein on the Beach* (1976) and *Satyagraha* (1980).

OPERA

Claudio Monteverdi

1567–1643

Italian composer Claudio Monteverdi began his musical career as a choirboy and a violinist. By the age of 15 he had published his first compositions. In 1607 he composed one of the first great operas, *Orfeo*. Monteverdi was appointed Music Master of St. Mark's in Venice, Italy, in 1613, where he also continued writing church music. However, Monteverdi is best known for his operas. His ideas and compositions helped develop the expressive art of opera in its early days.

Notable compositions: *Orfeo* 1607; *The Return of Ulysses* 1641; *The Coronation of Poppea* 1642

Richard Wagner

1813–1883

German composer Richard Wagner's early work was not popular, and after a brief period conducting at a theater in Riga, Latvia, he moved to Paris, France, where he worked as a journalist. The performance in Dresden, Germany, of his opera *Rienzi* in 1842 launched his career. Because of his revolutionary politics, Wagner lived in exile in France and Switzerland from 1848–1861. In 1876 he opened a theater in Bayreuth, Germany, where he staged his *Ring Cycle* series based on German myths and legends.

Notable compositions: *Lohengrin* 1848; *The Valkyrie* 1856; *Ring Cycle* 1876

Guiseppe Verdi

1813–1901

Verdi's musical training began at his local church in Roncole, Italy. His education was sponsored by locals, who paid for him to study in Milan. But in 1832 Verdi was rejected by the Milan Music Conservatory, and he studied privately. After the performance of his first great operatic work, *Nabucco* (1842), Verdi was in demand by Italy's top theaters. Many of his operas are based on the plays of Shakespeare (p. 120). *Aida* was written especially for the opening of the new opera house in Cairo, Egypt, in 1871.

Notable compositions: *Rigoletto* 1851; *La Traviata* 1853; *Falstaff* 1893

Nellie Melba

1861–1939

Nellie Melba was born Helen Mitchell in Melbourne, Australia. Her parents were musical, and she had some singing lessons as a young girl. It was not until 1882 that she decided to sing professionally. She studied in Paris, France, and chose the stage name Melba because she was from Melbourne. Her first performance was in Brussels, Belgium, in 1887 as Gilda in Verdi's *Rigoletto*. Melba was the prima donna of London's Covent Garden and performed in cities around the world. Her voice was admired for its purity and high range, and she took the lead roles in *La Bohème* and *Aida*. She also made some of the earliest gramophone recordings and enjoyed a long singing partnership with Italian tenor Caruso (p. 187).

Notable performances: *Rigoletto* 1886; *Romeo and Juliet* 1889; *La Bohème* 1923

▼ Nellie Melba often sang at London's Covent Garden Opera House. It was there in 1926 where she gave her final performance.

HENRY PURCELL 1659–1695
At the age of 20 English composer Henry Purcell became the organist at Westminster Abbey in London. He wrote music for the coronations of James II (1633–1701) and William III (p. 17). Purcell's only opera was *Dido and Aeneas* (1689). He also wrote church music and music for the plays *King Arthur* (1691) and *The Fairie Queen* (1692).

GEORGES BIZET 1838–1875
French pianist and composer Georges Bizet was nine when he went to study at the Paris Conservatoire. He went on to win the Grand Prix de Rome in 1857 for his miniopera *Le Docteur Miracle*. Bizet is best known for the opera *Carmen*, which was first performed in his native city of Paris in 1875 and is still popular today.

GIACOMO PUCCINI 1858–1924
Italian composer Puccini won a scholarship to study at the music conservatory in Milan in 1880. His first major success was the opera *Manon Lescaut* (1893). Puccini is best known for his operatic masterpieces—*La Bohème* (1896), *Tosca* (1900), *Madame Butterfly* (1904), and *Turandot*. The latter was completed after his death.

Richard Strauss

1864–1949

German composer Richard Strauss studied music in Berlin and went on to become a conductor in Bayreuth. He also wrote many tone poems, including *Also sprach Zarathustra* (1895–1896). His first opera, *Guntram*, was staged in 1894. When Strauss' operas *Salome* and *Elektra* were performed, audiences were shocked by their violence. His works after that, such as the comedy opera *Der Rosenkavalier*, were more traditional.

Notable compositions: *Salome* 1905; *Elektra* 1909; *Der Rosenkavalier* 1911

Benjamin Britten

1913–1976

English composer Benjamin Britten won a scholarship to the London Royal College of Music in 1930. His first successful and most-famous opera is *Peter Grimes*. Britten adapted many pieces of English literature to opera. His famous orchestral works include *The Young Person's Guide to the Orchestra* (1946) and *War Requiem* (1962).

Notable compositions: *Peter Grimes* 1945; *Noyes Fludde* 1958; *Death in Venice* 1973

Great Tenors

Enrico Caruso 1873–1921
Luciano Pavarotti b. 1935
Placido Domingo b. 1941
José Carreras b. 1946

Italian tenor **Enrico Caruso** first sang in the opera *L'Amico Francesco* in Naples in 1894, and at the age of 25 he became world famous when he appeared in *Fedora* in Milan (1898). He went on to appear in nearly 40 operas and made some of the very earliest recordings.

Also born in Italy, **Luciano Pavarotti** made his first appearance in 1961 as Rodolfo in *La Bohème*, and it became his favorite role. In 1990 he recorded the aria "Nessun Dorma" as the theme tune for the soccer World Cup. Pavarotti's magnetic personality has introduced a much wider audience to opera.

Spanish-born **Placido Domingo** studied music in Mexico. He first sang tenor in 1960 as Alfredo in *La Traviata*. He has performed in all of the major opera houses and founded the Los Angeles Opera in 1986.

Another Spanish tenor, **José Carreras** began singing at the age of six and was studying music two years later. He became a tenor when he was 18, and in 1974 he made his debut international performances in London and New York.

Pavarotti, Domingo, and Carreras have also appeared together many times as the "Three Tenors." Their first concert, held in Rome in 1990, was one of the highlights of 20th-century opera.

▲ Domingo, Carreras, and Pavarotti singing together as the "Three Tenors."

MARIAN ANDERSON 1902–1993
African-American contralto Marian Anderson began singing as a girl in her local Union Baptist church choir. Members of the congregation funded her private lessons. She became the first African-American woman to perform at the New York Metropolitan Opera, where she played Ulrica in Verdi's *The Masked Ball* in 1955.

MARIA CALLAS 1923–1977
U.S. soprano Maria Callas left the U.S. at the age of 14 to study in Athens, Greece. There she mastered the Italian *bel canto* style of singing. After her debut in *La Gioconda* in Italy in 1947 Callas sang in all of the main opera houses around the world. Her last performance was in *Tosca* at New York's Metropolitan Opera in 1965.

KIRI TE KANAWA b. 1944
New Zealand soprano Kiri Te Kanawa moved to London, England, to study opera in 1965. Her debut performance at Covent Garden's Royal Opera House in 1971 was followed by leading roles around the world. She achieved fame with her solo version of "Let the Bright Seraphim" at the wedding of the Prince and Princess of Wales in 1981.

POPULAR MUSIC

Musicals

▶ Richard Rodgers and Oscar Hammerstein II wrote many musicals, including *Oklahoma* (1943), *South Pacific* (1949), and *The King and I* (1951).

One of the earliest musical writing partnerships was between the two Englishmen **William Gilbert** (1836–1911) and **Arthur Sullivan** (1842–1900). Gilbert was a government employee who started writing comic verse for magazines. He went on to write plays, burlesques, and comedies before teaming up with Sullivan in 1871. Prior to their 18-year partnership Sullivan trained as a classical musician but is best known for the 14 light operas that he wrote with Gilbert. Still popular today, these include *HMS Pinafore* (1878) and *The Pirates of Penzance* (1880).

In 1928 U.S. composer **Jerome Kern** (1885–1945) joined forces with lyricist **Oscar Hammerstein II** (1895–1960) to create the popular Broadway musical *Showboat*. One of the most successful duos in the history of the musical is that of U.S. composer **Richard Rodgers** (1902–1979) and Hammerstein. Many of their hit musicals, including *The Sound of Music* (1959), were also made into highly successful movies.

New York composer George Gershwin (1898–1937) is best known for the musicals that he wrote with his brother, Ira (1896–1983). *Porgy and Bess* (1935) is considered to be their best work and includes the song "Summertime."

Probably one of the most-famous and popular musicals of all time is *West Side Story* (1957). This modern version of Shakespeare's (p. 120) *Romeo & Juliet* was written by two Americans—classical composer and conductor **Leonard Bernstein** (1918–1990) and composer and lyricist **Stephen Sondheim** (b. 1930).

Recently some of the best musicals of London's West End and New York's Broadway have been written by lyricist **Tim Rice** (b. 1944) and composer **Andrew Lloyd-Webber** (b. 1944). Since 1965 they have written the rock operas *Joseph and the Amazing Technicolor Dreamcoat* (1968), *Jesus Christ Superstar* (1971), and *Evita* (1978).

▶ *Starlight Express* was written by Andrew Lloyd-Webber and Richard Stilgoe (b. 1943) and first performed in 1984 at the Apollo Theater in London.

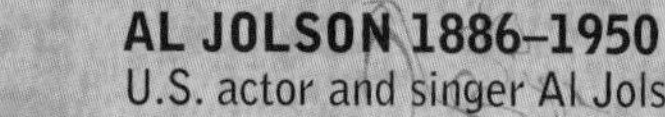

AL JOLSON 1886–1950

U.S. actor and singer Al Jolson starred in the first-ever talking picture, *The Jazz Singer* (1927). His real name was Asa Yoelson, and his family moved to the U.S. from Russia in 1893. In 1911 Jolson made his Broadway debut and soon became known as the "world's greatest entertainer" with songs such as "Mammy" and "Sonny Boy."

COLE PORTER 1891–1961

U.S. composer Cole Porter studied law and wrote shows for a college drama group. He went on to study music in Paris, France. By the late 1920s Porter's musicals, such as *The Gay Divorcée*, were big hits. He also wrote many hit songs, including "Every Time We Say Goodbye" (1944). His biggest success was the musical *Kiss Me, Kate* (1948).

Irving Berlin

1888–1989

Born Israel Baline in Russia, U.S. songwriter Irving Berlin emigrated to the U.S. in 1893. His first international hit was "Alexander's Ragtime Band" (1911). Berlin went on to write over 1,000 songs for shows, movies, and musical comedies. He retired in 1962.

Notable musicals: *Top Hat* 1933; *Annie Get Your Gun* 1946; *Easter Parade* 1948
Notable songs: "God Bless America" 1939; "White Christmas" 1954

Edith Piaf

1915–1963

Born Edith Gassion in France, Piaf began her singing career on the streets of Paris and was discovered by nightclub owner Louis Leplée in 1935. He called her "Le Même Piaf," Parisian for "the little sparrow," and Edith Piaf became her stage name. She performed many times in the U.S. and acted in plays and movies.

Notable song: "Non, je ne regrette rien" 1960

Frank Sinatra

1915–1998

Frank Sinatra was born in New Jersey and became one of America's most popular singers. A teenage heartthrob, his concerts were sellouts, and he also began appearing in movies such as *Anchors Aweigh* (1945). Rumors of Mafia connections damaged his career in the late 1940s and early 1950s until he won an Oscar for Best Supporting Actor in *From Here to Eternity* (1953). Top screen roles followed, and Sinatra's singing career took off again. Over the next two decades "Ol' Blue Eyes," as Sinatra was affectionately known, recorded classic swing albums and many top-selling singles such as "My Way." Sinatra last performed live in 1995 at his 80th birthday celebrations, singing "New York, New York."

Notable movies: *The Man with the Golden Arm* 1955; *High Society* 1956; *The Manchurian Candidate* 1962
Notable albums: *Songs For Swingin' Lovers* 1956; *Come Fly With Me* 1959; Notable songs: "Strangers in the Night" 1966; "My Way" 1969

Chuck Berry

b. 1926

American guitarist and singer Chuck Berry had a troubled upbringing, spending time in jail for armed robbery before embarking on a singing career in 1955. His blues-based music features a distinctive four-bar opening riff that has been widely copied but never surpassed. Berry's music has influenced the work of performers such as The Rolling Stones (p. 191).

Notable songs: "Maybellene" 1955; "Roll Over Beethoven" 1956

◀ During his career as a singer and actor, Frank Sinatra sold tens of millions of records, received nine Grammys and two Oscars, and made around 60 movies.

PAUL ROBESON 1898–1976
African-American singer and actor Paul Robeson began his stage career in 1922. His most notable role was in the London performance of Shakespeare's (p. 120) *Othello* in 1930. Robeson toured worldwide singing Negro spiritual music. In 1936 he impressed audiences with his version of "Ol' Man River" in the musical *Showboat.*

BILL HALEY 1925–1981
U.S. musician Bill Haley began playing country music in bands. However, it was with his own band, The Comets, that he found success. He wrote and recorded some of the first rock 'n' roll hit songs, notably "Rock Around the Clock" and "Shake, Rattle, and Roll" (both 1954), and became the first rock 'n' roll star to sell one million records.

LITTLE RICHARD b. 1935
As a child U.S. rock 'n' roll singer and pianist Little Richard sang in his local church choir, and by the age of 14 he was performing in vaudeville. He did his first recording in 1952, and in 1955 he had his first big hit with "Tutti Frutti." His stage acts are very distinctive and unusual, and he sometimes even plays the piano with his feet.

Elvis Presley

1935–1977

Born in Tupelo, Mississippi, Elvis Presley became the most successful recording artist in the world.

He was discovered in 1953 by Sun Records, who sold his contract to RCA in 1955. He was managed by Colonel Tom Parker (1909–1967) from 1955 to 1967. By blending country music with gospel and rhythm and blues, Presley made music that attracted huge numbers of young people at a time when the U.S. was emerging from the shadow of World War II. His first number-one single was the song, "Heartbreak Hotel," and it was followed by a string of others, including "Hound Dog" (1956), "Jailhouse Rock" (1958), and "King Creole" (1958). Presley caused a sensation with his dancing, which involved swiveling and gyrating his hips. Between 1958 and 1960 Presley served in the U.S. Army in Germany, but his record company had enough of his material to keep the public happy.

During most of the 1960s Presley also made a career in movies, starring and singing in two or three every year. In 1968 he emerged as a successful nightclub performer in Las Vegas. In 1977 Presley died of heart failure brought on by his excessive lifestyle. His mansion, Graceland, in Memphis is now a shrine for his millions of fans throughout the world.

Notable songs: "Heartbreak Hotel" 1956; "Blue Suede Shoes" 1956; "Love Me Tender" 1956; "All Shook Up" 1957; "His Latest Flame" 1961; "Return to Sender" 1962; 'Suspicious Minds" 1969

▶ Elvis Presley was known as the King of rock 'n' roll. During his career he recorded 94 hit singles, 40 hit albums, and starred in 27 movies.

Buddy Holly

1936–1959

U.S. singer and songwriter Buddy Holly was an early pioneer of rock 'n' roll. With his backing band, The Crickets, he combined country music with rhythm and blues and Mexican styles. In 1957 Holly had his first hit with "That'll Be the Day." He was killed in a plane crash.

Notable songs: "Peggy Sue" 1957; "Oh Boy" 1957; "Rave On" 1958; "Heartbeat" 1958

Marvin Gaye

1939–1984

U.S. soul singer Marvin Gaye's first hit was "A Stubborn Kind of Fellow" (1962). Many hits followed, including duets with Tammi Terrell (1945–1970) and Mary Wells (1943–1992). Gaye's musical maturity peaked with his album *What's Going On* (1971). He was shot dead by his father in an argument.

Notable songs: "I Heard it Through the Grapevine" 1968; "Sexual Healing" 1982

Bob Dylan

b. 1941

Born Robert Zimmerman, Bob Dylan is regarded as one of the most influential U.S. songwriters of the late 1900s. He shot to fame in the early 1960s with "protest" songs such as "A Hard Rain's A-Gonna Fall" (1963). In 1965 he teamed up with The Band to produce folk–rock songs such as "Like A Rolling Stone."

Notable songs: "Blowin' in the Wind" 1963; "Mr. Tambourine Man" 1965

HANK WILLIAMS 1923–1953
In his short caree, U.S. songwriter and singer Hank Williams became the greatest country singer of all time. His first hit was "Lovesick Blues" in 1949. Williams had a stormy marriage and health problems but produced some great songs such as "Your Cheatin' Heart." He died of a drug and alcohol overdose on the way to a concert.

JOHN WILLIAMS b. 1932
U.S. composer John Williams began as a session pianist, but he turned to writing music for television and then for movies. In 1971 he won an Academy Award for his music for *Fiddler on the Roof.* Since 1974 Williams has written the music for many of Steven Spielberg's (p. 152) movies, including *Jaws, Star Wars, E.T.*, and *Schindler's List.*

The Beatles

John Lennon 1940–1980
Ringo Starr b. 1940
Paul McCartney b. 1942
George Harrison 1943–2001

In 1960 four young musicians from Liverpool, England—John Lennon, Paul McCartney, George Harrison, and Pete Best (b. 1941)—formed The Beatles.

Pete Best was replaced as drummer by Ringo Starr. The band first played in small clubs in Liverpool and in Hamburg, Germany. From 1962 their popularity grew in the U.K. with the release of hit songs like "Love Me Do" and "She Loves You." The phenomenon known as Beatlemania took off when The Beatles first played in the U.S. in 1964. They attracted huge audiences who screamed so loudly that often the band could not hear themselves play. The Beatles also made several movies, and as their music matured the two main songwriters, Lennon and McCartney, showed they could write in a wide range of styles. In 1967 the band flirted with Indian mysticism and drugs before producing their groundbreaking album *Sergeant Pepper's Lonely Hearts Club Band*. The Beatles split up in 1969, and each member achieved solo success. Lennon was shot dead by a crazed fan in 1980, and Harrison died of cancer in 2001.

Notable albums: *Rubber Soul* 1965; *Revolver* 1966; *Sergeant Pepper's Lonely Hearts Club Band* 1967; *The Beatles* (*The White Album*) 1968; *Abbey Road* 1969
Notable movies: *A Hard Day's Night* 1964; *Help* 1965

Jimi Hendrix

1942–1970

U.S. guitarist and singer Jimi Hendrix first played with various American groups. In 1966 he moved to England, where he formed his band, The Jimi Hendrix Experience. He was an exciting performer, often playing the guitar with his teeth or behind his head. One of the most influential of the rock musicians, Hendrix died of a drug overdose.

Notable songs: "Purple Haze" 1967; "Hey Joe" 1967; "Voodoo Chile" 1968

Mick Jagger

b. 1943

English rock musician and songwriter Mick Jagger is the energetic lead singer of The Rolling Stones. Founded in 1961 by Jagger and Keith Richards (b. 1943), the band's original lineup also included Bill Wyman (b. 1936), Charlie Watts (b. 1941), and Brian Jones (1944–1969). Their early records were inspired by blues, soul, and country music.

Notable songs: "Satisfaction" 1965; "Jumpin' Jack Flash" 1968; "Brown Sugar" 1973

JAMES BROWN b. 1933
African-American singer James Brown mixed gospel, blues, and rhythm and blues music to produce highly influential songs. By the mid-1960s songs like "Papa's Got a Brand New Bag" (1965) earned him the nickname "Soul Brother No. 1." Brown has had over 100 hits in the U.S., and his influence can still be heard today in hip-hop, rap, and jazz.

JERRY LEE LEWIS b. 1935
Born into a poor white family in Louisiana, Lewis was playing the piano at the age of nine. With his frenzied stage act and songs like "Whole Lotta Shakin" and "Great Balls of Fire," he quickly established himself as one of the true originals of rock 'n' roll. Lewis' music career suffered after he married his 13-year-old cousin in 1958.

BOB MARLEY 1945–1981
Born in Jamaica, reggae singer, guitarist, and composer Bob Marley formed his band, The Wailers, in 1965. With a fierce political, social, and religious stance Marley soon achieved major international success with both white and black audiences with songs like "No Woman, No Cry" and "I Shot the Sheriff." He died of cancer in 1981.

Elton John

b. 1947

Flamboyant English songwriter and pianist Elton John was born Reginald Dwight. From the age of four he showed incredible talent on the piano, and by 11 he had won a scholarship to the British Royal Academy of Music. Teaming up with lyricist Bernie Taupin (b. 1950) in 1967, they became the most successful songwriting duo of the 1970s. In 1979 John became the first western popular musician to play in Moscow, Russia. His rewrite of "Candle in the Wind" for the funeral of Princess Diana (p. 236) in 1997 was the best-selling single ever.

Notable songs: "Your Song" 1970; "Rocket Man" 1972; "Candle in the Wind" 1974

ABBA

Björn Ulvæus b. 1945
Anni-Frid Lyngstad b. 1945
Benny Andersson b. 1946
Agnetha Fältskog b. 1950

ABBA was the first Swedish band to win the Eurovision song contest with their song "Waterloo" in 1974. Ulvæus and Andersson first met in Stockholm, and with their girlfriends, Anni-Frid and Agnetha, they formed ABBA in 1972. Following their Eurovision win, they had many other international hits. Both couples married but later divorced, and although the band split up in 1982, their music remains popular today. Andersson and Ulvæus went on to write the musical *Chess* (1984) with Tim Rice (p. 188).

Notable songs: "SOS" 1975; "Mamma Mia" 1975; "Dancing Queen" 1975; "Voulez-Vous" 1979; "Super Trouper" 1980

Freddie Mercury

1946–1992

British singer Freddie Mercury was born Frederick Bulsara on the island of Zanzibar and grew up in India. In 1963 he moved to England, where he studied design at Ealing College of Art in west London. After playing in a series of bands he formed the rock band Queen in 1971 with Brian May (b. 1947), Roger Taylor (b. 1949), and John Deacon (b. 1951). "Killer Queen" (1974) was their first hit, and the operatic "Bohemian Rhapsody" was their most famous. Mercury's performance at the Live Aid concert in 1985 stole the show. He also recorded an album, *Barcelona* (1988), with Spanish soprano Montserrat Caballé (b. 1933). Mercury died of an AIDS-related illness.

Notable songs: "Bohemian Rhapsody" 1975; "We Are the Champions" 1977

▲ Freddie Mercury performs with Queen.

PAUL SIMON b. 1942
In 1957 U.S. singer-songwriter Paul Simon teamed up with Art Garfunkel (b. 1941). Their first big hit was "The Sound of Silence" (1965), and their successful partnership included the songs for the movie *The Graduate* (1968). As a solo artist Simon went on to record his hugely successful, antiapartheid album *Graceland* (1986).

BRIAN WILSON b. 1942
With other members of his family U.S. musician and composer Brian Wilson formed the Californian band The Beach Boys in 1961. Hugely successful in the 1960s, their hits included "Surfin'" (1962) and "Good Vibrations" (1966). Wilson's biggest achievement was the highly creative and acclaimed album *Pet Sounds* (1966).

David Bowie

b. 1947

Born David Jones in London, England, David Bowie became interested in jazz as a teenager and played the saxophone. After graduating from art college he formed a series of bands. His first hit was "Space Oddity" (1969) and was followed by many more hits in both the U.K. and the U.S. During the 1970s his career rocketed, and he became known for his alternative personalities and disguises such as the sci-fi character Ziggy Stardust. Bowie has also acted in movies, including *The Man Who Fell to Earth* (1976), *Merry Christmas Mr. Lawrence* (1983), and *Labyrinth* (1986).

Notable albums: *The Rise and Fall of Ziggy Stardust and the Spiders from Mars* 1972; *Diamond Dogs* 1974

▲ David Bowie, disguised as Ziggy Stardust, performing in London, England, in 1972.

Michael Jackson

b. 1958

U.S. singer Michael Jackson has been performing since the age of four. In 1965, with his four brothers, he was part of The Jackson Five. During 1969–1971 they had four No. 1 hits, including "I'll Be There." Jackson went solo in 1972, and in 1979 he released his first solo album, *Off the Wall*. It was a big hit and was followed by the album *Thriller*, which broke all records, selling 38 million copies worldwide. Jackson now lives a reclusive life.

Notable albums: *Off the Wall* 1979; *Thriller* 1982; *Bad* 1987; *Dangerous* 1991; *Invincible* 2001

Carlos Santana

b. 1947

Born in Mexico, rock guitarist Carlos Santana was taught traditional Mexican music by his musician father. The young Santana also liked rock 'n' roll and used to play along with his favorite guitarists on the radio. He moved to San Francisco, where he formed the Santana Blues Band in 1966. In 1969 Santana played the Woodstock Festival, and his mixture of blues and Latin was an instant success. His hit singles include "Evil Ways" (1969) and "Black Magic Woman" (1970). Santana's recent album, *Supernatural*, won an amazing nine Grammy awards in 2000.

Notable albums: *Santana* 1969; *Abraxas* 1970; *Caravanserai* 1972

Madonna

b. 1958

U.S. singer and actress Madonna Louise Ciccone studied dance at Michigan University before moving to New York City in 1979. There she formed the group Breakfast Club and then in 1980, with drummer Steve Bray, another group, Emmy. Madonna had her first No. 1 hit single in 1984 with "Like a Virgin." Probably the most successful female singer ever, she has had a string of hits, and her total album sales have exceeded 100 million worldwide. She has also starred in movies, including *Desperately Seeking Susan* (1985) and *Evita* (1996).

Notable albums: *Like a Virgin* 1984; *You Can Dance* 1987; *Like a Prayer* 1989; *Ray of Light* 1998; *Music* 2000

▲ Madonna in one of her unique stage outfits.

ERIC CLAPTON b. 1945
As an art student English virtuoso rock and blues guitarist Eric Clapton loved American blues music. His music career began in the 1960s with The Yardbirds and John Mayall's Bluesbreakers. In 1966 Clapton formed the influential group Cream. "Tears in Heaven" (1992), which won Clapton a Grammy, was written after the death of his son.

STEVIE WONDER b. 1950
American soul singer Stevie Wonder was born blind but displayed a talent for singing and playing the piano. Wonder's first album, *Little Stevie Wonder: the 12-Year-Old Genius*, was an instant hit in 1962. His most notable album is *Songs In The Key of Life* (1976). He performed "Ebony and Ivory" with Paul McCartney (p. 191) in 1992.

GARTH BROOKS b. 1962
U.S. country singer Garth Brooks' debut album, *Garth Brooks*, was recorded in 1988. In 1991 his album *Ropin' the Wind* became the first country music album to enter both Billboard's country and popular charts at No. 1. Since then over 60 million copies of his albums have been sold, making Brooks the most successful country singer ever.

Whitney Houston

b. 1963

By the age of 11 U.S. soul and popular singer Whitney Houston was singing in the gospel choir of her local Baptist church. In 1985 her album *Whitney Houston* brought her instant success, and three of the singles on it, including "Saving All My Love For You," reached No. 1 in the U.S. charts. Her next album, *Whitney* (1987), was an enormous hit, and Houston became the first artist to have seven No. 1 singles in a row. She has also starred in movies, including *The Bodyguard* with Kevin Costner (b. 1955).

Notable songs: "The Greatest Love of All" 1986; "Where Do Broken Hearts Go" 1988; "One Moment in Time" 1988; "I Will Always Love You" 1992; "I'm Every Woman" 1993

▶ Robbie Williams performing at a concert in Birmingham, England, in 2000.

Robbie Williams

b. 1974

English popular singer Robbie Williams started out as the lead singer in the boy band Take That. After a string of seven hit singles in the early 1990s he left the band in 1995 to pursue a successful solo career. A versatile and humorous stage performer, his most popular songs include "Angels," "Let Me Entertain You," "Millennium," and "Rock DJ."

Notable albums: *Life Thru a Lens* 1997; *I've Been Expecting You* 1998; *Sing When You're Winning* 2000; *Swing When You're Winning* 2001

Kylie Minogue

b. 1968

Actress and singer Kylie Minogue first achieved stardom in 1986 as Charlene in the Australian soap opera *Neighbors*. Her singing career took off when her single "I Should Be So Lucky" topped the U.K. charts in 1987. The following year she had her second hit with Jason Donovan (b. 1968) with "Especially For You." 1999 saw her return to the top spot with the disco hit "Spinning Around." Kylie also performed a duet with Robbie Williams (above) in their hit single "Kids" in 2000.

Notable songs: "I Should Be So Lucky" 1988; "Can't Get You Out Of My Head" 2001

Britney Spears

b. 1981

At the age of eight U.S. popular singer Britney Spears was auditioned for the Disney Channel's Mickey Mouse Club. However, she was too young and had to return to school. During her summer vacations Britney attended classes at New York City's Off-Broadway Dance Center and the Performing Arts School. She eventually joined the Mickey Mouse Club as a child star at the age of 11. At the age of 17 her debut single and album, "...Baby One More Time," topped the U.S. charts. She repeated this with her next single, "Oops!...I Did It Again."

Notable songs: "...Baby One More Time" 1999; "Oops!...I Did It Again" 2000

JOHNNY ROTTEN b. 1956
Johnny Rotten, born John Lydon, was the lead singer of the English punk rock band The Sex Pistols. His sulky interviews and dyed-green hair made him a hero to the world's rebellious youth. During his short career with the band Rotten sang some memorably outrageous numbers, including "Anarchy In The U.K." (1976) and "God Save The Queen" (1977).

PRINCE b. 1958
Born Prince Roger Nelson, U.S. singer Prince made his first album, *For You*, at the age of 20. He first gained international recognition with his album *1999* (1982). His second album, *Purple Rain* (1984), with the song "Little Red Corvette," made him one of the biggest stars of the 1980s. For a while he was known as "The Artist formerly known as Prince."

Girl Bands

Girl groups emerged during the 1950s in the U.S. when rock 'n' roll music was the new craze.

Formed in 1959 as The Primettes, this U.S. girl band became **The Supremes** when they signed up with Motown. Their catchy "Where Did Our Love Go" went to No. 1 in 1964. In 1970 their lead singer, Diana Ross (b. 1944), went on to pursue a successful solo career.

Also formed in the late 1950s, the American girl group **The Ronettes** were discovered by producer Phil Spector (b. 1940) and had several big hits, including "Be My Baby" (1963).

During the disco craze of the 1970s the Philadelphia girl group **The Three Degrees** had a big hit with "When Will I See You Again?" (1974). Another U.S. girl group **Sister Sledge** had a huge success with their album *Lost in Music* (1979).

In 1996 the British girl group **The Spice Girls**—Victoria Adams (b. 1975), Melanie Brown (b. 1975), Emma Bunton (b. 1976), Melanie Chisholm (b. 1974), and Geraldine Halliwell (b. 1972)—reached No. 1 in the U.K. and 22 other countries with their hit "Wannabe." All five members have since gone on to pursue solo careers.

The latest U.S. girl group **Destiny's Child** first got together at a young age in the early 1990s. In 1998 they scored a massive international hit with their first album, *Destiny's Child*.

▲ Hailing from Detroit, Michigan, The Supremes became a big hit in the 1960s.

▼ The Spice Girls were one of the most successful girl groups of all time

BONO VOX b. 1960
Bono Vox, lead singer of the Irish rock band U2, was born Paul Hewson in Ireland. He has led the band through two decades of triumphs, from the critically acclaimed album *The Joshua Tree* (1987), which sold 12 million copies and reached No. 1 in 22 countries, to their legendary 1992 *ZooTV* tour. U2 have sold over 100 million albums.

JENNIFER LOPEZ b. 1970
U.S. singer and actress Jennifer Lopez started her show-business career as a dancer in New York City. By 2000 she had appeared in 20 TV series and movies, including Oliver Stone's *U-turn* (1997). In 1999 she launched an equally high-profile career as a singer, releasing two platinum-selling albums, *On The 6* and *J-Lo*.

CRAIG DAVID b. 1981
At the age of 14 Craig David was DJing and rapping in his hometown of Southampton, U.K. He later added record producing, singing, and songwriting to his list of talents. At the age of 19, with his second single, "Fill Me In," he hit No. 1 in the British charts. His debut album, *Born To Do It*, confirmed Craig as the leading light of the U.K.'s R&B scene.

BLUES AND JAZZ

Scott Joplin

1868–1917

U.S. pianist and composer Scott Joplin is best known for his ragtime music. He first started composing in the 1890s, and his first and most successful tune, "Maple Leaf Rag," sold over one million copies of sheet music and made him a wealthy man. However, the lack of success of his operatic compositions led to his depression. His ragtime music became popular again in 1973, following the release of the movie *The Sting*.

Notable compositions: "Maple Leaf Rag" 1899; "The Ragtime Dance" 1902

▲ Leadbelly plays his famous 12-string guitar.

Leadbelly

1888–1949

Born Huddie Ledbetter, U.S. folk-blues singer and guitarist Leadbelly went to prison twice—for murder in 1917 and for attempted murder in 1930. While in prison in 1933 Leadbelly was discovered by the music archivist Alan Lomax (1867–1948). Upon his release from jail Lomax launched Leadbelly onto the New York City folk scene and even recorded his music for the U.S. Library of Congress. Leadbelly's earthy blues music greatly influenced other rock musicians.

Notable songs: "Goodnight Irene" 1933; "Midnight Special" 1934

◀ Duke Ellington is considered to be the greatest of all orchestral jazz composers.

Duke Ellington

1899–1974

Born Edward Ellington, U.S. jazz band leader, composer, arranger, and pianist Duke Ellington formed his first dance band in New York City in 1924. By 1927 the band had become a 10-piece orchestra and was playing for white-only audiences at the famous Cotton Club in Harlem. Through the medium of radio Ellington's fame grew, and he had many hit records around the world. Over the next 40 years he composed over 2,000 pieces, including many suites and concert-length compositions such as "Brown, Black, and Beige" (1943).

Notable numbers: "Hot and Bothered" 1928; "Mood Indigo" 1930; "It Don't Mean A Thing" 1932; "Take the A Train" 1941

▲ Glenn Miller and his dance band entertained the troops during World War II.

Glenn Miller

1904–1944

American trombonist and bandleader Glenn Miller played in school bands and dropped out of college to pursue his musical career. He played in several bands before forming the Glenn Miller Orchestra in 1938. From 1939 to 1942 he had over a dozen top-10 hits, including the million-copy-selling "Chatanooga Choo Choo." During World War II Miller joined the U.S. Air Force and formed the Glenn Miller Army Air Force Band. In 1944 the band entertained Allied troops in Europe. After performing in Paris, France, Miller was flying to London, England, when his plane disappeared over the English Channel.

Notable numbers: "Moonlight Serenade" 1939; "A String of Pearls" 1941

Louis Armstrong

1901–1971

American jazz singer and trumpeter Louis Armstrong spent his early years in poverty. Labeled a juvenile delinquent, he was put in a children's home, where he learned to play the cornet. When he left the home in 1914, he played in local bars, and he got his first full-time musical job playing on Mississippi riverboats. In 1922 he joined a jazz band in Chicago and began accompanying soloists and singers. In 1926 Armstrong pioneered a new style of jazz known as "scat" singing—imitating instruments with the voice. By the late 1920s "Satchmo," as he was known, was playing the trumpet for big bands and had hits with numbers like "West End Blues" (1928). In 1947 he formed the Louis Armstrong All-Stars, a sextet that played to sellout audiences. In later life, lip problems forced him to turn to singing. He toured the world, usually sponsored by the U.S. State Department, and appeared in over 50 movies.

Notable songs: "Star Dust" 1931; "Hello Dolly" 1964; "What A Wonderful World" 1968

◀ While playing the trumpet Louis Armstrong always carried a handkerchief to mop up his brow.

Billie Holiday

1915–1959

At the age of 15 U.S. jazz singer Billie Holiday was singing in New York City clubs. She had her first recording session with Benny Goodman (1909–1986) in 1933. Holiday went on to record over 100 songs, including "Easy Living" (1937). She also sang with the big band of Count Basie (1904–1984) and with saxophonist Lester Young (1909–1959). Her early death was brought on by drug abuse.

Notable songs: "They Can't Take That Away From Me" 1937; "Strange Fruit" 1939

Thelonius Monk

1917–1982

U.S. jazz pianist and composer Thelonius Monk began playing in church at the age of 11. He played for many bands in New York City, making his first recordings in 1944. At this time the jazz style known as "bebop" was created, and Monk was a key figure, performing it at its birthplace—Minton's Playhouse. He took jazz to a new level, playing with jazz virtuosos such as saxophonist John Coltrane (1926–1967).

Notable numbers: "Round Midnight" 1947; "Straight No Chaser" 1957

▲ Ella Fitzgerald, the "First Lady of Song."

Ella Fitzgerald

1917–1996

As a shy 16-year-old U.S. jazz singer Ella Fitzgerald won first prize in an amateur singing competition in New York City. She was spotted by bandleader Chick Webb (1909–1939) and started singing with his Savoy Swing Orchestra. In 1938 she had her first hit record *A Tisket, A Tasket*, and in 1942 she started her solo career. Ella's voice suited a wide variety of music, and her interpretation of songs by composers such as Gershwin (p. 188) and Jerome Kern (1885–1945) in her *Songbook* albums made them classics.

Notable songs: "I'm Making Believe" 1944; "Dream a Little Dream of Me" 1950; "I Can't Give You Anything But Love" 1960

Charlie Parker

1920–1955

American jazz saxophonist, composer, and bandleader Charlie Parker learned to play the saxophone at school. In 1939 he moved to New York City, where he played with many bebop-jazz bands. In 1945 "Bird," as he is known, formed his own quintet and created a definitive form of bebop. Over the next three years he played with jazz giants like Miles Davis (1926–1991). Addictions and mental problems eventually killed him.

Notable numbers: "Anthropology" 1946; "Yardbird Suite" 1946; "Ornithology" 1946

Stan Getz

1927–1991

Born in Philadelphia, American jazz saxophonist Stan Getz went professional at the age of 15 and worked with many important figures in the jazz world. In the late 1940s he moved to the West Coast to join the band of Woody Herman (1913–1987). Getz then led a number of small groups and went on to develop the "bossa nova" style of jazz. He worked with many other musicians, including Canadian jazz pianist Oscar Peterson (b. 1925), and his light tenor saxophone style continues to be influential.

Notable numbers: "Early Autumn" 1948; "The Girl From Ipanema" 1963

Fats Domino

b. 1928

Born in New Orleans and influenced by blues and traditional jazz, U.S. pianist and singer Fats Domino joined his first band in 1945. During the early 1950s he had hits with "Goin' Home" and "Going To The River." Domino's career peaked in the mid-1950s with hits like "My Blue Heaven." He continued recording and touring into the 1990s.

Notable songs: "Ain't That a Shame" 1955; "Blueberry Hill" 1956

▲ Charlie Parker was a great saxophonist.

BESSIE SMITH 1894–1937
U.S. blues singer Bessie Smith began her career singing in traveling shows. She moved to New York City, and during the 1920s she sang with a number of leading jazz musicians, including Louis Armstrong (p. 197). She recorded some classic blues numbers, including "Downhearted Blues" (1923). Smith also appeared in the 1929 movie *St. Louis Blues*. She died after a car accident in Mississippi.

BIX BEIDERBECKE 1903–1931
U.S. jazz pianist and cornettist Bix Beiderbecke became a jazz enthusiast as a teenager. After being thrown out of a military academy in 1922 he worked with professionals and quickly made a name for himself with classics such as "In A Mist" (1927). He was the first white musician to make a major contribution to jazz music, but his career was cut short when he died from alcoholism and pneumonia.

DIZZY GILLESPIE 1917–1993
Born in South Carolina, American jazz trumpeter and composer Dizzy Gillespie began his career playing in swing bands. However, he spent much of his spare time playing with musicians like Charlie Parker (left) and Thelonious Monk (p. 197) to create the "bebop" jazz style. His 1945 rendition of "I Can't Get Started" is a classic from that period. He was also one of the founders of Afro-Cuban jazz. Gillespie is considered the greatest jazz trumpeter of all time.

WYNTON MARSALIS b. 1961
Born in New Orleans, U.S. trumpeter and composer Wynton Marsalis learned to play at the age of eight. He mastered both jazz and classical music and played with jazz musicians like drummer Art Blakey (1919–1990) and pianist Herbie Hancock (b. 1940). In 1983 he became the first musician to win Grammy awards for jazz and classical albums.

DANCE

Isadora Duncan

1877–1927

Acknowledged as one of the founders of modern dance, American dancer and choreographer Isadora Duncan founded several dance schools in Europe. In 1922 she married the Russian poet Sergei Yesenin (1895–1925). They could not speak each other's languages, and later Yesenin committed suicide. Duncan died when her scarf became entangled in the wheel of a car.

Notable dances: Strauss waltzes *Southern Roses* and *Blue Danube* 1903–1923

Vaslav Nijinsky

1890–1950

From the age of nine Russian ballet dancer and choreographer Vaslav Nijinksy trained at St. Petersburg's Imperial Ballet School. In 1909 he became famous as the leading dancer in Diaghilev's (right) Ballets Russes when they performed in Paris, France. He achieved considerable success in 1911 in Fokine's (right) *Spectre de la Rose* and Stravinsky's (right) ballet *Petrushka*. Nijinsky suffered from mental illness and retired in 1917. He is considered to be one of the greatest male ballet dancers of all time.

Notable performances: *L'Après-midi d'une Faune* 1912; *Sacre du Printemps* 1913

Fonteyn and Nureyev

Margot Fonteyn 1919–1991
Rudolf Nureyev 1938–1993

Margot Fonteyn and Rudolf Nureyev became the world's best-known ballet partnership when they danced together during the 1960s.

Born Peggy Hookham, English ballerina Margot Fonteyn spent her childhood in Hong Kong. She returned to England and joined the Sadler's Wells Ballet in 1934. Fonteyn made her solo debut in *The Haunted Ballroom* (1939), and she was Britain's leading ballerina for almost 30 years. Russian ballet dancer and choreographer Rudolf Nureyev studied dance from the age of 11 and joined the Leningrad Ballet School in 1955. By 1958 he was a soloist with the Kirov Ballet, but not wanting to join the Communist Party he defected to Paris, France, while on tour in 1961. In 1962 Nureyev made his debut with Fonteyn at London's Covent Garden. He became an Austrian citizen in 1982.

Notable ballet partnerships: *Giselle*; *Marguerite, and Armand*; *Swan Lake* 1962–1964

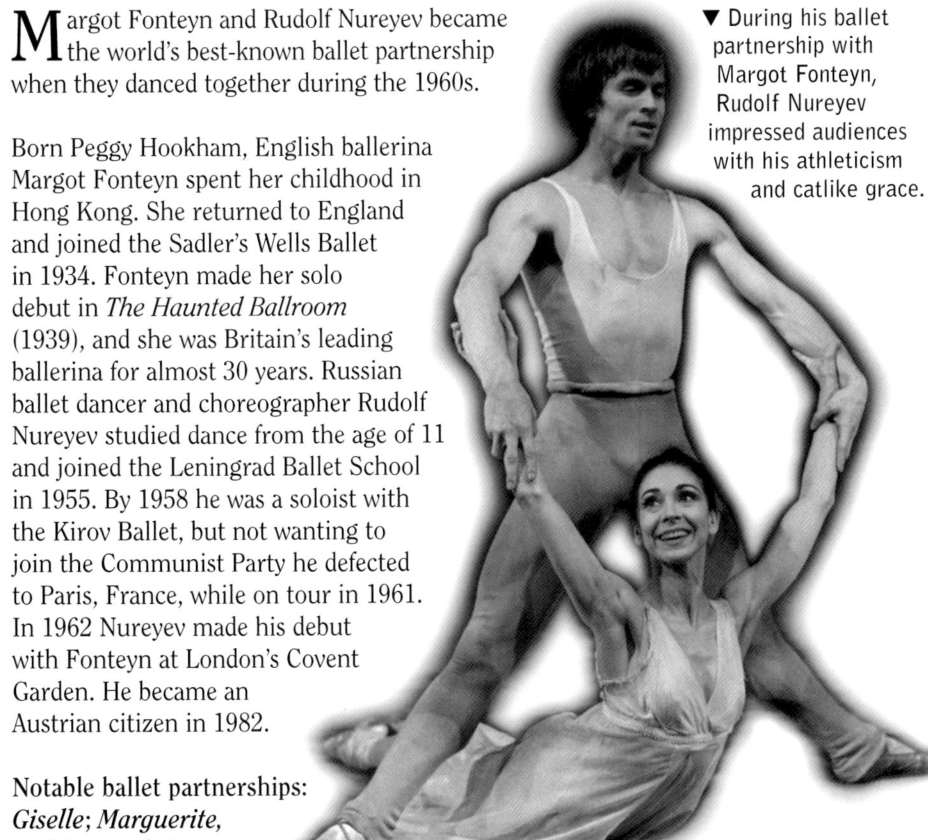

▼ During his ballet partnership with Margot Fonteyn, Rudolf Nureyev impressed audiences with his athleticism and catlike grace.

FLORENZ ZIEGFELD 1869–1932
American theater producer Florenz Ziegfeld was the man behind the popular *Ziegfeld Follies*, a glamorous theatrical show that ran every year from 1907 to 1931. Audiences flocked to see the spectacular sets and wide variety of performers, from comedians to the famous chorus lines of beautiful women singing and dancing. He also produced musicals such as *Show Boat* (1927) and *Bittersweet* (1929).

SERGEY DIAGHILEV 1872–1929
Born in Russia, Sergey Diaghilev became a very important figure in the arts between 1897–1906, organizing concerts and exhibitions of Russian music and art. Diaghilev founded the Ballets Russes in 1911 and began performances in Paris, France. He directed spectacular ballets and introduced Russian dancers, such as Nijinsky (left), to European audiences.

MICHEL FOKINE 1880–1942
American dancer and choreographer Michel Fokine was born in Russia. At the age of nine he went to study at St. Petersburg's Imperial Ballet School. In 1909 Fokine went to Paris, France, where he worked as a choreographer for Sergei Diaghilev's (above) Ballets Russes. He moved to the U.S. in the 1920s, becoming a U.S. citizen in 1932. He choreographed ballets including *Les Sylphides* (1909) and *Petrushka* (1911).

IGOR STRAVINSKY 1882–1971
As a young child in Russia, American composer Igor Stravinksky showed musical talent, but his parents sent him to study law. However, he met the composer Rimsky-Korsakov (p. 182), who taught him and encouraged him to pursue a musical career. He wrote great music for Sergei Diaghilev's Ballets Russes, including *The Firebird* (1910), *Petrushka* (1911), and *The Rite of Spring* (1913). Stravinsky became a U.S. citizen in 1945.

MARIE RAMBERT 1888–1982
Born in Poland, Marie Rambert went to Paris, France, to study medicine but changed to dance instead. In 1913 Diaghilev asked her to work on the choreography for the *Rites of Spring* ballet, and she joined the Ballets Russes. Rambert moved to England, where she became a citizen in 1918. In 1935 she founded the Ballet Rambert in London.

Michael Flatley

b. 1958

Michael Flatley was born in the U.S. to Irish parents. At the age of 11 he went to dance classes and showed a natural talent. In 1975 he became the first American to win the World Irish Dance Championships in Ireland. Flatley's modern style of Irish dancing and his *Riverdance* performance in the 1994 Eurovision song contest made him an overnight sensation. He toured with the *Riverdance* show for six months and then in 1997 Flatley created his own, very successful *Lord of the Dance* show.

Notable dance: *Riverdance* 1994

▲ Irish-American dancer Michael Flatley.

Gary and Diana McDonald

Gary b. 1967, Diana b. 1971

Since their early 1920s U.S. dancers Gary and Diana McDonald have represented the United States in over 20 amateur and professional World Championships. They were the first Americans to win the World Professional 10 Dance Championship.

Notable achievements: World Professional 10 Dance Champions, U.S. Professional Latin Champions 1997

Joaquín Cortés

b. 1969

Spanish flamenco dancer Joaquín Cortés joined the Spanish National Ballet at the age of 15. He soon became a soloist and toured the world. In 1992 he left the ballet and formed his own company, touring the world with his first show, *Cibayí*. Cortés' dramatic, modern dance style, choreography, and music has become an enormous hit worldwide.

Notable dances: *Cibayí* 1992; *Pasión Gitana* 1995

▲ Joaquín Cortés performing "Gypsy Passion Show" at the Royal Albert Hall in England in 1996.

MARTHA GRAHAM 1894–1991
U.S. dancer and choreographer Martha Graham was a pioneer of the modern dance movement. In 1927 she founded the School of Contemporary Dance in New York City. There she tried new ways of staging dance and choreographed contemporary dances based on themes ranging from Greek tragedies to Native American legends. Graham's groundbreaking work includes *Vision of the Apocalypse* (1929).

GEORGE BALANCHINE 1904–1983
Born in Russia, U.S. choreographer George Balanchine trained at the Imperial Ballet School. In 1924 he defected and never returned to Russia. Balanchine choreographed ballets such as *Apollo* (1928) for Diaghilev's (p. 199) Ballets Russes in Paris, France. He settled in the U.S., where he founded New York City's School of American Ballet in 1934. He also wrote musicals, and from 1948, as choreographer for the New York City Ballet, Balanchine created over 100 new works.

FREDERICK ASHTON 1904–1988
Born in Ecuador, English ballet dancer and choreographer Frederick Ashton took secret ballet lessons while working as a businessman in London, England. With Marie Rambert (p. 199) he founded Ballet Rambert. In 1935 Ashton became choreographer for the Sadler's Wells Ballet and then director of the British Royal Ballet. There he created many new ballets, including *Cinderella* (1948) and *Ondine* (1958).

MIKHAIL BARYSHNIKOV b. 1948
U.S. ballet dancer and choreographer Mikhail Baryshnikov studied dance at St. Petersburg's Kirov Ballet in Russia. He defected to the West in 1974 and became lead dancer at the American Ballet Theater (1974–1978) and the New York City Ballet (1978–1979). Between 1980 and 1989 Baryshnikov returned to the American Ballet Theater as the artistic director.

DARCEY BUSSELL b. 1969
English ballerina Darcey Bussell studied at London's Royal Ballet School. In 1987 she joined the British Royal Ballet, where she became a soloist. In 1989, at the age of 20, Bussell became the youngest-ever principal dancer with the Royal Ballet, taking the lead role of Rose in *The Prince of the Pagodas*.

CHAPTER NINE

SPORTS STARS

Sports before 1000

We do not know the names of the first great sportsmen and women. Sports have existed since prehistoric times and long before written communication could record names and deeds. Running, jumping, and fighting were all skills required by people to hunt, fight, and flee, and over thousands of years these skills have developed into the many sports we know today.

Many sporting events developed out of humankind's desire and curiosity to test themselves against the world and other humans. Races and tests of strength among different members of the same group or tribe go back thousands of years. Wrestling is one of the most ancient recognizable sports practiced in Asia, Africa, South America, and Europe.

The ancient Sumerians wrestled more than 4,000 years ago, and the oldest-recorded sports event was a wrestling contest between Egyptian and foreign soldiers held in front of the pharaoh **Ramses III** (1100s B.C.) in 1160 B.C.

Although most ancient people probably played sports, only a few civilizations have left behind artifacts. The richest treasure trove of ancient sports scenes comes from the Egyptians, who played many sports, including high jumping, fencing, and prototypes of ball games like handball and hockey.

THE ANCIENT OLYMPICS

Long before the modern Olympics became the four-yearly highlight in today's sports calendar, the ancient Olympics existed. Before A.D. 1000 they were the most famous and well documented of all sports contests. Dedicated to Zeus, the father of the gods according to the ancient Greeks, the ancient Olympics were both a festival and a sporting event. A truce was declared during the games, all battles were stopped, and no one was allowed to carry weapons. The first games that we know of took place in Olympia in Greece in 776 B.C. They featured just one event, the *stadion*, a race over a distance called a stade (approximately 590 ft./180m). This first race was won by **Coroebus**, a young cook from Elis, the state where Olympia was situated. Continuing once every four years for over one thousand years, more and more events were added to the games. In 724 B.C. the *dialus*, two lengths of the stadium in Olympia (just under 1,310 ft./400m), was introduced, and in 720 B.C. the long-distance *dolichus* (12 circuits around the stadium—around 2.8 mi./4.5km) was added. Boxing (688 B.C.), chariot racing (680 B.C.), and a race in full armor (520 B.C.) also became part of the games. The ancient Olympics featured many great champions, including the runner **Leonidas of Rhodes** (100s B.C.), who won the stadion race and two others in four successive games. One of the most legendary athletes in the ancient world was the wrestler **Milo of Kroton** (500s B.C.). Born in southern Italy, Milo won the boys' wrestling contest at the ancient Olympics in 540 B.C. and returned eight years later to win the first of five consecutive titles.

RACING WITH HORSES

The taming and riding of horses is believed to have began in Arabia over five thousand years ago, and racing horses or using them to pull chariots in races was popular in many ancient civilizations. One of the most famous of all ancient charioteers was **Cynisca** (200s B.C.), the daughter of Agesilaus II, the king of Sparta. She is the first recorded woman to win at an ancient Olympics in 396 B.C. **Eurylon** (200s B.C.), another woman from Sparta, followed her and won an ancient Olympic victory in the two-horse chariot race.

▲ The ball game of the ancient Mayas involved teams and a heavy ball that was passed through stone hoops attached to the walls of the court.

BALL SPORTS

Football

Walter Camp

1859–1925

Camp, an American, excelled in several sports as a young man, but he became infatuated with football while studying at Yale University. He established many of the game's rules, including the scoring system and having 11 players per side. Playing for Yale from 1877 to 1882, Camp was an all-around player with strong kicking, tackling, and running skills.

Captained Yale to 25 wins, 6 ties, and only 1 loss

Jim Brown

b. 1936

U.S. athlete Jim Brown was the leading basketball scorer for Syracuse University and is in the Lacrosse Hall of Fame. But it was as a football running back that Brown found fame. Standing 6' 2" (1.9m) tall and weighing 230 pounds, he had explosive speed and great strength. Brown played nine seasons for the Cleveland Browns before embarking on a movie career, making 32 movies.

126 touchdowns scored; 1963 NFL Championship winner

Walter Payton

1954–1999

Playing his entire NFL career for the Chicago Bears, Payton was an excellent running back who thrived on gaining territory in crowded and heavily defended parts of the field. He went on to become the record holder for rushing yards gained, with a career total of 16,726.

Ran over 100 yards in 77 games, gained 1,000 yards or more in 10 out of his 13 seasons; 125 touchdowns

Joe Montana

b. 1956

JOE MONTANA

Montana became one of football's greatest quarterbacks through his passing accuracy, bravery, and lightning-quick reactions. He played football for Notre Dame before going professional and joining the San Francisco 49ers. From 1981 Montana proved to be the master of winning games, often from difficult positions. In 1993 he joined the Kansas City Chiefs.

Four times Super Bowl winner with the San Francisco 49ers; 3,409 completed passes; 273 touchdowns

Dan Marino

b. 1961

The greatest football quarterback to never win a Superbowl, Dan Marino grew up in Pittsburgh, Pennsylvania. As a child he used to dodge around parked cars and used telephone poles as targets at which to throw the football. An excellent pitcher, Marino was sought by professional baseball teams, but instead he went to the University of Pittsburgh to play football, and from there he was drafted into the NFL to play for the Miami Dolphins. In a 17-year career with the Dolphins, Marino broke almost every quarterback record and retired at the end of the 1999 season.

1984 Super Bowl finalist; record holder for most career touchdowns (420), most career yards gained (61,361 yards), and most career completed passes (4,967)

Baseball

Babe Ruth

1895–1948

When he was seven, Ruth's parents handed custody of their unruly son over to a missionary orphanage and reform school because they could no longer take care of him. There he was guided into baseball by Brother Mathias.

Ruth quickly developed into an excellent pitcher and batter, playing for the Baltimore Orioles, the Boston Red Sox, and in 1919 the New York Yankees.

Before Ruth's arrival the Yankees had never won a championship or World Series. With him they won seven championships and four World Series, between 1920–1933. For ten out of the first twelve seasons Ruth scored more home runs than all of the players of his former team, the Red Sox, put together. Ruth became the biggest draw in American sports, and in 1923 the Yankees built a new stadium to help fulfill the huge demand to see him play.

714 home runs; .847 batting average 1920; .846 batting average 1921; four World Series wins

◀ By the time he was 26 Babe Ruth had hit more home runs than any player in baseball history. In 1927 he scored 60 home runs, 14 percent of the total scored by all players of all teams in his league that year.

Ty Cobb

1886–1961

In a 24-year, controversial career, Cobb, a right-arm thrower and a left-handed batter, emerged as one of baseball's best-ever players. Fiercely competitive, Cobb intimidated opposition fielders and was not above off-field arguments and brawls. Despite this, few discounted his achievements, which included 1,938 runs batted in and 4,189 hits. When the poll for baseball's Hall of Fame took place in 1936, Cobb received more votes than Babe Ruth.

Lifetime .367 batting average (the highest ever); led the American League in hits eight times; stole 892 bases

Joe DiMaggio

1914–1999

Joe DiMaggio was one of baseball's most graceful and popular players. Joining the New York Yankees in 1936, his powerful batting helped them win four World Series in a row. In the late 1940s DiMaggio suffered from injuries and retired tearfully in 1951. Not long after he began a romance with movie star Marilyn Monroe (p. 143). They got married in 1954 but were divorced nine months later.

Nine World Series; 56 games in a row hitting streak 1941; 361 home runs

▲ DiMaggio was named baseball's greatest living player at the 1969 Centennial Celebration,

Soccer

Pelé

b. 1940

Pelé was born in the Brazilian village of Três Coroções. He played for a number of amateur sides until he was spotted by Valdemar de Brito (b. 1913), a member of Brazil's 1934 World Cup team, who took him to Club Santos, a top Brazilian team.

In his first full game for the team Pelé announced his arrival by scoring four goals. Making his international debut against Argentina in 1957, Pelé burst onto the global stage at the 1958 World Cup finals in Sweden, scoring seven goals to help Brazil win the World Cup. A strong team player and a natural goal scorer, Pelé was capable of surprising opponents with moments of daring, vision, and finesse. When Pelé retired from Santos in 1974, the club honored him by retiring the number 10 shirt from their line up. Pelé came out of retirement to play for the New York Cosmos to help promote professional soccer in the U.S., and he has since gone on to be Brazil's Sports Secretary.

Winner of three World Cups with Brazil 1958, 1962, 1970; capped 93 times, scoring 77 international goals; scorer of 1,280 first team goals; winner of eight Brazilian national league titles, three Brazilian Cups, and two World Club Cups with Santos

▶Pelé always wore the number 10 team shirt. By 1969 he had scored 1,000 goals as a professional player.

FERENC PUSKAS b. 1926
A member of Hungary's best team—Honved—and the national team in the early 1950s, Puskas was short, stocky, and had an incredibly powerful left-foot shot. In 1956 Puskas was in his thirties when he joined Real Madrid, but he continued scoring heavily, four times heading the Spanish league goals table and scoring seven goals in two European Cup Finals. Retiring in 1966 to try managing teams with only limited success, Puskas was welcomed back to Hungary in 1993 as the national team's assistant coach.

EUSEBIO DA SILVA FERREIRA b. 1942
Born in the Portuguese colony of Mozambique, Eusebio was subject to a fierce contest between two Portuguese sides—Benfica and Sporting Lisbon. In 15 years with Benfica there were only two in which the team did not win an honor. Eusebio proved to be a powerful and fast forward and was the top goal scorer in the Portuguese league for five seasons in a row. A serious knee injury cut his career short, leaving him with an international total of 41 goals in 64 matches.

FRANZ BECKENBAUER b. 1945
Beckenbauer was playing for the top German team, Bayern Munich, by the time he was 18 and the German national team less than two years later. An excellent reader of the game, Beckenbauer changed the position of sweeper from an ultra-defensive role to one that linked defense to attack. He won a World Cup and European Championship with Germany, for whom he played 103 times. After a spell in the U.S. with the New York Cosmos, Beckenbauer began managing with equal success. He is now the president of Bayern Munich.

Lev Yashin

1929–1991

The Moscow-born Yashin was working in a tool factory until he was spotted by Soviet Union soccer giants Moscow Dynamo in 1950. Sitting on the bench for more than a season, Yashin became frustrated and almost switched to ice hockey. However, by 1953 he became his team's—and in 1954 his country's—first-choice goalkeeper. A spectacular shot stopper, Yashin possessed superb anticipation and dominated his goal area. Although records are sketchy, it is also recorded that he saved over 150 penalties in his career. He is the only goalie to win the European Footballer (Soccer Player) of the Year trophy.

Olympic Gold medalist with Soviet Union 1956; European Championship winner 1960; European Footballer (Soccer Player) of the Year 1963; won five Soviet national league titles

Johan Cruyff

b. 1947

Cruyff grew up in Amsterdam, Holland, almost overlooking the Ajax stadium, the team with which he was to win over 20 trophies. Joining Ajax's youth academy at age 10, Cruyff progressed quickly, debuting for Ajax at 16. A striker blessed with enormous skill and vision, he became famous for leading a new style called Total Soccer. Devised by Ajax and later the Dutch national coach Rinus Michels (b. 1928) this saw players swapping positions quickly and easily. None more so than Cruyff, who followed Michels to Barcelona before spells in the U.S., an emotional return to Ajax, and a successful career in team management.

Three times European soccer player of the year; winner of 16 Dutch league or cup titles and three European Cups with Ajax

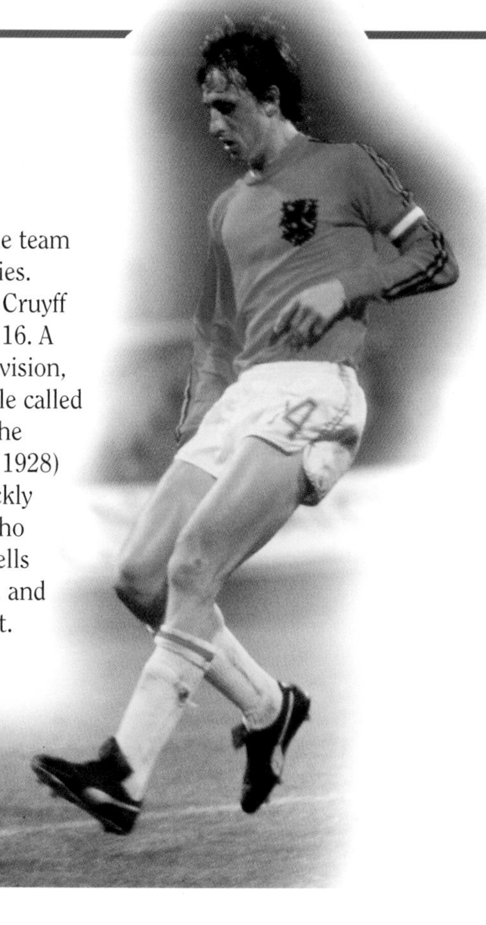

Diego Maradona

b. 1960

Diego Armando Maradona was born on the outskirts of Buenos Aires, Argentina. Taking up soccer at an early age, Maradona became known in his local area as *El pibe de oro* ("the golden boy") before becoming his country's youngest-ever international player when he played against Hungary aged only 16.

Two years later he captained the World Youth Cup winners and moved to Europe—first to Barcelona, Spain, and then to the Italian club, Napoli, with whom he won two Italian championships. An excellent dribbler of the soccer ball, Maradona had a magnificent 1986 World Cup, scoring two of the best-ever World Cup goals and leading his team to victory. The following World Cup saw Maradona and Argentina again reach the final, only to lose to Germany. The latter stages of Maradona's soccer career were blighted by controversy and two failed drug tests that were followed by bans. He officially retired on his 37th birthday.

World Cup winner and 1986 man of the tournament with five goals; winner of Italian league and cup double 1986–7; South American Footballer (Soccer Player) of the Year 1979 and 1980

Mia Hamm

b. 1972

Hamm made her U.S. national team debut at 15 and dominated the women's game during much of the 1990s. In 1999 she became the first female to score over 100 goals in internationals.

Women's World Cup winner 1991, 1999; Olympic Games gold medalist 1996

David Beckham

b. 1975

Born in London, England, Beckham made his debut for Manchester United as a substitute in 1992. A gifted midfielder with world-beating, set-piece shots, Beckham captained England to World Cup qualification in 2002 and attracts media publicity for his marriage to Spice Girl Victoria Adams (p. 195).

1999 Champions League winner; 1999 FIFA World Player of the Year Runner-up

Tennis

Fred Perry

1909–1995

Born in Stockport, England, Frederick John Perry played table tennis as a teenager and did not take up tennis until he was 18. A major force in 1930s tennis, Perry became the first player to win all four grand slam events, and in 1933 he led Great Britain to its first Davis Cup triumph for 21 years. His 1936 Wimbledon win remains the last time a male singles winner was British.

Wimbledon singles champion 3 times; U.S. Championship winner 3 times; twice winner of the Davis Cup

Rod Laver

b. 1938

Australian Rod Laver's slight physique belied his enormous arm strength. In the 1962 season he won all the Grand Slam tournaments. Because he went professional in 1963, he could not enter Wimbledon until the late 1960s. In 1969 he won an incredible 17 tournaments and notched up a second Grand Slam.

Only player to win the Grand Slam twice 1962, 1969; Wimbledon champion 4 times; 11 Grand Slam singles titles in total

Billie Jean King

b. 1943

An outstanding softball player, Billie Jean King was born in Long Beach, California. She became the world tennis number four when she was 17 and went on to win six Wimbledon singles titles. She has been a powerful campaigner for equal rights for women and has done more than anyone else to raise the profile of women's tennis and sports in general.

20 Wimbledon titles in total; 5 U.S. Open doubles and 4 U.S. Open singles titles

▲ Björn Borg is credited with inspiring several generations of Swedish tennis stars, including Stefan Edberg (b. 1966) and Mats Wilander (b. 1964).

Martina Navratilova

b. 1956

Born in Czechoslovakia, Navratilova was a natural athlete as a child and loved competing against boys in skiing, hockey, and soccer. But coming from a tennis-loving family, tennis was always her main passion. Bringing a new level of athleticism to the women's game, Navratilova dominated women's tennis. Ranked world number one for seven years, Navratilova was at home on all surfaces. The grass of Wimbledon, however, became her second home as she managed the incredible feat of winning nine singles titles there. In 1975 she defected from Czechoslovakia and waited over five years before being granted U.S. citizenship. Retiring in 1994, she now supports many charities.

168 singles titles and 165 doubles titles; 18 Grand Slam singles and 31 Grand Slam doubles titles; 9 Wimbledon singles titles

Björn Borg

b. 1956

Borg captivated crowds in the late 1970s and early 1980s, winning five Wimbledon titles in a row and six French Opens. His 1980 Wimbledon final victory against McEnroe (b. 1959) is regarded as one of the most exciting games ever. After losing to McEnroe at the 1981 Wimbledon final Borg took time off from tennis and retired in 1983. He attempted a comeback in 1991, still using his favorite wooden tennis racket when other players were using advanced and more powerful graphite rackets. He was not successful, but he became a huge draw on the seniors tour for older players, where he resumed his rivalry with McEnroe.

11 Grand Slam titles; 44 singles titles; four times U.S. Open finalist

▲ In the 1987 U.S. Open Martina Navratilova managed the rare feat of winning the singles, doubles, and mixed doubles.

Steffi Graf

b. 1969

Born in Mannheim, southern Germany, Graf had won the German and European under-18s championships by age 13. In 1982 she went professional and played in the French Open. By the age of 19 she had won a Grand Slam and went on to become the only player to win each of the major tournaments four times each. Nicknamed "Fraulein Forehand" for her powerful shots, she also had an accurate serve and dominated women's tennis for almost ten years before retiring at the age of 30. In 2001 she the married tennis star Andre Agassi (b. 1970).

22 Grand Slam titles; ranked No. 1 in the world for 374 weeks; Golden Grand Slam winner in 1988, when she won all major championships and the Olympic tennis gold medal

▲ Steffi Graf's first tennis racket was given to her before her fourth birthday. By the age of 16 she was ranked as one of the top 10 tennis players in the world.

Pete Sampras

b. 1971

The son of Greek immigrants in the U.S., Pete Sampras dominated tennis in the 1990s. Moving to California when he was seven, the family joined the Peninsula Racket Club and quickly discovered that one of their four children was a prodigy. Sampras qualified for the adult tour when he was just 16, made the top 10 at the age of 18, and when he was 19 years, 28 days old, he became the youngest-ever winner of the U.S. Open, beating Ivan Lendl (b. 1960), John McEnroe (b. 1959), and Andre Agassi (b.1970). A further 12 Grand Slam titles and over 60 other titles fell to Sampras —proof that behind the mild, self-effacing manner lay a fierce and determined competitor.

Ranked No. 1 in the world for 6 consecutive years; 7 Wimbledon titles 1993–1995 and 1997–2000

Rugby

Barry John

b. 1945

Welshman Barry John electrified audiences with his dazzling attacking play, vision, and accuracy of his passing and kicking. He played halfback for Llanelli and Cardiff teams and debuted for Wales in 1966. He was hugely influential in the 1971 British Lions series win over the New Zealand All Blacks. After scoring 180 points against national and local teams John retired at 27.

Masterminded British Lions series win over New Zealand 1971; 25 Welsh caps

BARRY JOHN

J.P.R. Williams

b. 1949

Williams was a talented all-around sportsman who competed at Junior Wimbledon, but he chose rugby, making his debut for Welsh team Bridgend in 1969. Over the following 12 years he became arguably the best fullback in the world. Fast and fearless, he was an aggressive tackler and a powerful runner. Winning 55 caps and playing in a superb Welsh national team during the 1970s, he won six Five Nations Championships and three Grand Slams with Wales. He played England 11 times and was never on the losing side. During his rugby career he also qualified as a surgeon.

8 Lions caps, losing only once; 6 Five Nations Championships

Jean-Pierre Rives

b. 1952

Easily spotted on the field by his long, blond hair, Rives was a tough, highly competitive forward graced with the speed and flair of a defender. Although small for a flanker, he more than made up for it with a desperate desire to succeed and great skill and bravery. Making his debut for France in 1975 when they beat England 27–20, Rives became a vital part of an enormously talented and exciting French side. Made captain in 1978, Rives went on to lead his country a record 34 times, securing a Grand Slam against England, Wales, Ireland, and Scotland in 1981.

59 caps for France; 2 Grand Slams with France 1977 and 1981

Squash

Jahangir Khan

b. 1963

Jahangir, from Pakistan, son of Roshan Khan, the 1957 British Open Champion, became the youngest-ever winner of the World Amateur title at 15. After his brother, coach, and mentor Torsam (1950– 1979) died Jahangir dedicated himself to becoming the best in the world. In the 1981 British Open he lost to Australian Geoff Hunt in an epic contest. That was the last time he lost a game for five years and eight months. His fitness, work pace, and calmness under pressure became legendary, and it was a major news event when his record fell to a New Zealander, Ross Norman, in 1986. Khan then went unbeaten for another nine months and only retired in 1993 after leading Pakistan to win the World Team Championship.

10 consecutive British Open titles; 6 World Open titles

Jansher Khan

b. 1968

Jansher Khan's early career featured many exciting contests against his Pakistan countryman, the legendary Jahangir Khan (above). Jahangir was the victor in their first three meetings, but this was followed by two successes for Jansher, the latter on the way to winning the World Open title for the first time. In 37 games Jansher won 19 to Jahangir's 18, but no other player would push Jansher so close as he dominated much of the 1990s. Succumbing to injuries, Jansher retired in 2001.

6 British Open titles in a row; 8 World Open titles 1987, 1989, 1990, 1992–96

Basketball

Wilt "the Stilt" Chamberlain

1936–1999

After attending Kansas University the muscular, 7' 2" (2.2m) Chamberlain entered the NBA in 1960. He did not just rely on his extreme height but was also a tremendous athlete, shooter, and defender who dominated games. In his 13-year NBA career he never fouled out of a game and won the NBA's MVP award four times.

Averaged over 50 points per game over an entire NBA season 1962; won NBA titles with the Philadelphia 76ers 1967 and Los Angeles Lakers 1972; scored 100 points in one game 1962

Julius Erving

b. 1950

Erving played for the American Basketball Association league (ABA) for five seasons (winning two league titles and three MVP awards) before joining the NBA in 1976. In his 11 seasons with the Philadelphia 76ers he thrilled the public with his power shooting and all-around court play. The 76ers retired his No. 6 shirt after he retired in 1987.

Scored 30,000 points in NBA and ABA; record ABA highest average scorer (28.7 points per game); NBA career scoring average 22.0 points per game

Magic Johnson

b. 1959

Earvin Johnson, Jr. was dubbed "Magic" at the age of 15 by a sports reporter after he had scored 36 points in one game. Entering the NBA with the L.A. Lakers in 1979, his exuberance and outstanding talent helped transform his side into one of the best teams of the 1980s. In 1991 he announced that he was HIV-positive and retired from the NBA. He won an Olympic gold medal as part of the 1992 U.S. basketball team. Still in excellent health, Johnson made a surprise return in 1996, again firing up the Lakers into winning 29 of their last 40 games.

Winner of 5 NBA Championships with L.A. Lakers 1980, 1982, 1985, 1987, and 1988; elected to play in 12 All-Star games

◀ Magic Johnson (left) evades the opposition.

Michael Jordan

b. 1963

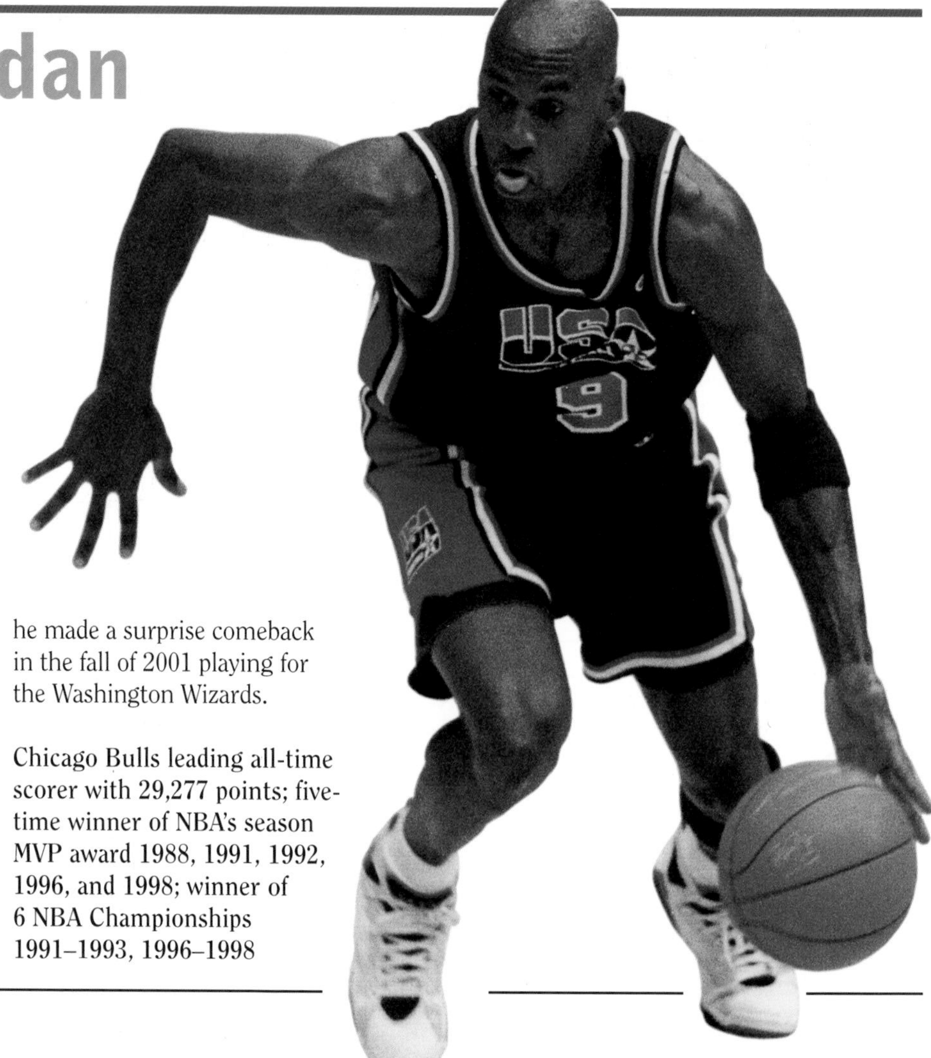

Today accepted as the world's most famous basketball player, the young Michael Jordan was not initially picked for his own high school basketball team.

Still an amateur, the 6' 5" (1.98m) tall Jordan was picked to play for the U.S. at the 1984 Olympics in Los Angeles, winning the first of two Olympic golds. The same year he was drafted into the NBA and began a long association with the Chicago Bulls. Season after season, he continued to impress and was voted the most valuable player in six different NBA finals. Tragically, his father was murdered in 1993, and Jordan retired from the NBA. He returned to playing baseball for the White Sox with limited success. The pull of basketball was too strong, however, and Jordan returned to the Bulls. In 1997 he broke a famous record, scoring more than 10 points for the 788th consecutive game. Retiring from the Bulls in 1999, he made a surprise comeback in the fall of 2001 playing for the Washington Wizards.

Chicago Bulls leading all-time scorer with 29,277 points; five-time winner of NBA's season MVP award 1988, 1991, 1992, 1996, and 1998; winner of 6 NBA Championships 1991–1993, 1996–1998

Cricket

Robert Colchin

1713–1750

In the 1700s the first cricket clubs in England were forming to play the game, often with wealthy landowners as the patrons or organizers. Many players were amateurs, although some teams run by the nobility started employing professional cricketers. Colchin was considered the leading player of the best cricket team of the time—the London Club—who played at the Artillery Ground in central London. Colchin was famed mainly as a powerful batsman.

Robert Colchin was the most successful professional cricketer of his time, although records of his scores have been lost to history

W. G. Grace

1848–1915

The greatest English cricketer of the 1800s, Grace made his professional debut in 1865 at 17. Three years later he became the first player to score a 100 in every inning of a match. A formidable figure, he continued playing cricket for another 40 years while following in his father's footsteps as a doctor. He was a founder of the Bowls Association, and in 1903 he captained England against Scotland in the first-ever international bowls match.

First player to ever score 1,000 runs in May 1895 at the age of 47; professional totals of 54,896 runs, taking 2,876 wickets and 887 catches

Don Bradman

1908–2001

Born in Cootamundra, Australia, Donald Bradman dominated cricket like no other player before or since. A right-handed batsman, he developed his hand-eye coordination as a youngster by hitting golf balls against a wall with a cricket bat. He averaged one century every three innings throughout his 20-year domestic career, with a highest test score of 452 not out. As captain he steered Australia to four successive Ashes wins between 1928 and 1948. His career test average of 99.94 was 40 runs higher than any other player.

117 centuries and 37 double centuries in professional cricket; averaged 201.5 runs per inning in the 1931 series against South Africa

Garfield Sobers

b. 1936

Gary Sobers is considered the finest all-around player to ever play cricket. Born in Barbados, he was a multitalented sportsman, playing soccer, basketball, and golf for Barbados. He made his test debut for the West Indies at the age of 17, and from 1956 to 1973 he played 86 test matches. An attacking yet precise batsman with a large range of shots, Sobers totaled 8,032 test runs, averaging 57.78 runs per inning. He was also an excellent natural athlete with over 100 test-match catches, and he could bowl both spin and deceptively fast spells, collecting 235 test wickets.

Record highest test score of 358 1958; hit six sixes in one over in English county cricket 1968

► In 1968 Sobers became the first player to hit six sixes in an over.

Ian Botham

b. 1955

Ian Botham was English cricket's most charismatic star and one of the game's greatest all-rounders. His impressive test statistics of 383 wickets, 120 catches, and 5,200 runs do not tell the whole story. His swashbuckling batting, fast-medium bowling, and superb close catching and outfield skills frequently transformed games. Botham debuted for the county of Somerset in 1974, and in 1977 he played his first test, taking five Australian wickets in one inning. He played many of his best matches against the Australians. In the 1981 Ashes series Botham became a national hero with a series of thrilling, match-winning displays. Since retiring in 1994 he has raised large sums of money for charity.

Man of the series, recapturing the Ashes for England in 1981. England's leading, all-time wicket taker with 383 test wickets and 5,200 runs

Vivian Richards

b. 1952

Born in Antigua, Viv Richards was the most-feared batsman of his time. His batting featured a huge range of shots that helped him collect over 8,500 test- and 6,700 one-day international runs. Richards thrilled English crowds, playing for Somerset and Glamorgan in England before retiring in 1992.

291 highest test score 1976; 189 not out in One-day International 1984

Shane Warne

b. 1969

Since his test debut in 1992 this extroverted Australian has terrorized batsmen with ferocious spin and a formidable array of unplayable balls. He bats late in the inning and has the ability to score quickly. He has taken over 230 wickets in one-day internationals.

Australia's leading test wicket taker 2000; passing 400 test wickets in the test series against England 2001

Golf

Bobby Jones

1902–1971

American Robert Jones never had a formal golf lesson, instead learning by copying a course professional. Winning his first major, the U.S. Open in 1923, he won 13 out of 21 major tournaments and retired at just 28. He then became a golf course and club designer, creating the Augusta National course in Georgia, home to the Masters tournament.

Only amateur to win U.S. Open and British Open in the same year twice 1926 and 1930

Jack Nicklaus

b. 1940

Jack Nicklaus was born in Colombus, Ohio. At the age of 10 he played his first nine holes and took 51 strokes, an impressive start to a career that would make him the most successful golfer of all time. At the age of 19 Nicklaus became the youngest winner of the U.S. Amateur Championship for 50 years. At 21—and after winning his second U.S. Amateur title— he went professional. He swept all before him, winning 100 tournaments, including 18 majors. Nicklaus has also become a renowned golf course designer.

6 Masters; 5 PGA Championships; 4 U.S. Opens; 3 British Opens; 2 U.S. Amateur Championships; playing member of the U.S. team that won five and tied one of six Ryder Cup competitions

► Tiger Woods heads for victory in the 1997 U.S. Open Championship.

Tiger Woods

b. 1976

Nicknamed "Tiger" after a Vietnamese soldier who was a friend of his father, Eldrick T. Woods, this young American was a genuine child prodigy at golf. At the age of two he appeared on a national TV show, where he putted golf balls against comedian Bob Hope (p. 137). At eight he won the Optimist International Junior Championship, repeating this victory five out of the next seven years. Since that time Woods has become the best golfer on the planet, and at 21 he smashed the record for youngest-ever, number-one ranked golfer by eight years.

Only three-time winner of the U.S. Amateur Championship; youngest winner of the Masters; won three majors in one year 2000

BEN HOGAN 1912–1997
Giving up his job as a bank teller to become a professional golfer, Hogan, born in Texas, went on to win 63 tournaments, including four U.S. Opens and four Masters. However, in 1949 a terrible car crash almost killed him. Fighting his severe injuries, he was able to return to golf and win another 13 tournaments because of his enormous willpower.

ARNOLD PALMER b. 1929
Palmer, born in Pennsylvania, surged through the junior and amateur ranks, winning the U.S. Amateur Championship in 1954. He went on to win seven majors, including four Masters, but his impact in the TV age was far greater than his victories. His swashbuckling style, together with his likable nature, inspired thousands to take up the game.

Track and Field

Babe Didrikson

1914–1956

The daughter of Norwegian immigrants in the U.S., Mildred Didrikson was a phenomenal all-around sportswoman. She was a star basketball player, whose baseball prowess earned her the nickname "Babe" (from baseball giant Babe Ruth p. 204). At the U.S. National Amateur competition in 1932, she entered herself in the women's team event and came first in the competition, winning six different events and setting four world records in a single afternoon. At the 1932 Olympics she won the 80-m hurdles, the javelin, and a silver in the high jump. She also helped found the Ladies Professional Golf Association and won many tournaments before succumbing to cancer.

2 Olympic golds and 1 silver; 10 major professional and 55 amateur golf titles

Jesse Owens

1913–1980

James Owens was born in Alabama to a poor family who moved to Cleveland, Ohio, when he was eight. Owens turned to track and field after a school visit by the Olympic champion Charles Paddock (1900–1943), and by the time he was 18 he ran the 100-m sprint in 10.3 seconds.

At a track-and-field meet in May 1935 Owens broke three and tied a fourth world record in little over an hour. At the infamous 1936 Olympics held in Germany, Hitler (p. 22) expected his white athletes to triumph. Owens stunned spectators with victories in the 100-m, the 200-m, and the long jump. He was also one of the winning U.S. 4 x 400-m relay team. After this success Owens still struggled financially and made public appearances, even entering sideshow races against animals. Eventually he became a leading spokesman for the Olympic movement and encoraged sports as a way out of poverty.

Set 3 world records; won4 gold medals at 1936 Berlin Olympics

◀ Jesse Owens in action at the 1936 Olympics in Germany.

EMIL ZATOPEK 1922–2000
Born in Czechoslovakia, Zatopek went to work in a shoe factory at 16. He excelled at factory race meetings and received specialist coaching. At the 1948 Olympics, Zatopek won the 10,000-m race, coming second in the 5,000-m final the following day. In the 1952 Olympics he won the 5,000-m, 10,000-m, and the marathon.

ROGER BANNISTER b. 1929
An accomplished middle-distance runner, British athlete Bannister became fascinated by the science of running while studying medicine at Oxford University. On May 6, 1954, he became the first to run a mile in under four minutes. He retired at the end of 1954 to pursue his medical studies full-time, finally becoming a neurologist.

Fanny Blankers-Koen

b. 1918

Born Francina Koen in Amsterdam, she represented the Netherlands in her first Olympics in 1936, coming sixth in the high jump and fifth in the 4 x 100-m relay. It was 12 years before the next Olympics in London, England. By that time she had married her coach, Jan Blankers, and had two children. Despite coming to the games as the holder of six world records, many felt she was too old to compete. But she triumphed, winning four Olympic golds in the 80-m hurdles, the 100-m and 200-m sprints, and the 4 x 100-m relay. She did not enter the other two events she held world records for because the long jump clashed with the hurdles and she did not enjoy the high jump. Revered in her native country, she still rides bicycles and plays tennis.

First woman to win 4 gold medals at one Olympic Games

Kip Keino

b. 1940

Kipchoge "Kip" Keino was one of the bravest and most versatile middle-distance runners and a massive inspiration to new generations of successful athletes in his native Kenya. At the 1968 Olympics, Keino was laid low by a gallbladder infection and collapsed during the 10,000-m race, yet he insisted on completing it. A few days later he won his first Olympic medal—a silver in the 5,000-m. For the 1,500-m final Keino had to jog 1 mi. (1.6km) to the stadium because his taxi got stuck in traffic, yet he managed to win the event. He repeated his success at the 1972 Olympics with a silver in the 1,500-m and a gold in the 3,000-m steeplechase. Now president of the Kenyan Olympic Committee, Keino and his wife run a home for abandoned children in Kenya.

Triumphed over adversity to win 1 gold and 1 silver medal in 1968 Olympics

Ed Moses

b. 1955

Born in Dayton, Ohio, Moses was a top student as a child and went on to achieve degrees in physics and business administration. In 1976 he stormed onto the world stage, winning an Olympic gold in the 400-m hurdles at his first-ever international competition. Moses then went on one of the longest winning streaks in track-and-field history. Between August 1977 and June 1987 he won every single 400-m hurdles race he entered, collecting 107 awards in the process.

2 Olympic gold medals 1976, 1984; 3 World Championships; 9-year unbeaten run

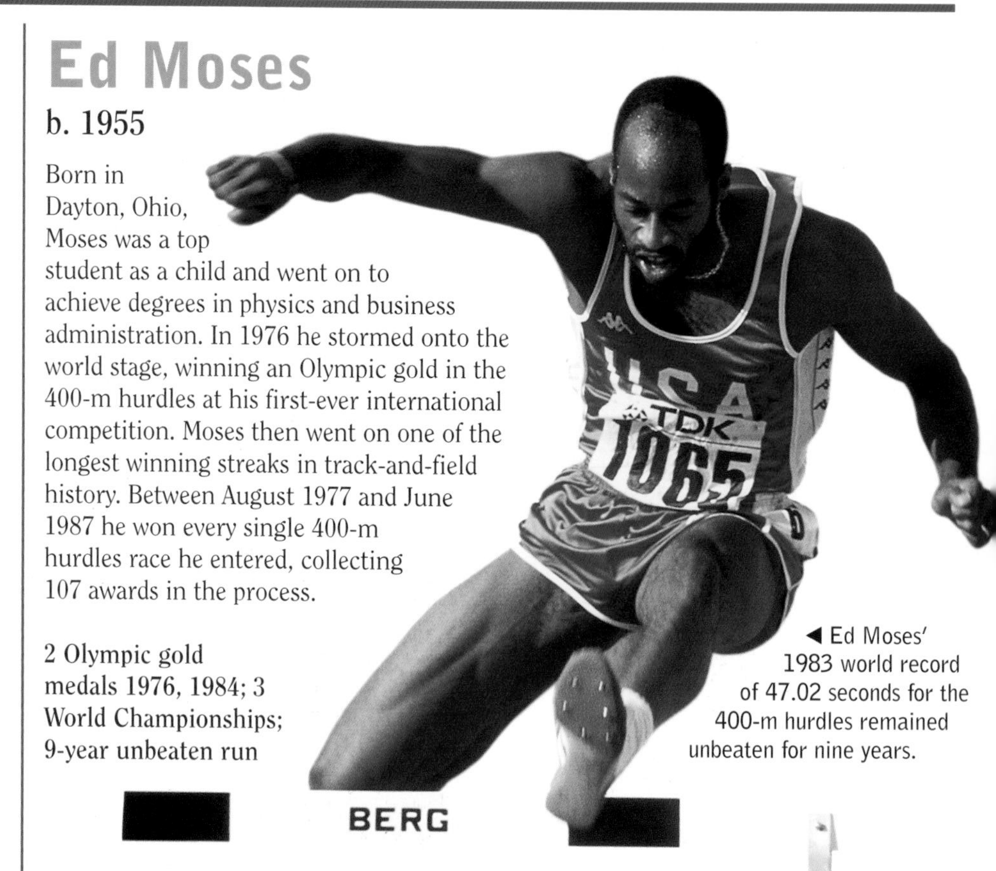

◀ Ed Moses' 1983 world record of 47.02 seconds for the 400-m hurdles remained unbeaten for nine years.

▲ Carl Lewis is rated as one of the greatest athletes of all time.

Carl Lewis

b. 1961

Born in Birmingham, Alabama, Frederick Carlton Lewis was a late bloomer and was bullied for being a weakling. He met Jesse Owens (p. 213) when he was 12, and this inspiration, plus a growth spurt of 4 in. (10cm) during his teens, helped him become a star athlete. Running 100 yards in 9.3 seconds in 1976, Lewis enrolled at Houston University. The U.S. boycott of the 1980 Moscow Olympics prevented Lewis from competing, but he made up for it in 1984. At the Los Angeles Olympics, Lewis equaled Owen's feat by winning four gold medals. Possessing great charisma, Lewis was an excellent sprinter and long jumper who remained unbeaten in the long jump for 10 years. He won four more Olympic gold medals before retiring in 1997.

9 Olympic gold medals in track-and-field competitions; unbeaten in long jump for 65 consecutive competitions

Daley Thompson

b. 1958

Broke decathlon world record 4 times; 2 Olympic golds 1980, 1984; holder of the Olympic, World, European, and Commonwealth titles and world record all at the same time

In many countries the heptathlon (seven events for women) and the decathlon (ten events for men) are considered the height of track and field.

One of the finest decathletes of all was Daley Thompson. Born in London, England, to a Scottish mother and Nigerian father, Thompson discovered an aptitude for sports while at boarding school. Winning the first decathlon he entered and breaking the British Junior record in the process, he took part in the 1976 Olympics, where he finished 18th on his 18th birthday. At the Commonwealth Games in 1978 he won the gold and then came second in the European Championships. It was the last time he was beaten in a competition for nine years. His personality occasionally upset the authorities, but it endeared him to the public, and he became one of the world's best-known athletes. Plagued by injuries before and during the 1988 Olympics, Thompson still managed to finish fourth, but injuries stopped him from qualifying for the 1992 competition, and he retired.

Sergei Bubka

b. 1963

Born in the Ukraine, Bubka showed promise as an athlete at an early age. His first attempt at pole vaulting when he was 11 saw him clear over 8.8 ft. (2.69m). Despite finishing only eighth in the Soviet championships, he was included in the team for the first World Track-and-Field Championships in 1983. Bubka astonished everyone, clearing 18.67 ft. (5.69m) to win the competition. The following year he broke the world record, the first of 35 indoor and outdoor vaulting world records he obtained over a long career. Bubka, who speaks Ukranian, Russian, English, and German, retired after the Sydney Olympics in 2000.

6 consecutive World Championships; 1 Olympic gold medal 1988; holder of world record for pole vaulting

Michael Johnson

b. 1967

With an upright, short-stepping running style not found in any coaching manual, Michael Johnson, born in Dallas, Texas, dominated the 200-m and 400-m events throughout the 1990s. Injury and illness deprived him of likely Olympic gold medals in 1988 and 1992, but in 1996 he won both and shattered Pietro Mennea's (b. 1952) 200-m world record that had stood for an amazing 17 years. Johnson has also broken the 400-m world record with a time of 43.18 seconds. After a spectacular victory in the 2000 Sydney Olympics 400-m final Johnson announced his retirement at the end of 2001.

World record holder for the 200-m, 300-m, and 400-m; twice Olympic gold medalist at 400-m, twice at 4 x 400-m relay, once at 200-m

SPORTS ON WHEELS

Bicycle Racing

Eddy Merckx

b. 1945

The Belgian bicyclist was the greatest racer of his era, winning 525 races over both short and long distances. In his first Tour de France in 1969 Merckx astonished everyone by winning the grueling competition by a large margin. Over the next four years Merckx, nicknamed "the Cannibal" for his sheer willpower to succeed, won consecutive Tours de France as well as many other races. However, in the 1975 event Merckx lagged behind the leaders and did not achieve his dream of becoming the first winner of six tours. He retired and founded his own bicyclemaking company.

5 Tours de France;
5 Tours of Italy; 3
World Championships;
7 Milan–San Remo
Classics

Miguel Indurain

b. 1964

Spaniard Miguel Indurain first rode a bicycle at the age of nine, and three years later he won the second local race he entered. Indurain did not complete his first two Tours de France and came 97th in the third, but in 1991 he won. This signaled the start of a remarkable period in which he won five tours in a row. Indurain won the 1996 time-trial Olympic gold medal and retired shortly afterward.

Tour de France winner 1991–1995; breaking the World hour record in 1994; Olympic gold medalist 1996

Lance Armstrong

b. 1971

Texas-born Lance Armstrong began his sports career as a triathlete, but he gradually focused solely on bicycling. With the encouragement of the person he most admires—his mother—he roared through 1993, winning 10 titles, including the World Championship. In 1996 he was diagnosed with cancer. Undergoing an arduous but successful treatment, Armstrong returned to bicycling in 1998 and won three consecutive Tours de France.

Won 3 Tours de France 1999–2001;
1993 World Championships winner;
Olympic bronze medalist 2000

MIGUEL INDURAIN

Car Racing

Juan Fangio

1911–1995

The son of Italian immigrants living in Argentina, Fangio was originally a car mechanic before racing on the lethal Argentine race circuits of the 1930s. Twice the Argentine National Champion, Fangio finally achieved his dream to race in Europe in 1947. He was over 40 when he won his first World Championship, but he then went on to dominate much of the 1950s. His 24 wins from 51 starts has rarely been bettered. In 1952 he broke his neck in an accident and missed two seasons. Fangio retired abruptly in 1958.

5 times Grand Prix World Champion 1951, 1954–1957

Ayrton Senna

1960–1994

When he was a child, Senna's coordination was so poor that he was taken to see medical specialists, but behind the wheel of a motorized go-cart he showed nothing but grace and skill. Racing from the age of eight, Senna won the British Formula Three championship in 1983 and 1985. He scored his first Grand Prix victory in Estoril, Portugal. Another 40 victories and over 80 starts from the front row of the grid followed. Senna was leading the San Marino Grand Prix in 1994 when he crashed. He died of his injuries shortly after.

Grand Prix World Champion 1988, 1990, and 1991

Michael Schumacher

b. 1969

A cart powered by an old lawnmower engine was four-year-old Schumacher's first racing vehicle. In 1984 and 1985 he won the German junior carting title and in 1987 the adult title. He made his Formula One debut at the 1991 Belgian Grand Prix, but he did not finish the race. He soon moved to Benetton, and on the first anniversary of his debut he won his first race. A perfectionist and a ruthless driver, Schumacher ruffled feathers with his dominant racing style that saw him win two World Championships for Benetton. Switching to Ferrari in 1995, he endured a number of lean years before giving Ferrari the Constructors' Championship in 2000 and 2001, as well as winning the Drivers' Championship.

51 Grand Prix race wins; 4 Grand Prix World Championships 1994, 1995, 2000, 2001

TAZIO NUVOLARI 1892–1953
Nuvolari was a driver in the Italian army before he began racing motorcycles at the age of 28. Switching to cars in 1924 and signing up to Alfa Romeo in 1928, Nuvolari quickly became a legend. He was incredibly fast, courageous, and passionate about racing. He won many races, including Le Mans, and continued racing well into his fifties.

STIRLING MOSS b. 1929
The greatest Grand Prix driver to never win the World Championship, Moss was the child of two race-car drivers. Moss made his name in Formula 3, competed in Le Mans, and was the first British winner of the Mille Miglia race in 1955. He won 16 Grand Prix and was beaten to the 1958 World Championship by another British driver, Mike Hawthorn (1929–1959).

NIKI LAUDA b. 1949
Lauda was born in Vienna, Austria. In 1974, driving for Ferrari, he won two World Championships. In the 1976 season he nearly died in a crash, suffering terrible injuries and burns to his face and body. He quickly recovered to race ten weeks later, narrowly losing the 1976 championship to James Hunt (1947–1993). Retiring in 1979 to concentrate on his airline business, he made a dramatic comeback in 1982, spending three seasons with McLaren and winning his third World Championship in 1984.

KENNY ROBERTS b. 1951
Born in California, Kenny Roberts won the AMA Grand National Championship in 1973 and 1974, the prestigious Daytona 200 three times, and the World 500cc Grand Prix series three times in a row before retiring in 1983.

DALE EARNHARDT 1951–2001
Dropping out of school at an early age, Dale Earnhardt entered NASCAR racing in 1975. He was victorious over 70 times in the top-flight Winston Cup competition, earning the nickname "the Intimidator" for his relentlessly determined racing style. The winner of seven NASCAR championships, he crashed while competing in the Daytona 500 and died shortly after owing to his injuries.

WATER AND WINTER SPORTS

Swimming and Diving

Johnny Weissmuller

1903–1984

Hungarian-born Peter Jonas "Johnny" Weissmuller moved to the United States at a young age. Taking up swimming seriously at the age of 16 Weissmuller won 52 national championships and set over 60 world records in an incredible nine-year swimming career. He retired from competitive swimming in 1929, and after a brief period giving lessons and working as a swimwear model he began a long movie career as Tarzan.

5 Olympic gold medals 1924 and 1928

◀ Johnny Weissmuller took the leading role in 19 Tarzan movies between 1932 and 1948.

Dawn Fraser

b. 1937

Australian-born Fraser suffered from asthma as a child and was encouraged to swim by her older brother. Spotted by coach Harry Gallagher, Fraser won the 100-m freestyle at the 1956 Melbourne Olympics. She followed up with wins in the same event at two more Olympics—the first person to do so. Fraser often clashed with officials, and after a prank at the 1964 Olympics she was banned from all competitive swimming for ten years. This event ended her career.

3 Olympic gold medals; first woman to swim 100-m freestyle in under one minute

▲ Mark Spitz will always be remembered for his astonishing 1972 Olympic performance.

Mark Spitz

b. 1950

Although he was studying dentistry at Indiana University, Mark Spitz's greatest talent was swimming. At the Pan-American Games in 1967 he won five gold medals and followed this up with two Olympic gold medals in 1968. In the 1972 Olympics, Spitz outshone all other competitors, entering seven different swimming events and winning them all in world-record times. In total he set 23 world records during his career. A 1991 comeback attempt at the age of 41 was not successful.

9 Olympic gold medals 1968 and 1972

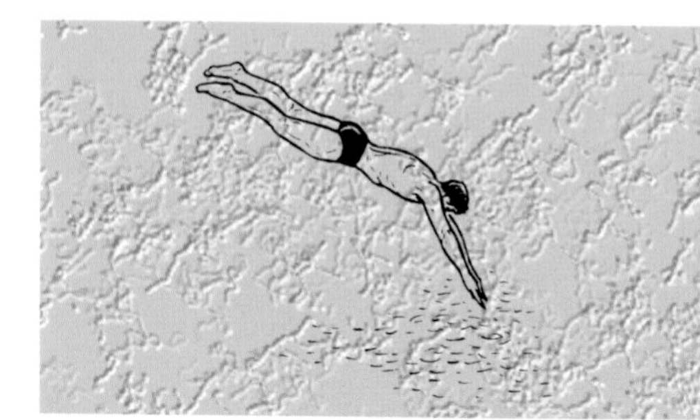

GREG LOUGANIS b. 1960
Winner of five World Championships and 47 U.S. national diving titles, Greg Louganis was born to Swedish and Samoan parents living in the U.S. who gave him up for adoption. Winning a 1976 Olympic silver at the young age of 16, Louganis won both springboard and platform diving events at the 1984 and 1988 Olympics. He retired in 1989.

IAN THORPE b. 1982
In 1997, aged only 14, Ian Thorpe swam for Australia in the Pan-Pacific Games, coming second in the 400-m. He was only 16 when he triumphed at the 1998 World Championships, winning both the 400-m freestyle and the 4 x 200-m freestyle relay. At the 2000 Olympics in Sydney, "The Thorpedo" won three golds and two silvers.

Rowing

Steve Redgrave

b. 1962

British rower Redgrave won a gold in the coxless fours at the 1984 Olympics before switching to pairs and winning a gold in 1988 with Andy Holmes. After Holmes retired Redgrave partnered with 19-year-old Matthew Pinsent (b. 1970). The pair had a record 61 wins in a row, including gold medals at the 1992 and 1996 Olympics. Switching back to a coxless four, Redgrave triumphed again in a close final to win in Sydney in 2000.

5 Olympic gold medals;
9 World Championship gold medals;
3 Commonwealth Games gold medals

▲ Steven Redgrave (third from left) about to win the 2000 Olympics coxless four.

Yachting

Dennis Conner

b. 1942

A native of California, Conner has sailed for the U.S. since 1963. He won the Star Class World Championship in 1971, an Olympic medal in 1976, and has taken part in two Whitbread Round-the-World Races. However, he is best known for his exploits in seven Americas Cup competitions. Conner won in 1980, lost in 1983, but triumphed by winning the cup back in 1987 and defending it the following year. He is preparing another Americas Cup challenge for 2003.

Three times Americas Cup winner 1980, 1987, 1988

Hockey

Wayne Gretzky

b. 1961

Wayne Gretzky started skating on a makeshift ice rink in his family's backyard in Ontario, Canada. The leading scorer in the 1977 Junior World Cup, he became professional at 17. In his first eight years in the National Hockey League he led the league in points scored each year and led the Edmonton Oilers to win four Stanley Cups. Moving to the L.A. Kings in 1989 and the New York Rangers in 1997, Gretzky retired in 1999 and is now a part owner and advisor to the Canadian national team.

10 times NHL scoring champion;
led Edmonton to 4 Stanley Cups;
all-time NHL leader in points (2,857) with 894 goals and 1,963 assists

KING CHARLES II 1630–1685
After the execution of his father English king Charles II was exiled in Europe, where he took great interest in the small, fast boats—called Jachts—that were built for races by Dutch noblemen. In 1660 Charles II was restored as king and popularized yachting in Great Britain. He is said to have owned 28 different yachts throughout his reign.

BOBBY ORR b. 1948
Canadian-born Orr revolutionized hockey's defensive position through skillful, attacking moves. Playing most of his career for the Boston Bruins, he remains the only defensive player to be the leading scorer in the National Hockey League, a feat he managed twice. At the age of 31 he was elected into the Hockey Hall of Fame.

Skiing

Jean-Claude Killy

b. 1944

Dominating skiing in the late 1960s, Frenchman Killy collected the first World Cup competition in 1967, winning 12 races. In front of his home crowd, he took all three skiing competitions at the 1968 Olympics—the downhill, slalom, and giant slalom.

Twice World Cup champion 1967 and 1968; 3 Olympic gold medals 1968

Ingemar Stenmark

b. 1956

Born in northern Sweden, Stenmark became one of the most successful and famous skiers of the 1970s and 1980s. He was a master technician who competed in slalom and giant slalom and won an impressive 86 World Cups. In 1978–1979 he set a record, winning 13 World Cup races in a single season. In 1989 the man known as the "Silent Swede" hung up his skis for good.

3 World Cup Championships 1976–1978; 2 Olympic gold medals 1980

Franz Klammer

b. 1953

Born in Austria, Klammer became the fastest downhill skier in the world. After triumphing in the 1976 Winter Olympics he was deeply affected by a skiing accident that left his brother confined to a wheelchair. Yet Klammer did return in the early 1980s to win again.

◀ Klammer exhibited a daredevil's flair for skiing, taking many risks in order to win races.

Olympic Downhill gold medal 1976; World Cup Downhill title 1975, 1976–1978, and 1983

Annemarie Moser-Pröll

b. 1953

Born into a large Austrian farming family near Salzburg, Austria, Moser-Pröll was encouraged by her local priest to take up skiing. Making her international debut in 1969, Moser-Pröll dominated women's downhill skiing between 1970 and 1975, retiring aged 22. She returned to win the 1978 World Championships, a sixth World Cup, and a gold medal in the 1980 Olympics.

Winner of 6 World Cups; Winter Olympic gold medalist 1980

Skating

▲ Irina Rodnina and her partner, Aleksandr Zaitsev, got married in 1975.

Irina Rodnina

b. 1949

Born in Moscow, Russia, Rodnina, with her partner Alexei Ulanov (b. 1947), won the 1972 Olympics' pairs skating competition. Ulanov fell in love with skater Lyudmila Smirnova, so Rodnina found another partner, Aleksandr Zaitsev (b. 1952). They won the 1973 European Championship with perfect 6.0 scores from all 12 judges and went on to win every World Championship they entered. She was the oldest winner of a gold medal at the 1980 Winter Olympics.

3 Olympic gold medals 1972, 1976, 1980

Eric Heiden

b. 1958

Born in Wisconsin, Heiden won the overall world championship speed skating title in 1977, 1978, and 1979. In the 1980 Winter Olympics he won every men's speed-skating event, breaking Olympic or world records in each. He retired afterward, turning first to bicycle racing and then to medicine.

5 Olympic gold medals 1980

BOXING

John L. Sullivan

1858–1918

John L. Sullivan was an Irish-American born in Boston, Massachusetts. He had strength, endurance, and a tremendous punch, the former vital in contests that could last 30 rounds or more. After beating American and British champions in the early 1880s Sullivan toured around the United States, offering $1,000 to anyone who could last four rounds with him. The public had not seen anything like this before and flocked to dance halls and theaters to see Sullivan. In 1887 he traveled to Europe to fight in England and France, again with great success. His career ended after he was knocked out by Jim Corbett (1866–1933) in 1892.

Beat American Champion Paddy Ryan 1882; beat British Champion Charley Mitchell (1861–1918) 1883

Jack Dempsey

1895–1983

Born in Colorado, Dempsey started his working life as a traveling miner who made extra money by challenging all-comers to boxing contests in saloons in rough mining towns. In 1914 he went professional, and in 1919 he knocked out the 250-lb (113-kg), 6' 5" (1.98-m) giant Jess Willard (1881–1968) to win the heavyweight title. Known as the "Manassa Mauler," he defended his title six times before losing twice to Gene Tunney (1897–1978). After the defeats Dempsey continued boxing, mainly in exhibition bouts, but retired in 1940.

A record of 60 professional victories, 49 by knockout

Sugar Ray Robinson

1920–1989

Born in Ailey, Georgia, and considered the greatest non-heavyweight boxer of all time, Sugar Ray Robinson turned professional in 1940 and won his first 40 fights in a row before losing to Jake LaMotta (b. 1921). He did not lose again for eight years, during which he became World Welterweight Champion. In 1951 he fought in a heavier weight category against LaMotta to win the middleweight title. In 1952 he retired as champion. In 1955 he tried again, regaining the middleweight title, and out of a career total of 19 defeats, 16 occurred during his comeback.

World Welterweight Champion 1946–1951; World Middleweight Champion 1951; 174 professional fight wins with 109 knockouts

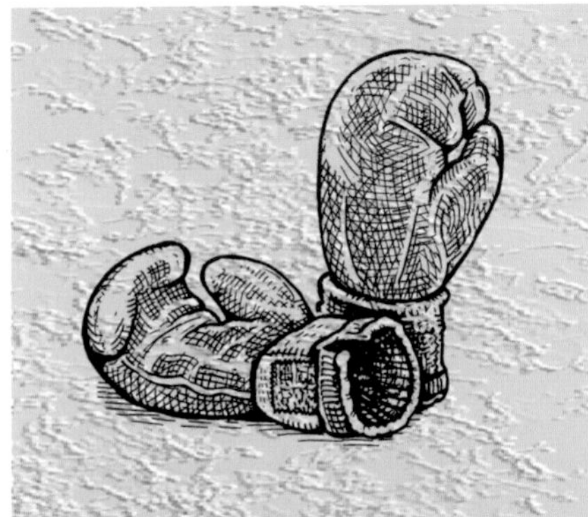

JAMES FIGG 1696–1734
A master fencer and wrestler, the 5' 9"- (1.8-m) tall Figg became the first recognized champion of England at bare-fist fighting. He fought all-comers and is believed to have lost only one fight when he was sick, although some believe he was undefeated until he retired in 1730. In 1719 he opened a school for boxing and fencing in London known as Figg's Amphitheater. The success of his academy prompted more boxing schools to open and members of the nobility to take up boxing as a sport.

JOE LOUIS 1914–1981
Born Joseph Louis Barrow in a shack near Lafayette, Alabama, Louis' father was committed to a mental institution when Joe was two, and the young boy's early life was difficult. Boxing as an amateur under the name Joe Louis so that his mother would not find out, he won 50 out of 54 amateur fights before turning professional in 1934. "The Brown Bomber" became a huge celebrity as the unbeaten heavyweight champion for 12 years and 25 fights. This is still a record.

ROCKY MARCIANO 1923–1969
Growing up in Massachusetts, Rocky was introduced to boxing by his uncle and boxed in the U.S. Army during World War II. Turning professional in 1947, Marciano was shorter and lighter than other heavyweights and had a crude brawling style. Yet his immense energy reserves, willpower, and belief took him to a professional record of 49 fights—49 wins, 43 by knockout. In 1952 he knocked out Jersey Joe Walcott (1914–1994) to win the World Heavyweight Championship, and four years later he retired with back pain as the undefeated world champion. The day before his 46th birthday he died in a plane crash.

Muhammad Ali

b. 1942

Cassius Marcellus Clay was born in Louisville, Kentucky, and started boxing at the age of 12. He won Olympic gold medals at the age of 18, but many boxing experts were not impressed with his ring style and his ultraconfident boastfulness—"I am the greatest."

When Cassius Clay fought the heavyweight champion Sonny Liston (1932–1970) in 1964, few gave him a chance, but he easily beat Liston. He then announced that he had accepted the teachings of Islam and would be known as Muhammad Ali. Ali was blessed with phenomenal hand and foot speed, and he brought a level of grace to heavyweight boxing not seen before. Outside the ring the bright, funny, and handsome Ali generated unprecedented interest in boxing. In 1967 Ali refused to serve in the U.S. Army in Vietnam. He was arrested, stripped of his title, and banned from boxing for over three years. The 1970s are considered a golden age in heavyweight boxing with champions such as Joe Frazier (b. 1947), Ken Norton (b. 1943), and George Foreman (b. 1949). Ali's epic contests with these boxers, which he usually won, have gone down in history as among the best ever. Ali beat Foreman to win the title in 1974, and after losing to Leon Spinks (b. 1953) in 1978 he recaptured the title six months later. Now past his prime, Ali had two more fights, which led to defeats by Larry Holmes (b. 1949) and Trevor Berbick (b. 1952), before he retired in 1981.

Olympic gold medal 1960; won the World Heavyweight title three times; won 56 out of 61 professional fights, including 37 knockouts

▲ Married four times and with nine children, Ali now suffers from severe Parkinson's disease, but his face is still one of the most recognized in the world.

► In 1974 at the famous "Rumble in the Jungle" in Zaire, Ali beat George Foreman to regain the World Heavyweight title.

OTHER SPORTS

Gymnastics

Olga Korbut

b. 1956

Born in Belarus, U.S.S.R, Olga Korbut was the smallest in her class, yet she could outrun and outjump larger children. She came to the attention of coach Renald Knysh, and the pair formed a partnership that generated a series of new moves in gymnastics, including the backward somersault on the balance beam, which was called a Korbut Salto. At the 1972 Olympics she captivated audiences with her bold, imaginative routines, winning four gold medals. She retired in 1977 and was the first person to be inducted into the International Gymnastics Hall of Fame in 1988.

4 gold and 2 silver medals at the 1972 and 1976 Olympics

Nadia Comaneci

b. 1961

Born in Moldova, Romania, Nadia Elena Comaneci competed in her first national championships at the age of eight. Attending her first Olympics in 1976 as a 14 year old, Comaneci scooped three gold medals, one silver, and one bronze. She was also the first gymnast in Olympic history to be awarded a perfect "10" when she performed on the uneven bars. She retired in 1984 and became an international judge and a coach to the Romanian national team. In 1989 she defected to the United States.

First perfect "10" at an Olympics; 5 Olympic golds, 3 silver, and 1 bronze

▲ Nadia Comaneci received a second perfect "10" on the balance beam in the 1976 Olympics.

Fencing

Camillo Agrippa

c. 1530–c. 1575

Agrippa was an Italian Renaissance architect, philosopher, and amateur swordsman. He studied swordplay and wrote a definitive book about the sport. Agrippa emphasized thrusting with the point of the blade, and he described and detailed many of the stances and grips still used in fencing today.

Wrote *Trattato di Scientia d'Arme* (*Treaty on the Science of Arms*) 1500s

Weightlifting

Naim Suleymanoglu

b. 1967

Turkish Suleymanoglu began lifting weights when he was 10, and at 14 he came within 5.5 lbs (2.5kg) of a world record. At 16 he achieved his first adult world records and later won gold medals at three Olympics, retiring in 2000.

3 Olympic golds 1988, 1992, and 1996

Judo

Masahiko Kimura

1917–1993

Kimura became All-Japan Open Weight Judo Champion at 20 and kept this title for 13 years, during which he never lost a bout. Standing 5'6" and weighing 185 lbs (84kg), Kimura often had to fight taller, heavier opponents. His training regime included 1,000 nonstop push-ups.

All Japan Open Weight Judo Champion 1937–1950

Sumo wrestling

Kajinosyke Tanikaze

1750–1795

The sport of sumo wrestling started around 2,000 years ago, but the late 1700s saw what is described as Sumo's golden age. One of the leading sumo wrestlers during this period was Kajinosyke Tanikaze. Born in Sendai, Japan, Tanikaze rose through the ranks to become the Grand Champion, or *Yokozuna,* in 1789. In the highest class of wrestling, the upper division, Tanikaze won 258 bouts and only lost 14. He won 21 titles, and statues commemorating his achievements exist in Japan to this day.

Won 21 titles; won 63 bouts in a row; *Yokozuna* (Grand Champion) 1789

Mitsuga Chiyonofuji

b. 1955

At 280 lbs (127kg) Mitsuga Chiyonofuji was light for a top-class Japanese sumo wrestler, but he countered this with explosive speed and strength. Spotted by scouts in 1974 who took him from Hokkaido to Tokyo, Chiyonofuji earned the nickname "the Wolf" because of an intense stare that helped him win the mental battle with an opponent. In 1987 "The Wolf" recorded 53 victories in a row, the most since World War II. Two years later he had won 968 victories, the highest number on record. After many shoulder dislocations he retired to national acclaim in 1991. He is now the head of the Kokonoe stable of sumo wrestlers where he coaches.

Winner of 31 Grand Sumo tournaments; 1,045 victories, the highest ever recorded

Horseback riding

Willy Shoemaker

b. 1931

As a teenager Billie Lee Shoemaker cleaned out the stables at a Californian ranch to earn a living. By the age of 18 he was racing professionally and had developed a smooth riding style that proved very successful. He broke the U.S. record of 6,033 winners in 1970, and he reached 8,833 winners before retiring in 1990. Shoemaker then became a trainer, but was left confined to a wheelchair after a car accident in 1991.

Rode 6 winners in one day, 6 times in his career; 4 Kentucky Derby wins; 11 Triple Crown wins

Lester Piggott

b. 1935

English jockey Lester Piggott collected over 5,300 wins in the U.K. and in 27 other countries. Shy and reluctant to give interviews, he was an aggressive rider who had a number of run-ins with the racing authorities. However, he remained the people's champion from the moment he won the Derby as an 18 year old. In 1985 he retired and started training horses, but in 1987 he was sent to prison for three years for tax evasion. After one year in prison Piggott made a successful comeback as a jockey.

Champion Jockey of England 11 times 1960, 1964–1971, 1981, and 1982; won the Derby a record 9 times

◀ Mark Todd on The Irishman at the Badminton Horse Trials in 1989.

Mark Todd

b.1956

Born in New Zealand, Mark Todd won the three-day eventing competition at the 1980 Badminton Horse Trials as a relative unknown. In 1984 he won the three-day eventing gold medal at the Los Angeles Olympics. He repeated the feat at the next Olympics, also winning a bronze in the team event with New Zealand. After many competition wins throughout the 1990s he was voted the three-day eventer of the 20th century.

Two golds, one silver, and two bronzes in Olympic three-day eventing; winner of three Badminton Horse Trials

CHAPTER TEN

MOVERS AND SHAKERS

Movers and Shakers before 1000

In the ancient world the movers and shakers were the founders and prophets of religions. Some of their names are lost in the past. Hindus, for example, see their faith as one that has always existed. The prophets of Judaism also lived long ago, but because of the Bible, their names are recorded, and their deeds have inspired Christians and Muslims as well as Jews.

▲ Confucius was a Chinese philosopher whose sayings are still quoted today.

THE PROPHETS OF JUDAISM
Judaism is a religion with three main founders. **Abraham**, the father of the Hebrew people, probably lived between 2000–1650 B.C. He is seen as a key ancestor by all of the great faiths that believe in one God—Judaism, Christianity, and Islam. Next came **Moses**, the man who led the Jews out of slavery in Egypt and to the Promised Land of Canaan. Moses also received the Divine Law from God. As with Abraham historians are not sure exactly when Moses lived, but he was probably alive between 1400–1200 B.C. The third founder was **Ezra**, who led the Jews out of another period of captivity, this time in the city of Babylon. A scribe of the 500s B.C., Ezra arranged and wrote down the sacred Jewish writings that make up the Torah, the first five books of the Hebrew Bible. The biblical Book of Ezra describes how the Jews returned from Babylon to Jerusalem and rebuilt their temple there.

▲ The elephant god, Ganesh, is one of the most popular Hindu gods.

TEACHERS IN THE EAST
The origins of Hinduism go so far back in time that its founders are unknown. But the greatest philosopher of Hinduism, **Shankara**, lived much later, probably around A.D. 788–820. Shankara lived the life of a wandering scholar and sage and attracted many students. He wrote commentaries on sacred Hindu writings and founded numerous temples and monasteries. But much of his life is shrouded in legend. At the end of his life he is said to have disappeared into the Himalayas, near the mountain where the god Shiva was supposed to live.

Another great Indian religious leader, the **Buddha**, lived between c. 563–c. 483 B.C. Born into the royal family of the Sakya tribe in Nepal, the Buddha's original name was Prince Gautama Siddhartha. But when he was about 30 years old, the prince turned his back on the luxurious ways of the royal palace and followed a life of poverty and meditation. He is said to have reached a state of heightened religious awareness—known as enlightenment—and it was at this point that he was given the name of the Buddha (the "enlightened one"). From that time on he taught his companions how to follow the path of peace, suffering, and contemplation, which leads to the enlightened state. His followers spread throughout Asia—and later around the rest of the world—showing others how to follow the Buddhist path.

At around the same time as the Buddha the great philosopher **Confucius** (551–479 B.C.) lived in China. Confucius was a representative of the Chinese government before he gave up his job for a life of contemplation and teaching. In his teachings he showed how virtues, such as hard work, politeness, wisdom, and respect for others, helped people live better lives. His teachings won many followers in China and were developed by later philosophers and sages, such as **Mencius** (c. 372–289 B.C.), into a complete religious system. Confucianism was the state religion in China for many centuries.

▲ Revelations from the angel Gabriel were written down as the Koran, the book of Islam.

CHRISTIANITY

The influence of **Jesus** (c. 6 B.C.–c. A.D. 30) only became widespread after his death by crucifixion. Belief that Jesus was the son of God, that he ascended to heaven on his death, and that he would one day return to earth as the Messiah was spread around the Mediterranean by preachers such as St. Paul (died c. A.D 64). At first Christians were persecuted by the Romans who ruled the area at the time. But during the reign of the emperor **Constantine I** (c. A.D. 274–337) Christianity became a state religion of the Roman empire. From then on it spread quickly in Europe and elsewhere.

▲ The Buddha's teachings are now read by people all over the world.

One of the most important early Christians was one of Jesus' original disciples, **St. Peter**. According to a tradition that goes back to the A.D 100s, Peter traveled to Rome, where he was crucified. Roman Catholics regard him as the first bishop of Rome and therefore also as the first pope. Many remarkable men led the early Church. The most famous included **Pope Gregory I** (Gregory the Great, c. A.D. 540–604), who reorganized the Church and sent missionaries to convert the people of Spain and England, and **Saint Augustine of Hippo** (A.D. 354–430), a Numidian bishop in North Africa who produced some of the best-known of all early Christian writings.

◀ On Palm Sunday Jesus rode into Jerusalem triumphantly.

ISLAM

The most recent of the great world religions to become established, the Islamic faith, was revealed to the prophet **Muhammad** (c. A.D. 570–632). In around A.D. 610 Muhammad began to receive revelations from the angel Gabriel about the word of God, which were written down as the Koran, the sacred book of Islam. During his lifetime the Islamic faith spread throughout the Arabian peninsula. After Muhammad's death an Islamic empire grew in western Asia and North Africa, spreading the faith farther. In more recent centuries Islam has spread all over the world, and it is today's most rapidly expanding religion.

WRONGDOERS

This chapter also looks at some of the most notorious wrongdoers and lawbreakers in history. The ancient world had its fair share, and some of them were very powerful people. Among the Roman emperors, for example, two men have earned their reputations for making evil use of their power. **Caligula** (A.D. 12–41) murdered his relatives, had citizens of Rome executed so he could take over their property, and showered himself with honors in the hope that he would be treated as a god. **Nero** (A.D. 37–68) behaved in a similar way, first murdering his mother and his wife, Octavia (d. 62), and then his second wife, Poppaea. He is then alleged to have set fire to Rome so that he could use the land to build a grand palace. Christians were blamed for the fire, and Nero had them killed. The other notorious ruler of the ancient world was **Attila**, king of the Huns (c. A.D. 406–453). Attila killed and pillaged his way from the Black Sea to the Mediterranean Sea, carving out a huge empire. He died the day after marrying Ildeco, a princess from Burgundy. It is believed that she murdered Attila in revenge for his horrible treatment of her own people.

▲ Roman emperor Caligula was one of the most notorious rulers of the Roman Empire.

MOVERS AND SHAKERS

Peter Abelard

1071–1142

French-born theologian Peter Abelard became Headmaster of the Notre Dame School in Paris, France, in 1115. He had an affair with Héloïse (c. 1098–1164), his young pupil, and married her. Because of the scandal, Abelard was forced to become a monk and Héloïse a nun. As a monk he continued his work, impressing many with his arguments but worrying others with his unorthodox views.

Wrote a collection of letters to Héloïse 1115–1120; author of *The History of My Misfortunes* 1130s

Eisai

1141–1215

A monk from Japan, Eisai traveled to China to study a type of Buddhism called Ch'an. He brought Ch'an back to Japan, where it became Zen, a form of Buddhism that strictly trains monks and uses meditation. From Japan, Zen has spread around the world to become one of the most popular forms of Buddhism.

Founded the Rinzai school of Zen Buddhism 1190s

Thomas Aquinas

1225–1274

Thomas Aquinas was born into a rich family near Aquino, Italy. Against his family's wishes he left his wealth behind, joined the Dominican friars, and soon became the best-known teacher in Europe. Aquinas wrote a number of theological books that tried to match the theology of his time with the scientific beliefs of ancient Greek writers such as Aristotle (p. 106). After his death the Church made Aquinas a saint for his philosophical and theological work.

Wrote *Summa Theologiae* 1266–1273

Niccolò Machiavelli

1469–1527

Machiavelli was an Italian politician whose ruthless ideas made him world-famous. He was born in Florence, Italy, which was then an independent city-state, and he became one of the city's most powerful leaders in 1498.

Over the next few years he was one of those in charge of the city's foreign policy, and he went on diplomatic missions to meet most of Europe's influential rulers. However, in 1512 he lost his job, and the following year he was arrested and tortured, suspected of treason. Although he was released, Machiavelli did not return to politics. Instead, he became a full-time writer, producing books about ancient history and warfare. His most famous work was *The Prince*, a short book explaining exactly how Machiavelli thought a ruler, or prince, should behave. *The Prince* draws on Machiavelli's experience in government and his wide reading of other writers, and it offers all kinds of advice to the ruler. Its most famous idea is that a prince should be prepared to do wrong if he believes that good will come of his actions. This idea, summed up in the famous phrase "the end justifies the means," has led some to praise Machiavelli's common sense, while others see him as an evil influence on politicians.

Influential Italian politician 1498–1512; political writer 1513–1532

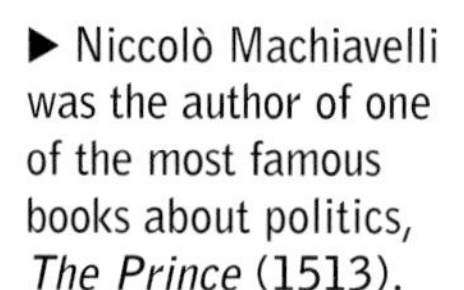

▶ Niccolò Machiavelli was the author of one of the most famous books about politics, *The Prince* (1513).

▲ John Wesley preached to Native Americans during his visit to Georgia.

John Wesley

1703–1791

Born in England, John Wesley was a pious Christian who became a priest in the Church of England in 1728. Wesley began to preach increasingly dramatic sermons to convince others of his faith. His zealous approach was disapproved of by the Church, which banned him from their sermons. As a result Wesley, with his brother, the hymnwriter Charles Wesley (1707–1788), started a religious movement—Methodism. Wesley traveled widely, preaching to huge crowds, often outside, and converted millions of people around the world.

Founded Methodism 1720s; traveled 250,000 mi. around Great Britain, preaching around 40,000 sermons 1739–1789

John Jacob Astor

1763–1848

German-born John Jacob Astor settled in the U.S. in 1784 and went into the fur trade. His companies made huge profits, especially after the U.S. government bought Louisiana from the French in 1803, opening up trade with the west. Astor used the money he made to buy property in New York City and ended up owning around half of southern Manhattan. When he retired, he was the richest man in the U.S. and left large sums to pay for facilities in New York City.

Made a fortune of over $20 million by property speculation 1808–1848; founded the settlement of Astoria, Oregon, 1811

Cornelius Vanderbilt

1794–1877

New Yorker Cornelius Vanderbilt began working at the age of 16 when he bought a boat and started a ferry service between Staten Island and New York City. Over the next 24 years he bought more and more boats, eventually becoming the U.S.'s most successful steamship operator. In 1862 he sold all of his ships and started over—building railroads. He was soon in control of many railroad companies, with lines running all over the U.S. In his lifetime, he amassed a vast fortune of over $100 million.

U.S. steamship operator 1810–1862; built extensive U.S. railroad empire 1862–1877

POCAHONTAS 1595–1617
The daughter of a Native American chief, Pocahontas worked to keep the peace between her people and the English settlers in Virginia. She is said to have twice saved the life of John Smith (1580–1631), an English settler, when her people threatened to kill him. In 1613–1614 she was captured by the English and finally released in exchange for the freedom of English prisoners and stolen goods. While being held by the English, she converted to Christianity and married Englishman John Rolfe (d. 1622). She went with Rolfe to England in 1616 but died before returning to America.

GEORGE FOX 1624–1691
George Fox was a Puritan who rejected the approach of the established Church in his native England. He traveled around England preaching and attracting many followers. He said that men should love each other like brothers, and he and his followers called themselves the "Friends of Truth." Their organization later became known as the Society of Friends (or Quakers) and is still admired for its campaigns of religious tolerance and peace.

STAMFORD RAFFLES 1781–1826
Born in Jamaica when it was ruled by Great Britain, Raffles was one of the thousands of English who worked abroad running Great Britain's large empire. When he was sent to Southeast Asia, he led an expedition against Java in 1811, captured the island, and became its vice governor. A few years later he stopped working because of sickness and wrote a notable *History of Java.* In 1818 he returned to Asia and founded the British settlement of Singapore, which eventually became one of the world's most important cities and trading centers.

Brigham Young

1801–1877

New Yorker Brigham Young converted to Mormonism in 1832. He quickly became an elder of the Mormon church and was appointed the head of the Mormon settlement in Nauvoo, Illinois. When Joseph Smith (below), Mormonism's founder, died in 1844, Young took over as President of the Church. In 1847 he led the Mormons to Utah and was appointed governor. However, in 1857 there was widespread objection in the U.S. to the Mormon custom of polygamy (one husband marrying several wives), and a new governor was appointed.

Mormon leader 1844–1877; founder of Salt Lake City 1847; governor of Utah 1850–1857

Joseph Smith

1805–1844

In 1827 Joseph Smith, a young man from Sharon, Vermont, claimed to have been given a hidden gospel written on sheets of gold. This work—*The Book of Mormon*—claimed to tell the history of North America up to A.D. 400. It was said to have been written by a prophet named Mormon, and it inspired Smith to start a new church, the Church of Jesus Christ of the Latter-day Saints. Followers of his religion became known as Mormons. The church quickly grew and founded settlements in Ohio and Missouri. Many people disliked the Mormons, and in 1838 they were forced to leave Missouri for Illinois. Smith was arrested for conspiracy, imprisoned in Carthage, Illinois, and shot when a violent crowd broke into the jail.

Founder of the Mormon Church 1830

▲ Florence Nightingale was known as the "Lady with the Lamp."

Florence Nightingale

1820–1910

Born in Florence, Italy, Florence Nightingale was the daughter of rich British parents. She wanted to become a nurse, but her parents would not allow this. However, in 1853 she began working as the superintendent of a hospital for women in London, England. The following year she read in newspapers about the appalling conditions suffered by wounded soldiers in the Crimean War. Nightingale volunteered to help and sailed to Turkey with a group of 38 nurses. When she arrived at the military hospital in Scutari, Turkey, she changed the way the place was run, making it hygienic, improving the soldiers' comfort levels, and reducing the death rate.

Reformed army nursing practice 1850s–1870s; reduced death rate at Scutari military hospital 1854–1856; founded the Nightingale School of Nursing, London, England, 1856

William Booth

1829–1912

Born in Nottingham, England, William Booth was a Methodist minister and preacher. With his wife, Catherine (1829–1890), he went on a preaching tour overseas before returning to England to set up a mission in London. This was aimed mainly at the poor in London's East End and was originally called the East London Revival Society, but it eventually became the Salvation Army. Booth's lively preaching style converted thousands to the new religious movement, but he also tackled more worldly problems. Poverty, child abuse, poor health, and alcoholism—common in East London—were all reduced as a result of the work of Booth, Catherine, and their eight children, all of whom played important roles in running the Salvation Army.

Founder of the Salvation Army 1878

Andrew Carnegie

1835–1919

As a young man Scottish-born Andrew Carnegie worked for the Pennsylvania Railroad. He was promoted to head of the railroad's western division and then introduced the first Pullman sleeping cars. In 1865 he left the railroads to start up his own steel company, which made him a multimillionaire. He sold his company in 1901 and devoted himself to a wide range of charitable causes.

Founded over 2,500 libraries; gave over $350 million to good causes 1901–1919

John D. Rockefeller

1839–1937

John D. Rockefeller was born in New York but learned the oil business while working at a refinery in Cleveland, Ohio. In 1870 he and his brother, William (1841–1922), founded the Standard Oil Company, an organization that grew to become the world's biggest oil refining company and made the Rockefellers one of the world's richest families. In 1911 the U.S. Supreme Court decided that Standard Oil was too large, and it was broken up into 39 separate companies. By this time John D. Rockefeller was already worth around $1 billion.

Cofounded Standard Oil Company 1870; donated over $500 million to education and medical research 1911–1937; founded the Rockefeller Foundation 1913

▼ William Booth's Salvation Army was well known for its music making. This was one way of attracting attention on the streets.

MARY BAKER EDDY 1821–1910
Born and raised in New England, Mary Baker Eddy's adult life began unhappily. Her first husband died young, her second marriage ended in divorce, and she suffered continual pain from a spinal injury. But in 1866 she was suddenly healed while reading the New Testament. From this point on she developed Christian Science, a new religion based on a linking of spirituality and healing. The movement grew quickly and has many followers.

JOHN PEMBERTON 1831–1888
Pharmacist John Pemberton was selling a variety of homemade remedies in Georgia when he came up with a cure for headaches made from a mixture of coca leaves, fruit syrup, and the extract of kola nuts. His business partner, Frank Robinson, thought up the name Coca-Cola Syrup. The drink sold well but did not make a profit, so Pemberton sold his share of the business to another pharmacist, Asa Candler (1851–1929), making very little money from his invention.

JOHN PIERPONT MORGAN 1837–1913
The son of a banker in Hartford, Connecticut, John Pierpont Morgan transformed his father's business into the biggest bank in the U.S. He became so rich that during the 1895 depression he could support the U.S. Federal Reserve. In 1901 he was able to buy Andrew Carnegie's (above left) huge steel corporation. Morgan gave a lot of money to good causes and collected art on an enormous scale.

HENRY HEINZ 1844–1919
The son of German parents who settled in Pennsylvania, Henry John Heinz founded the Heinz Company to produce pickles and similar foods in 1876. Proud of the range of his products, he invented the slogan "57 varieties." His company was highly successful and also had a reputation for taking care of its staff.

Thomas Barnardo

1845–1905

Irish-born Barnardo moved to England to study medicine with the aim of working as a missionary and doctor in Africa. Shocked by the number of orphaned children in London, he decided to open children's homes in the city. The first—the East End Mission—opened in 1867.

Founded Dr. Barnardo's Homes caring for 60,000 children 1867–1905

Sigmund Freud

1856–1939

Austrian neurologist Sigmund Freud moved to Paris, France, in 1885, where he made a scientific study of mental disorders. Back in Vienna, Austria, Freud developed the technique of psychoanalysis, where he treated patients with mental disorders by investigating the conscious and unconscious workings of their minds. By listening to his patients, Freud was able to help them come to terms with their hidden fears.

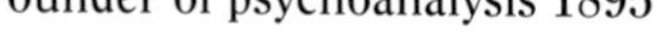

Founder of psychoanalysis 1895

William Randolph Hearst

1863–1951

The son of a newspaper publisher, Hearst took over the *San Francisco Examiner* from his father, and by buying or starting up other newspapers he eventually owned a chain of them stretching right across the U.S.

Hearst increased his readership with popular features. Some of his dubious articles about the Cuban fight for independence even helped start the Spanish–American War of 1898. Hearst, by now a rich man, was also known for his lavish lifestyle. He built a castlelike house in California that he packed full of artwork that he collected.

Publisher of U.S. newspapers with "banner" headlines and large pictures 1890s; built 165-room San Simeon mansion that he filled with artwork 1922–1947

▼ Hearst's mansion on the Pacific coast in San Simeon, California.

WILLIAM KELLOGG 1860–1951
U.S. manufacturer William Kellogg and his brother John (1852–1943), a physician, teamed up to produce a nourishing breakfast food for John's patients at the Battle Creek Sanitarium in Michigan. Their cornflakes were so successful that they were soon selling them across the country, first by mail order and then to shops locally and worldwide.

FRANK WOOLWORTH 1852–1919
A store assistant from Rodman, New York, Frank Woolworth heard about a new store in Lancaster, Pennsylvania, in 1879. All the store's goods sold for either five or ten cents. In 1905 Woolworth began building a chain of similar stores. They were very successful, and by the time he died Woolworth owned over 1,000 stores in North America and England.

Coco Chanel

1883–1971

Born into a poor family and then orphaned, Coco Chanel worked for a milliner before opening a shop in Deauville, northern France, to sell clothes that she had designed and made herself.

She became famous when she opened a shop in Paris, France, in 1924 and began designing clothes that transformed women's fashions. Coco Chanel's clothes were casual and simple but elegant, and many of her designs remained popular for decades. The chemise dress and the cardigan sweater without a collar were two of her most popular designs, and she came up with the term "little black dress" to describe a simple evening dress that could be worn on many different occasions. Chanel also had a great flair for accessories, such as scarves and costume jewelry, which she used to complement the clothes she designed. She also began companies to produce fabrics, jewelry, and perfumes, becoming France's richest couturier.

Opened couture house in Paris, France, 1913; designed first chemise dress 1920; introduced Chanel No. 5 perfume 1921; transformed women's fashions 1924–1938

▶ Coco Chanel produced designs that still inspire fashion designers today.

Edith Cavell

1865–1915

In 1907 British nurse Edith Cavell became the matron of a training school for nurses at the Berkendael Medical Institute in Belgium. When World War I began in 1914, the school was turned into a Red Cross hospital to treat the wounded. Cavell nursed all soldiers sent to the hospital, whatever country they came from. She was also involved in working for the Resistance, helping Allied soldiers escape from German-occupied Belgium to the Netherlands, a neutral country at the time. In 1915 she was discovered by the Germans, court-martialed, and executed.

Nursed hundreds of wounded soldiers during World War I; helped many soldiers escape from occupied territory 1914–1915; executed by Germans 1915

GIOVANNI AGNELLI 1866–1945
Italian army officer Giovanni Agnelli founded the Fiat company in 1899. Fiat produced highly original car designs and became Italy's leading car manufacturer. The company also produced equipment for the Italian Army during World War II, and Agnelli, also an Italian senator, helped promote Italy's industry during this period.

HELENA RUBINSTEIN 1870–1965
Born in Kraków, Poland, Helena Rubinstein was living in Australia when she realized that her Polish face cream was ideal for the local climate. She began selling the cream and soon had a successful business. By 1917 Rubinstein had opened beauty salons in major cities, following these up with laboratories and factories worldwide.

MAX BEAVERBROOK 1879–1964
Lord Beaverbrook was born in Canada but emigrated to England. He was a successful manufacturer and politician before he took over the British newspaper the *Daily Express* in 1919. It soon became the world's most successful newspaper. Beaverbrook was appointed Minister of Supply to help bolster Great Britain's war effort in 1941–1942.

Catwalk Kings

Guccio Gucci 1881–1953
Christian Dior 1905–1957
Pierre Cardin b. 1922
Hubert de Givenchy b. 1927
Giorgio Armani b. 1935
Yves St Laurent b. 1936
Gianni Versace 1946–1997
Alexander McQueen b. 1969

The great couturiers began by making clothes for a handful of very rich women, but they influenced design in many different directions.

The great age of the catwalk kings began after World War II, when **Christian Dior** launched his first collection, introducing the "New Look," a narrow-waisted, full-skirted style using lots of fabric. Soon every clothing manufacturer was producing women's clothes like Dior's—a very welcome reaction to the drab wartime, tailored, uniform-like style. Later couturiers developed their own unique styles. The brightly colored, futuristic, 1960s clothes of **Pierre Cardin**, the elegant tailored designs of **Hubert de Givenchy**, **Giorgio Armani**'s muted colors and soft fabrics, even **Yves St. Laurent**'s fashions, often based on modern art, and **Versace**'s striking colors—all had an influence on the way ordinary people dressed.

Many of these designers produce all kinds of products, from **Gucci**'s fine leather goods to Dior's perfumes. Less expensive, ready-to-wear ranges were started in the late 1960s by Givenchy. With more recent designers, such as **Alexander McQueen**, whose outrageous designs often make the headlines, the tradition is carried on. In 1997 Gianni Versace was shot dead outside his Florida home. His sister, Donatella (b. 1955), is now the Versace company's creative designer.

◀ Versace on the catwalk with his sister, Donatella (right), and models.

Conrad Hilton

1887–1979

U.S. hotelier Conrad Hilton began his working life as a banker before taking over the family inn when his father died in 1918. He then built up a successful chain of hotels in major U.S. cities. Hilton's hotels became known for high-quality, reliable service and for their luxurious rooms and facilities. After World War II, Hilton merged all of his businesses to form the Hilton Hotels Corporation and expanded overseas under the name Hilton International.

Founder of the Hilton hotel chain 1919

Jean Paul Getty

1892–1976

The son of a U.S. oil executive, Jean Paul Getty also went into the oil business. He was very successful, and by the late 1960s he had built up a fortune that made him one of the richest people in the world. Getty spent a lot of his money buying art. Much of this collection went to the Getty Museum in California, along with a gift of money that made it the world's most generously funded art gallery.

Founded the Getty Museum 1954; Personal fortune of over $1 billion by 1968

Benjamin Spock

1903–1998

Benjamin Spock was a U.S. physician who specialized in pediatrics and published the world's most-popular childcare book in 1946. Spock's book expressed his views on how children should be brought up, encouraging parents to be gentle and affectionate with their children. It was extremely popular, selling over 30 million copies, and it changed the way parents raised their children.

Wrote *The Common Sense Book of Baby and Childcare* 1946

◀ Howard Hughes designed and built a wooden seaplane, the *Spruce Goose*, in 1947. It was the largest one ever built but made only one flight.

Howard Hughes

1905–1976

Hughes' father built up a successful business making oil-drilling equipment. Hughes, born in Texas, inherited this business and built up an enormous financial empire. He used his profits to make movies before beginning to build, design, and fly aircraft. During the 1960s Hughes became a total recluse with a fear of disease, and as a result his later life is shrouded in mystery.

Inherited Hughes Tool Company 1924; broke air speed records 1935–1938; designed world's largest seaplane 1947

Rupert Murdoch

b. 1931

Born in Australia, Rupert Murdoch inherited the Adelaide *News* before expanding abroad, taking over the British *Sun* and other popular titles before buying the London *Times*. He founded the Sky satellite broadcasting company in 1989, bought the movie studio 20th Century Fox, and added many U.S. publications to his empire. His huge empire has made him perhaps the most powerful media tycoon in the world.

Owner of newspapers and TV stations that reach 40% of U.S. population 2002

Billy Graham

b.1918

Billy Graham was born in North Carolina and became a minister of the Southern Baptist Church. In 1949 he began a series of "crusades" where he preached to huge congregations. Many of his listeners were captivated by Graham's dramatic preaching style, and he quickly began to win converts to Christianity. He traveled all over the world, even converting people in places where authorities frowned on organized religion.

Founded Billy Graham Evangelistic Association 1950; notable crusades: Greater London 1954, New York 1957

▼ Billy Graham's preaching has attracted millions of converts to Christianity.

SOICHIRO HONDA 1906–1991
The man who became one of Japan's most famous manufacturers began working as a mechanic in 1922. By 1934 he owned a factory making engine piston rings. In 1948 he became President of the Honda Corporation, which began by making motorcycles. These were soon selling well overseas, and Honda repeated the pattern with cars, helping make Japanese technology popular in the U.S. and Europe.

ALFRIED KRUPP 1907–1967
The Krupp business empire was already huge when Alfried Krupp inherited it from his father in 1943. The younger Krupp built the business up even more, developing the firm's iron, steel, and arms factories but using forced labor during the Nazi period. After the war his success continued, and he built factories overseas. Not until 1959 did he finally pay compensation to some of the victims of his forced labor practices.

KERRY PACKER b. 1937
The Australian tycoon Kerry Packer is best known for being the owner of the media group Australian Consolidated Press. He upset the world of cricket in 1977 when he invented World Series Cricket, a season of international games—broadcast on Packer's Channel Nine—where cricketers wore colorful uniforms. In spite of the protests, many of his innovations, including brightly colored uniforms and playing under floodlights, are still used in games today.

ANITA RODDICK b. 1942
Born in England, Anita Roddick founded the chain of stores called Body Shop in 1976 to sell cosmetics made from natural ingredients. Her products and the success of her business have shown that it is possible to be successful while respecting the environment and without exploiting suppliers in the developing world.

Bob Geldof

b. 1954

Irish rock musician Bob Geldof worked for a while as a journalist in Canada before returning to Ireland to form his band, The Boomtown Rats, in 1975.

In 1984 Geldof's life changed. He had seen television news coverage of the famine in Ethiopia and was determined to do something to help. He formed a charity, the Bandaid Trust, to raise money for the famine victims. Geldof gathered together a group of well-known musicians and made a record, "Do They Know It's Christmas?," which topped the charts in December 1984 and raised millions for Ethiopia. The next year he launched an even bigger scheme, Live Aid, with live fundraising concerts in Europe and North America. Even more money was raised for the famine victims in Africa.

Formed Boomtown Rats 1975–1986; raised $12 million through Bandaid 1984; raised $77 million through Live Aid 1985

▶ In 1985 Bob Geldof organized Live Aid, the world's biggest rock benefit event.

Richard Branson

b. 1950

Born in London, England, Richard Branson is one of Great Britain's most successful businessmen. At the age of 16 he published a student magazine. In 1969 he founded Virgin to sell records by mail order. Virgin record-producing business was set up in 1973. The success of this led to other ventures. Branson expanded into many areas—rail and air travel, publishing, broadcasting, real estate, and soft drinks. He sold Virgin Records for £560 ($840) million in 1992. Branson's record-breaking hot-air balloon journeys have also gained him major publicity.

Founded Virgin Music 1969; first hot-air balloon crossings of Atlantic Ocean 1987 and Pacific Ocean 1991

Bill Gates

b. 1955

Born in Seattle, Washington, Bill Gates founded Microsoft in 1975 to produce software for the desktop computers that were just beginning to appear in stores. In 1980 Microsoft designed a computer operating system and licensed the giant corporation IBM to use it in all personal computers they produced. The system, MS-DOS, caught on, and either it or Microsoft's later, more user-friendly Windows, which was introduced in 1983, have been included in the majority of personal computers in the world. This, together with other ventures, such as Internet software, have made Gates one of the world's richest men.

Founded Microsoft Corporation 1975; made his first $1 billion in 1986; richest man in the world ($42 billion) 1997

Diana, Princess of Wales

1961–1997

Lady Diana Spencer worked in London, England, as a nursery school teacher until she married Prince Charles, heir to the British throne, in 1981. They got divorced in 1996. Diana was well known for her work with good causes, including children's charities and AIDS victims. She also campaigned against the use of land mines. She was killed in a car accident in Paris, France, in 1997.

Campaigned for children, AIDS victims, and land-mine victims 1980s and 1990s

LAWBREAKERS

Tomás de Torquemada

1420–1498

Torquemada was a Dominican monk who was the personal confessor of Ferdinand and Isabella of Spain (p. 14). In 1483 he was given the job of heading the Inquisition, a Catholic court set up to find and punish people with different religious beliefs. Under Torquemada the Inquisition ruthlessly sought out men and women (especially former Jews and Muslims) who had been forced to convert to Christianity but were suspected of keeping their old beliefs. Torquemada personally ordered about 2,000 people to be burned at the stake.

Head of Spanish Inquisition 1483–1498; encouraged the Spanish king Ferdinand to expel 200,000 Jews 1492

Married three times by the age of 21, Lucrezia Borgia is also alleged to have committed incest with her brother and father.

The Borgias

Rodrigo 1431–1503
Cesare c. 1476–1507
Lucrezia 1480–1519

The Borgias were one of the most powerful families in Italy in the 1400s and 1500s. Rodrigo, who was born in Spain, became Pope Alexander VI, a position he achieved by bribery. Cesare and Lucrezia were his illegitimate children. Cesare was made a cardinal by his father but gave up the Church to become a soldier, carving out a kingdom for himself in central Italy. He murdered Alfonso of Aragon (d. 1500), Lucrezia's second husband. Lucrezia also has a reputation for corruption and vice, but this is based mainly on rumors.

Corrupt rulers of Italian city-states late 1400s and early 1500s

Khayr ad-Din Barbarossa

c. 1483–1546

The name Barbarossa means "red beard," and Barbarossa's face was feared on the Mediterranean Sea in the early 1500s. He was one of the most notorious pirates of his time.

His original name was Hizir, and he was born on the Greek island of Lesbos. He was also known by the Arabic name of Khayr ad-Din (which means "gift of God"). Barbarossa preyed on ships belonging to the Christian countries of western Europe, plundering Spanish warships, merchants, and even ships belonging to the pope. With his brother, Arouj (c. 1474–1518), also a pirate, he had various bases along the coast of North Africa, and he was so successful that the people of Algiers made him regent (ruler) in 1530. Although Khayr ad-Din lost control of the city of Tunis in 1535, he had notable victories in Majorca and Nice. He was especially popular with the Muslim rulers of the Ottoman Empire in Turkey, defeating the combined fleets of the pope, Venice, and Spain in 1538 that looked likely to attack them.

Mediterranean pirate early 1500s; ruler of Algiers 1518–1535

▼ Barbarossa and his men force a Spanish soldier to watch as they steal valuables from his ship.

▼ Guy Fawkes and fellow conspirators in the Gunpowder Plot.

Guy Fawkes

1570–1606

Born an English Protestant, Guy Fawkes became a fervent Catholic. He joined a conspiracy to blow up the British House of Lords during the official opening of Parliament on November 5, 1605, when the Protestant king and all of the government officials would be present. Before they could carry out their deed Fawkes and his fellow conspirators were captured and executed.

Plotted to blow up English Parliament 1605; executed 1606

Mary Read and Anne Bonny

Early-1700s

Disguised as a man, English-born Mary Read was serving on a ship bound for the West Indies. The vessel was captured by pirates, and Read joined them. With "Calico" Jack Rackham (d. 1720), Irish-born Anne Bonny terrorized shipping in the Caribbean before capturing Read's ship. Read and Bonny became close friends and worked together as pirates before they were captured in 1720.

Female pirates early-1700s

Madame Cheng

Active 1807–1810

Madame Cheng was the wife of one of the most powerful pirates on the South China coast. When her husband died in 1807, she took over his pirate fleet. Those who disobeyed her were executed, and victims were shown no mercy. In the end the Chinese navy had to enlist the help of the British and Portuguese to force Madame Cheng to give up her life of crime. She was captured in 1810.

Commander of 50,000 pirates on the South China Sea 1807–1810

▲ On board a large Chinese junk Madame Cheng gives her pirates their orders.

Jesse James

1847–1882

Well known because he has featured in many songs, stories, and movies, Jesse James grew up during the Civil War (1861–1865). At the young age of 15 he fought on the Confederate side with a band of guerrillas, and when the war finished with the defeat of the Confederates, he became an outlaw. For years Jesse, his brother Frank (1843–1915), and their gang of outlaws robbed banks and trains in the wild west. Finally the authorities put up a large reward for his capture—dead or alive. The temptation was too much for Robert Ford, one of the James gang, who shot Jesse in 1882 with the hope of claiming the money. Frank gave himself up, served a prison sentence, and worked on the James family farm until his death.

Leader of a gang of outlaws in the wild west 1866–1882

THOMAS BLOOD c. 1618–1680
Irishman Thomas Blood had fought against the Royalists in the English Civil War, and Charles II (1630–1685) had seized his land. In 1663 Blood launched an unsuccessful plot to capture Dublin Castle. In 1671 he broke into the Tower of London and stole the Crown of England. He was captured but was pardoned by the king, who returned his land.

HENRY MORGAN c. 1635–1688
As a child Welshman Henry Morgan was kidnapped and ended up in the Caribbean. There he became a pirate, raiding Spanish and Dutch ships and capturing Panama in 1671. When the Spanish complained of Morgan's conduct, he was taken back to England. But when war broke out with Spain, he was pardoned by the British.

DICK TURPIN 1705–1739
English highwayman Dick Turpin was a burglar, smuggler, and cattle thief. He was also a killer who was finally hanged in York, England, for the murder of an innkeeper. He is said to have ridden from London to York in 15 hours on his famous mare, Black Bess, but this feat was probably achieved by highwayman John Nevison (1639–1684).

▼ In 1873 Jesse James and his gang of outlaws held up and robbed a passenger train of the Chicago & Rock Island Railroad near Adair, Iowa. They escaped with $2,000 and passengers' valuables.

Billy the Kid

1859-1881

William Bonney, known as "Billy the Kid," was one of the most notorious thieves and murderers of his time. He killed his first man for insulting his mother when he was only 12. By 1877 he was taking part in a war between two feuding cattle-ranching families before taking up a career of killing and cattle rustling in the southwestern U.S. and Mexico. In 1881 he was cornered and shot by sheriff Pat Garrett (1850–1908) in Fort Sumner, New Mexico. By this time he was the most-wanted man in the U.S.

Murdered 21 men 1871–1881; most-wanted man in the U.S. 1881

◀ To protect himself Ned Kelly made a suit of armor, its strange metal helmet becoming his trademark.

Ned Kelly

1855–1880

The son of an Irish convict, Australian outlaw Ned Kelly went to prison for the first time in 1870 for assault. When he was released, he became a cattle thief and returned to prison for three years. After his release in 1874 Kelly's mother was jailed for three years for allegedly attempting to murder a policeman. Swearing vengeance for this, Kelly, his brother Dan (1861–1880), and two others, Steve Hart and Joe Byrne, hid out in the Australian bush. There they shot three policemen sent to capture them. On the run and with a price on their heads the Kelly gang began robbing banks. They were finally tracked down in a hotel. After a fierce fight with the police Kelly was caught and hanged.

Australian outlaw, robber, murderer, and folk hero 1878–1880

Henri Landru

1869–1922

Henri Landru was one of France's most notorious serial killers. When his story became known, he earned the nickname "Bluebeard" after the famous fairytale character who murdered his wives. The reason for the nickname was the way Landru went about luring his victims. He would befriend a woman, tell her that he was in love with her, make a promise of marriage—and then kill her for her money. In 1919 Landru was finally arrested for his crimes. There was a long court battle, but Landru denied that he was a murderer. However, he had kept a detailed notebook of the profits made from his crimes, which led to his downfall. In 1922 he was found guilty and sent to the guillotine.

Murdered 11 women after promising to marry them 1915–1919

WILLIAM HARE 1790–1860 AND WILLIAM BURKE 1792–1829
Burke and Hare were a pair of murderers who lived in Edinburgh, Scotland. They made money from their crimes by selling the corpses to a professor of anatomy, Robert Knox, who needed the bodies for dissection. Hare eventually owned up to the crimes, and Burke was hanged as a result.

JOHN WILKES BOOTH 1839–1865
U.S. actor John Wilkes Booth supported the Confederates during the Civil War. When the Confederates lost, Booth took revenge by shooting and killing President Abraham Lincoln (p. 19) at Ford's Theater in Washington, D.C., in 1865. Booth escaped to Virginia and was shot dead when he refused to give himself up.

LIZZIE BORDEN 1860–1927
In August 1892 Lizzie Borden was accused of murdering her father and stepmother with an ax. She always denied the crime, saying that she had been outside the barn where the killings took place. After a long trial she was eventually found not guilty and went back to live in her hometown of Fall River, Massachusetts.

Hawley Crippen

1862–1910

Born in Michigan, Hawley Crippen trained as a doctor and moved to London, England, with his first wife, an opera singer named Cora Turner (1875–1910). Crippen was not happy with Cora and fell in love with his secretary, Ethel Le Neve (1883–1967). He decided to poison Cora and cut up her body before burying what was left in the cellar. Then Crippen and Ethel fled, boarding a ship to the U.S. and traveling under false names as a father and son. The ship's captain was suspicious and contacted the British police by radio. The couple were arrested, and Crippen was executed.

Murdered his wife Cora 1910; the first criminal to be caught as a result of the police use of radio 1910

▲ U.S. outlaw "Ma" Barker poses with a friend while on the run from the police.

"Ma" Barker

1872–1935

The notorious gangster "Ma" Barker was born Donnie Clark in Missouri. She, her husband, George (1859–1941), and their four sons formed a criminal gang that terrorized the Midwest. They built up a fortune from kidnapping and armed robbery. By the 1920s the police were offering large rewards for members of the family, either dead or alive. In 1935 "Ma" and her son Arthur were killed in a gun battle with the FBI at Lake Weir, Florida. Her other three sons all died violently—Herman committed suicide, Fred was killed escaping from prison, and Lloyd was killed by his wife.

Staged a series of raids, netting more than $3 million 1920s

Grigori Rasputin

1871–1916

Rasputin was born to a family of poor Siberian peasants. He became a monk and gained fame as a faith healer. In 1905 he traveled to St. Petersburg, Russia, where he was introduced to Czar Nicholas II (p. 18) and Empress Alexandra (1872–1918). They were both impressed by Rasputin because he appeared to be able to cure their son Alexis (1904–1918), who suffered from hemophilia. Rasputin gained favor in the royal household and persuaded the czar to give him control over appointing and firing government ministers. In 1915, when Nicholas was away leading the army, Rasputin virtually took charge of the government, hiring and firing ministers at will. In 1916 disgruntled noblemen poisoned him, shot him, and then drowned him in a river.

Extreme influence on the Russian royal family 1907–1916; assassinated 1916

▼ Rasputin, Alexandra, and her son, Alexis.

Mata Hari

1876–1917

Originally named Margaretha Zelle, the woman now known as Mata Hari was born in the Netherlands, where she married Rudolph Macleod, a Scottish officer serving in the Dutch army. The couple traveled widely before separating in 1905, when she trained as a dancer. She impressed audiences in Paris, France, where she appeared under the stage names of Lady Macleod and Mata Hari, a name that means "the sun" in Malay. Mata Hari attracted many lovers, including some in the armed forces. In 1907 she is said to have become a spy. Her lovers before World War I included both Germans and high-ranking army officers on the Allied side. She claimed to be a double agent, pretending to spy for Germany but in fact passing secrets to the Allies in France. She was arrested by the French and executed in Paris in 1917 for spying for the Germans.

Exotic dancer in European music halls, seductress, and spy 1907–1917

► Gavrilo Princip killed Archduke Franz Ferdinand of Austria as the ruler was driven through the streets of Sarajevo, Bosnia.

Gavrilo Princip

1895–1918

Born in Bosnia, Gavrilo Princip fought for Serbian independence at a time when Serbia was part of the Austro–Hungarian Empire. A member of a Serbian terrorist group called the Black Hand, he assassinated Archduke Franz Ferdinand of Austria (1863–1914) and his wife in Sarajevo, Bosnia, in 1914. As a result, Austria declared war on Serbia and World War I began. Princip was sent to prison in Austria, where he died in 1918.

Assassinated Archduke Franz Ferdinand of Austria 1914

John Christie

1898–1953

Born in England, John Christie was convicted and hanged in 1953 for the murder of his wife. At his trial he also confessed to the killing of six other women, including a Mrs. Evans. Christie was also suspected of killing her baby daughter, despite of the fact that the child's father, Timothy Evans (d. 1950), had been hanged for this murder. As a result of this tragic mistake, the British Parliament eventually abolished the death penalty for murder.

Murdered at least six women 1940s

"Lucky" Luciano

1897–1962

Charles Luciano, known as "Lucky" because he escaped prosecution for years, was a famous Mafia boss. Born in Sicily, Italy, he emigrated to the U.S. in 1907 and grew rich from prostitution, protection rackets, and drug dealing. He was finally imprisoned in 1936, but he kept control of his crime operations from prison. Upon his release from prison he was deported from the U.S. and spent most of the rest of his life in Italy.

Mafia godfather 1920s–1930s; founder of the Crime Syndicate of Mafia Families 1936–1946

▲ Mafia godfather "Lucky" Luciano was eventually arrested by the FBI in 1936.

Al Capone

1899–1947

Perhaps the most notorious of all American gangsters, Alphonse Capone was born in Brooklyn, New York, to parents who had emigrated from Italy. As a teenager he joined street gangs, and by the time he was a young man he had a scar from a razor cut, which gave him the nickname "Scarface."

Capone became powerful during the 1920s when the sale of alcohol was banned in the U.S.—a period known as the Prohibition. Operating in Chicago, Capone made huge sums of money from the illegal sale of alcohol, gambling, and other criminal activities. He was ruthless with his rivals, mowing them down with machine guns if they tried to muscle in on his turf. On February 14, 1929, he organized the killing of seven members of a rival gang. This became known as the Valentine's Day Massacre. He dealt with the police by bribing them, and they could never find enough evidence to convict him of his greatest crimes. In the end, though, he was convicted for nonpayment of taxes and sent to prison for 11 years. He was released in 1939 because of poor health and spent the rest of his life in Florida.

Made a fortune from gambling, prostitution, protection rackets, and the illegal sale of alcohol 1920–1931; killed seven rivals in the Valentine's Day Massacre 1929

▲ Al Capone was known all over the world as Chicago's biggest racketeer.

John Dillinger

1903–1934

U.S. gangster John Dillinger began his criminal career with an attempted robbery in 1923. In 1933 he was the mastermind behind a series of bank robberies, during which he and his gang ruthlessly killed anyone who got in the way. By then he was known as "Public Enemy Number One." In 1934 he was arrested. He escaped from custody, but an informer told the FBI where he was. The police shot him dead in Chicago.

Gangster accused of 16 murders 1930s

Marie Besnard

c. 1905–c. 1970

Frenchwoman Marie Besnard poisoned her first husband in 1927. She then quickly married Léon Besnard, and together they planned to poison their relatives and inherit their money. They began by ingratiating themselves with close family members to ensure that they were included in their wills. Then they killed Marie's father, Léon's father and sister, two cousins, as well as a rich couple they had befriended. Finally Marie killed Léon. During her trials the prosecution case was poorly presented, and she was acquitted in 1961.

Murdered nine people 1927–1949

Adolf Eichmann

1906–1962

Austrian Nazi Adolf Eichmann joined the SS and planned German anti-Semitic policies during World War II. He organized the Holocaust—sending Jews and others to concentration camps where they were murdered. In 1945 Eichmann was imprisoned, but he escaped to Argentina. He was tracked down by Israeli agents, who took him to Israel where he was tried and executed.

Nazi official responsible for genocide 1939–1945; executed by Israelis 1962

Bonnie and Clyde

Clyde Barrow 1909–1934
Bonnie Parker 1911–1934

Texas-born gangsters Bonnie and Clyde had a glamorous image, but they committed horrific crimes all over four U.S. states.

They met in 1932 and became lovers. Soon after this Clyde was arrested, tried for numerous counts of burglary and theft, and sent to prison for two years. When Bonnie visited him in prison, she smuggled in a gun, and Clyde escaped. Bonnie and Clyde, along with gang members Raymond Hamilton, W. D. Jones, Clyde's brother, Marvin, and his wife, Blanche, pursued their career of crime. Most of their robberies—in Texas, Oklahoma, Missouri, and New Mexico—were on a small scale, but the pair killed anyone who got in their way. Bonnie wrote a poem called "The Story of Bonnie and Clyde," which made the pair even more notorious, and it predicted a horrible end for the couple. This came true when they were shot dead at a police roadblock in Louisiana.

Carried out a series of murders and robberies in the U.S. 1932–1934

▲ This staged photograph of Bonnie and Clyde while on the run from the police was taken by one of their gang members in 1933.

Joseph Mengele

1911–c. 1979

Joseph Mengele was a German physician at the Auschwitz concentration camp during World War II. There he selected inmates for death in the gas chambers. He also carried out research, including "experiments" involving procedures such as injecting harmful chemicals into children's bodies and performing operations without anesthetics. After the war Mengele fled to South America and changed his identity. He is known to have died in Brazil in around 1979.

Multiple murderer and torturer of children at Auschwitz 1942–1945

▲ At Auschwitz, Dr. Joseph Mengele was known as the "Angel of Death."

Kim Philby

1911–1988

British spy Kim Philby was educated at Cambridge University. He became a Communist and an agent for the Soviet Union and later began working for the British Secret Service. Philby was given a job in the British Embassy in Washington, D.C., where he also worked for the CIA. All the time, however, he was passing Western secrets to the Russians. He admitted his deception in 1963, fleeing to Moscow.

Double agent who deceived Western intelligence agents 1944–1956

The Rosenbergs

Ethel 1915–1953
Julius 1918–1953

The Rosenbergs were an American couple who were part of one of the world's most powerful spy rings.

Ethel Rosenberg had a brother, David, who worked for the nuclear research station in Los Alamos. Julius worked for the U.S. Army. Together they gathered U.S. nuclear secrets and passed them to a courier, who in turn gave them to a Soviet diplomat. The spy ring was uncovered when another nuclear scientist and Soviet spy, Klaus Fuchs (1912–1988), was put on trial in England. Ethel's brother gave himself up and confessed in order to save his own life. The Rosenbergs were put on trial, found guilty, and sentenced to death. After many failed appeals for mercy they were finally executed.

Led a network of spies passing U.S. secrets to the Soviet Union 1943–1950

◀ Ethel and Julius Rosenberg were the first spies in the U.S. to receive the death penalty during peacetime.

Caryl Chessman

1921–1960

Born in Michigan, Caryl Chessman was wanted for a string of robbery, rape, and kidnapping offenses by the time he was in his late twenties. Known as the "Red-Light Bandit," he was caught in California, sentenced to death but given stays of execution that kept him on death row for 12 years. During this period he learned four languages and wrote several books, including *Trial by Ordeal* and *The Face of Justice*, campaigning against the death penalty. He was finally executed in 1960, but this made many people unhappy with the way the U.S. legal system works.

Sentenced to death for 17 violent crimes 1948; given eight stays of execution

James Earl Ray

1928–1998

Born in Alton, Illinois, James Earl Ray was a little-known, small-time criminal. In 1968 he murdered civil rights leader Martin Luther King, Jr. (p. 128) in Memphis, Tennessee. In 1969 Ray was arrested in London, England. He confessed to the murder of King, stood trial in the U.S., but withdrew his confession when he was sentenced to a 99-year prison term. From that time on various people, including friends of Ray and members of Martin Luther King, Jr.'s family, campaigned for a retrial, but this did not take place, and Ray died in prison of liver failure in 1998.

Alleged assassin of civil rights leader Martin Luther King, Jr. 1968

◀ James Earl Ray swears the oath in court.

▼ Ronnie Biggs soon after his arrest for his part in the Great Train Robbery in 1963.

Ronald Biggs

b. 1929

Ronald "Ronnie" Biggs was an English thief who shot to fame in 1963 as one of the gang who carried out the Great Train Robbery. The gang held up a London-to-Glasgow mail train, beat up the driver, and took mail bags that contained £2.5 ($3.75) million. Biggs was caught, tried, and sentenced to 30 years in prison. In 1965 he escaped and went first to Australia. The British police pursued him there, so he headed to South America. Biggs settled in Brazil, and the British police began trying to get him extradited. Biggs' girlfriend was expecting a baby, and under Brazilian law the fathers of Brazilian children cannot be forced to leave the country. Biggs remained in Brazil until 2001, when, a sick man, he decided to return to Great Britain. He was arrested by the authorities and is now back in prison.

Took part in the Great Train Robbery 1963; escaped justice for 36 years

Kray twins

Ronnie Kray 1933–1995
Reggie Kray 1933–2000

Born in England in London's East End, the Krays became two of the city's most feared criminals. Modeling themselves after the mobsters of Chicago, they built up an empire of organized crime that profited from illegal gambling, drinking clubs, and protection rackets. Although the Krays were involved in violence and gang warfare, the police failed to convict them of murder until 1969, when each was given prison sentences of at least 30 years. Ronnie died in prison. Reggie died in a hospital shortly after his release.

Powerful London gang leaders 1960s

Charles Manson

b. 1934

Kentucky-born Charles Manson carried out his first armed robbery when he was 13. Through his teens and early twenties the crimes continued, with theft and fraud added to the string of offenses. Manson spent seven years in prison in the 1960s, and upon his release he set up a hippy commune in California. There he became the leader of a criminal "family," committing many murders, including that of the actress Sharon Tate (1943–1969), her friends, and neighbors. He was imprisoned in 1979.

Murdered nine people 1969

Ulrike Meinhof

1934–1976

Ulrike Meinhof worked as a left-wing journalist in Germany. Her life changed when she met Andreas Baader (below), who persuaded her that it was necessary to use violence to bring about changes in society. With Baader she became a leader of the Red Army Faction, leading terrorist attacks against German targets. In 1974 she was sent to prison, where she committed suicide.

Joint head of underground guerillas in Germany 1970–1972

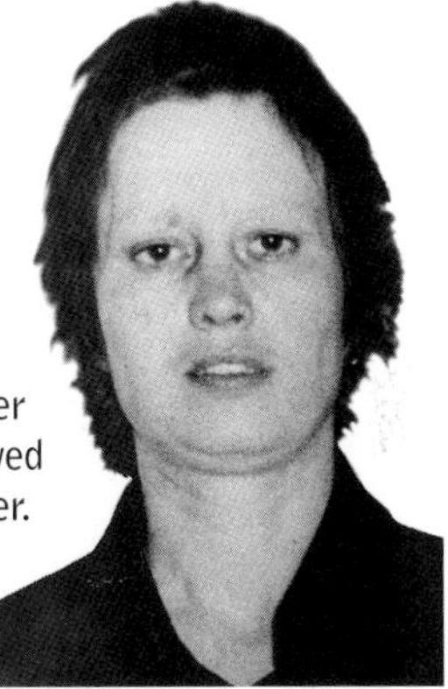

► Ulrike Meinhof met Andreas Baader when she interviewed him for a newspaper.

Andreas Baader

1943–1977

Born in Munich, Germany, Andreas Baader founded a terrorist guerrilla group called the Red Army Faction. They carried out various terrorist acts and political killings to try to bring about change. Eventually, Baader was caught and put in prison, but the Faction helped him escape. When he was caught again, the Faction tried to release him by hijacking an airliner, but they failed. Baader killed himself in prison.

Founder and leader of Red Army Faction 1970–1977

► Baader began his political life as a student protester before turning to terrorism.

Lee Harvey Oswald

1939–1963

Lee Harvey Oswald was born in New Orleans, Louisiana. He served in the U.S. Marines, but he was also a Marxist and lived in the U.S.S.R. for a while.

Oswald became famous in November 1963 when he was accused of killing President John F. Kennedy. Oswald was said to have taken up a vantage point on the sixth floor of the Texas School Book Depository in downtown Dallas, shooting Kennedy as he and his wife, Jackie (1929–1994), passed below in a motorcade. But Oswald's guilt was never proven in a criminal court. Two days later Oswald was shot by Jack Ruby (1911–1967), a nightclub owner who said that he was taking revenge on behalf of Kennedy's widow. Since then there have been many unproven stories claiming that Oswald's death covered up the involvement of another assassin. It was also alleged that Oswald was connected with the Mafia and the U.S. Secret Service. A committee set up by the U.S. government to investigate Kennedy's death said that it was probably because of a conspiracy, but the precise truth may never be known.

Allegedly assassinated President John F. Kennedy November 22, 1963

▲ Two days after the assassination of President John F. Kennedy, nightclub owner Jack Ruby shot Lee Harvey Oswald before his guards could intervene.

▼ On November 22, 1963, the Kennedys were traveling through Dallas in an open car when the president was assassinated.

JAMES HANRATTY c. 1936–1962
English criminal James Hanratty was convicted of murder in 1962. He was identified by his victim's girlfriend but said he was innocent. At his trial Hanratty was found guilty and then hanged. Witnesses said later that Hanratty had been somewhere else at the time of the murder and an inquiry decided that he had been wrongly convicted.

ANDREI CHIKATILO 1936–1994
One of the world's worst serial killers, Russian Andrei Chikatilo murdered over 50 children in Rostov, Russia, between 1982 and 1990. He killed his victims by stabbing them repeatedly. Chikatilo was finally linked to the crimes after a leading expert produced a psychological profile of him. He was found guilty and executed in 1994.

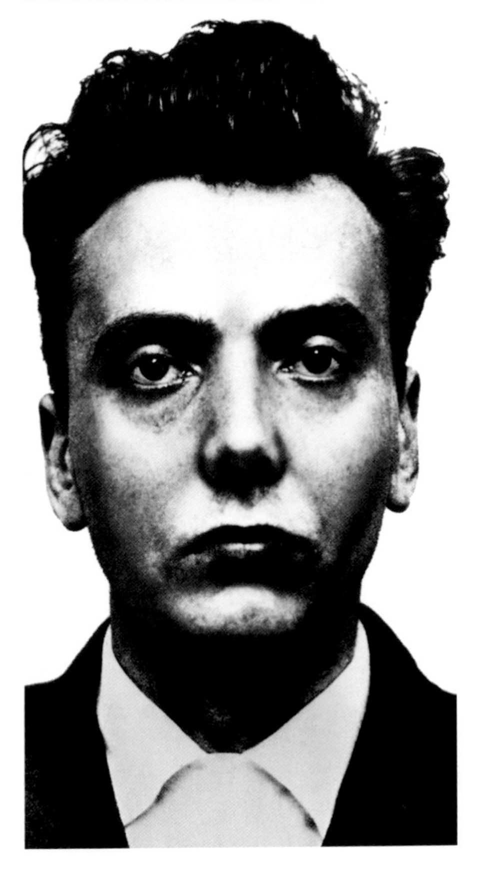

The Moors Murderers

Ian Brady b. 1938
Myra Hindley b. 1942

Ian Brady, born in Glasgow, Scotland, was a stock clerk who was obsessed with Nazi Germany. He and Myra Hindley, an office worker from Manchester, England, became lovers in 1961 and began a life of crime that shocked the world. Brady and Hindley lured small children to their home, tortured them, and killed them. They buried most of the children on Saddleworth Moor in northern England, which is why they became known as the Moors Murderers. The truth about their crimes was revealed in 1965 when Hindley's brother-in-law told the police that the couple were killers. The following year Brady was found guilty of three murders—two small children, John Kilbride and Lesley Ann Downey, and a 17-year-old, Edward Evans, whose body was found at the couple's house. Hindley was also found guilty of two murders, and the pair were sent to prison for life. Hindley later confessed to two more murders. Since then Hindley has claimed that she has totally reformed, but she has remained in prison, as has Ian Brady.

Murdered and tortured at least five young people 1963–1965

Gary Gilmore

1940–1977

Brought up in Oregon, Gary Gilmore turned to crime at a young age. After numerous offenses—including robbery, car theft, and violence—he spent more than half of his life in prison before he reached his early 30s. He committed his first murder in 1976, shooting a gas station attendant in a robbery. The second murder, of a motel manager, followed soon after. Gilmore was quickly caught, tried, and sentenced to death. Many people protested, but Gilmore demanded to be executed. He was shot by a firing squad at Utah State Prison. Gilmore's execution paved the way for widespread use of the death penalty in the U.S.

Psychopath and double murderer 1976

Harold Shipman

b. 1946

Shipman was a British doctor who practiced in West Yorkshire and later in Greater Manchester, both in England. For the 24 years following the start of his career, Shipman's patients suffered a much higher death rate than those under other doctors. No one saw this as suspicious until another doctor, a relative of Shipman's, raised the alarm in 1998. A police investigation revealed that Shipman had been systematically killing many of his older female patients, mostly with lethal injections. He was convicted of 15 murders, although the actual total was probably much higher.

Murdered perhaps as many as 300 victims 1977–2000

PETER SUTCLIFFE b. 1946
Peter Sutcliffe was a truck driver from Yorkshire, England, who murdered 13 women. His brutality earned him the nickname of the "Yorkshire Ripper." After being questioned several times by the police he was finally convicted in 1981 of the murders (as well as seven attempted murders) and was sent to prison for life.

JOHN HINKLEY b. 1955
At the age of 21, Oklahoma-born Hinkley became obsessed with actress Jodie Foster and the movie *Taxi Driver*, the story of a psychopath who stalks a politician. In 1981 Hinkley shot and wounded President Ronald Reagan (p. 23), hoping that this would impress Foster. He was arrested, found to be insane, and sent to a mental institution.

NICK LEESON b. 1967
Leeson was a young financial trader who worked for the 200-year-old British merchant bank Barings. While working in their Singapore branch, he lost over £600 million ($900 million) of Barings' money trading on the Tokyo Stock Exchange. His actions brought about the collapse of the bank, and he was sent to prison for six years.

David Berkowitz

b. 1953

Calling himself the "Son of Sam," David Berkowitz began a reign of terror in New York City in 1976. Over a one-year period he shot at lone women and couples, killing some and wounding others. He seemed impossible to catch, and the New York City police had to organize a squad of 200 officers to find him. When he was arrested, he insisted that evil voices were telling him to kill his victims. He was given a 365-year prison sentence.

Murdered six people and injured another seven 1976–1977

Guy Georges

b. 1962

Born in Angers, France, Guy Georges lived in Paris, where he became known as the "Beast of the Bastille." Georges murdered a number of women in the Bastille area of Paris, France, during the 1990s. He stalked his victims for days before tying them up, torturing them, and cutting their throats. Georges was caught following France's largest-ever manhunt. He began by denying his crimes, but he later confessed when confronted with the evidence in court in 2001. He was sent to prison for life.

Murdered around ten women in Paris, France 1991–1997

Timothy McVeigh

1968–2001

On April 19, 1995 a bomb destroyed the Federal Building in Oklahoma City, Oklahoma. New York-born McVeigh planted the bomb. He had served in the U.S. Army during the Gulf War (1991) and had become obsessed with guns. In 1995 he rented a truck, packed it with explosives, and parked it outside the Oklahoma Federal Building. Half the building collapsed, killing many. McVeigh was caught and sentenced to death.

Killed 168 and injured some 500 others in the Oklahoma City bombing 1995

Osama bin Laden

b. 1957

Osama bin Laden was born in Saudi Arabia. He is the youngest of 24 siblings in a rich family whose wealth comes from a construction company founded by his father, Mohammed.

When studying at college in Saudi Arabia, Bin Laden learned about the world of Islamic politics. In 1979 the U.S.S.R. invaded Afghanistan. Bin Laden left Saudi Arabia to fight the Russians in Afghanistan, supporting the Afghan resistance and recruiting thousands of Muslims from all over the world to fight for Islamic causes. By this time he had formed an organization called Al Qaeda ("the Base"), which is believed to have over 5,000 members in 50 different countries. In 1991 Bin Laden moved to Sudan, where he organized attacks on U.S. soldiers in Yemen and Somalia. Under pressure from the U.S. government he was expelled from Sudan in 1996 and returned to Afghanistan. There he was given tacit support by the Islamic fundamentalist leaders of that country—the Taliban—and allowed to run training camps for terrorists. He continued his campaign against the U.S., bombing U.S. embassies in Kenya and Tanzania. In 1998 Bin Laden called for a *jihad* ("holy war") against Americans and Jews.

Osama bin Laden and Al Qaeda are now considered responsible for the attacks on September 11, 2001, when terrorists hijacked four U.S. airliners and used two of them to destroy the twin towers of New York City's World Trade Center. Another hijacked jet was crashed into the Pentagon building in Washington, D.C. The total number of dead or missing people has been put at around 3,200. The United States' "War on Terrorism," begun as a result of these actions, continues.

▲ A hijacked jet about to hit the second of the Twin Towers on September 11, 2001.

Founded Al Qaeda 1988; implicated in terrorist action that caused the death of over 3,000 people in New York City and Washington, D.C., on September 11, 2001

▲ Saudi Arabian-born Osama bin Laden, leader of the Al Qaeda organization, is one of the CIA's most-wanted men. He has also become a hero to many young Arabs.

Index

INDEX

C

D

M

NO

PQ

INDEX

UV

W

XY

Z

Websites

Readers can find websites with any search engine (ie *http://www.mamma.com/* or *http://www.google.com/*) simply by typing in the name of any of the people in this book. However, there are some general websites listed below that readers may find useful.

http://www.famouspeople.com/ A biographical reference
http://www.biography.com/ A biographical reference
http://www.imdb.com Internet movie database
http://www.gomilpitas.com/homeschooling/explore/biography.htm A to Z Home's Cool Homeschooling
http://www.kcls.org/hh/biographies.html Homework help, famous people/biographies
http://www.amillionlives.com/ Lives, the biography resource
http://www.famouspeopleworldwide.com/ General biographies
http://www.s9.com/biography/ Biographical Dictionary
http://www.freality.com/biograph.htm Freeality biographies – important people
http://www-groups.dcs.st-and.ac.uk/~history/BiogIndex.html Indexes of biographies
http://www.distinguishedwomen.com/ Women's biographies
http://www.cappelloart.com/ Hollywood stars, sports heros and political personalities
http://www.laser-imprints.com/famous.htm Famous people homework and reference site
http://www.aboutfamouspeople.com/ biographies of historical people
http://www.libraryspot.com/biographies/ Biographical information
http://www.peoplespot.com/ People search

Acknowledgments

The publishers wish to thank the following for their contribution to the book:

Photographs

(t = top; b = bottom; m = middle; l = left; r = right)

Page 1 Magnum; 3 Art Archive; 6 Kobal; 13 *bl* Art Archive; 17 *t* Art Archive; 17 *br* Art Archive; 18 *tl* Illustrated London News; 18 *m* Illustrated London News; 19 *m* Illustrated London News; 19 *b* Illustrated London News; 20 *m* Art Archive; 21 *tr* Illustrated London News; 21 *br* Illustrated London News; 22 *m* Illustrated London News; 22 *bl* Corbis; 22 *br* Corbis; 23 *m* Magnum; 23 *b* Popperfoto; 24 *bl* Magnum; 24 *m* Popperfoto; 25 *tl* Popperfoto; 25 *tr* Magnum; 28 *ml* Art Archive; 29 *br* Illustrated London News; 30 *bl* Illustrated London News; 30 *t* Illustrated London News; 30 *br* Illustrated London News; 31 Popperfoto; 32 *tr* Corbis; 32 *b* Popperfoto; 33 Royal Geographical Society; 36–7 Art Archive; 37 *br* Bridgeman Art Library; 38 *tr* Bridgeman Art Library; 38 *bl* Mary Evans Picture Library; 41 *b* Mary Evans Picture Library; 43 *br* Popperfoto; 44 *mr* Royal Geographical Society; 50 *t* Popperfoto; 50 *b* Corbis; 51 *bl* Corbis; 51 *tr* Popperfoto; 52 *mr* Illustrated London News; 53 *ml* Popperfoto; 53 *br* Popperfoto; 54 *t* NASA; 54 *bl* NASA; 55 *tl* Popperfoto; 55 *mr* Popperfoto; 56 (background) NASA; 56 *tr* Popperfoto; 56 *b* NASA; 57 Art Archive; 59 *br* Corbis; 60 *t* Corbis; 61 Art Archive; 62 *br* Hulton; 65 *bl* Corbis; 66 *b* Popperfoto; 69 *b* Corbis; 70 *bl* Corbis; 72 *l* Science & Society Photo Library; 72 *br* Hulton; 73 *t* Corbis; 73 *bl* Corbis; 74 *tr* Mary Evans Picture Library; 74 *b* Art Archive; 75 *br* Corbis; 76 Illustrated London News; 78 Art Archive; 79 Natural History Museum; 80 *ml* Popperfoto; 80 *br* Corbis; 81 Illustrated London News; 86 *bl* Corbis; 86 *br* Corbis; 87 *t* Hulton; 89 Rex Features; 90 Mary Evans Picture Library; 91 *m* Mary Evans Picture Library; 92 *br* Hulton; 93 *t* Hulton; 93 *b* Corbis; 95 *t* Hulton; 95 *b* Corbis; 96 *t* Corbis; 97 *tr* Corbis; 97 *b* Corbis; 98 *bl* Rex Features; 99 *tr* Art Archive; 99 *b* Science Photo Library; 100 *tr* Corbis; 102 *br* Hulton; 103 *tr* Art Archive; 104 *br* Science Photo Library; 105 Hulton; 108 *tr* Art Archive; 109 *bl* Bridgeman Art Library; 110 *t* National Portrait Gallery; 111 *tl* Illustrated London News; 111 *b* Art Archive; 112 *tr* Illustrated London News; 113 *t* Corbis; 113 *b* Illustrated London News; 114 *bl* Art Archive; 115 Art Archive; 116 *t* Kobal; 116 *b* Popperfoto; 117 Hulton; 118 *t* Art Archive; 118 *b* Bridgeman Art Library; 119 *tr* Corbis; 119 *b* Corbis; 120 *t* Art Archive; 121 *bl* Corbis; 121 *m* Bridgeman Art Library; 122 *b* Hulton; 122 *tr* Hulton; 126 *tr* Corbis; 126 *mr* Corbis; 126 *b* Art Archive; 127 *bl* Corbis; 127 *tr* Hulton; 128 *t* Popperfoto; 128 *b* Corbis; 129 Kobal; 131 *t* Art Archive; 131 *br* Art Archive; 132 *t* Corbis; 132 *bl* Kobal; 133 Kobal; 134 *t* Kobal; 134 *b* Kobal; 135 *t* Kobal; 135 *bl* Kobal; 136 *bl* Kobal; 136 *br* Kobal; 137 Kobal; 138 *tl* Kobal; 138 *br* Corbis; 139 *bl* Kobal; 139 *m* Kobal; 140 *t* Kobal; 140 *b* Kobal; 141 *t* Kobal; 141 *br* Kobal; 142 *t* Kobal; 142 *bl* Kobal; 143 *m* Kobal; 143 *tr* Kobal; 144 *t* Kobal; 144 *br* Kobal; 145 *bl* Kobal; 145 *tr* Kobal; 146 *t* Kobal; 146 *b* Kobal; 147 *t* Kobal; 147 *bl* Kobal; 148 Kobal; 149 Kobal; 150 *l* Kobal; 150 *r* Kobal; 151 *t* Kobal; 151 *l* Kobal; 152 *tl* Kobal; 152 *tr* Kobal; 152 *b* Kobal; 153 Art Archive; 156 *tl* Art Archive; 156 *br* Art Archive; 157 Art Archive; 158 Art Archive; 159 Art Archive; 160 Art Archive; 161 *bl* Art Archive; 161 *tr* Bridgeman Art Library; 162 *t* AKG; 162 *br* Art Archive; 163 © Succession H. Matisse/DACS 2002 Art Archive; 164 *t* Illustrated London News; 164 *b* Art Archive; 165 *m* Art Archive; 165 *b* AKG; 166 *bl* Illustrated London News; 166 *tr* © ADAGP, Paris and DACS, London 2002 Art Archive; 167 *bl* © The Andy Warhol Foundation for the Visual Arts, Inc/ARS, NY and DACS, London. Trademarks licensed by Campbell Soup Company. All rights reserved. Bridgeman Art Library; 168 Bridgeman Art Library; 170 *br* Corbis; 171 *t* Art Archive; 171 *bl* Bridgeman Art Library; 172 *t* Corbis; 172 *b* Victoria & Albert Museum; © Richard Avedon 1955; 174 *tr* Bridgeman Art Library; 175 *b* Bridgeman Art Library; 176 *t* Arcaid; 176 *b* Arcaid; 177 Redferns; 179 *t* Bridgeman Art Library; 179 *b* Art Archive; 180 *m* Corbis; 180 *b* Corbis; 181 *ml* Hulton; 181 *t* Art Archive; 182 *bl* Hulton; 182 *tr* Bridgeman Art Library; 183 *bl* Hulton; 183 *tr* Hulton; 184 *ml* Hulton; 184 *t* Redferns; 184 *br* Redferns; 185 *t* Hulton; 185 *b* Redferns; 186 Corbis; 187 *t* Hulton; 187 *br* Retna; 188 *tr* Hulton; 188 *b* Donald Cooper; 189 *ml* Redferns; 189 *br* Retna; 190 Redferns; 191 *t* Redferns; 191 *b* Redferns; 192 *tl* Redferns; 192 *br* Redferns; 193 *t* Redferns; 193 *br* Redferns; 194 *t* Redferns; 194 *bl* Redferns; 195 *tr* Redferns; 195 *b* Kobal; 196 *ml* Redferns; 196 *tr* Redferns; 196 *b* Hulton; 197 *m* Redferns; 197 *bl* Redferns; 198 *tl* Corbis; 198 *b* Redferns; 199 Hulton; 200 *t* Corbis; 200 *b* Rex Features; 201 Colorsport; 203 *t* Colorsport; 203 *br* Colorsport; 204 *bl* Hulton; 204 *br* Hulton; 205 Allsport-Hulton; 206 *bl* Colorsport; 206 *tr* Colorsport; 207 *t* Colorsport; 207 *br* Colorsport; 208 *tl* Colorsport; 208 *bl* Colorsport; 209 *tl* Colorsport; 209 *br* Allsport; 210 *tr* Colorsport; 210 *b* Colorsport; 211 *bl* Colorsport; 211 *tr* Colorsport; 212 *bl* Colorsport; 212 *tr* Colorsport; 213 *tl* Hulton; 213 *br* Hulton; 214 *tr* Colorsport; 214 *b* Colorsport; 215 *tr* Corbis; 215 *br* Colorsport; 216 Colorsport; 217 Allsport; 218 *t* Hulton; 218 *b* Allsport; 219 *tr* Colorsport; 219 *b* Colorsport; 220 *m* Empics; 220 *tr* Associated Press; 221 *m* Corbis; 221 *b* Hulton; 222 *tr* Allsport; 222 *b* Allsport; 223 Allsport; 224 Colorsport; 225 AKG; 227 *br* Art Archive; 228 Bridgeman Art Library; 229 Hulton; 230 *tl* Popperfoto; 230 *bl* Popperfoto; 230 *t* Illustrated London News; 231 *ml* Hulton; 232 *ml* Hulton; 232 *tr* Hulton; 232 *b* Corbis; 233 *tl* Hulton; 233 *br* Hulton; 234 Retna; 235 *t* Hulton; 235 *b* Popperfoto; 236 *t* Corbis; 236 *br* Popperfoto; 237 *t* AKG; 240 *t* Corbis; 241 *tl* Bridgeman Art Library; 241 *br* Popperfoto; 242 Popperfoto; 243 *bl* Popperfoto; 243 *mr* Hulton; 244 *bl* Hulton; 244 *br* Hulton; 245 *tl* Popperfoto; 245 *mb* Corbis; 245 *mr* Hulton; 245 *br* Hulton; 246 *tr* Popperfoto; 246 *b* Popperfoto; 247 *tl* Popperfoto; 247 *mt* Popperfoto; 248 *bl* Associated Press; 248 (background) Associated Press; 248 *br* Corbis

Artwork

Jonathan Adams; Nemesh Alles; Marion Appleton; Owain Bell; Peter Bull; Norma Burgin; Vanessa Card; Nigel Chamberlain; Peter Chesterton; Peter Connelly; Peter Cornwell; Peter Dennis; Jeff Farrow; Chris Forsey; Terry Gabbey; Luigi Galante; Jeremy Gower; Nick Harris; Nick Hewitson; Adam Hook; Christian Hook; Richard Hook; John James; Peter Jones; Jack Keay; Chris Lyon; Kevin Maddison; John Martin; D. Mayer; Angus McBride; Chris Molan; Teresa Morris; Doug Post; Bernard Robinson; Rodney Shackell; Bob Venables; Mike White